MIDDLE EAST STUDIES
HISTORY, POLITICS, AND LAW

Edited by
Shahrough Akhavi
University of South Carolina

A ROUTLEDGE SERIES

Middle East Studies
History, Politics, and Law
Shahrough Akhavi, *General Editor*

DIPLOMACY AND DISPLACEMENT
Reconsidering the Turco-Greek Exchange of Populations, 1922–1934

Onur Yıldırım

Routledge
Taylor & Francis Group

NEW YORK AND LONDON

Routledge
Taylor & Francis Group
711 Third Avenue
New York, NY 10017

Routledge
Taylor & Francis Group
2 Park Square
Milton Park, Abingdon
Oxon OX14 4RN

Routledge is an imprint of Taylor & Francis Group, an Informa business

First issued in paperback 2012

International Standard Book Number-13: 978-0-415-97982-5 (Hardcover)
International Standard Book Number-13: 978-0-415-64907-0 (Paperback)

Library of Congress Cataloging-in-Publication Data

Yıldırım, Onur, 1966-
  Diplomacy and displacement: reconsidering the Turco-Greek exchange of populations, 1922-1934 / Onur Yıldırım.
      p. cm. -- (Middle East studies : history, politics, and law)
      Includes bibliographical references (p.   ) and index.
  ISBN 0-415-97982-X (alk. paper)
      1. Population transfers--Turks--History--20th century. 2. Population transfers--Greeks--History--20th century. 3. Turkey--Emigration and immigration. 4. Greece--Emigration and immigration. 5. Turkey--History--1918-1960. 6. Greece--History--1917-1944. I. Title. II. Series: Middle East studies (Routledge (Firm)).

DR590.Y53 2006
304.8'495056109042--dc22   2006011237

Visit the Taylor & Francis Web site at
http://www.taylorandfrancis.com

and the Routledge Web site at
http://www.routledge-ny.com

For Süreyya Deniz

Table of Contents

List of Tables

A Note on Sources

This study makes extensive use of official documents obtained from the Historical Archives of the Greek Ministry of Foreign Affairs and the Turkish Republican Archives. The published minutes of the Turkish Grand National Assembly are also utilized all throughout. The documents obtained from the Archives of the Foreign Ministry are found in folios (*fakeloi*) that contain documents ranging in size from a few pages to hundreds. These folios are named according to the subject matter and assigned a letter and number that indicate the specific section of the ministry (e.g., A, B, and Γ stand for political section) with which each folio is related. The folios especially in A and B groups contain a wide range of classified documents such as the official correspondence to and from various Greek consulates, ministries and army divisions, individual reports, blueprints of League of Nations documents, secret reports of various Greek agents, newspaper clippings, translations of articles published in Europe, the United States and Turkey, the minutes of the official sessions of refugee-related institutions, the Council of the League of Nations and the League of Nations Higher Court of Justice, etc. In referring to these folios only pertaining numbers are quoted throughout the book. Individual document citations are given in quotations. Each quotation contains information on the persons involved and/or the title of the report as well as the date on which the document was originally written, **not** the date on which it was received by the Ministry. The folio number succeeds the closing quotation mark. Some of the documents whose authors are not identified are referred to as anonymous.

As for the Turkish sources, the great majority of the documents were obtained from the Republican Archives where the classification process is still under way. Classified documents have been assigned official numbers that indicate the institution from which they originated or the subject matter they address. In endnotes, these numbers are given at the end of citations in brackets. Most of these documents also have attachments, to which separate numbers have been assigned. Unclassified documents, mostly government resolutions, and their attachments are cited only with their original number of issuance. The minutes of the Turkish Grand National Assembly are available in print and they are cited according to the information on the cover page of each volume. This information consists of the 'assembly term' (*devre*), the conveying year of this assembly (*içtima senesi*), the volume number (*cilt*) and the dates covered by the volume; the dates that are quoted in endnote citations throughout the book are those that are indicated on the front cover of each volume.

A Note on Dates

The sources used throughout this book are dated according to various calendar systems. Greek official documents that were obtained from the Historical Archives of the Greek Ministry of Foreign Affairs for the pre-1923 period carry the dates written according to the 'old' (Julian) and 'new' (Gregorian) systems.[1] The Julian calendar is 13 days behind the Gregorian one. With the exception of a few important documents, only Gregorian dates are given in footnote citations throughout the book. As for the Ottoman and Turkish sources of this study, they are dated mostly according to the fiscal (*Rumi*) calendar and to a lesser extent the Islamic (*Hijri*) calendar.[2] Some of the published material is also dated according to the Islamic calendar. For all practical purposes, the Islamic and fiscal dates are almost always given together with the corresponding dates in the Gregorian system in brackets in endnote citations throughout the book.[3]

Acknowledgments

To the extent that this book is successful in its efforts to offer a new perspective on the Turco-Greek Exchange of Populations and to contribute to both Turkish and Greek historiographies, much credit must go to many individuals and institutions that have helped me in this project over the years.

I was fortunate to receive comments, guidance, encouragement and various forms of assistance from a number of friends and colleagues among whom it is a pleasure to mention Şükrü Hanioğlu, Peter Loizos, Faruk Tuncay, Stavros Anestides, Socrates Petmezas, Dimitri Gondicas, Alex Lampou, Nikos Marantzides, Frederic Shorter, Michael Dark, Eyüp Özveren, Kürşad Ertuğrul, Erkan Erdil, Ozge Senay, Pinar B. Toker, Sheila Pelizzon, Fikret Şenses, and Amal Muhammad. I am particularly indebted to Mark Mazower and Bruce Clark for encouraging me to conceive this book and to Suraiya Faroqhi and Norman Stillman for their intellectual support. I also would like to express my sincere thanks to several students who have provided me with various forms of assistance at different stages of the project: Seven Ağır, Sibel Atasoy, Özge Özay, Gökçer Özgür, Deniz Taner Kılınçoğlu, and Burcu Çıngay.

I am grateful to the following organizations and their administrators for facilitating my research as well as writing process: The Department of Near Eastern Studies at Princeton University, the Program in Hellenic Studies at Princeton University, the Center for Mediterranean Studies at Rethymnon (Crete), the Alexander Onassis Public Benefit Foundation in Athens, and my current institution the Department of Economics in the Middle East Technical University, Ankara. As for the archives and libraries, in particular, the Historical Archives of the Greek Ministry of Foreign Affairs, which often hesitates to grant permission to Greek citizens, deserves much credit. The review committee of this institution has never turned down my applications. The Center for Asia Minor Studies in Athens has the best documentary and book collections on the subject of this study and I was granted unlimited access to these materials. Using the collections of the Firestone Library at Princeton was a luxury that I exploited to the best of my ability. I thank all these institutions for being very helpful and generous.

I also would like to thank Benjamin Holtzman and Randy Burling, both of Routledge: Taylor and Francis Group, and Eleanor Chan of IBT Global for their meticulous work during the production process of the book.

Finally, I offer my sincere thanks to my parents, Firdes and Hüsnü Yıldırım as well as my sister Derya and my brothers Uğur and Hayati for their moral support for this and other projects. My wife, Gözde, deserves a wholehearted thank for her tolerance I tended to abuse, but often to no avail. Lastly I feel extremely fortunate to have a humorous two-year old daughter, Süreyya Deniz, who brought me a brand new look at life. This book is dedicated to her.

Introduction

On the first Sunday of September 1922, the male residents of Kozbeğli (Κοζμβεϊλη), a small village located on a hilltop commanding the Ali Ağa Bay on the road to Yeni Foça (Νεα Φοκεα) gathered for the last time in the cozy village church in order to discuss plans for evacuating their village for the port of Izmir. While the women and children stayed at home to pack up their few remaining possessions, the village men carried on their meeting for a few hours and concluded with the final sermon by village priest. Once the meeting was over, one of them carved the date of their last mass on the left-hand side of the entry gate to make the moment memorable. The carving, which still reads today as 'XXI.8.1922'[1] marked the total evacuation of Kozbeğli as well as the placement of the village residents' fate at the mercy of the neighboring village communities. The oral evidence suggests that during their twenty-mile-long march, the residents of Kozbeğli were subject to constant attacks by bandits who stripped them of what little they were carrying. The few old men and women, left behind in the village, suffered death at the hands of bandits from the neighboring villages, who were on the rampage for '*pılıçka*' (from the Greek word '*πλιατσικο*' which means pillage). The surviving witnesses anonymously reiterate the story of an old Greek woman, left in the village, who was savagely put to death by looters.[2]

In the early days of December 1923, one year after the aforementioned event, Tevfik Ahmed Efendi, one of the leading Muslim landowners in the Greek town of Florina, bordering Albania, received the first official notification from the local authorities to evacuate the town and join his extended family of thirteen members in the stream of refugees who had been in motion for the last several months. While negotiations at Lausanne over the fate of minority populations were still in progress, the Greek government ordered the evacuation of Muslim populations from its territories with a view to resettling in their stead the incoming Greek refugees from

1

Asia Minor and eastern Thrace. After having used up all available options to prevent it from happening, the Muslim populations of Greece became aware of their prospects and accordingly began to liquidate their properties. In a very short period of time, many large landowners sold off their lands to seasonal laborers or other locals at prices well below their market value. Those who could find purchasers were considered fortunate for most of them failed to do so. As incoming Greek refugees from Asia Minor were granted some of those lands without any legal warning, and many local Greeks illegally came to occupy them, local Muslim landowners were rushing off to cash in their holdings.

Tevfik Ahmed Efendi was one of the lucky few who could sell at least a small portion of his holdings and convert the money into gold. When the final notification was delivered on the last week of July 1924, the extended family of Tevfik Efendi completed their preparations for departure from Florina to the port of Salonica. Gold coins were carefully placed in large shawls and tied around the bellies of the small children, who were thought to be the least likely to be searched by Greek officials and possibly highway robbers. Tevfik Efendi also hid a small bag of gold coins to be used for daily expenses inside his umbrella. Despite all kinds of harassment by soldiers and incoming refugees, the family managed to reach the port of Salonica and after a two-week wait, finally boarded a boat destined for Turkey. Having spent money on accommodation and boarding in Salonica and boat tickets, little remained for the members of the family to start a new life in their destination. After their arrival, the family had to resettle several times within a year. The family, having refused the option of temporal settlement (*iskan-ı adi*), had to waive all the rights granted by the Exchange Convention in order to obtain the right to free settlement. The difficulties the family of Tevfik Efendi faced in such a short period of time quickly exhausted what was left in the chest and they had to start life anew wherever they went. One of the remaining two members of the family bitterly remembers the pain and suffering the whole family experienced during the first years after their arrival in Turkey.[3]

These two stories are reconstructed on the basis of data collected during my long journey into the history of Turkish and Greek refugees. They concern perhaps the most dramatic event of the history of modern Turkey and Greece, namely the exchange of populations between the two countries. Following the bloody encounter of Turkish and Greek armies in Anatolia, both sides were summoned by the Allied States, namely Great Britain, France and Italy, to an international peace conference at Lausanne on November 13, 1922. The conference, which opened on November 20, 1922, lasted with disruptions until the middle of the following year. The first phase of the conference concluded with the signing of a convention on January 30, 1923, which stipulated the exchange of Muslims of Greek nationality (excluding the Muslim populations of Western Thrace) established in Greece for the Greek Orthodox of Turkish nationality (excluding the Greeks of Constantinople) established in Turkey. Nearly one year after the conclusion of the Lausanne meetings, approximately 700,000 people were removed by virtue of the Exchange Convention from their native soil and made refugees, and this agreement also confirmed the refugee status of an additional more than one million people, displaced since the Balkan Wars, especially in the later stages of the Turco-Greek War of 1920–1922. The implementation of the Exchange Convention took nearly a full decade to complete, in the course of which it brought about a multitude of social, economic, cultural and political constraints not only upon Greece, as the conventional view of this event suggests, but also upon Turkey. For both countries, the decade of 1923–1933 was a period of national reconstruction at the center of which stood thousands of homeless, jobless, and hungry refugees. Adopting a notion of the Exchange as a pervasive and complex process that loomed equally large in the modern histories of Turkey and Greece, the current study maps outs out the progression of this event from the diplomatic negotiations behind the making of the Exchange Convention at Lausanne in 1922–1923 to the official conclusion of the implementation process after laborious negotiations in Athens and Ankara in the later months of 1933.

MINORITY INTO REFUGEES: HISTORICAL BACKGROUND

The process that turned minorities into refugees in southeastern Europe originated during the late nineteenth century and gathered momentum during the Balkan Wars, when the Ottoman presence in the region was further debased by Greek, Serbian, Bulgarian, and Albanian nationalists.[4] The de-Ottomanization of former Ottoman territories by the Balkan nationalists and the growing nationalist fervor of the ruling party, namely, the Committee of Union and Progress (from now on CUP), in the Ottoman Empire took their toll on the local minorities. This was particularly true with regard to the fate of two major minorities, namely the Muslim population in the Ottoman territories (principally Salonica, Kavala, and Florina) newly captured by Greece and that of the Greek population in Ottoman Anatolia. As the last minority groups akin in race, language, or religion to the neighboring state, both communities entered a long period of uncertainty characterized by frequent migrations and deportations. It was not until the elimination of these minorities that the Greek and Turkish nationalisms retreated to their home bases.

In the immediate aftermath of the Balkan Wars, the ruling elite in the Ottoman Empire decided to embark on "on a new policy of eradication, with the object of creating an ethnically homogeneous State."[5] At the ideological level, this development marked the shift from Ottomanism to Turkish nationalism, which found its best expression in the sloganish formula, "A Turkish Empire for the Turks and by the Turks."[6] This proclamation then metamorphozed into another public catchword, "Turkey for the Turks," which was later inherited by the Republican leaders. Earlier attempts to define a broad Ottoman identity embracing all the populations of the Empire had been ineffectual, and Ottomanism as a state policy was a failure.[7] This became obvious as early as the turn of the century when the fine lines between the Ottomanist and Turkist traits of the Young Turk ideology nearly disappeared.[8] In the background of a multi-ethnic and multi-confessional Parliament[9], the CUP's move to a more nationalistic platform during and after the Balkan Wars marked the final twist in the Young Turk ideology. From this point on, the leading members of the CUP openly promoted nationalist policies at home and abroad. The immediate aftermath of the Balkan Wars saw increasing complaints especially by Greek members of the Ottoman Parliament about the local incidents perpetuated by the growing nationalist fervor (boycotts, etc.).[10] Where the security of the Greek communities was concerned, both Greek Members of Parliament as well as the Patriarchate often intervened on their behalf and petitioned the Ministry of Justice, thereby generating further controversy with leading contemporary intellectuals affiliated with the CUP.[11]

In the same vein, the annexation of former Ottoman territories by the Greeks witnessed nullification of long-standing policies towards ethnic minorities in these regions. A large majority of these areas' Muslim populations, now reduced to minorities, shared the fate of other minority groups such as the Bulgarians.[12] They were subjected to a wide range of discriminative policies, especially regarding property rights. All kinds of property transactions by the Muslim populations were prohibited and the hitherto deserted estates were confiscated with the aim of redistributing them among the local Greek populations. Many Muslim landowners who had been living in towns as absentee landowners and using sharecroppers to till their *çiftlik* (large estates) lands were threatened with the redistribution of their agricultural lands to the share-croppers if they did not return.[13] In the early stages of the Balkan Wars, the Greek entry into Salonica was marked by the formulation and application of strict rules regarding primarily the Bulgarian and Muslim populations of the city.[14] The ensuing developments proved that the Greek nationalists acted the same way as their Turkish counterparts in terms of their plans for ethnic homogeneity at the expense of the local minorities. Under the provocative leadership of Venizelos, the Greek aspirations of 'Greater Greece' were remolded into a new vision of Greek society where a homogeneous population was considered as the only viable means of statehood.

It is at this political conjuncture, dominated by the activities of Greek and Turkish nationalists, that the fates of minorities in the remaining territories of the Ottoman Empire and within the expanding borders of Greece were determined. Against this background, the triumvirate of Enver, Cemal, and Talat Pashas, having already made a deal with the Bulgarians for a voluntary exchange of minorities, now approached the Greeks with an offer of a formal exchange of populations which would involve the populations of the Greek villages in Thrace and in the district of Izmir in return for the Turkish-Muslim populations of Macedonia and Epirus. The idea of population exchange was not novel to the history of the region, but this time the form of exchange implicated in this discussion was not simply the old form of wholesale expulsion still being implemented with the Armenians.[15] It involved certain guarantees that would provide for the disposal of immovable property and the liquidation of estates abandoned by the emigrants. The option of partial or complete removal of the minorities along these lines was welcomed by the governments of the adversary states concerned. The triumvirate, which had already signed an accord to this effect with Bulgaria in 1913,[16] signed another one with Greece the following year,[17] stipulating a geographically limited and "voluntary-based" exchange of populations. Since negotiations on both of these exchange plans were conducted on an informal basis, there is little evidence as to the details of the agreement process and much scholarly controversy ensued concerning their formulation and the degree of application. Alexander Pallis, who points to Venizelos as the initiator of the exchange project, records the following on the Turco-Greek exchange:

> An exchange of populations between Greece and Turkey was first suggested by M. Venizelos in 1914 as a way of solving the difficulties which had arisen at the beginning of that year between the two countries. Relations had become strained owing to the refusal of Turkey to recognize the Greek annexation of the Aegean Islands opposite the Anatolian coast. In order to put pressure on the Greek government, the Turks proceeded to expel the Greek inhabitants of a large number of towns and villages in Eastern Thrace and on the Western Anatolian littoral, installing in their place Moslem emigrants from Macedonia. These Greeks, amounting to 270.000 were forced to take refuge in Greece.

It was useless to expect that these refugees would ever be allowed to return, and even if the Turkish Government had given its consent, it is more than doubtful whether they could ever have been reinstalled in their homes, seeing that these had already been occupied by Moslem emigrants. The only solution was therefore to accept the fait accompli and to regularize the situation by an agreement which would have enabled the property abandoned on both sides to be properly liquidated, and also isolated communities which had remained behind, and were in danger of annihilation by the surrounding population, to be removed under proper safeguards.[18]

As early as June 1914, the Greeks began to flee under duress in massive numbers from such coastal settlements as Çesme and Urla.[19] In response to a petition by leaders of local Greek communities, a commission made up of representatives from foreign embassies in Istanbul came to inspect the situation in *locus* and hear the complaints. The Mixed Commission, which had been established according to the Athens Accord for the Exchange of Populations, was assigned to look into the matter. At the end of June in 1914, two Greek and two Turkish members of the Commission under a neutral arbiter from a European state met in Izmir. In the presence of members of the Commission, the local Greeks complained that the Turkish populace had stopped shopping in their stores in accordance with a systematic boycott plan. They also noted that Muslim day laborers were no longer tending their fields due presumably to low wages. Thus, according to the testimonies of local Greeks, many fellow Greeks who had lost their economic bases were compelled to move out of these areas. During the interviews, local Turks vehemently argued that those Greeks who had left should never be allowed to return. The Greeks, on the other hand, insisted that people should be left to make their own decisions. Having heard both sides of the story, the members of the Commission returned to Istanbul to discuss the terms of a wholesale liquidation of the abandoned properties. Certain arrangements were eventually made to complete this process.[20] Such plans, however, were not realized due to the outbreak of WWI and the Athens Accord for a voluntary exchange of populations between Greece and the Ottoman Empire turned out to be abortive.

During the 1915–1918 period, wartime conditions facilitated further escalation of pressure by the nationalists on the respective Greek[21] and Muslim populations and uncertainty concerning the fate of these populations was further increased. While the Greeks in Anatolia came to build hopes on the discourse of "redemption" promoted by their elected representatives[22] as well as the Greek politicians in Greece, the Muslim populations of Greece waited patiently for the recapture of their lands by the Ottoman army. As the pressure from governmental channels and by brigands mounted, many Greeks took refuge in the mountains of Anatolia where they were to stay for years[23] while some Muslims gave into the suppressive policies of the Venizelist government by emigration to Anatolia.

Ever since the last decades of the nineteenth century, such sporadic migratory movements had been all too familiar to Ottoman Anatolia and, to this effect, many offices specializing in refugee affairs had already been created both in the center and outlying provinces of the Ottoman Empire.[24] Although these institutions functioned ineffectively, the refugees who came in small groups fended for themselves by producing their own solutions to the problem of resettlement sometimes by way of seizing the abandoned properties of the Armenians and Greeks who had departed or been expelled from the country. In Greece, the territorial claims, entrenched in the project of 'Great Idea' (*Μεγαλη Ιδεα*),[25] barred massive migrations from the Ottoman Anatolia, especially from the Aegean coast. Although certain governmental offices were established to deal with refugee affairs, their functions were limited for the most part to provisioning the incoming refugees and providing them with sanitary services.

Later on, these developments were to have major effects on the governments of both Greece and Turkey. The immense influx of refugees from the Anatolian hinterland during the Turco-Greek War of 1920–22 caught the Greeks unprepared as far as resettling and accommodating a massive number of refugees were concerned. In Turkey, the Ottoman institutions in charge of refugee affairs were to be adopted unchanged by the new State, but their services would soon prove to be ineffectual due to the size of the incoming population and the inefficient regimentation and supervision of the resettlement process by the government.

The conflict between the Ottoman Empire and Greece, which had entered an unsteady phase of development after the outbreak of WWI, contingent on the military and diplomatic conjuncture, lasted until the Greek occupation of the *Vilayet* (Province) of Aydın in 1919. The Greek annexation of the region intensified the national sentiments against a perceived anti-Turkish conspiracy. Many public demonstrations were organized in Istanbul as well as in other major cities throughout Anatolia.[26] Having gained momentum after the annexation of the Aydın region, Greek irredentist aggression, formerly embedded in the rationale of "redeeming the unredeemed brethren," took on an expansionist character towards the Anatolian interior. This development in turn brought the Greek nationalists up against their Turkish counterparts, who were struggling to attain territorial and ideological consolidation of the alternate state in the making. The

conflict between Turkish and Greek nationalists in Anatolia came to an end
with the military defeat of the latter, which led to a general flight of Greek
inhabitants from Anatolia to Greece during the latter part of 1922. The
wholesale uprooting of the Greek population from Anatolia was mirrored
by that of their Muslim counterparts in Greece. Almost a decade later than
the abortive exchange plan and the two abortive diplomatic steps taken in
Paris in 1919 and in Sèvres in 1920 and initiated principally by the Greek
statesmen (primarily by Venizelos himself), the ruling elite in Turkey and
Greece which anonymously saw respective minorities as a major source
of friction finally found a legitimate platform upon which to renegotiate
and ultimately adopt, albeit on a compulsory basis, the earlier project of
1914. Thus, under the patronage of the Allied states, the ruling classes of
Turkey and Greece proceeded with the forceful removal of the minorities,
silhouettes of the Ottoman past, in order to consolidate the formation of
their respective states. Accordingly, in the early stages of the peace negotiations at Lausanne, the two sides reached a quick agreement on an agenda
to exchange the majority of their minorities and signed, to this effect, the
Convention Concerning the Exchange of Greek and Turkish Populations
on January 30, 1923.

The rush that characterized discussions between Turks and Greeks
at Lausanne on the issue of minorities emanated as much from the pressure of the representatives of the Allied States in the conference as from the
concerns of both parties to return to the domestic scene, which had long
been plagued by political and economic instability and to which was added
another major challenge of great magnitude, namely, the refugee problem.
After having been moved on to a formal platform, the latter now found
itself a safe place at the top of both countries' agendas due to its highly
complicated nature in the character of which were manifested all the political, social and economic problems of both countries accumulated since the
Balkan wars. Seen from this angle, it would not be too far-fetched to conclude that the Treaty of Lausanne not only confirmed the refugee problem
but also formalized and enlarged it.

The Convention concerning the Exchange of Greek and Turkish Populations as the first annex of the Lausanne Treaty laid down the principles
for the transfer, resettlement and rehabilitation of the Greek and Muslim
refugees in their destined countries. The application of the most preliminary provisions of the Convention proved at the outset that the task was
more sophisticated and challenging than either of the parties had entertained. The provisions of the Convention were far from providing an effective solution to the immediate practical concerns of the refugees such as
their shelter, health, food and clothing. More difficulties sprang from the

language of the Convention, which left considerable room for interpretation. First and foremost, the Convention was very confusing in terms of its designation of the people to be covered, and thus both Turkish and Greek political leadership tried to entangle the "unwanted" minorities (Albanians and Roma in Greece, the remaining Armenians and Assyrians in Turkey) in their countries with the exchange. Moreover, many people who had voluntarily emigrated or were forcefully uprooted from their homes before and/or after WWI, despite the fact that they were not being treated as equal partners in this process, forcefully included themselves. In this chaotic environment, many other groups took advantage of the vacuum. While in Greece, the native populations, be they local elite (*tsorbadjidhes*) or poor peasants, occupied the properties of the departed Muslims, in Turkey, the refugees of the Balkan Wars (*Balkan harbi muhacirleri*) and the 'eastern refugees' (*Şark muhacirleri*) together with the members of native populations seized, at the outset, most of the abandoned movable and immovable properties (*emval ve emlak-i metruke*) that had been earmarked for the incoming refugees. In Turkey, many soldiers and local governmental officials also participated in this "property rush." Accordingly, the refugee problem, which now surfaced due to the formal agreement, came to secure itself a safe seat in the general public opinion as well as in the agendas of governments in Greece and Turkey, and with its multi-faceted nature promised to play a major role in the reconstruction of the two countries in the years to come.

WHY STUDY THE EXCHANGE?

Only one year after the conclusion of the Lausanne meetings, the British diplomatic historian H. W. V. Temperley asserted that "the Treaty of Lausanne with its Annexes, seemed destined, in all human probability, to inaugurate a more lasting settlement, not only than the Treaty of Sèvres but than the Treaty of Versailles, St. Germain, Trianon, and Neuilly."[27] The assumption that the settlement at Lausanne—a freely negotiated and not an imposed treaty unlike the other five post-WWI treaties—represented a success story from the viewpoint of international politics and diplomacy has provided the chief leitmotiv to the study of this event by later scholarship. Many diplomatic historians treated this settlement with a view to clarifying the growth and maturation of a distinctive international state-system against the background of the Eastern Question and Great Power rivalry in the region.[28] When they concerned themselves with the domestic repercussions of this event upon the countries primarily concerned, namely Greece and Turkey, they devoted their efforts largely to appraising the role of this covenant in consolidating the territorial limits and national sovereignty of their states, and in laying down the foundations of a peaceful coexistence between them. In all these efforts, the accent was placed manifestly upon the performance of diplomats during the decision-making process.[29]

Thus, the copious literature in diplomatic history, with its strict adherence to reported fact, brought the diplomatic and political aspects of this event, not to mention the virtues of the peacemakers, to the forefront of historical analysis. Obviously, this emergent scholarly attitude dwarfed certain dimensions of this historic agreement, such as the Exchange Convention, which had enormous impact upon the domestic conditions of Greece and Turkey. The Exchange entered the agenda of this scholarship only to the extent that it presented opportunities to these countries in terms of homogenizing their ethnic and national outlooks, and providing them with territorial security while the many social and economic constraints it generated for them were pushed to the background. Perhaps even more importantly for the purpose of this study, the above attitude tended to relegate enormous suffering, including the loss of homes and livelihoods and the disruption of social, cultural and economic ties that the Lausanne settlement inflicted on minority populations on both sides by turning most of them into refugees.

The depiction of the Turco-Greek Exchange of Populations as an autonomous historical event in scholarly literature dates from the inter-war era when an international scholarship flourished in Europe and the United States to explain and produce resolutions to the then ameliorating problem of minorities. Operating largely within the boundaries of the nation-state as the primary unit of analysis, this scholarship, represented by such scholars as Stephen P. Ladas,[30] Sir John H. Simpson,[31] C. A. Macartney,[32] and Joseph B. Schechtman,[33] among many others, was collated by a tendency to integrate the Exchange dimension of the Lausanne settlement into the study of the then newly formed League of Nations system of minority protection. These scholars considered in unanimity the reciprocal exchange of minorities between Turkey and Greece as the first **organized** transfer of large ethno-religious groups by means of which minorities were **forcibly** uprooted under the aegis of international law to contribute, in turn, to the reconstitution of ethnically 'pure' homogenous states. Against the background of rising prospects in Europe for the adoption of similar practices, the pattern of Turco-Greek Exchange was presented as an operational device to be pursued in the settlement of minority problems, that is to say, in support of local actors to create 'pure' national homelands.

Moreover, this scholarship tended to portray Great Power involvement in the formulation and execution of the Turco-Greek Exchange scheme merely as a 'humanitarian' endeavor. To this effect, many scholars studied the execution of the Exchange Convention exclusively with respect to Greece, the only side of the event in which the League of Nations had directly intervened on behalf of the Great Powers to orchestrate the resettlement of refugees through the medium of an autonomous institution, namely the Refugee Settlement Commission. Although certain students of the subject, such as Stephen Ladas and C. A. Macartney, referred to various impediments that arose during the implementation of the Exchange Convention,[34] the traditional scholarship, clearly biased towards the Greek side, judged the success of this settlement on the basis of its written provisions and general outcome. Accordingly, it hastened to consider the scheme of the Turco-Greek Exchange to be on the whole a success story. As a specialist would put it later "the success achieved by this solution to the Greco-Turkish dispute allowed the concept [Exchange] to take root in international relations theory as a mechanism for solving international disputes and settling minority problems."[35]

The scholarly attempts that attached a success paradigm to the Turco-Greek Exchange of Populations made their imprints momentarily on the international arena as they inspired putative policy-makers in Europe and elsewhere in the world to adapt the Turco-Greek scheme to their authentic situations. By the mid-1930s, several totalitarian governments in Europe, more particularly the Nazi regime in Germany, had already launched their nationalist programs, which had significant ramifications upon minorities, to the extent of persecution and then genocide in the case of Jews. The contents and consequences of these programs, especially their implications for the Jewish minorities, have been the subject of numerous publications, but they are outside the scope of this study.[36]

What is important for the purpose of the current discussion is the extent to which the exchange of populations was used as part of population transfer programs to address the question of minorities. After the breakup of the Austro-Hungarian and Russian Empires, many minority groups (e.g., Germans, Poles, Slovaks, Magyars, etc.) in the existent or newly established nation-states (e.g., Germany, Austria, Poland, Czechoslovakia, Estonia, Latvia, Lithuania, Finland, etc.) had been granted the status of 'national' through a series of treaties in 1919 and 1920 under the auspices of the League of Nations. These groups had opted to stay in their homelands instead of moving into the territory of another state with which they were akin in race and language. The triumph of fascism in Germany and Italy in the 1930s went hand-in-hand with the ethnic purification of these geographies (i.e., the creation of *Lebensraum*). In disputed regions where the prospects for the assimilation of minorities or the application of frontier revision were null, and the practicality of international law had already been rendered impossible, the exchange appeared to the policy-makers as one of the methods to address the question of minorities. The most concrete example was the German-Italian agreement on the transfer of the German minority from South Tyrol on June 23, 1939, which marked the beginning of the far-reaching transfer program of the Third Reich. This arrangement was modeled in terms of its compulsory character and accompanying procedures explicitly after the Turco-Greek example.[37]

The case of South Tyrol portended the population exchanges of various scales that were to take place during the1939–1941 period. Several population exchanges were conducted between Germany and the Soviet Union, whereby many Germans living in the Soviet-occupied territories such as Estonia, Latvia, Wolhynia, Bessarabia, Lithuania etc. were transferred to Germany through terms similar to the Turco-Greek agreement. At the end of the war, when the peacemakers at Postdam decided to apply the national principle in all its simplistic power in formerly German-occupied areas such as Czechoslovakia, Romania, Poland, Hungary, and Yugoslavia, the exchange also appeared as a workable solution to certain territorial disputes.[38] The exchange agreement between Poland and the Soviet Union in 1944 and the exchange of populations between Czechoslovakia and Hungary in 1946 were all fashioned after the Turco-Greek model.[39] Thus nearly two decades after its introduction to the agenda of world history, the exchange of populations was appropriated by policy-makers as one form of population transfer to pattern the map of Europe according to prevalent ideologies.

The information gleaned from the available literature suggests that various official and independent research attempts undertaken at the time to investigate the situation involved scholars whose names were recounted above and who were quite familiar with the Turco-Greek case. It should be mentioned that these scholars were among those who presented the Turco-Greek pattern as an "instructive" precedent and success story in their general studies on the population transfers and the refugee phenomena. Given the institutions under the patronage of which these scholars conducted their research and published their books, the policy implications of such research efforts were all too obvious especially when the political climate of the era is taken into consideration. As a matter of fact, the policy-oriented nature of this scholarship is often acknowledged by the authors themselves as in the case of John H. Simpson who remarks on the very first page of his oft-quoted survey, "it was hoped that the facts disclosed by the survey might be helpful to those with whom these decisions rest."[40]

Elsewhere in the world, two separate occasions of exchange are spotted where the decision-makers had at their disposal the available literature on the Turco-Greek Exchange of Populations. The pattern of the Turco-Greek Exchange was quoted in 1937 by the British Royal Commission on Palestine (i.e., the Peel Commission) as a model to be integrated to the partition package that was then drawn up to resolve the Arab-Jewish conflict over Palestine.[41] The Commission recommended "in view of the manifest advantage for both nations of 'reducing the opportunities of future friction to the utmost,' the Arab and Jewish leaders 'might show the same high statesmanship as that of the Turks and the Greeks and make the same bold decision for the sake of peace.'"[42] Although the British Government, which held the League of Nations Mandate over Palestine, adopted a favorable position on the idea of a compulsory exchange of populations, it pulled back later in recognition of the great disturbances it was bound to create amongst the Arab populations of the region. The idea had also been concurrently taken up by the principal Zionist organization, namely, the Jewish Agency, which formed various research committees to investigate the feasibility of such a project and even dispatched some of its members to Greece to gather further information about the Greek experience.[43] But the Zionist project also proved inconclusive due to the belated realization of geographical and demographic obstacles before the implementation of such a project, the anticipation of a concerted Arab opposition to such an idea, and perhaps more concretely due to the British Government's retreat from the idea of exchange.

The second case, where the decision-makers cast their eyes back to the Turco-Greek Exchange as an instructive precedent, was the exchange of populations between India and Pakistan in 1947, which was to register in history pages as the largest exchange of populations ever by involving more than 11 million Hindus and Muslims.[44] The available information suggests that the leaders of the respective states often alluded to the Turco-Greek case while formulating their ideas about the demographic dimension of the partition process. Mr. Neogi, Minister for Relief and Rehabilitation in India, had the following to say on the Turco-Greek experimentation: "In the case of Greece and Turkey—which were the first in modern times to have a similar experience of mass movements of population—the time taken for rehabilitation of a fraction of the population with which we are concerned today was five years, and they seem to take pride that it was accomplished in that period (my emphasis). . . . Greece took five years: we have not had as many months in India."[45]

These two cases suffice to conclude that owing largely to the scholarly literature of the inter-war period, the Turco-Greek Exchange of Populations as a 'precedent-setting event' was turned into a catchword whenever inter-ethnic or inter-religious conflicts, forced migrations and refugee phenomena came to threaten peace at national, regional or international levels. The best-known student of the Turco-Greek Exchange, Dimitri Pentzopoulos, who were concerned with Greece's worsening relations with Yugoslavia and Turkey at the time, would explain the objective of his Princeton dissertation in the early 1960s as follows: "National minorities still exist and refugees still plague the world and stigmatize the Twentieth Century civilization. Moreover their repercussions and the danger they present acquire ominous dimension in the context of the present day "cold war." In the light of the Greek-Turkish experiment, can this method, the exchange of minorities, be used to minimize some of the perils and, if so, what are the necessary prerequisites for its successful application?"[46]

When during the Cold War era, the ideological bipolarization unleashed open warfare to generate further refugees in different corners of the world from Vietnam to Afghanistan, push and pull factors were also in full operation to spawn further displaced populations around the globe.[47] However, the word 'exchange' does not seem to have been pronounced by scholars or circumspect by decision-makers[48] as anticipated by Pentzopoulos. It is only over the past few decades in parallel to the escalation of ethnic conflicts and forced migrations in various parts of the world, more particularly in the Balkans, due to the demise of the Cold War and the collapse of Yugoslavia, and in the Middle East due to the growing conflict between the Jews and Arabs that the term "exchange" and thus the Turco-Greek experience has begun to appear frequently in scholarly publications as well as in political rhetoric.[49]

A group of scholars, who are interested in explaining and producing strategies to resolve current conflicts in the Balkans and the Middle East, looked up the conditions that configured in the Turco-Greek Exchange. Dressed up with the conceptual elegance of 'engineered ethnic unmixing,' the Turco-Greek Exchange of Populations was referred to in this literature as an ample illustration of ethnic unmixing caused by ethnic cleansing.[50] Alluding to the Turco-Greek example, scholars argued that in the absence of an opportunity to carve out a new state (partition) for the minorities under threat, the reciprocal transfer of minority populations on both sides could be resorted in order to provide security to these groups, on the one hand, and to eliminate the potential for the two parties to engage in large-scale military conflicts in the long run, on the other. Thus similar to its interwar antecedent, this scholarship pondered the idea of eliminating 'ethnic' minorities from national or nationalizing states via an exchange, considering it as a justifiable option should there be a need.

With their varying orientations, all the scholarly strands recounted above had their unique contributions to the study of the Turco-Greek Exchange of Populations and its integration to the general framework of world history. Common to all these studies was, however, a tendency to stick to 'reported fact' and neglect the actual effects of such an arrangement on people's lives. On a more specific level, the two most obvious shortcomings are noted especially in the studies in which the causes and consequences of the Exchange are treated with some detail. Firstly, they pass over centuries of generally peaceful coexistence between the Greeks and Turks under the Ottoman rule and assume that all the Greeks in Anatolia and the Muslim Turks in Greece, subjected to the Exchange Convention, were constantly involved in the perpetration of ethnic violence against one another. It is true that frictions between the two communities were of common occurrence in the aftermath of the Balkan Wars and some individuals and groups amongst these communities gave direct support to the respective nationalist elites. However, the great majority of the people whose fate was sealed definitely with the Exchange Convention were far from being involved. As the first part of this book on the diplomatic process shows, the decision for a compulsory exchange was taken by the nationalist cadres without any pretense of consulting the populations concerned[51] and without any anticipation of the problems that such a decision was bound to generate. Secondly, it is generally assumed that the implementation of the provisions of the Exchange Convention, including the questions of property liquidation and refugee compensation (e.g., indemnification) took place as stipulated by the Exchange Convention. This presumptuous opinion is placed in the center of the second part of this book, where it is contended on the grounds that both Greek and Turkish refugees suffered from numerous predicaments generated by the discrepancies between the formula and the reality during the application of the Exchange Convention. It is our contention that all these problems, especially those encountered in the recently flourishing scholarly literature, are closely related to the fact that these scholars, not having read Turkish and Greek histories, take for granted all the findings, and sometimes even the arguments, of the traditional scholarship on the subject and simply regenerate them, with all their flaws and deficiencies, under the mantle of a new terminology.

More recently, several scholars, affiliated with the newly emergent field of refugee studies,[52] have concerned themselves with the human dimension of population transfers, more particularly, refugees, who bore the brunt of the staggering cost entailed by this settlement.[53] These scholars treated the Turco-Greek Exchange legitimately as emblematic of minority rights violations and forced migrations throughout history. In this history, which harkens back to the Middle Ages, if not to Biblical times, the Turco-Greek case holds a special place since it illustrates "the formation of a new type of refugee, stemming from the organization of a largely involuntary unmixing of people under the aegis of international law."[54] Accordingly, they placed the undertaking of the Turco-Greek Exchange, with its causes and consequences, within the long history of refugee movements as a background to the emergence of an international regime for refugees.[55] In this context, they focused on the particular policies that the states adopted in compliance with this regime and the linkages between the processes governing the formation of refugees and international politics.

It is obviously beyond the scope of this study to assess the bulky literature on the refugees. Suffice it to say that when the refugees appeared in these studies, they were treated as subservient to the practices of the nation-state as they had been in the traditional scholarship of various sorts, a criticism raised by some scholars of post-modern inclinations from within the same field.[56] Critics have argued that refugees have been portrayed in the traditional scholarship as people who constituted a commonly recognized problem in the context of the sovereign territorial state, an approach that made them a dependent variable, more acted upon than actors.[57] In other words, where refugees figured in the picture, they were studied not on their behalf but due to the importance of their activities to the cause of the political agency, namely the nation-state. However, as two well-known students of refugee studies would state in the preface of a collected volume, "the refugee is as real as the nation-state is real."[58]

The approach of attributing agency to the refugees was most concretely applied to the refugees of the Turco-Greek Exchange of Populations by Renée Hirschon.[59] The author presented a totally different 'history' of the Greek refugees whose lives were characterized, upon their arrival in Greece, by constraints ranging from educational and economic disadvantages to spatial segregation, which combined to make them a Greek minority ('strangers at home') within the larger Greek society. Hirschon's study, which will be frequently referred to in this book, certainly brought a new spirit to the study of the Exchange, at least for its Greek side, by challenging some of the established paradigms such as that of "the twin myths of ethnic and national homogeneity"[60] which has long crippled the study of the subject. Nevertheless, the anthropologically grounded approach, including that of Hirschon, runs the risk of reducing in importance the role of the political and diplomatic process that led to the making of the refugees. Therefore, like all the other strands of scholarship, it suffers from the chronic partiality that has dominated the representation of the Exchange in scholarly literature.

Nowhere has the representation of the Turco-Greek Exchange of Populations been more problematic than in the official histories of Greece and Turkey. Written from the vantage point of the nationalistic ideological concerns of the ruling elite, the official histories in both countries appropriated the historical setting of this event from the very beginning and molded along the way the local ramifications of the Lausanne Treaty as a whole into the master narratives of their respective nations. Whereas Greek official historiography looked upon the events which led to and were associated with Lausanne as a collective tragedy and sanctioned them under the rubric of the Asia Minor Catastrophe, Turkish scholarship viewed these events as a triumphant recreation and epitomized them as the National War of Independence. These two attitudes engendered, in turn, two discernible and diametrically opposed patterns in the representation of the Exchange, pointing at best to the use of history as an instrument of manipulating collective memory. An eminent historian has noted this function of history to be in the service of dominant social groups in order to attain such objectives since the beginning of the age of nationalism and nation-states. He stated: "Collective memory has been an important issue in the struggle for power among social forces. To make themselves the master of memory and forgetfulness is one of the great preoccupations of the classes, groups, and individuals who have dominated and continue to dominate historical societies. The things forgotten or not mentioned by history reveal the mechanisms for the manipulation of collective memory."[61]

In Greece, the remembrance of the Asia Minor Catastrophe constituted the backbone of political rhetoric on the past, present and future of Greek nation-state, not to mention Greek national identity.[62] This event, having derailed the entire course of Greek history by ending the hopes for a Greater Greece and therefore closely linked with the fate of Hellenism, secured for itself from inception a distinguished, if not autonomous, place in the early historiography of modern Greece.[63] Many politicians and historians set out to read this traumatic event into the existing biography of the Greek nation in the 1920s. The Exchange and more particularly the refugees as the most concrete manifestation of this national disaster provided politicians and historians alike with "a forceful tool with which to decry the persecutions of Greeks in general"[64] and were conveniently incorporated into this discourse as reminders of the defeat, humiliation and victimization inflicted by Turks.[65] These people also sought to illustrate, often through selective quotation, the quality of Greek statecraft in absorbing over a million displaced individuals as well as the contributions of the latter to the economic and cultural development of Greece. This double-edged tendency to fit the Exchange within the neatly woven pattern of nationalist narrative became a permanent feature of Greek historical writings and dominated the studies of various Greek scholars, established in Greece or living in the Diaspora.[66] Their indispensable contributions to the documentation and reconstruction of the Exchange for Greece notwithstanding, these standard accounts have not only rendered the Turkish side of the story nearly obsolete but have also reduced the whole discussion, through an utterly nationalistic discourse, to a one-sided appraisal for Greece. On the whole, these studies tend to overlook the problems of the refugees with the native populations and assume that since the incoming refugees were ethnically of a common origin, they were immediately accommodated into the existing social and national framework. More than eighty years after the Exchange, this traditional tendency among historians, especially within the Greek academic establishment, remains in effect, albeit to a lesser extent.[67]

As for Turkey, the nationalists, who emerged triumphant from the struggle for independence, adopted an opposing tendency and subordinated specific occurrences such as the Exchange to the success story of the War of Independence and the making of the Turkish nation-state. The emergent attitude in the Turkish nationalist historiography tended to portray the Turco-Greek War as an event that marked the unification and independence of the Turkish nation while viewing all the rest as trivia. But even the trivia were considered inseparable from the success story and thus were molded, preserved, and defended. Thus, during the formative as well as the later phases of Turkish national history, the Turco-Greek Population Exchange among many other topics of the period was overshadowed by the preordained literature of "the Turkish Revolution" and eventually marginalized to the historical narrative of the nation.[68] If the Exchange was ever spelled out in this narrative, it was either portrayed as identical to the expulsion of the enemy from a homeland that was not there before or has been subjected to false generalizations. In this context, some scholars even got the date wrong, and there has been some understandable confusion about the exact number of people involved in the Exchange.[69] This was not at all surprising since what is called the Early Republican period has from the very beginning fared embarrassingly poorly at the hands of professional historians.[70] Thus, it can be argued that inasmuch as Greek historiography embraced "remembrance" as the essence of its pursuit, Turkish mainstream historiography adopted "forgetting" as the guiding line in appropriating such occurrences as the Exchange while tailoring a brand new history for the Turkish nation.

By and large, both Greek and Turkish mainstream historians invariably entangled all the historical events of the 1920s with the affairs of their respective nationalisms and engendered from the beginning a body of scholarship bound up principally with the dominant political discourse. Accordingly, the episode of nearly two million people, who were subjected to the provisions of the Exchange Convention annexed to the Lausanne Treaty, was either *remembered* or *forgotten* in a manner pertinent to the ideological goals of the political leadership. Whereas Greek historians from the very outset *remembered* the Exchange as a turning point in the consolidation of the country's ethnic and national homogeneity, their Turkish counterparts, carried away by the foundation of the new state, tended to *forget* by treating it as hardly more than a footnote—despite its immediately visible effects on the social, economic, and political conditions of the country—in the master saga of the Turkish nationalist struggle and the quest for statehood. Therefore, it was not necessarily the relative impact, whether quantitative or qualitative, of the Exchange upon the countries concerned, though it might have been, but rather the relative specificities and historical contingencies of the political discourse that conditioned the representation of this topic in Greek and Turkish mainstream historiographies.

In contrast to earlier ones, the recent anniversaries of the Lausanne Treaty coincided with the rise of new scholarly voices, mostly of a "revisionist" tone, in Greece and Turkey as well as abroad. This new trend originated largely from amongst Greek and Turkish scholars disenchanted with the nation-state paradigm and the explanations of political history, a universal trend in social sciences in this era of global revolutions. This "revisionist" tendency is characterized by its critical approach to the recent past and its overt emphasis on the role of social and cultural factors in historical analysis. Thus, the Lausanne Treaty, which has been epitomized as a major watershed in the recent history of Turkey and Greece,[71] is now exposed to a critical reading and reassessment by social scientists,[72] who have traditionally been reluctant to undertake such attempts owing to the strong grip of the state on the writing of history. Accordingly, hitherto neglected effects of the Treaty, such as the social and cultural ramifications of the Exchange Convention on the modern history of Greece and Turkey, have recently begun to receive their due scholarly attention in both countries as well as abroad. Our current level of knowledge on the consequences of the Lausanne settlement, and more particularly of the Exchange, which suffers a great deal from a state-centric perspective operating on the premises of a nationalist historiography, promises to undergo substantial revisions in the light of new sources and approaches.

The deficiencies in the traditional interpretations of the Exchange mentioned above have provided the departure point for the recent approaches to the subject. On the Greek side of the event, scholars coming from the disciplines of anthropology and sociology produced, on the basis of oral history material, pioneering studies regarding the cultural, social and economic aspects of the Exchange. Under the leadership of such prominent figures as Michael Herzfeld[73], Renée Hirschon,[74] Maria Vergeti,[75] and more recently Anastasia Karakasidou,[76] the anthropological approach to the relations between the refugees and Greek nationalism has modified quite a few of the widely-held opinions on the subject and brought attention to the voice of refugees.[77] These studies have unpinned the multiple ramifications of the refugee identity and demonstrated that from the beginning Greek nationalist ideology has played a vital role in the suppression of the distinct identity represented by these people. In the same critical tradition, a few political scientists and economic historians have concerned themselves respectively with the participation of the refugees in mass politics and their integration with economic life.[78] They tracked the impediments experienced by the refugees in political and economic realms and their continued grievances of social and economic nature with the native populations during the first years of arrival. These studies have been particularly critical in order to debunk a set of scholarly attitudes such as the "twin myths of ethnic and national homogeneity" that had been promoted through the combined efforts of politicians and scholars during the post-Lausanne era with a view to playing down the effects of the military defeat in Asia Minor.

As for Turkey, in the 1990s, critical trends in the social sciences, especially in regard to the role of the nation-state, were combined with political developments unfolding in the Balkans[79] and rising critical voices in Turkey and abroad over the issues of democratization, minority rights and the larger question of human rights[80] to wield significant bearings on many scholars established in Turkey or abroad and who are specialized in the Early Republican Period of Turkish history. In this context, many scholars and journalists produced a large body of publications on a selective list of topics concerning the institutions and policies of the Early Turkish Republic, largely as a background "to understand the present situation."[81] The discovery of the Exchange as a proper subject of historical research took place as part of these revolutionary trends when the power of the nation-state began to be questioned in Turkey. Then several studies cropped up to explore the foundations of the Republic with reference to specific occurrences such as the Exchange in order to highlight the process of the making of the Turkish state. However, while the plethora of publications in Greek historiography has begun to challenge various theses of nationalistic historiography concerning the Exchange from all directions, Turkish domestic historiography, perhaps due to the fact that it had just discovered the subject, has become home to two contradictory tendencies. On the one hand, a group of scholars undertook original archival research with a view to fitting the Exchange into the master saga of the Turkish Revolution.[82] On the other hand, several scholars attempted to reread the existing secondary sources with the objective of portraying the Exchange as an independent event with all its opportunities and constraints upon Turkey, paying due attention to the predicaments experienced by the refugees.[83]

The former tendency is of a piece with the state-centric approach that has long crippled Greek national historiography on the role of Exchange and the refugees in Greek history. This view can be summarized as such: While the state benefited greatly from the Exchange in terms of providing the ethnic homogeneity of the country and the nationalization of the country's physical and human geographies, not to mention the economy, on the one hand, the incoming refugees came to contribute a great deal to the economic and cultural development of the country on the other. It is possible to argue in this sense that the first category of recently developing Turkish scholarship on the Exchange represents a mode of thinking that has long been phased out or marginalized in Greek scholarship.

As for the latter trend, it is represented by scholars who are well grounded in the most recent scholarly currents and methodologies in social sciences, and who are aware of the ongoing scholarly research with revisionist overtones on the subject in Greece and abroad. Unlike those representing the first mode of scholarship, the scholars in this category tend to adopt a critical approach to the formation of the nation-state in Turkey, underpinning the social, cultural and economic consequences of the Exchange for the country as a whole. In this context, the significance of the Exchange is attributed not so much to its role in the eradication of an allegedly potentially dangerous minority, thus the homogenization of the country's population, as to its transformative impact upon the physical and human geography of the country by restructuring its property map as well as by reshaping its composition of the human capital and class structure (e.g., the formation of a Muslim-Turkish bourgeoisie, etc.). These issues are treated in detail throughout this book with due attention paid to the relevant bibliography. Suffice it to point out here that regardless of their orientations, both these scholarly trends should be appraised for having played an important role in bringing the topic of the Exchange to public attention in Turkey.

Against this historiographical background to the study of the Exchange, the present study has a twofold purpose. Firstly, it aims to contribute to the recently flourishing critical scholarship on the Early Republican Period of Turkish history by introducing the Turco-Greek Exchange as a proper research topic to the agenda of modern Turkish historiography. In this regard, it documents and investigates, in juxtaposition to the well-documented Greek side of the event, the manifold dynamics of this event as unfolded in Turkey. Secondly, it aims to contribute to the general literature on the Exchange by incorporating aptly the Turkish dimension of the event, more particularly the Turkish side of the decision-making process and the episode of the Muslim refugees that have been left outside the scope of the research agenda, to the broader picture, thereby, breaking up the established notion of the Exchange skewed to the Greek side. By doing so, this book aims to provide a comprehensive, relatively balanced, and factually grounded narrative of the Turco-Greek Exchange of Populations as a historical event that has been the subject of much distortion in the historiographical traditions of nationalist lore in Greece and Turkey and scholarly publications of various sorts at an international level over the span of more than eighty years.

SOURCES, METHODOLOGY, AND THEMES

As discussed above, the status ascribed to the Exchange in both Greek and Turkish national histories is embedded in the historicist presuppositions of the nationalistic-minded historiography, which have been inseparably associated with the ideological tenets of the ruling elite. Accordingly, most of the historical developments which led to and were associated with Lausanne have been the subject of much distortion in the national historiographies of Turkey and Greece. Therefore, their documentation presents major hurdles to the researchers. Under these conditions, establishing the facts and the chronology of the Exchange necessitated the use of original material scattered throughout a wide and varied range of sources. In the absence of authentic sources on the Turkish refugees, the greater portion of the information concerning the public attitude towards the population exchange and particularly towards the problems of the refugees was gleaned from newspaper reports of the period. The current study also made extensive use of the official sources obtained from the documentary collections of the Historical Archives of the Greek Ministry of Foreign Affairs (*Ιστορικο Αρχειο του Υπουργειου Εξωτερικων της Ελλαδας*) in Athens and the Republican Archives of the Turkish Prime Ministry (*Cumhuriyet Arşivi*) located in Ankara. The author was fortunate to be given permission to consult and use freely the archival collections of the Foreign Ministry in Greece. This material is used to trace some of the developments concerning the refugee policies of the Greek State prior to and during the Lausanne negotiations and to shed light on various aspects of the ensuing refugee problem.

The Republican Archives is the most valuable repository for sources on the early history of the Turkish Republic. It provided the resolutions of the government on many aspects of the Exchange and the problems faced by incoming refugees. Many sources available at this repository are still in the process of being classified, therefore could not be utilized. However the author was granted the privilege of seeing some of these uncatalogued documents, which will certainly become the most vital sources from which to study the social and economic history of the Early Republican period in the near future. As for the archives of the Ministry of Foreign Affairs in Ankara, this institution permits only a select few researchers to consult these collections. Therefore, only the published documents from this repository were used in this study.

In addition to the collections at the above-mentioned repositories, the Turkish Military Chief of Staff Archives (*Askeri Tarih ve Stratejik Etüdler Başkanlığı*, abbreviated as ATASE) contains many documents on the military affairs in the region, especially during the Balkan Wars and WWI, but fewer for the post-WWI period. Since the decade of the 1910s falls outside the scope of this study, very limited use of this material was made. Several documents from this location were especially helpful in tracing the frequent migratory movements between the Western shores of Anatolia and the islands as well as some of the early policies concerning the expulsion of the Greeks towards the interior of Anatolia. Finally, the Library of the Turkish Grand Assembly (*Türkiye Büyük Millet Meclisi Kütüphanesi*) furnished the author with copies of some of the booklets that had been prepared by the Ottoman government to regulate refugee affairs after the Balkan Wars. The same institution donated to the present institution of the author a set of the proceedings of the Turkish Grand Assembly that covers the 1920–1928 period. They were used extensively to trace the development of the refugee problem in Turkey. The picture is admittedly incomplete. The lack of data or the unreliability of available material is responsible for most of the gaps.

In addition to written historical sources, oral sources were also researched for this study. A recent study reminds us that "oral history is simply one among several primary sources. It is no worse than written documents."[84] Such sources have only recently begun to receive their long overdue respect in the study of modern Turkish and Greek histories. The current study makes a very preliminary attempt to utilize these sources. The Center for Asia Minor Studies archives in Athens remains the repository with the most valuable collections on the experiences of Greek refugees before and after the Exchange. Unfortunately, the experiences of Turkish refugees remain for the most part unrecorded, and attempts to locate the surviving refugees were not successful, with the exception of a few cases. These cases certainly offer a different perspective to the study of the subject, but one only wishes that more survivors could have been located. Therefore, in terms of its empirical sources, the current study is based primarily on official sources, which usually present very clear images of how the situation unfolded. The very few oral accounts that were found are used to fill in the gaps of the picture.

Needless to say, the author's investigations have by no means exhausted the stock of material lying in the various archival collections in Greece, Turkey and elsewhere. Due to financial constraints and the limited scope of the study, many sources were not used directly in this study. But as will be obvious in the following pages, the research conducted by other students on the subject and the material collected in these archives have benefited the present work in a variety of ways. Among the major collections in the League of Nations' archives located in Geneva, the documents concerning the Lausanne Conference have been widely used by scholars and proven to be of particular value.[85] Leading scholars of the Exchange, such as Stephen Ladas and Dimitri Pentzopoulos, have based their accounts primarily on these sources. But perhaps more important are the archival collections located in various cities of Greece and Turkey, especially the documentary collections of the General State Archives (*Γενικο Αρχειο του Κρατους*)in Athens, which includes, among others, the archives of the Refugee Settlement Commission. Furthermore, repositories like the National Institute of Research (*Εθνικο Ιδρυμα Ερευνων*) in Athens, hold manuscript collections of historical figures such as Alexander Pallis, who was officially involved in the Exchange. In the same way, the private archives of Venizelou located in the Bennaki Museum (*Τμημα Ιστορικων και Χειρογραφων)*in Athens is known to house many documents relevant to the topic of this study. The Historical Archives of Macedonia located in Salonica contains the material of the General Administration of Macedonia (*Αρχειο Γενικης Διοικησης Μακεδονιας*), and has been used mainly by the Salonica-based scholars. As for Turkey, the only locations with material relevant to the subject are the archival collections of the Provincial Bureaus of Village Affairs (*Köy Hizmetleri Müdürlükleri*) and the archives of the Turkish Red Crescent (*Kızılay Arşivi*) which have recently come to the attention of scholars in Turkey.[86] With the efficient use of these local Greek and Turkish archives, which have started to be exploited by some Ph.D. students in recent years, the lacuna in the study of the Exchange will hopefully be minimized in the near future.

In terms of its methodological concerns, the current study adopts a narrative approach in covering the diplomatic process behind the formulation of the Exchange Convention, and tracing comparatively the development of the refugee problem in Turkey and Greece from its genesis to the turn of the decade. However, it should be remarked at the outset that by studying the Exchange, the current study aims to open up a previously neglected area in the historiography of Turkey and to show its importance for the history of the country as whole. As it was briefly mentioned above, the topic remains to date much like many other topics of history, another *terra incognita* in modern Turkish historiography, which unfortunately unlike its Greek counterpart, has not had the luxury of developing along multiple directions. Thus, the slightly lopsided orientation of this approach towards the Turkish side stems more from a historiographical necessity than the chronic parochialism characterizing the field. Even then, the current study offers some novel insights into the Greek side of the Exchange by placing the whole event within its broader historical context. It is the author's genuine commitment to the latter goal that should make the present book of some interest to Turkish and Greek scholars alike. Furthermore, although present day decision-makers are more circumspect in advocating the exchange of populations than their predecessors at Lausanne (Paris and Postdam as well, for that matter), the attraction of the exchange as an instrument to putative peacemakers and ardent nationalists remains fully intact.[87] Therefore, a more thoroughly told story of the Turco-Greek Exchange of Populations should offer some lessons to decision makers.

With the aim of reconstructing the broader picture, the current study proceeds through two levels of inquiry. The first part, which is an attempt at rereading the Lausanne discussions with special reference to the Exchange, focuses on the Lausanne meetings and maps out the dynamics of the negotiation process. This part traces for each side the formation of the idea of exchange with all its fluctuations. There is specific reference to the developments that took place away from Lausanne in Greece and Turkey and had a particular impact on the course of discussions during the negotiation process. While surveying some of the political developments in both countries, this section also looks at some of the other issues of debate at Lausanne (e.g., the issue of the Patriarchate) in relation to the ongoing discussions surrounding the Exchange.

In general, the principal arguments of this part can be recapped as follows: the diplomatic teams of both states were determined to pursue an argument for a compulsory exchange of populations upon their arrival in Lausanne. The only exceptions to their anticipated plans were the Greeks of Constantinople for the Greek delegation and the Karamanlı Greeks of central Anatolia for the Turks. The Turks considered the Greeks of Constantinople to be subjected unconditionally to the Exchange while viewing the question of Turkish Muslim population in Western Thrace as a territorial matter in line with the principles of the National Pact (*Misak-ı Millî*). A plebiscite was the best they hoped for. For the accomplishment of these goals, both diplomatic teams had strict instructions from Ankara and Athens to follow, but their positions wavered greatly during the negotiations depending upon the maneuvers of the other side. The entanglement of the

Exchange with other issues (e.g., the Armenian question, the status of Patri-archate, etc.) during the negotiations modified the plans of the two sides and the drafted plan came to include the Karamanlides in the exchange scheme while leaving out the Greeks of Constantinople. The Turkish claims over Western Thrace were met with an orchestrated opposition of the confer-ence and the whole question was ultimately resolved by the full annexation of this region to Greece, as the Turkish Muslim population of the region was exempted from the Exchange in return for the Greeks of Constanti-nople. Since the conference focused a major part of its work concerning the Exchange on these issues, the decision-makers paid little attention to the formulation of the rules and regulations that would govern the regimenta-tion and implementation of the Exchange.

Having examined the diplomatic underpinnings of the decision for the Exchange on both sides, the current study moves on to trace the unfolding of the exchange from the conclusion of the negotiation process to the aboli-tion of the international and local institutions in charge of its execution in both countries. It has been claimed all along, perhaps rightfully so, that the Lausanne Treaty radically solved the most persistent questions between Turkey and Greece, such as territorial and minority issues.[88] Where Greece is concerned, it is also established that the treaty gave rise to a domestic problem of immense proportions in the character of refugees during the first decade of the Exchange. Thus, the refugee problem as a subject of study has retained a special place in Greek historiography. By arguing that the refugees suffered numerous predicaments and came to pose as much of a challenge to Turkey as they were to Greece during this period, the pres-ent study introduces the refugees as a novel social category to the field of Modern Turkish studies.

Accordingly, the second part of the book focuses primarily on the ref-ugee problem. The three consecutive chapters (5–6–7) examine the process from the implementation of the provisions of the Lausanne Convention to the Ankara Convention of 1930, which transferred the ownership of all the sequestered property into the hands of the two national governments and thus bypassed the refugees' claims completely. Chapter Eight adopts a mul-tiple view of the refugee problem with emphasis on the laborious efforts of Turkey and Greece to cope with the Exchange. While surveying the devel-opment of the refugee problem in Turkey, this section pays particular atten-tion to some of the key issues with regards to the implementation of the Convention's terms, such as compensation for the property losses of the refugees. Those who filed charges against the Turkish state in the immedi-ate aftermath of the Athens Agreement of 1926 are a good case in point. On the basis of the scanty evidence obtained from the Historical Archives of the Greek Ministry of Foreign Affairs and the Republican Archives in Ankara, it will be shown that the majority of the charges filed against the Turkish state were dismissed outright due to insufficient documentation or some unknown reason. Chapter Eight also looks at the institutional mechanisms and policies of the Turkish and Greek governments regarding the minority-turned-refugees. The principal argument here is that the institutions and practices envisaged by the Exchange Convention proved to be too unrealistic to address the complexities of the transfer, resettlement, and rehabilitation of the refugees. The Mixed Commission, which had been instituted to oversee the implementation of the Convention, more particularly its terms concerning the liquidation and proper indemnification of the refugees, became mired in such questions as the status of *établis* and neglected to address its principal obligations. In the same vein, both in Greece and Turkey, local institutions devised by the respective governments proved ineffectual in providing for the resettlement of the refugees. The Greek case registered some degree of success—using the language of the Greek revisionist scholarship, 'ambiguous success'—at the outset due to the very fact that an autonomous institution, namely, the Refugee Settlement Commission, handled not only the resettlement but also most of the exchange-related issues. The Commission, using its bargaining power underscored by the schemes of foreign loans under the aegis of the League of Nations, managed to resettle most of the Greek refugees. But the resettlement scheme focused largely on the physical accommodation of the refugees, failing to address adequately the social and economic needs of these people. Where Turkey was concerned, the establishment of a highly bureaucratic body, namely the Ministry of the Exchange, Reconstruction and Resettlement (*Mübadele, İmar ve İskan Vekaleti*), to deal with the exchange as well as the absence of necessary funds prolonged the attempts to address the problems of the refugees. The Ministry, which had inherited most of its institutional apparatus from the Ottoman State, failed in most of its policies concerning the resettlement of refugees. Thus, it was soon abolished and all its functions were transferred to other governmental offices, creating a major havoc in the handling of refugee affairs. In the final analysis, the minority-turned-refugees on both sides shouldered the heavy burdens of an ineffectual agenda put forward by the Exchange Convention.

Part Two also rewinds the narrative and turns to early developments. Chapter Seven provides an overview of the developments from the transportation of the refugees to their settlement and economic integration. It examines various socio-economic aspects of the refugee problem with emphasis on the difficulties encountered by the refugees during their integration to the respective countries. Although the study does not specifically address the question of refugee identity, it suggests certain explanations about its formative process. In this respect, the conclusion (Chapter Nine) looks at the political participation of the refugees in their respective countries. This process offers a piecemeal explanation as to why Greek refugees came to have a permanent refugee identity, while Turkish refugees gave up their cultural bearings right away and became absorbed into the existing cultural framework.

In this study, the author is situated, of necessity, in modern Turkish historiography. In his seminal work, "The Identity of France," Fernand Braudel remarked that "the historian can really be on an equal footing only with the history of his own country; he understands almost instinctively its twists and turns, its complexities, its originalities and its weakness."[89] The assumption that native scholars have some inherent knowledge about their own culture is not without its critics. However, the present author has the firm conviction, after his long engagement with historical research, that this assumption should be credited for its great merits. Speaking only for Turkish history, the everyday implications of a highly ideologized and falsified history are learnt by living, using Karakasidou's words, through "the intimacy of childhood socialisation and native enculturation."[90] In other words, most of the peculiar behaviors of the state raised and criticized throughout the following pages were not learnt by reading or simple observation. Braudel had also stated, perhaps referring to himself, that "what we need is for someone to bring our history out from behind the walls, or rather ramparts, in which so many other people have enclosed it."[91] Given the richness of the diverse historiographical traditions behind the writing of French history, it can be assumed that Turkish history requires battalions of historians to fulfill the same mission, to reconstruct and explicate historical reality freed from the oppression of myths. To the ordinary citizens of Turkey, the past has now become largely, using David Lowenthal's famous dictum, "a foreign country"[92] colonized from within, and imaginations and myths continue to fill in the lacunae where the historical reality remains under the prerogative of the select few. Not forgetting that the historical reality or "Truth always remains beyond our grasp, and we can only arrive at some approximation to it,"[93] this book will not have failed its purpose should it provide the reader with some sense of this approximation.

Part One
Diplomacy

Chapter One
Introduction

> Turkey, her treasury fattened with rubles, her forces accoutred with
> French, Italian and Bolshevist arms, has conquered Greece and will
> appear, paradoxically, at Lausanne in the role of a victor, although she
> was cast for the part of a vanquished nation treating with her conquer-
> ors. An ambitious and unscrupulous clique at Angora, having defied
> the great European powers, having overridden the religious and politi-
> cal authority of the Sultan, is aflame with arrogance and greed.[1]

Lausanne provided the venue for the peace conference that was designed to
negotiate the outcome of the Turco-Greek war and to settle the grievances of
the Allies—namely Great Britain, France, and Italy—with Turkey. Although
the Ankara government insisted on hosting the conference in its own territory, preferably in Izmir, the Allies, abandoning their earlier plans for Ven-
ice, eventually designated Lausanne as a neutral site for holding the peace
negotiations.[2] In the meantime, the Allies convened with the representatives
of the Ankara government and the Greek delegates in the Turkish town of
Mudanya to officially declare the end of the Turco-Greek war with an armistice. Despite the serious objections of the Greeks, the Armistice was signed
between the Allied commanders and Turkish military representatives on
October 11, 1922, and it was accepted by the Greeks three days later. Thus,
the Armistice paved the way to the peace conference, which was originally
scheduled to open on November 13, 1922 but was able to meet a week later.

UPON ARRIVAL

The Turkish delegates came to Lausanne in a very conspicuous position. Not
only were they considered a "band of marauders" and an "unscrupulous

clique"³ by the leading figures of world diplomacy, but they were also in a precarious situation due to the mounting dissension within Turkey over the nature of the new regime.⁴ While Bolshevik support and recent agreements with France and Italy had brought home the victory, they had hardly settled the other grievances with these countries.⁵ Moreover, the most recent Chanak crisis added yet another moment to the history of Anglo-Turkish tension. When the official sessions convened at the Conference, the Turkish delegation found the Allies united⁶ and the situation back at home approaching a political schism between Istanbul (still under Allied occupation) and Ankara.⁷ Thus, the Conference proved to be a double-edged sword for the newly developing state, in that the Ankara government had to use the platform cast by the victory as an occasion to impose itself upon the international public on one hand, and to cultivate public confidence at home, on the other.

On the side of the "vanquished," the Greek delegates arrived at Château d'Ouchy, where the conference was held, with concerns more or less similar to those of their Turkish counterparts on international and national affairs. Greece was as internationally isolated as Turkey, and "since December 1920, all Allied help had been withdrawn and official and public opinion in Britain and France had been totally estranged by the restoration of King Constantine because of his anti-Entente politics during the World War."⁸ On the domestic front, the newly empowered military government, not recognized by the Allies, was in search of ways to settle the accounts with the alleged culprits of the Asia Minor Disaster, while the schism between Royalists and Venizelists (*Εθνικος Διχασμος*) with its profound repercussions continued to plague the country's politics.⁹ Much like their Turkish contenders, the Greek delegation came to Lausanne against the backdrop of a precarious political scene at home. The head of the Greek diplomatic team, Eleftheros Venizelos, who had represented Greece in all the major diplomatic meetings over the past decade, was perhaps Greece's sole advantage at the Lausanne Conference. Although in the eyes of European diplomats, his country's economic and political credentials were at their lowest ebb,¹⁰ the experienced politician still maintained on the eve of the Conference his distinct reputation among the European diplomatic elite.¹¹ As some scholars keenly argued later, Venizelos was in fact equipped with all the diplomatic skills to turn the military defeat into a diplomatic victory and then perhaps translate it into a strong come-back in Greek political life.¹²

THE OPENING

The Turkish side made its case at the Conference when the head of the Turkish delegates, İsmet Paşa, took the floor as the third speaker after the

President of the Swiss Confederation M. Habb, and the British Foreign Minister Lord Curzon. With what Curzon later called, "some very partisan and rather truculent remarks,"[13] İsmet Paşa proceeded to outline the history of the Turkish war for independence with frequent references to the Turkey's war-torn population. Against the backdrop of the principles of the National Pact (*Misak-ı Milli*) of January 28, 1920, İsmet Paşa centered his "off-the agenda" speech around two major issues; territorial consolidation of the new state in the making and the defiance of all the capitulary agreements of the Ottoman Empire. Both conditions were vital to the definition of the sovereign state, which İsmet Paşa later described in one of his political speeches: "a homogeneous, unified homeland; within it, freedom from the obligations imposed by foreigners and from privileges of a nature creating a state within a state; freedom from imposed financial obligations; a free, rich homeland with a recognized absolute right of self-defense."[14] It is upon this basis that İsmet Paşa demanded complete equality of representation with all the participating countries in the Conference before the "star chamber proceedings" and "steamroller methods" of Lord Curzon could come to dominate the course of negotiations.[15]

The National Pact had become the canon of Turkish foreign policy since the beginning of the decade. After the litmus test of the Mudanya Armistice, which declared the end of the Turco-Greek war, the principles of the Pact now came to govern the Turkish position at the Conference.[16] This became firmly established during the second day when the work of various commissions was underway. In the first session of the Territorial and Military Commission, the efforts of which were devoted fully to Thrace, İsmet Paşa, claiming all the pre-war Thracian territory, brought up the issue of a plebiscite in Western Thrace.[17] The third article of the National Pact clearly stated that "the juridical status of Western Thrace, which has been dependent on the Turkish peace, shall be effected in accordance with a free plebiscite."[18]

İsmet Paşa's adamant remarks, which were intended for the protection of the large Muslim population living in that area and for the security of eastern Thrace, sparked off a duel with Lord Curzon, a frequent occurrence throughout the Conference. The latter confronted him immediately and asked for quantitative evidence in support of his arguments and clarification of some of the geographical issues he had referred to in his presentation.[19] In reply, İsmet Paşa said he would have to consult with his advisers, which he did immediately by wiring Ankara.[20] Following the reply of Hüseyin Rauf on behalf of the government,[21] İsmet Paşa persisted in his position and a commission was established by the Conference to look into this matter.[22] It was obvious from the beginning that İsmet Paşa and the other members of the Turkish diplomatic team were determined to pursue negotiating from strength as the victors in order to dictate the conditions of the peace despite the fact that the Allies viewed them as the losers of WWI and therefore felt they should be conciliatory.[23] To this effect, the Turkish plenipotentiaries observed very closely the guidelines listed by the government in Ankara.[24]

The Greek side found the occasion to make its case on the program of the Conference immediately after İsmet Paşa's speech. Venizelos, the head of the Greek diplomatic team, stood up to respond to İsmet Paşa's long list of allegations and demands. Refraining from any personal polemics with his opponent, Venizelos crafted a speech that was on the whole an unruffled evaluation of the historical developments that brought Greece to Lausanne.[25] Two major themes ran through his discourse. The first one was, though only by implication, the abortive nature of the Greco-Entente alliance, which he described as follows,

> The Greek government had asked for eastern Thrace, for Smyrna and its hinterland, because it was convinced that its claims were in conformity with the principles for which the allies fought. . . . Greece only entered the war in order to keep her promise towards her allies and in order to defend the principles upheld by the Allies, and entirely approved by himself.[26]

Venizelos' carefully crafted statements included no open criticisms of the Entente politics before his defeat in the elections of November 1920, but emphasized the developments after the breaking point when the Greco-Entente friendship was disrupted by the accession of the King Constantine to power. To him, it was from this very point onwards that the Greek advance into Asia Minor, which had been carried out "in the name of the Entente" turned into a duel between Greece and Turkey, eventually resulting in the loss of Asia Minor to the latter.[27] With these remarks, in which there was no criticism of the Allies for leaving Greece alone during the war with Turkish nationalists, Venizelos, in fact, gave the first major message in the conference that "the Greece of Venizelos was different from that of the King," a particular reference to the unfolding conflict over the nature of the regime as well as a confidence building message to the Allies for Greece's future relations with them.

The second theme was the state of the refugees in Greece, a subject that in fact enveloped all the other issues raised in his speech. According to Venizelos, the demand of İsmet Paşa to secede further portions of Western Thrace beyond the west of Maritsa from Greece was inconceivable due the very fact that this would cause the uprooting of many more Greeks settled in this region.[28] And Greece was not in a position to shelter and feed more refugees than those who were already present in the country. The decision for such an arrangement would drag Greece into an unprecedented situation of great social, political and economic repercussions, an argument he was to pursue for the Greeks of Constantinople in the later stages of the conference. Thus, any consideration of territorial concession on the part of Greece was not only unacceptable but also unfeasible.[29]

Venizelos, having started his speech with the remark that "it was not Greece who started the war which was just finished, although she might have been driven to such a step by the desire to realise her national unity"[30] concluded it by saying "Greece had already paid for her faults and no more could be asked of her."[31] Thus, the national project of the Great Idea (*Μεγαλη Ιδεα*) that had governed both the internal and the foreign policies of Greece under the leadership of Venizelos himself over the entire last decade was formally denounced first hand at the very outset of the Conference. With this position, Venizelos assured the conference participants that his side would adopt, in complete contrast to his opponent, a constructive approach during the negotiations. Perhaps more important than its impact on the conference was the far-reaching implication of this declaration on Greek political life. The official denunciation of the Great Idea, which had become the chief column of Greek politics since the turn of the century, would turn the Greek political life "largely to the sterile attribution of blame and the cynical maneuvers of personal followings for office and patronage."[32]

THE CONFERENCE AGENDA

The peace conference was designed as two settlements in one. For the Allies it was held with the aim of restoring and formulating the terms of peace in the geographical areas, which had been under Ottoman rule for many centuries. These areas had been in turmoil since WWI and the first comprehensive diplomatic settlement, namely Sèvres, had been aborted by the resistance of Turkish nationalists. As for the Greeks and Turks, the conference was viewed as a way to settle their own conflict.

The settlement of the grievances of the Allied countries with Turkey was of vital importance to the fulfillment of the goals of the Conference. Although some countries, such as India, Spain, and Denmark had applied to participate in the Conference, the official list came to include, besides Turkey and Greece, Great Britain, France, Italy, Japan, Romania, and the Kingdom of the Serbs, Croats and Slovens. On the status of the Straits, the Soviets were to participate in the conference at a later date. With the exception of

Japan, each of these countries, in fact, had its own specific set of issues to settle with Turkey. The major parties, principally concerned with fostering their own interests, took different attitudes during the negotiations. Lord Curzon deemed three issues as significant to his country's position. These were the internationalization of the Straits, the Mosul question, and the future of the newly formed alliance between Ankara and Moscow. Unless these issues were effectively handled, there would be no reason to claim success.[33]

Of the major parties, France and Italy had, in addition to their common concerns over the Straits, unique interests at stake, for which they were to argue vehemently throughout the Conference. While the former sought to restore its capitulary privileges in Turkey, the latter was primarily concerned with the re-endorsement of its complete suzerainty over the Dodecanese,[34] islands off the coast of Asia Minor. The United States, which was not officially part of the Conference at the beginning,[35] had determined its position long before. As early as October 5, 1922, Admiral Bristol, the American High Commissioner in Istanbul had wired the Secretary of State (Hughes) that "as the United States is one of the capitulatory powers with extensive vested interests in Turkey, we can not afford to remain inactive while the Allies give their consent to important changes in the capitulatory regime."[36] Whether the Americans were interested in becoming a major player in the Aegean area is hard to say. But it was certain that they cared about the oil reserves in the Mosul district, whose status was yet to be decided. It should also be emphasized that the preservation of the juridical privileges of American citizens and institutions, whether cultural or economic, in Turkey, which had been guaranteed under the capitulations, was also among the primary goals of the American mission at Lausanne.[37]

Minor parties, such as Bulgaria, did not lag behind France, Italy, Great Britain and the United States. Thus, the Bulgarian representatives were involved intensively in all discussions pertaining to territorial issues between Turkey and Greece. As early as the second day of the meetings, the head of the Bulgarian delegation, Stamboulisky, presented the Conference with his country's position over the Thracian problem, thereby making the discussions even more complicated.[38] Bulgaria was determined to regain an outlet to the Mediterranean by any means possible, including the declaration of Western Thrace as an autonomous zone under Allied control, a solution considered by the Turks as well.[39] Therefore, from the beginning, the Conference was pregnant with many diplomatic and political twists on the part of all the major and minor parties involved in the process.

During the plenary sessions, the heads of the Turkish and Greek delegations presented the foundations of their arguments in the Conference with special references to their governments' concerns over current domestic and foreign affairs. But, in none of their speeches was there any mention of the word "Exchange." Only in the third meeting (November 23, 1922) was the name of Dr. Nansen spelled out by Venizelos to support some of his earlier points concerning the size of the refugee population in Greece.[40] This name was by then synonymous with refugees.[41] Otherwise, despite their frequent references to the prevailing refugee problem in their countries, both Turkish and Greek delegates remained silent on the fate of the people caught up in the uncertainty of the post-war environment. In their stead, the head of the Bulgarian delegation, Stamboulisky, urged the Conference participants to find an immediate solution to the mounting refugee problem on both sides of the Thracian border.[42] Nevertheless, other items of the Conference agenda, overloaded with many controversial issues of the past decade, came to dominate the course of discussions during the initial sessions.

The issues on the Conference agenda were referred to various commissions and sub-commissions for examination. As a subject that cut across much of the conference agenda, the topic of an exchange was first raised in a meeting of the Territorial and Military Commission, the chief commission of the Conference, on December 1, 1922. It decided to establish a sub-commission on the Exchange of Prisoners and Populations. The issue was made a concomitant part of the agenda of the sub-commission of the Minorities, which brought the results of its work to the Territorial and Military Commission on December 14, 1922. The sub-commission of the Exchange of Prisoners and Populations concentrated its activities around the topic of the exchange and presented its report before the chief commission on January 9, 1923.

METHOD AND SOURCES

It is certainly beyond the scope of the present chapter to survey each and every one of the issues that was raised at the negotiation table by all these commissions at the Conference. Such a task has been fulfilled by many scholarly publications, and many studies on various aspects of the Conference continue to appear.[43] The existing literature, however, is characterized predominantly by the study of the issues that were important to the major parties. In this respect, such issues as the status of the Straits, the Mosul question, and capitulations received wider attention at the expense of some others, such as the Thracian question, the minority problem, or the population exchange, the implications of which were limited exclusively to the minor parties. Thus, the author of the most widely quoted study on the Lausanne Conference, Briton C. Busch, considered the whole diplomatic process with respect only to the settlement of Britain's 'Eastern Policy' while Harry N. Howard treated the Lausanne negotiations only within the context of American interests in the question of the Straits.[44] In his extensive coverage of the Conference issues, Busch made only a passing remark about the Exchange, while the rest of his treatment is devoted to the examination of the issue of capitulations and the Mosul question.[45] Whereas Howard neglected to mention the subject, the late Roderic Davison, in probably the best essay on the diplomatic history of the early Turkish Republic, adopted an indifferent attitude to the subject in favor of the aforementioned issues.[46]

The representation of the Exchange as marginal to the general agenda of the Conference has emanated as much from the scholarly orientation as from the nature of available sources. The memoirs of British, French and American diplomats coupled with the *Official Journal* and other official publications of the League of Nations have practically drawn scholars into their orbit. The later-time tendency of the general scholarship to crown the proceedings of the conference and the newly-opened French or British archives as the canonical sources of the subject was shared by local scholars in Turkey and Greece. As discussed briefly in the Introduction, the two eminent scholars of the Exchange, namely Stephen P. Ladas and Dimitri Pentzopoulos, based their coverage of the making of the Exchange agreement almost completely on the European sources, whether primary or secondary, with very limited utilization of the available Greek sources and virtually no use of the Turkish sources.

The difficulties involved in the study of the decision-making process behind the Exchange are compounded by the general trends in the national historiography of the "minor" parties. Again, as discussed briefly in the Introduction of this study, Turkish national historiography has remained indifferent to the subject owing to a variety of historiographical and historical factors (e.g., poor documentation, the State factor, the relative impact of the Exchange). In the absence of a commensurate counterpart, Greek scholarship has taken the liberty of usurping the Exchange for its own reasons, as a unique component of Greek national historiography, and has laid claim to the representation of the other side of the story, as well. This trend has not only made the Turkish viewpoint nearly obsolete but has also turned the topic of the Exchange into a subject of redundant discussion.

Against this background, the present chapter juxtaposes the Greek and Turkish cases with a view to providing a more complete picture of the negotiation process by which the Exchange Convention was made. To this effect, it brings to the fore some of the hitherto neglected objective conditions of the Exchange, often treated as "accomplished facts," which had direct bearing on the stance of both sides on the issue. Where Greece is concerned, these conditions ranged from the emergency of the social and economic problems associated with the refugees to the relief and evacuation efforts of the Greek government, which were conducted in a way that made the prospect of repatriation an unattainable task from the very outset. As for Turkey, the firm commitment to the ideals of national sovereignty as the basis of newly-emerging nation-state encouraged the adoption of certain radical measures, among which the ethnic homogenization of the population ranked as one of the priorities. These conditions, some of which had been laid down irreversibly, provide insights into the genesis and development of the views of both sides on the Exchange. In light of these facts, the current chapter proceeds to argue that both Greeks and Turks had come to Lausanne intending to realize a compulsory exchange, and the Conference became merely a setting to negotiate their reservations on the nature of the project. It is owing to their restless entanglement with the latter instead of the particulars of the exchange process (the issues of property liquidation, refugee indemnification, etc.) that the resulting agreement would prove ineffectual in terms of accommodating the situation of the refugees, as reflected in the ensuing difficulties during the application phase of the Convention. This argument is developed more fully in Part Two of the present book.

In arriving at peace settlements, it is generally recognized that the negotiations outside are as important as discussions in a conference hall. The Lausanne Conference was no exception. Accordingly, the current study makes extensive use of information drawn from intensive caucus in the hotel corridors, rooms, and lobbies at the conference site. İsmet Paşa's meetings with Poincaré, Mussolini, and Tchitcherin as well as Venizelos' meetings with Lord Curzon and the same figures were conducted informally. It was during İsmet Paşa's meeting with Poincaré (the Turkish and French delegations were staying in the same hotel) that the latter assured his colleague of the settlement of the Exchange to the satisfaction of the Turkish side.[47] Again it was in İsmet Paşa's conversation with Lord Curzon that the unyielding position of the Allies on the issue of the Patriarchate first became pronounced.[48] Thus, a significant portion of the informal conversations of the Greek and Turkish delegates with their colleagues on the subject of the Exchange has remained off-the-record, making their way into the personal accounts of the diplomats or the telegrams.

The existing two wire lines at the conference site were used intensively by the members of the Greek and Turkish delegations in order to exchange views with their governments on the details of the Exchange plan.[49] Where the minutes of the official sessions fail to provide a full explanation of the maneuvers on both sides concerning such issues as minorities and the Exchange, the facts emerging in these sources contribute to the completion of the jigsaw puzzle. These facts also help us understand how many adjustments and accommodations on the part of the Greeks and Turks during the preparation, discussion and endorsement stages of the Exchange Convention were affected by the developments outside the conference room, which have been neglected by the literature. Insofar as the study of the subject has been bound strictly to the contents of the conference proceedings and foreign sources, the formulation of the Exchange Convention remains partially explained, carelessly treated, or passed unnoticed. It is no coincidence that the most basic question as to who initiated the idea of an exchange continues to be an enigmatic question.

THE NANSEN DEBATE

The name Dr. Nansen is almost always identified with the Turco-Greek population exchange. Many Greek historians studying the Exchange in its immediate aftermath credited Dr. Nansen as the originator of the idea.[50] Even during the Lausanne discussions, Venizelos and İsmet Paşa, having accused each other of being the first to propose the Exchange, had eventually named Nansen, ironically in his absence, as the initiator of the idea.[51] In the very limited existing literature on the Turkish side of the subject, the Norwegeian samaritan also emerges as the principal figure behind the idea.[52] It is also known, however, that Nansen declined to see himself as the first to bring up this option and held the Turks and Greeks responsible.[53]

As a matter of fact, the previous decade had several times seen the plan for an exchange become a subject of diplomatic negotiations. The first attempt was in 1913 when the Ottoman government signed a convention with the Bulgarian government as a follow-up to the Treaty of Constantinople of September 29, 1913. The two sides signed a "Convention concerning the exchange of populations" at Edirne on November 15, 1913. With this agreement, some 48,570 Muslims from the Bulgarian territory were exchanged for 46,764 Bulgarians from eastern Thrace (e.g., Kırk Kilise and Edirne). Shortly after, a similar agreement was reached between the Ottoman and Greek governments for the Muslims in Macedonia and Greek Epirus in return for the Greeks in the *Vilayet* of Aydın. The implementation of this plan, which had in fact been adopted to sanction the official process for a *de facto* situation, was aborted due to the outbreak of WWI. The importance of these two agreements consists in the fact that they laid down the institutional foundations (e.g., the creation of a Mixed Commission for the appraisal of the people and property subject to the Exchange) for similar arrangements at Neuilly and Lausanne. During the same decade, the idea of an exchange was brought up twice in 1915 and 1918 by Venizelos, first for the exchange of Greeks and Bulgarians, which failed due to the refusal of the King,[54] and the second time again for the Greeks and Bulgarians before the Paris Peace Conference, which was integrated in the form of a separate "Convention for the Reciprocal and Voluntary Emigration of National Minorities between Bulgaria and Greece" to the Treaty of Neuilly of November 27, 1919.[55] Article 143 of the Treaty of Sèvres, the application of which was aborted due to the outbreak of hostilities in Anatolia, also included, if only by implication, a provision for the exchange "of the Greek and Turkish populations in the territories which were ceded to Greece or remained in Ottoman possession respectively."[56]

As for the formulation of a plan for an exchange of Greek and Turkish populations after the Turco-Greek War, the basic story begins with the appointment of Fridtjof Nansen[57] by the League of Nations to look into the matter of the refugees in the region in the immediate aftermath of this war. Having been charged with a mission "to reach an agreement with regard to an exchange of populations between the Greek and Turkish governments," he entered into negotiations at various levels with the two governments in order to arrange an immediate solution for the refugees.[58] The impression among the European diplomats at the time was that due to the urgency of the situation after the Izmir events, Greece and Turkey would convene to negotiate an immediate exchange independent of all the other issues pending settlement between the two sides. The evidence suggests that as early as October 13, Venizelos was prepared to come to the negotiation table with the Turks.[59] However, the circumstances under which the Mudanya Armistice was signed diminished the prospects for a forum that would bring the two sides together. Therefore, the subject was placed on the table at the Lausanne Conference.[60]

In line with the view circulating among the Turkish population that "the cure for the Greek populations of the coastal regions is the exchange and for those in the interior is [the establishment of] an Anatolian Patriarchate" (*sahil Rumlarının ilacı mübadele, dahil Rumlarının ilacı Anadolu Patrikliğidir*),[61] the then Minister of Foreign Affairs, Yusuf Kemal Bey, had brought up the issue of a Turco-Greek population exchange in his meeting with Lord Curzon as early as March 1922.[62] The latter had considered the project as insufficient to solve the minority problems in the region and persisted in the opinion that a minorities treaty would still be needed to address the issue in a more comprehensive and effective manner.[63] The idea of an exchange heretofore remained part of the Turkish public opinion and the local newspapers and the Istanbul press continued to bring it up now and then.⁶⁴ The end of the war with Greece partially accommodated the Turkish public opinion by uprooting a great majority of Greek populations in Anatolia. However, the fates of the Greeks who were concentrated in the Anatolia littoral and those in the interior who had been unaffected by the war were still uncertain. It was not until Nansen's visit to Istanbul that the idea of an exchange met with more popular acceptance. In contrast to the general scholarly view that there is much uncertainty as to Nansen's visit to Turkey, Nansen's activities in Istanbul received much coverage in almost all the major newspapers throughout the country.

Nansen came to Istanbul for the first time on October 5, 1922 accompanied by Philip Noel-Baker, the High Commissioner of the League of Nations. He sought to arrange a meeting with Mustafa Kemal in Bursa and then to travel to Izmir.⁶⁵ While waiting for a response from Mustafa Kemal, he visited several refugee camps in Istanbul in the company of Hamdi Bey, the General Director of Refugee Affairs.⁶⁶ The Administrative Representative of the Ankara government in Istanbul, Hamid Bey, tried to persuade Nansen in the meantime to find a solution to the problems of the Russian refugees, and possibly provide their quick transfer to Bulgaria. On October 15, he met, upon invitation, with the High Commissioners of France, Great Britain, Italy and Japan in Istanbul, where he was asked "to take all possible steps to endeavor to reach an agreement with regard to an exchange of populations between the Greek and Turkish governments as soon as possible, independent[ly] of the peace negotiations."⁶⁷

On October 16, having been turned down by Mustafa Kemal, he decided to travel to Bulgaria and Romania and return at a later date to Istanbul.⁶⁸ On October 22, Istanbul newspapers wrote that the Greeks had agreed to an exchange of Muslim and Greek populations, and Dr. Nansen, in Athens at the time, was on his way to Mudanya in order to resume negotiations.⁶⁹ He arrived in Istanbul on October 23, and met with Hamid Bey and repeated his request to see Mustafa Kemal.⁷⁰ After apparently several inconclusive meetings with the former,⁷¹ Nansen actually met with Re'fet [Bele] Paşa, the governor of Thrace, for the second time on October 29. In a communication to the Prime Minister Rauf [Orbay] Bey, Re'fet Paşa states "I saw Nansen for the second time today. I told him my opinion that such an exchange especially for Western Thrace is out of question. He would like to discuss the issue with '*Başkumandan Paşa*' [Mustafa Kemal] and also with the central government. He is disappointed about not having received any reply from Hamid Bey to his communication. I believe that we should respond to him immediately and inform him of our positive or negative decision within four hours."⁷² The answer to this communication came the next day. Hamid Bey informed Nansen that "his instructions only permitted him to negotiate on the basis of a total and enforced population exchange, from which the population of Constantinople would not be excepted."[73] Only five days later, on November 4, Nansen made another attempt and presented Hamid Bey with a draft treaty based on the former Greco-Bulgarian exchange of populations.[74] Having not received any response, he left Turkey empty-handed.

It was not until the proposal of Nansen was presented at the conference, and Lord Curzon remarked that "good offices of the League be used in settling the issue of minorities" that the Turkish side made any official public announcement on its position concerning the Exchange. Thus, the first reaction to the proposal came from İsmet Paşa, who opposed it on the ground that since Turkey was not a member of the League, it would be inappropriate at that stage to consider using the League's machinery.[75] İsmet Paşa concluded his speech with the remark that "Dr. Nansen's statement is emanating from a private person. It was because of the private character attributed to Dr. Nansen's activities that it had proved impossible to carry his negotiations with Turkish officials beyond a certain point."[76] Lord Curzon challenged İsmet Paşa once again that "this point was unimportant. The real importance of the question lay in the fact that it vitally affected the interests of Greece and Turkey, no matter who brought it forward."[77] This debate between İsmet Paşa and Lord Curzon unleashed the negotiation phase of the Exchange at Lausanne.

Thus, the idea of a population exchange, which had been raised here and there by the Greeks and Turks since the Balkan wars, finally came to the brink of being materialized through the mediation of Nansen. The exchange negotiations, characterized by the maneuverings of both Turks and Greeks, lasted on multiple fronts until the signing of the Convention on January 30, 1923. Accordingly, legal analysis of the draft convention and other official procedures were carried out in haste and the Convention was finalized within a matter of weeks with a view to its taking effect on May 1, 1923.

Chapter Two
The Greek Case

The Greek delegation came to Lausanne with the idea of an exchange of populations in their agenda. However, they refrained from bringing it to the negotiation table until the presentation of the Nansen report at the conference on December 1, 1922.[1] The head of the Turkish delegation, İsmet Paşa, notwithstanding his reservations on the role of Nansen and the use of the League's machinery, commented that "in any case, if an exchange were effected, the Greek population of the whole of Turkey, including Smyrna and Contantinople, would be included."[2] Venizelos, who had anticipated this view earlier and conducted all his pre-conference negotiations to this effect, was unmoved by his opponent's comment. Except that the Greeks of Constantinople were included within the Turkish demand, he had no reason to oppose the idea of a compulsory exchange implied by İsmet Paşa's statement. According to John Petropoulos, İsmet Paşa's comment, in fact, constituted the essence of Venizelos' very presence in the conference.[3] Since Venizelos, as the head of the Greek delegation, "welcomed a compulsory exchange for his own reasons and wished for domestic and international political reasons, to have it appear that such a brutal process was forced upon him by the Turks."[4] Be that as it may, such an assumption, though it has its merits, fails to acknowledge the urgencies of the post-war situation manifested in the refugee reality, and discounts the position of the contending party to the extent of rendering it obsolete. It is the objective of the present chapter to highlight the background against which the Greek commitment to the idea of a compulsory exchange was formulated.

PRE-CONFERENCE DEVELOPMENTS

Venizelos' presence in Lausanne as the head of the Greek diplomatic team had been arranged upon the invitation of the newly instituted military government. On September 27, 1922, Venizelos, who had retired and gone into a self-imposed exile after being hurled from power by the elections of 1920, received a telegram from the Greek government saying that the "Revolution declares its absolute confidence and trust in you to deal with the conduct of foreign matters and asks for your immediate help."[5] Such an invitation was also supported by the Allies, as Venizelos would state during one of his earlier speeches at conference.[6] Having been furnished with full powers to deal with the foreign affairs of Greece, Venizelos launched his diplomatic campaign for the peace conference as of late September.

Upon his return, Venizelos became the diplomatic representative of the Greek government as part of the Hellenic Legation in London. From this point on, evidence in the form of intense wire communication between Venizelos and the government until the beginning of the peace negotiations suggests that he acted as the *de facto* Minister of Foreign Affairs.[7]

In his new mission, Venizelos underwent an immediate litmus test during the negotiations of the Mudanya Armistice, which he commanded from afar. Prior to the Armistice, he cultivated his old friendship with Lord Curzon with a view to appeasing the Turkish government in its harsh demands concerning the swift evacuation of eastern Thrace. He asked that the Turkish forces take over the administration of the region after the peace conference (Lausanne), thereby giving the Greek populations enough time to safely evacuate the area. Much to his dismay, his appeals were met with an indifferent attitude on the part of Lord Curzon. Despite the objections of the Greek generals, the Mudanya Armistice was signed by the military representatives of the Allied powers on October 11, 1922. In a follow-up to his earlier communication Venizelos wrote to Lord Curzon on October 13, 1922:

> Allow me to assure you that it is with greatest misgiving that I have read the protocol of [the] Armistice that has been signed. It would seem that the terms of this document are not in accordance with the request I made to you recently and which, from our last conversation in Paris, I thought had been granted. I had asked that the Turkish administration and gendarmerie be established in Thrace one month after the evacuation of that province by the Greek Army. This would give, to those of the unfortunate Christian populations who wanted to leave, time to do so. Instead of this, it appears that the Turkish authorities are to be restored immediately after the withdrawal of the Greek troops and that the whole transference of the Province to the Turks is to be accomplished in a month . . . I would be guilty of a lack of sincerity, my Lord, if I neglected to state that the Greek Nation feels that in this hour

of its misfortune, it has not been supported in its legitimate claims, to
the extent it was justified in expecting support from those of its former
allies with whom it shared the common sacrifices of lives, in order that
the liberty of the world might be safeguarded.[8]

Venizelos informed the acting minister of the coup government Nicholas
Politis of the position of Curzon and asked him to persuade the army to
comply with the requirements of the Armistice.[9] The persuasion of General
Mazarakis and Colonel Plastiras was considered a *sine qua non* by Venizelos to pursue his pre-conference negotiations, and finally the stronghold
of the Greek army in eastern Thrace was relinquished through the intervention of Athens.[10]

The situation of eastern Thrace was important in several respects.
Harry Psomiades argues that by accepting the terms of the Mudanya Armistice, Greece waived the last opportunity "to halt or modify the massive
movement toward the population exchange."[11] Based on the assumption
that the compulsory nature of the population exchange was imposed on
Greece at Lausanne, Psomiades postulates that "a firm stand on the eastern Thrace question by Greece during the Mudanya Armistice or at least
a refusal to evacuate the region until after the Lausanne peace conference,
would have undoubtedly strengthened the Greek position during the peace
negotiations."[12]

Venizelos' persistent call to comply with the Armistice was motivated
as much by the safe evacuation of the Greek populations from eastern
Thrace as by his concern to improve the image of Greece in the upcoming
peace negotiations at Lausanne. Since the early days of October, the British
and French legations in Athens had been receiving reports from the region
with details of the brutal treatment of the Muslim populations in the area.
For example, a memorandum sent by the British Legation to the Ministry
of Foreign Affairs stated that "Reports received from the Kırk Kilise district
accuse the Greek troops of the worst excesses and allege that twenty-eight
villages have been destroyed and the inhabitants driven away."[13] Venizelos
was well aware that the continuing presence of Greek troops in the region
would mean a potential renewal of war with Turkey or, at worst, the delay
or full abandonment of the peace negotiations. Also Venizelos' consideration
of the premises against which the Armistice was held might have played a
role in his assent to the terms of this settlement. Turkey had earlier agreed
that the minorities would be granted protection in the case of Greek evacuation of eastern Thrace, a point which would give Venizelos some ammunition to counter-argue the Turkish demands on the question of minorities.[14]
Thus, to the extent of threatening the government with resignation from his

duty to represent Greece abroad, Venizelos insisted on the withdrawal of the Greek army according to the terms of the Armistice. While the evacuation was underway, the British and French Legations in Athens sent separate *notes-verbaux* to inform the Greek Ministry of Foreign Affairs that "the installation of the Turkish administration in Gallipoli has been postponed until the 26th instant [November]," which gave the Greek troops and populations a safe passage for evacuation.[15] Accordingly and in line with the early agreement between Venizelos and the Foreign Ministry, the withdrawal of Greek troops was completed, a development that provided the Greek side with some leverage to counter-argue the Turkish position on a variety of issues, the most important of which being a plebiscite for an autonomous administration in Western Thrace. Since the majority of the population from eastern Thrace had been transferred to Western Thrace, it would be beyond comprehension to consider the removal of these people, an argument that Venizelos, with the backing of Lord Curzon, would devise at the outset of the negotiations on the Exchange.[16]

Prior to the Conference, Venizelos had to sort out another point of disagreement with the Greek government, which comes out in his correspondence with Nansen. This was related to the nature of a possible exchange. On October 10 and 11, Venizelos received two consecutive telegrams from Nansen asking him to mediate in his negotiations with the Greek government on the settlement of the refugee problem.[17] In his letter dated October 10, Nansen wrote:

> Everyone appears to agree that it is hopeless to expect either the Turks will agree to receive them again in Asia Minor, or that the refugees themselves would agree to go even if they were received. They must therefore be settled elsewhere and I presume that it will be the purpose of the Greek government either as a result of the Treaty for the exchange of populations with the Turkish government or without such a Treaty to settle them in the vacant lands of Macedonia on Western Thrace.[18]

In his reply to this letter on October 13, Venizelos, prompted by the verdict of the Mudanya Armistice, informed Nansen that the "Minister of the Interior of the Ankara government declared a fortnight ago that the Turks had decided not to allow further presence of Greeks on Turkish soil and would propose at the forthcoming conference the compulsory exchange of populations."[19] The letter continued, "I take the liberty of requesting that you endeavor to arrange that the transfer of the populations begin before the signature of peace." Thus, the housing problem of the refugees already present in Greece would be alleviated by the departure of some 350,000 Muslim Turks in Greece.[20] On October 17, in a follow up to this communication, Venizelos also mentioned that "perhaps if reasons of a higher order fail to persuade Mustafa Kemal, it will be possible to point out to him that if he does not concur in his migration of the Turks in Greece, the Greek government, under the pressure of unavoidable necessity, will be very probably compelled to impose this migration on the Turks living in the Greek soil."[21] Before he came to Istanbul for the second time on October 23, Nansen went to Athens to meet with Greek government officials on the subject. There he got confirmation that he could proceed with his mission "to establish an agreement on the subject of the exchange of population."[22]

Stephen Ladas, taking his cue from Nansen's meetings with the Government and communication with Venizelos, had tentatively argued that the Greek view on the subject implied a compulsory exchange of populations. This argument was later rejected by Dimitri Pentzopoulos on the very poor grounds that this ran contrary to the general policy of the Greek state as manifested during the conference, which had favored a voluntary exchange from the beginning.[23] The confusion is caused mainly by Nansen's separate negotiations with Venizelos and government officials in Athens. Unlike Venizelos, who seemed to entertain the idea of a complete population exchange including the Greeks of Constantinople and the Muslims of Western Thrace, the government in Athens, which had been conducting its evacuation of refugees from Asia Minor and eastern Thrace in a decisive manner, vehemently opposed the idea that the Greeks of Constantinople would be included in a such a project. Also, the Turkish view, based on the exclusion of the Muslims of Western Thrace and the inclusion of the Constantinople Greeks in the exchange, had only recently surfaced in Nansen's negotiations with Turkish government authorities. On November 4, Nansen sent a telegram to Venizelos indicating that the Greek government "could not contemplate taking into Greece the enormous Greek population of Constantinople or admit the principle that the Turks should expel it."[24] It is very likely that at this moment in time Venizelos and Nicholas Politis reached a consensus on the terms of the exchange project, which included a provision for the exemption of the Greeks of Constantinople. They mobilized thenceforward all available means to find an optimum solution to the issue before the Turkish authorities declared their take-over of the city from the Allied administration. The issue remained pending until the Lausanne Conference, which had been scheduled to begin its work on November 13, but "due to a number of considerations arising out of the political situation [vis-à-vis Turkish authorities] in Constantinople"[25] the Conference was postponed till the latter part of the month. This delay gave Venizelos more time to work out his conference strategy for the settlement of other grievances (e.g., Western Thrace, war reparations) which Greece had with Turkey, among which the population exchange was undoubtedly the most urgent. In the meantime, he sorted out his further differences with the government in Athens on the nature of the Exchange, and eventually attached the provision on the Greeks of Constantinople to his conference strategy.

"THE REFUGEE GREECE"

Venizelos' commitment to a compulsory exchange was prompted by factors that were manifest in the social, economic and political life of Greece. First and foremost, the mounting public pressure in Greece on the settlement of the refugee problem, which had culminated in the last few months due the continuous influx of Greek and non-Greek refugees from Asia Minor, was instrumental in the Greek government's consideration of the population exchange as a primary issue to be settled quickly. Secondly and perhaps more importantly, the immediate aftermath of the Smryna disaster had shown, from the very beginning, that the Greek government had organized its efforts to evacuate the Greeks from Asia Minor in such a way that rendered repatriation an unattainable task. Thus, it was important to take the issue to the negotiation table before the *de facto* situation became the norm.

Reciprocating the above situation were the immediate developments in the territories deserted by the Greek populations in Turkey. The seizure of abandoned Greek properties and intensive looting in these areas by the local populations or, as in the case of Smyrna and its environs, their confiscation by the Turkish authorities, preceded the quick Turkification of these areas.[26] A great number of debates in the Turkish Grand Assembly in Ankara were concerned with measures to prevent such incidents from happening, but the majority of the looters were either local officials or soldiers. Thus any systematic plan, such as the establishment of "Independence Tribunals" (*İstiklal Mahkemeleri*)[27] throughout these areas, to discourage looting was doomed to failure from its inception.[28] Moreover, the government issued a resolution on October 1, 1922 concerning the movable and immovable properties abandoned (*emval ve emlak-ı metruke*) by the Greek residents of the city. Local governmental authorities in collaboration with the newly established Committees (*fen heyetleri*) were asked to prepare inventories of these properties (including those of the Greek nationals) with the aim that the Government could use them as security against the reparations to be demanded from Greece in the upcoming peace conference.[29]

The refugee problem, with its multi-faceted nature, had already secured for itself a firm place in the social, economic and political life of Greece since the Balkan Wars. Long before Venizelos discovered in the character of the refugees the dismal end of the Great Idea, the romantic tag attached to the rhetoric of the "unredeemed brethren" had been abandoned in favor of a more realistic and sometimes hostile attitude towards the former populations of Asia Minor. Several major power cliques of Antivenizelist orientation, some of which were associated with Royalism and others with the nascent Socialist Party, drew attention to the less popular aspects of the refugee phenomenon. Mavrogordatos gives utterance to the Antivenizelist–represented largely in the People's Party–attitude towards the refugees:

> Antivenizelism not only appeared indifferent to the plight of the refugees but actually became the vehicle for native hostility and aggression, even systematically exploited and manipulated such hostility, using the refugees as a conventional scapegoat. Throughout the first decade of the refugee presence in Greece after 1922, Antivenizelism was not only absent, or excluded, from the great task of refugee relief and settlement, but actually attacked it and often explicitly promised to reverse, once in power.[30]

This hostility was manifested in the discourse of certain intellectuals (e.g., G. Vlachos, N. Kroniotakes). On more than one occasion, the deputies of Thrace, having expressed concern over the Greek populations in Asia Minor, were met with the hostile stance of the royalist deputies in the Parliament.[31]

As the royalists declined to pay respect to the refugees for their own reasons, the socialists had better reasons to approach the refugees. The quick organization after WWI of the socialist movement in Greece under the banner of the Socialist Labor Party of Greece (*Σοσιαλιστικον Εργατικον Κομμα της Ελλαδος*) had high hopes built on the urban labor populations among which the refugees occupied a significant portion.[32] Before the Smyrna disaster, the Greek Communists had drawn attention to the Greek state's submission to the imperialist ambitions of the European states as well as to the social and economic impact on Greece of the Asia Minor campaign. The Communists, preoccupied by their internal problems and still carried away with the idea of a Balkanic Federation, failed to find much support for their anti-bourgeois discourse among the refugees in Greece but gained some ground among the Greek soldiers in Asia Minor, who had been in the battlefield for nearly the entirety of the previous decade.[33] Against the

mounting economic and social problems of the country, their messages cir-
culated widely in the later stages of the Asia Minor campaign. In the view
of Communists, the campaign had begun to drain the sources of the country
and curb economic development,[34] a fact that struck the Greek soldiers and
the refugees immediately upon their arrival in Greece. Not only did they
encounter a devaluated drachma but also they had to compete against each
other over the few existing jobs. All these facts combined to constitute a
cultivable environment for the Communists as well as a major potential for
popular unrest with profound repercussions. Thus, on November 22, 1922,
the Greek Minister of Foreign Affairs, Nicholas Politis, reminded Venizelos
that the increasing number of refugees (referring specifically to the incoming Greeks from Constantinople) as sources of social cleavage "would provide excellent ammunition for the Communist organizations in Greece."[35]

The military *coup d'état*, which ousted King Constantine in favor of
his son George in late September, was as much a response to the military
defeat in Asia Minor as to the worsening political and social situation in
the country. It might have failed to cause a major change in Greek political
life[36] but it was effective in bringing a major social problem, namely the
plight of the refugees, into the forefront of public opinion, if not among the
intellectuals. The early political agenda of the new government remained
limited, for the most part, to diverting public attention away from the army
for the Asia Minor Disaster. Meanwhile, it undertook "a series of drastic
and bold measures for the relief and settlement of the refugees,"[37] as well
as for the appeasement of the public reaction. While the Lausanne negotiations were in progress, the trial of those held responsible for the defeat in
Asia Minor concluded with the severe punishment of the six alleged culprits.[38] This dramatic event is considered as "the settling of accounts with
Antivenizelism"[39] and the triumph of Venizelism throughout the country.
The military government, by cultivating public confidence,[40] created the
conditions for the effective return of Venizelos to the political scene, a fact
that was confirmed by the appointment of Venizelos as the head of the
Greek delegation to the "mission impossible" at Lausanne.

THE MYTH OF REPATRIATION

The principal explanation offered for the adoption of the Exchange at Lausanne as the only solution to settle the minorities question between Greece
and Turkey is that it "was a result of the declaration of Turkey that it would
refuse to allow the repatriation of over a million Greeks who were driven
from or left Turkey between 1912 and 1922."[41] At a more specific level,
Alexander Pallis argues that "if a repatriation would have been worked out

immediately after the Smyrna disaster, the Exchange would not have been necessary. [Since] the Greek government had no interest in getting rid of the Moslems of Macedonia."[42] Such a view fails to take into account not only the developments summarized in the previous section but also the efforts of the Greek government, in collaboration with several international relief agencies, to provide for the quick removal of the thousands of refugees throughout the Anatolia littoral, who had been subjected to various forms of violence by the local populations as well as the members of the Turkish para-military groups.

The political and social conjuncture in Greece prompted a quick settlement of the refugee problem through government mobilization of all available resources for the evacuation, relief, and settlement of the refugees. Early on, the relief efforts of the government were organized in such a way that they rendered the refugees' hope for repatriation to Asia Minor far from realistic. In addition to the establishment of a Refugee Relief Fund, the government worked in cooperation with several international relief organizations, and its own agencies throughout Asia Minor and the Islands off the cost of Asia Minor. It organized a very effective network of information through its various consulates as well with the offices of the Greek Patriarchate. Especially in the immediate aftermath of the military defeat, the Patriarchate in Constantinople played a vital role in reporting to Athens the situation of the Greek populations throughout Asia Minor. The local church officials, on the other hand, compiled information on the people gathered in various ports of Asia Minor. Many reports were transmitted from Constantinople concerning the number of refugees gathering along the shores of the Black Sea and the Aegean Sea as well as on the Islands, where the preparations for the safe removal of the refugees who had moved from Asia Minor had been underway.[43] The government processed this information to mobilize its navy to certain ports. The military forces in eastern Thrace reported to the headquarters of the Ministry of Foreign Affairs in Athens the number of refugees shipped to various Greek ports, primarily Salonica.[44]

Once the implementation of the Mudanya Armistice began in mid-October, the uprooting of the Greek populations gained an irreversible character in Anatolia and eastern Thrace. The relief efforts of the Greek government were not limited only to the Greeks but also included the scattered groups of Armenians and the other Christian groups, which were trying to make their way out of Anatolia proper. Wherever the government was unwilling to do so, it faced the pressure of the Allies. The international relief organizations depended for the most part on the organizational efforts of the Greek government to evacuate all the Christian groups. The evacuation of the Armenian orphans from an orphanage in Istanbul was realized by the Greek authorities in early November, and they were transferred temporarily to Corfu, where they "were housed in barracks and that every facility has been offered" by the Armenian Refugees Lord Mayor's Fund.[45] At the peak of the negotiations at Lausanne, Greek ships were still transporting the Greek and Armenian refugees from the shores of the Black Sea.[46]

Early in September, the frenzied situation in Anatolia caused many Christians to depopulate their settlements. In this environment, there was actually no discrimination as to the creed. Christians of all sects constituted the refugee crowd, which was directed to certain urban centers along the Anatolian coast. For example, a group of 30,000 Greek refugees who had gathered in Edremid were not allowed by the Turkish authorities to embark on the Greek ships. There was much rumor that they were to be sent to the interior to be used as security against the Greek demands in the upcoming peace conference.[47] In mid-October 1922, the *mutasarrıf* of Antalya informed the Italian consulate in the city, who in turn passed the information on to the Greek consulate in Rhodes that "nearly 5,000 women and children of Christian faith who had come from [I]sparta and Burdur were awaiting their fate in the port of Antalya."[48] During the same period, representatives of the Italian government in the area informed the Greek consulate in Larnaca that the number of Greeks, Armenians and other Christians reached great numbers and that certain measures had to be taken before their lives were further threatened. The Italian consulate was also reminding its Larnaca office that "they [refugees coming from Asia Minor] should not be allowed to travel between Alexandretta and Aleppo for the reason that there are many robber bands in action."[49] To make it brief, the great majority of Greek populations of Anatolia as well as eastern Thrace had already been removed from their lands under the most appalling conditions and there was no way of reversing the situation and repatriating them.

The exchange reality made its presence felt in another area. Given the economic state of the country, the Greek government, from the beginning, mobilized all its mechanisms at home and abroad to raise funds to finance its relief efforts for the refugees. Greek ambassadors, consuls, and philhellenes throughout the world launched a systematic fund-raising campaign, whereby they sought assistance from the countries with large Greek populations. A small sum of 15,000 Francs was raised in Switzerland.[50] In a letter sent to the Orthodox archbishop of Lausanne, the ambassadors appealed for help for an estimated 700,000 refugees.[51] The systematic nature of those efforts owed much to the formation of many committees in these countries. These committees aimed not only to raise money but also, as in the case of the committee of Damascus, to provide temporary shelter for the refugees who were arriving from the eastern half of Asia Minor.[52] The Greek government sought to obtain as much assistance as possible from the international public.[53] In the meantime, many foreign countries donated funds to various agencies to be spent on the refugees. The call for aid went as far as Brazil. The Brazilian government donated 1,000 English pounds, while the Japanese government contributed 26,000 Swiss Francs to the Dr. Nansen Fund to be used for the relief of the Asia Minor Refugees.[54] High ranking bureaucrats and diplomats continued to make public fundraising speeches in major European capitals. They emotionally conveyed to their audiences hourly accounts, based fully on the newspaper reports, of the Turkish capture of Smyrna.

In cases where unsolicited help was concerned, the Greek government responded cautiously and did not hasten to accept it blindly. A Theodoros Portoli of Smyrna, an Italian citizen, asked the assistance of the Italian Embassy in Washington, D.C. to persuade certain South American countries (Brazil, Argentina, Chile etc.) to allow Greek refugees from Smyrna, who had been temporarily settled on various Aegean Sea islands, to emigrate to these countries. Many refugees of Christian and Muslim faiths had already found their way to South American soil for better economic conditions during the previous few decades, and Greeks and Armenian constituted large communities in major capitals of South America. When his intent was brought to the attention of the Greek government authorities, it was interpreted as an Italian conspiracy to reduce the size of Greek population on the islands and to create room for Italian settlers. The Italians had already begun to replace the Greeks in Smyrna and the islands of the Aegean Sea, where the Italian authority had already been established.[55]

The refugee reality was nowhere more apparent than in the landscape of Greece. Since their arrival, the refugees invaded schools, theatres, town halls, exposition buildings. In a report, it is said that "The ancient Royal Palace of Athens as well as those of Princes George and Nicholas have been occupied. It is impossible to shelter at least for the moment all the refugees in Athens."[56] Those who failed to find space in urban areas moved to the countryside, where they "maintained a fox-like existence in tents, wooden barracks, shelters of twigs, or of turf, even in caves."[57] In the cities, the refugees not only halted the functions of the public services but also took over industrial buildings, which looked convenient for settlement.[58] Various factories in districts of Athens were occupied by refugees, a development which sometimes led their proprietors to appeal to the Greek government for assistance in their evacuation as in the case of a citizen of

Czechoslovakia whose factory in Patissia-Podonifte employed 500 workers and was occupied by refugees.[59]

All the circumstances recounted above point to the fact the exchange had already gained an irreversible character on the eve of the Lausanne Conference and any project based on the repatriation of the refugees and the restoration of *status quo anti* was unrealistic. As Alexander Pallis remarks, "it was inevitable in these circumstances that M. Venizelos should revert to the old idea of an exchange of populations."[60] Whether Venizelos was as far-sighted as John Petropoulos claims, that the Greek statesman had long-term plans for using the refugees as a cause to secure foreign loans and use this financial assistance for the economic reconstruction of the country, is another matter, but it was certain that all the aforementioned facts had played a portentous role in persuading the Greek government and Venizelos to make their bid on the swift settlement of the refugee problem—the source of many other problems to be covered in the second part of this book—instead of prolonging the negotiations by diplomatic wrangling for an uncertain ending.

BACK TO LAUSANNE

Venizelos came to Lausanne equipped with all this information, and he continued to receive regular reports on the unfolding developments from the Ministry of Foreign Affairs. He integrated the emerging facts into his arguments and acted single-handedly on the settlement of the exchange. A cursory reading of the Conference minutes reveals that he sailed liberally from one extreme position to another on the issue of the exchange. He started with an ambiguous position of acceptance of the conditions outlined in the Nansen report and was prepared to discuss both compulsory and voluntary exchange.[61] However, he favored the idea of a voluntary exchange since "he did not wish to oblige the Turkish population to leave Greece," and "it would be best to settle this question in a definite and humane manner."[62] Then he agreed to a compulsory exchange "under the stress,"[63] a position from which he decided to withdraw multiple times in favor of a voluntary exchange for different reasons.[64] At some point, he decided that he wanted the full repatriation of all those who had been forced to leave Turkey.[65]

Venizelos, who participated in the sessions of the Sub-commission on Minorities, pursued his unique style of diplomatic conduct during the negotiations on the general principles and details of the Exchange with little or no intervention from Athens. With his "calm and cool evaluation of certain facts,"[66] he stood firm on his commitment to a compulsory exchange. In this regard, he maneuvered freely according to the arguments of his chief opponent, namely İsmet Paşa, who turned out to be stiffer and "deafer" than all the other parties had envisaged prior to the negotiations. The only stumbling block before his realization of the swift settlement of the Exchange was his government's provision concerning the exclusion of the Greek population of Constantinople from this project, which he soon adopted as one of his own.

Venizelos' early positive stance on the Exchange was bolstered by recent military and political developments. Since the problem of eastern Thrace had been settled and the region had been handed over to the Turkish forces on November 30, 1922, enough houses were created for the Turkish refugees from Greece. Should the Turkish side agree to the transfer of the Muslims from Greece, the transfer of remaining populations could be started immediately. There were also economic considerations facilitating the quick settlement of the issue. As Nansen had stated in his report "many fields are already ploughed and many only waiting their animal cultivation. It is vitally in the interest of both Turkey and Greece that in the coming summer they should have the maximum possible production."[67] Additionally there was already a well-formulated and executed plan for an exchange that was provided by the Greco-Bulgarian agreement at Neuilly.[68] By seconding the Nansen proposal, Venizelos did show his intent to resolve the problem in a quick manner since the removal of the nearly 400,000 Muslims would provide a quick solution to the refugee problem, which had begun to become a multi-faceted challenge.[69] Thus, at the outset of the conference, his lip-service to the idea that the exchange should take place on a voluntary basis, and the Greek government had no intention of expelling the Muslim population outside Greece seems to be only a diplomatic tactic.

Venizelos' position turned ambiguous once again when the Turkish side declared its firm commitment to the idea of the complete removal of the Greek population from Constantinople. Although İsmet Paşa had openly announced that his government would not take any action on the Greeks of the Anatolian interior, there was no reservation as to the removal of the Greeks from the City. Earlier in the conference, major friction had arisen over the proposal of a plebiscite, which the Turks insisted was the only solution to the problem in Western Thrace. The fate of some 124,000 Muslims in the region had been complicated by the Bulgarian arguments and the problem had been forwarded to a sub-commission. On December 12, Curzon combined the two problems to propose that "the Greek government is prepared to leave alone [the Muslims of Western Thrace] if the Greek population of Constantinople is also left undisturbed . . . If no such arrangement can be arrived at, then they also will be turned out, and there will be no Turkish population in Western Thrace for whom provision will be required."[70] Venizelos seconded Curzon's proposal without any hesitation.[71] The Turkish delegation, which had vehemently argued for the complete uprooting of the Greeks from Constantinople, adopted thenceforward a more reconciling attitude. As to be discussed in the following chapter, the twist on the part of the Turks had much to do with their unexpected entanglement with the larger question of the minorities, which started with İsmet Paşa's long speech describing the Turkish policy on the minorities.[72]

Both Curzon and Venizelos played a considerable role in pushing the Turkish side up against the wall on the question of minorities. Their most effective weapons in confronting the Turkish demands became the very weapons of the contending party. That was the provision of the National Pact (*Misak-ı Milli*) concerning the minorities and the pre-conditions of the Mudanya Armistice.[73] Both boldly stated that the rights of the minorities would be recognized upon their declaration of allegiance to the Turkish state. [74] The wise move of Lord Curzon to bring into play the provision of the Mudanya agreement that "the secession of eastern Thrace to Turkey was granted on the condition that the latter would honor its earlier commitments concerning the minorities" sparked off a concerted opposition of the conference participants to the stiff Turkish position regarding the Greeks of Constantinople and a "Home" for the Armenians.[75] Under the pressure of the conference participants and especially of the Americans, the following day İsmet Paşa reframed his tasks and wrote them to Ankara:

> The unconditional rejection of an [Armenian] Home and the [demands for] the exemption of the minorities from military service; the security of travel and property [rights] to be mentioned; the exchange of Greek[s] to be insisted on; special conditions for the exemption of the Greeks of Istanbul to be set forth; the refusal of the Minority Law to be abandoned in favor of the acceptance of the Law [concerning the minorities] written in the National Pact (*Misak-ı Milli*).[76]

This subject will be examined in the following chapter; it suffices to point out here that the Turkish agreement to the exemption of the Greeks of Constantinople constituted a turning point in the negotiations. The conference thenceforward witnessed lame discussions over the other points of the exchange such as the status of the Patriarchate, the issue of cemeteries, etc. A limited discussion on the situation of the abandoned properties also took place. But this issue was unresolved and presented a potential for further conflict between the two sides in the post-Lausanne era.

Venizelos made his last speech before the Territorial Commission on January 27, 1923, in which he stated that "the obligatory character of the exchange of populations between Turkey and Greece has been received by his government and the Hellenic delegation with particular antipathy. And he was prepared to dismiss the obligatory exchange in favor of voluntary exchange," which was opposed by the Turkish side.[77] As Ladas points out, the speech was intended more "to satisfy the Greek public than with a serious view to its consideration by the Commission."[78] On January 30 1923, the agreement on the Exchange was signed by the Greek and Turkish delegations. Kaklamanos informed Athens of the signature of the convention on the compulsory exchange of populations at 17:45 on 30/1/1923, which was received in Athens at 21:50 of the same day.[79]

The Lausanne negotiations give the impression that the Greek position on the exchange, despite Venizelos' maneuvers, did not undergo major revisions. Although the latter was determined to go for a swift settlement to avoid any further prolongation of the refugee problem, his plans were halted temporarily by the Turkish demands. The situation of the Constantinople Greeks complicated the course of negotiations as Turks accepted no arguments on the subject until mid-December. Through the intervention of the Allied representatives and the wise tactics of Venizelos, which made the Turkish position more difficult to defend, the stalemate was resolved and the exchange negotiations moved onto a more reasonable platform, where both sides even found reciprocal interests such as the exemption of anti-government figures from the Amnesty. Perhaps the only group of people that was victimized by this shift in negotiations was the Greeks of the Anatolian interior, namely, the Karamanlides, whom the Turks seemed not to consider for inclusion in the Exchange at the outset.[80] After the unyielding attitude of the Turkish side towards the Greek reservations on the Exchange was somewhat overcome, Venizelos' maneuvering was bolstered to make the best of the negotiations in order to solve the details of the Exchange, such as the status of Patriarchate, in favor of Greece.

Chapter Three
The Turkish Case

When they arrived at the venue of the conference neither İsmet Paşa nor the other members of the Turkish delegation were equipped with full authority to conduct negotiations as they wished.[1] Nor did they have experience in diplomacy commensurate with their rivals.[2] Due to his military background, İsmet Paşa, the head of the Turkish delegation, adopted a very stiff attitude throughout the negotiations and remained in constant telegraphic communication with Ankara.[3] As for the second Turkish plenipotentiary, Rıza Nur, who was the Minister of Health in the cabinet, he remained, several instances notwithstanding, bound to the commands of the former. He headed the Turkish delegation in the sub-commissions on the minorities and then the exchange of war prisoners and populations.[4] The Turkish delegation presumed that the question of minorities and thus the exchange would come to the negotiation table after territorial and capitulary matters.[5] However, the early stages of the conference showed that the contending party deemed the settlement of the minorities problem as a priority. Thus the topic of population exchange as a workable solution to this problem came up with the effective intervention of Lord Curzon, to the negotiation table earlier than the Turkish delegation had anticipated. Having failed to dominate the course of the negotiations at the outset, the Turkish delegation faltered in retracting the direction of exchange discussions according to their plan.

STRATEGY FOR THE EXCHANGE

Prior to Lausanne, the Turks had given signs that they would seek an unconditional exchange of populations at the conference. Although Nansen's communication with the Turkish officials in Istanbul had been inconclusive, Mustafa Kemal himself had given his consent to the proposal and supported the idea that the issue of the exchange be taken up at the upcoming peace conference. As Nansen acknowledges in his report, he had "made **some** progress in [his] negotiations with the representatives of Angora" after having received the reassurance of the Greek government in a series of official documents.[6] His four meetings with the governmental authorities in Turkey sufficed for Nansen to announce in the conference that "all the governments here represented are in favour of what I proposed."[7]

Although the Turkish side agreed in principle with the Nansen proposal, it had its reservations, as well. The early Lausanne telegrams demonstrate that the original plan of the Turkish side targeted an unconditional exchange of the Greeks of Asia Minor, with the exception of those of the Anatolian interior, namely the Karamanlides, and conceived no special consideration for the Greeks of Constantinople. The Turks also seemed to nourish the hope that the status of Western Thrace would be determined by a plebiscite and the fate of the Muslim populations in the region would not become a matter of negotiation for the exchange.[8] The telegrams reveal in addition that the government was still pursuing its war time policy of displacing Christian populations, this time, towards the coast. Many Christians were being gathered in various port cities (e.g., Trabzon, Mersin, and Antalya) to be deported, much to the dissatisfaction of İsmet Paşa. The latter warned the government numerous times to refrain from deportations and displacements (*tehcir ve teb'id yapılmamasını suret-i katiyyede istid'a ederim*) as they would "harm and create anti-opinion towards our current position."[9] Before the issue of the exchange came to the negotiation table, İsmet Paşa informed Ankara that, "with the participation of the Americans in the discussions on such issues as minorities (*ekalliyetler*) and Christians (*Hıristiyanlar*), I guess, we will face great difficulties."[10] Here the term "Christians" should be read as referring specifically to the remaining Armenian groups and perhaps Karamanlı Greeks in the interior of Anatolia, who had not yet been displaced. By considering the Karamanlides as 'Turks,' the Turkish government showed its intention to keep them, at least, as minorities. As for the Armenians (mainly those in Istanbul), the government was determined to expel them and had no willingness to accord them the status of a minority. The telegrams, though they contain rich information on the concerns of the government and İsmet Paşa, hardly offer any systematic information on the strategy that the Turkish delegation was to devise in pursuit of their formidable goals. Some valuable insights, however, are gained from the list of instructions (*talimatname*) that had been drafted in a cabinet meeting in Ankara.

The document provides certain clues as to the steps in achieving these goals.[11] The content of the document, embedded essentially within the framework of the National Pact, consists of 14 principles listed according to their relative importance and relation to one another. Each principle suggests, besides the main goal, an alternate solution or recommends complete withdrawal from the conference. In line with the *raison d'être* of the National Pact, almost all the principles had been drawn with a view to consolidating the territorial borders of the new state, and abolishing the economic concessions granted under the capitulatory regime. On the question of minorities, which ranks ninth in the list, the exchange is offered as the principal goal (*esas mübadeledir*) to be adopted in solving the problem without any alternate proposition. However, the problem itself was far from being clearly defined. If the understanding of minority was based on religious criterion, which was certainly the case on the part of the Turks, the larger question of minorities involved not only the Greeks but also the other non-Muslim groups like the Armenians, Jews, Nestorians and Assyrians. By looking at the relative place of the issue within the broad framework of the document, which follows the article concerning the capitulations, it seems plausible that the Turkish delegation had the intention of devising an economic argument. Justifying the exchange with special reference to the "destructive role" of minorities in the country's economy over the past decades, however, would hardly suffice to justify the expulsion of the Greeks alone. Nor would such an argument find any sympathy among the conference participants, who had their own interests at stake.

The performance of İsmet Paşa, who seemed to be very concerned about the international opinion, remained to be seen. If he pursued an argument along the above line, it was obvious that the discussion of the exchange was from the beginning bound to the raising of two, among other, major issues: the situation of the relatively large group of other minorities, mainly Armenians, and the judicial status of foreigners associated with the capitulary enterprises. Unlike the directive on the minorities, the instructions concerning the last two issues suggested complete withdrawal from the conference. Should there be any discussion of "an Armenian Homeland," considered an exclusively territorial matter, or any demand for the reinstatement of the capitulary privileges, the Turkish delegation could withdraw from the conference without informing Ankara.[12] Seeing the Armenian issue merely from a security perspective also conflicted with their arguments on the status of the Muslim minority in Western Thrace, for which they have been promoting a plebiscite. Thus, in opposing any demand to solve the minority question based on territorial claims, they would have to reassess their case against the Greek view concerning the Muslims in Western Thrace. The ambiguity of the Turkish policy, coupled with other reservations, presented major potential for further complications, which would lead them either to withdraw from the negotiations or revise their commitment to the unconditional exchange of all the minorities, except perhaps the 'Turkish Orthodox' (Karamanlides). The later negotiations showed that İsmet Paşa had opted for the latter.

Against this background, the success of the Turkish case, from the very outset, hinged on İsmet Paşa's ability to make an exchange argument for the Greeks alone without entangling the other minorities in the discussion. As he states in one of his earlier telegrams, "I think it is not possible to justify to the world the expulsion of the Armenians. We may rightfully speak of the exchange of the Greeks. To mention the expulsion of the Turkish Orthodox is not acceptable. I am looking forward to your approval of my points of view, and sitting next to the telegraph machine. Without any interference from outside, I have to conduct negotiations with the American representatives and the Armenian delegation on this ground, and [try] *to isolate the Greeks* [from the other minorities]."[13] In a follow-up to this message, he informed Ankara that "he will follow the principle of exchanging the Greeks and keeping the other minorities by exposing them to the minority rights in Romania[14] and similar examples" (*Fakat Rumları mübadele, diğerlerini muhafaza ve bu halde Romanya ve saire kavaidine tabi' tutmak esasını ta'kib edeceğim*).[15]

DOMESTIC BACKGROUND

The Turkish case on the exchange was pursued against the background of a parliamentary consensus on the expulsion of all the non-Muslim populations of the country. Prior to and during the Lausanne discussions, the members of the Turkish parliament often argued that the population exchange must include not only the Greeks and Armenians of Istanbul and Anatolia but also the Jewish populations of these regions.[16] Their rhetoric focused mainly on the political developments of the past decade with an emphasis on the role of the non-Muslims in the demise of the Ottoman Empire.

A different concern was voiced by the deputies of immigrant or refugee background with their personal interests at stake. They made passionate speeches with reference to the "atrocities" and other inhuman practices, to which their brethren had been exposed in the former Ottoman territories.[17] In their view, the remaining non-Muslims in the country did not deserve a less harsh treatment from the Turks. Similar ideas found much room for circulation among the Turkish public. Increasing public pressure, manifested in the press and major rallies, contributed greatly to the reinforcement of the idea of exchange as a form of punishment to the non-Muslims for "their past mistakes."[18]

The public pressure for a swift settlement of the minority question in the form of an exchange was reflected in the telegrams of Prime Minister Hüseyin Rauf to İsmet Paşa. In addition to the public reaction, Rauf [Bey] often presented İsmet Paşa with his personal opinion as "our obligation to the wretched peoples of Islam" (*milel-i mazlume-i İslamiye'ye karşı vazifemiz*) in the Greek-held territories.[19] He also transmitted details of the Greek military activities in the Western Thrace and Rumelia (Macedonia), as well as eastern Thrace, where the skirmishes between the Turkish forces and the Greek army were continuing.[20]

Since mid-September, similar information had been transmitted to the headquarters of the Greek Foreign Ministry by the foreign legations in Greece.[21] During the peak of the Asia Minor campaign, the systematic efforts of the Greek government to arrest the local Muslims with relatives in Turkish paramilitary nationalist forces (*Kuvay-i Milliye*) had somewhat reciprocated the Turkish efforts to purge the local Greeks on account of security measures. After the declaration of the Mudanya Armistice, the Greek irregulars joined by Circassian bands under the aegis of the Greek government continued to create great havoc in various parts of eastern Thrace. These groups remained *in situ* for a few more years after the conference, and they were later accompanied by the bands of refugees stationed on the Aegean Islands.[22]

As the Greek government appealed to the conference and the High Commissioner in Istanbul for the protection of the Christians and Greeks in Anatolia and Istanbul, so did the Ankara government try to intervene on behalf of the Muslim populations of Macedonia, Thrace, and Crete.[23] During the Lausanne negotiations, further information was transmitted to the Turkish delegation about incidents where the Muslim community of Crete was exposed to the pressure of Greek bands.[24] Included in the information transmitted to İsmet Paşa, there was also news that involved the kidnapping of Muslim girls and the execution of some local Muslim leaders.[25] In the meantime, the protest letters of the local populations in various parts of Greece were pouring into the conference. On December 23, 1922, the conference received a letter from the Turks, Vlachs, and Bulgarians of Florina who protested the Greek government for its policies against their communities.[26]

The situation of the Muslims in various parts of Greece, especially in Western Thrace, furnished the Turkish public with a claim to Western Thrace on one hand, and a reason to press for the wholesale expulsion of all the remaining "Christians" in Turkey, on the other. Having adopted this discourse, İsmet Paşa himself often referred to these facts in order to support his arguments on the Turkish claims to Western Thrace or to refute Venizelos' claims that Muslim populations in the area were in fact peacefully giving up their homes or even hosting the incoming refugees.[27] However, the telegrams reveal that İsmet Paşa did not nourish much hope for the feasibility of a plebiscite and accordingly included the populations of Western Thrace in a series of questions he posed to Ankara concerning the housing prospects for the would-be refugees from Greece.[28] During the first week of December, the idea that the Muslim populations of Western Thrace be held against the Greeks of Constantinople surfaced in the negotiations.[29] Thenceforward, the situation of the Muslims of Western Thrace became a marginal concern to the Turkish viewpoint.

ECONOMIC ARGUMENT

During the 1910s, in line with the shift towards economic nationalism, in response to increasing German influence and the growing discontent with the French and the British, the government of the ruling Committee of Union and Progress had redefined the empire's external economic relations in several areas. "First, it abrogated [after the outbreak of WWI] the capitulations and subjected foreign companies and individuals to Ottoman laws."[30] Then it went on to declare a "moratorium on payments of the country's large and crippling external debt, most of which was held by France, Germany, and Great Britain."[31] Many legislative measures were also taken to revive and expand domestic industry. Perhaps more importantly for the purpose of the present discussion, the assumption that the non-Muslim populations of the Ottoman Empire prospered at the expense of the majority populations and provided a channel by means of which foreign capital exploited the resources of the Ottoman territories became part of the political rhetoric on the eve of WWI. Correspondingly, the CUP government sought to embody a local bourgeoisie based on Muslim traders and artisans to the effect of which it openly favored the Muslim entrepreneurs over their non-Muslim counterparts, and created, for example, eight new joint-stock companies with the participation of the Muslim entrepreneurs. At the social level, this tendency found expression in systematic boycotts and other forms of government-organized protests (under the aegis of the *Teşkilat-ı Mahsusa*) against non-Muslim economic enterprises. Simultaneously, many Greeks along the Western coast of Asia Minor were forced to immigrate to nearby islands or mainland Greece, a development that had even led to the consideration of a limited exchange of populations between Greece and the Ottoman Empire. It was not until the placement of the Greek administration in the *Vilayet* of Aydın in 1919 that most of the Greek and Armenian entrepreneurs of this region operated their businesses outside Asia Minor.

The "economic nationalism" (*milli iktisat*) rhetoric of the Young Turk governments became fully adopted by the nascent Turkish state, which from the very outset tried to create a national economy within the borders of the National Pact (*Misak-i Milli*). Especially during the Turco-Greek War, the social machinery behind this policy resurfaced in an effective way. As Falih Rıfkı vocalized it "We will defeat the Greeks with bayonets in the field, and with our boycotts behind the war front. We will not allow any Turkish money to go to the citizens of the Greek army [*Yunan ordusunun vatandaşlarına*]."[32] In line with the CUP's position on the capitulations, Turkish authorities were obsessed with the idea that "the economic, financial and judicial independence of the country must be assured and freed from restrictions."[33] This rationale often surfaced in the speeches of the deputies in the Grand National Assembly in Ankara and made its way into the discourses of İsmet Paşa and Rıza Nur during the negotiations on the question of minorities and more specifically on the exchange of populations. Insofar as capitulations posed a threat to national sovereignty, so did the minorities.[34] Thus, in line with the then dominant view on a world scale that "a national economy is possible only through ethnic uniformity,"[35] capitulations and minorities were intertwined to support the Turkish thesis on the exchange.

The economic policy of the new Turkish State, with its exclusionist character, received much criticism outside the conference. Thus, Dr. Caleb Gates, who was the President of Robert College, wrote "the Kemalists have been making economic mistakes. They have laid very heavy duties upon articles of import that can be manufactured in the country with a view to encouraging home industries. They do not realize that it takes generations to produce an artisan and commercial class. . . . . It will not be long, also, before the Turks will realize very keenly their need of the Christian population, which has been driven out. The Christians were the producers and the Turks were the consumers, except for the Turkish peasantry, engaged in agriculture, and they are rather shiftless farmers."[36]

At the conference, the Turkish delegates faced similar criticisms. The Allies and Venizelos emphasized the indispensable role of the non-Muslims in the Turkish economy, which İsmet Paşa contradicted with simple explanations. At a later point in the negotiations, when Curzon raised the issue of the economic role of the Greeks of Constantinople, İsmet Paşa replied that "everyone knew that they formed a class of small traders (grocers, etc.), and that it would not be difficult to replace them."[37] In the face of harsh criticisms, İsmet Paşa eventually stated "On looking into the question of the exchange of the Greek population, [there is] no need for regarding the economic difficulties which might arise for the country in consequence as the only important factor. The transfer of any section of a population would naturally entail some disruption and change in the economic life of a country, but it was not fair to attribute superiority in a particular sphere to a certain element of the population on the strength of this fact."[38] Although İsmet Paşa acknowledged the indispensable role of the non-Muslim elements in the country's economy, he stuck to his military-driven position much like Young Turks (all the nationalist elites for that matter), who did not distinguish between political and economic.[39] Any room for the development of irredentist claims, as the Greek case proved, must be eliminated with a view to achieving complete national sovereignty, a point to be constantly reiterated by Rıza Nur during the negotiations.[40]

THE QUESTION OF MINORITIES

The first time the issue of the population exchange had been brought up by the Nansen proposal on December 1, İsmet Paşa stated in tandem with his instructions that "the question of the exchange of populations seemed to him to be bound up with the solution of the question of minorities in Turkey. If the conference recognized (as he hoped they would) the connection between the two problems—exchange of populations and minorities—the Turkish delegation would expound their view at a subsequent meeting."[41] It was not until Lord Curzon's *fait accompli* before the chief commission of the conference on December 12, 1922[42] that İsmet Paşa took any steps in this direction. On this very day, he presented the conference with a historical survey—in accordance with his given instructions—in which he laid out the Turkish government's view on the minorities and explained why the exchange should be considered within the larger problem of minorities. There were three major points:

1. That the amelioration of the lot of the minorities in Turkey depends above all on the exclusion of every kind of foreign intervention and of the possibility of provocation coming from outside.
2. That this purpose can only be affected by first of all proceeding to an exchange of the Turkish and Greek populations.
3. That the best guarantees for the security and development of the measures for reciprocal exchange would be those supplied by both the laws of the country and the liberal policy of Turkey with regard to all communities whose members have not deviated from their duty as Turkish citizens.[43]

The central message of İsmet Paşa's speech turned out to be the concern that the minorities had become weapons in the hands of foreigners, capable of being utilized for subversive purposes, and the Turkish State could not afford to take any risks against its national sovereignty. Thus, the speech as a whole gave the impression that the Turkish side was in fact committed to a wholesale exchange of all the minorities, excepting, by implication, the non-Hellenic Greeks, namely the Karamanlides.[44] Although some progress had already been made concerning the exemption of the Greeks of Constantinople from the exchange scheme in the sessions of the sub-commission, İsmet Paşa's earlier speech had been prepared in advance,[45] and he had failed to integrate the emerging facts of the conference into his text. As might be expected, the speech fuelled an orchestrated opposition on the part of the Allies and all the other members of the Commission, which centered mainly around İsmet Paşa's harsh remarks about the Armenians. In the face of a block reaction on this issue, prompted by Lord Curzon's provocative remarks concerning the question of minorities, which paid lip-service to the idea of "an Armenian national home,"[46] the Turkish delegation, despite the strict instructions of Ankara, waived the option of withdrawal from the conference.

The next day, İsmet Paşa's speech was more carefully crafted, as he itemized the broad category of minorities. Having slightly modified his view on the Greeks of Constantinople as well as the Armenians, who "must have recognized the unavoidable necessity of living as good citizens,"[47] he limited his exchange argument exclusively to the Greeks. But, where his commitment to the original plan was concerned, such a major maneuver was certainly not without its toll.

The three crucial variables that İsmet Paşa's earlier speech had introduced would significantly affect the rigid stance of the Turkish side on the exchange. These—the League of Nations, the Americans, and the Armenians—will be dealt with separately in the following pages; but it is important to mention at the outset that the Turkish view of the exchange came to be dependent on the individual performance of each Turkish representative in playing out these three variables, on which Lord Curzon and Venizelos would keep pondering during the rest of the negotiations. İsmet Paşa heretofore had been struggling to limit the discussions on the minorities only to the subject of the exchange while not alienating some of the parties (e.g., the Americans), which proved a piecemeal success. Accordingly, the firm commitment of the Turks to a compulsory exchange had to undergo certain revisions in the third week of the negotiations, which resulted in the exemption of the Greeks of Constantinople from the exchange.

Where the negotiations on the exchange were concerned, the settlement of the issue of the Greeks of Constantinople, having provided temporary relief to the Turkish delegation, turned out to be the key to the conclusion of the negotiations. Since the early days of the conference, the delegations of the Allies had shown their resentment on this particular aspect of the exchange. Already in the major newspapers in England and United States, long editorials and news items criticizing the Turkish position on the Greeks of Istanbul had appeared and there was enough public pressure in both countries to dismiss any counter-arguments by the Turks.[48] In line with the instructions of Ankara that kept reminding him that there would be no misgivings on the matter, İsmet Paşa ignored the Allied pressure and declined to make any concessions to his firm commitment.

Nevertheless, while he was vehemently arguing for the inclusion of the Constantinople Greeks in the exchange, he also carried a letter in his pocket dated December 7 sent by Rauf [Bey] saying "To include the Greeks of Istanbul in the exchange is in fact the principal goal. Despite the extraordinary importance of the matter, if this is not possible, their stay may be acceptable on the condition that they would not demand any privileges."[49] Keeping this option as his last resort, İsmet paid lip-service to the idea firstly in an addendum to his long speech of December 12 and the next day he announced, the exchange of the Greeks of Constantinople was a painful necessity, but logical—an operation which justice and equality required. It would also afford a means of housing the Moslems expelled from large Greek towns. Nevertheless, the humane feelings of Turkey led her to agree on the exclusion from the exchange, of the Greeks born in Constantinople."[50] This announcement, which was based on İsmet Paşa's considerations on the following issues, saved the negotiations from a deadlock.

THE LEAGUE FACTOR

The three days of negotiations from December 12 to 14 helped the Turks and Greeks sort out their major differences on the exchange issue. The first session of the Territorial Commission on the question of minorities turned into a battleground where İsmet Paşa and his team confronted a series of harsh criticisms for not cooperating with the Allied participants. The major emphasis was placed on the position of Turkey in regard to the role of the League of Nations. The reluctant position of the Turkish delegation concerning the signature of a minority treaty with the League of Nations, which by implication would affect the direction of exchange negotiations, engendered much controversy concerning the Turkish policies on minorities.

The major controversy sprang from the interpretation of the article regarding minorities in the National Pact. The fifth article of the National Pact stated that "the rights of the minorities will be confirmed [by us] on the same basis as is established in other countries by conventions hitherto concluded between the powers of the Entente, their adversaries and certain of their associates—in reliance on the belief that the Moslem minorities of other countries will benefit from similar guarantees."[51] The concepts of 'sovereignty' (*hakimiyet*) and 'independence' (*istiklal*) were extracted from the National Pact to be analyzed against the background of the Turkish policy towards minorities. These two concepts had been formulated under war conditions and their adaptation to international law required certain adjustments, one of which was undoubtedly related to the exclusive nature of these concepts, 'whose sovereignty and independence and at what and whose expense?' 'Was the Turkish government willing to honor international agreements as to the definition of these concepts?' Perhaps more importantly, 'was Turkey willing to sign a minorities treaty with the League of Nations?'

İsmet Paşa was not in a position to refute any of the arguments that came up on these issues because of the fact that they implied a major question, namely, 'if the Turks were to take part in the League of Nations.' İsmet Paşa had earlier mentioned in passing remarks that Turkey wanted to join the League, but he had abstained from making any commitment. Given the urgencies of the situation, he gave in to the pressure and pronounced that his government fully complied with the principle of the National Pact on minorities, and wanted to join the League. The latter was interpreted by the foreign press to mean that Turkey was accepting the conditions of the League of Nations on the issue of minorities.[52] If anything, this development helped calm down the tension which was making things more and more difficult to handle. In İsmet Paşa's own view, this maneuver "put the question of minorities to rest."[53]

Upon this announcement, İsmet Paşa immediately contacted the government in Ankara and expressed his intention to issue a proclamation saying "The Turkish government wants all the minorities to live in their homes and continue their engagements peacefully and safely under the protection of the State. Those who want to leave are not to be prevented. However, nobody will be forced to leave the country. For those who wish to leave, ships will be allowed to come to the Turkish ports for their transportation."[54] The government advised İsmet Paşa that "although we agree to the content of such a proclamation in principle, you should take into consideration that such an action would prevent many Greeks of Istanbul, who are currently in the process of moving, [from doing so]."[55]

THE AMERICAN FACTOR

As a diplomat, İsmet Paşa was certainly not as gifted and foresighted as Venizelos. However, given the limited range of possibilities, he carefully pondered the available opportunities in order to enhance his bargaining position over the exchange. Thus, from the early days of Lausanne, he tried not to alienate an influential, though "disinterested," party from his cause. When the Americans publicized their intent to officially participate in the minority negotiations, he tended to cultivate the idea on various grounds.[56] There was already the rumor that İsmet Paşa was not in favor of the American participation in these sessions, a rumor that apparently originated from a news item published in an American newspaper.[57] He tried to appease the American concerns through informal negotiations.[58] On November 24, 1922, the Americans informed the Turkish delegation that the American public was very concerned about the minorities, and the American institutions and nationalities in Turkey.[59] The Americans wanted to learn what policy the Turkish government was to adopt regarding the situation of the Armenians and the Greeks in the Anatolian interior. During the last week of November, there were several instances when the American delegates contacted the Turks to get assurances about the future of American institutions in Turkey.[60] İsmet Paşa received a telegram from the government saying that "as long as the American institutions agreed to operate within the framework of Turkish laws, there was no intention to expel them."[61]

The American interest in the question of minorities was initially prompted not so much by the plight of the Greeks as by that of the Armenians. In his telegram to the government on November 25, 1922, İsmet Paşa openly states that "the Americans and the British are trying to find out the conditions under which the Armenians are to be exchanged" and it would be difficult to justify to them the expulsion of the Armenians from the country.[62] He is of the view that any action to be taken on this issue should be postponed.[63] Thus, when Curzon presented İsmet Paşa with the information that "the Ankara government had decided to expel all the remaining Christians and there were one million men displaced in addition to the continuous transfer of orphans to Italy," he replied that "the decision about the expulsion of the Christians could not be true and one million men were using their right to freedom of travel."[64]

İsmet Paşa's persistent warning to the governmental authorities at home that unwanted incidents concerning minorities should be avoided was in part motivated by his desire not to totally estrange the Americans from his side. The American public kept a close eye on this matter and the eye of the whole world was on Turkey.[65] The Americans had been involved in relief efforts for the Greek refugees and had made substantial donations to this effect. Many relief organizations, such as the American Red Cross and the Near East Relief, were operating among the Aegean islands. American ships were also involved in the transportation of refugees. The Ankara government allowed access to Greek ships not flying the Greek flag, provided that they were accompanied by an American military ship, to pick up the Greeks along the Black Sea coast.[66]

On December 7, the Americans openly announced their position on the situation of the Greeks of Constantinople saying that "the American delegation is unable to approve the movement of the Greek population from Constantinople under conditions which will send an urban people used to artisanship and commerce to a rural district. We will not hesitate to express in pursuance of our legitimate humanitarian interest our protest at any such dislodgement of human beings."[67]

The American position on the question of minorities was shared by Lord Curzon. Perhaps driven by the guilt of his indifferent attitude towards the Greeks during the Mudanya negotiations, Curzon was totally committed to the fulfillment of the Greek reservations on the exchange. Thus, he repeated the "demand for a cession of territory by Turkey as a refuge for minorities."[68] And where the American official view was concerned, such a zone was conceived not for any other group but the Armenians. The members of the American delegation were constantly seeking to find out the position of Turkey on an Armenian Homeland. They took every opportunity to exchange views with members of the Turkish delegation.[69]

Besides their short-term interests, the Turks had long-term interests in the Americans. Given their rigid attitude on the capitulations, the Turkish side was aware that they would not get much assistance from the Allies during the post-conference era. The possibility of getting financial assistance from a "disinterested" country for economic rehabilitation seemed appealing, thus they tended to appease the American demands. It would not be a far-fetched assumption that the Turkish delegates, by conceding to the case of the Constantinople Greeks and adopting a more conciliatory attitude towards the Armenians, were able to accommodate the American demands on the minorities. From this point on, American pressure for an Armenian Homeland gradually decreased. This would pay off for the Americans at a later stage of the conference, since "a further play for American support" was made when on April 9 the Grand National Assembly ratified the Chester Concession, granted to the Ottoman-American Development Company.[70] Though American aid might be welcome in developing nationalist Turkey, ratification was undoubtedly a maneuver to win American support at Lausanne against European economic claims.[71]

THE ARMENIANS

The position of the Armenians at Lausanne was from the beginning very ambiguous for there were no Armenian representatives participating in the official sessions. The Armenian delegation headed by the ex-Ottoman minister of Foreign Affairs, Noradunghian, visited İsmet Paşa several times and repeated the demand for a buffer zone (no place specified) to resettle some 700,000 Armenian refugees, some of whom were residing in Anatolia and some others were scattered throughout the Middle East.[72] There were many American missionaries and representatives of various Armenian communities staying in hotels around the area where the official meetings were being conducted. They were being involved in large-scale lobbying efforts. Concomitantly, all the newspapers in England and the United States were publishing news on the movement of the Armenians.[73] Moreover, many Armenians were sending letters and telegrams to the conference. For example, the Armenians of Salonica, who feared expulsion, telegraphed the Secretary General of the Conference on December 23, 1922 to state that they wanted to live as *"les hommes sur leur territoire national."*[74] In the face of the active lobby efforts of the Armenians and international pressure, the Turks refrained from raising the issue of the exchange during the negotiations.

İsmet Paşa, who had been looking for an opportunity to settle the Armenian question through an exchange, wrote to Ankara "with whom shall I negotiate for the exchange of native Armenians with the Turks in Armenia?" (*yerli Ermenilerin Ermenistan'daki Türklerle mübadelesini kiminle görüşeyim?*).[75] On the other hand, as İsmet Paşa himself acknowledges in the same telegram, any discussion of this problem with the Allied States is bound to bring up the question of the eastern borders and the clauses of the Treaty of Moscow. To discuss this problem with the Russians would lead to the discussion of some other issues as well as a possible review of the provisions of the same treaty. Therefore, İsmet Paşa saw the restriction of the exchange to the Greeks only as a necessity.[76] He warded off all kinds of arguments for an Armenian Homeland, considering the question as a threat against the Turkish national sovereignty.

Having failed to find a party to negotiate the issue, the Turkish delegation continued to pursue its exchange policy against the Armenians outside the agenda of the conference and tried to negotiate with the Armenian government. On 28 November 1922, İsmet Paşa received a note from Hüseyin Rauf stating that "The Council of Ministers took the decision to exchange the Armenians in Turkey with the Turks in Armenia and allow the Turkish Orthodox (Karamanlides) in Turkey to stay with the provision that they would claim no 'privileged' (*mümtaz*) position."[77]

İsmet Paşa's success in limiting the situation of the Armenians to a territorial framework prevented the Armenian issue from being an obstacle before the fulfillment of his primary task. However, the Turkish commitment to the expulsion of the Armenians remained unchanged. The evidence suggests that the earlier plan of reducing the size of the Armenian minority through gradual emigration over several years would be adopted, should İsmet Paşa's proposal of repatriation of the Armenians be taken seriously. However, İsmet Paşa must have entertained the view that the conditions under which the Armenians left Turkey would certainly prevent them from considering the option of repatriation.

THE PATRIARCHATE

The removal of the Patriarchate from Istanbul was one of the principal goals of the Turkish delegation at Lausanne. Having failed to include the Greeks of Constantinople in the Exchange, the Turkish plenipotentiaries laid down the removal of the Greek Patriarch and all its institutions from Constantinople as the first condition for their consenting to allow the Greek population to stay in the city. This was in tandem with the recent policy of the Ankara government on the Patriarchate.

The Ankara government has long been trying to find out whether the institution of a new Patriarch within the structure of the state would be a solution to what they considered a long historical problem. Earlier it had researched the possibility of establishing an Anatolian Patriarchate (*Anadolu Patrikliği*). In a resolution dated 5 Kanun-i Sani 1337 [January 1921], the Minister of Justice (*Adliye Vekili*), Celaleddin Arif Bey is asked to "look into the possibility of establishing an Anatolian Patriarch by means of which it would be possible to distance the Christians of Turkish descent in Anatolia from the orbit of the Patriarchate in Istanbul"[78] The name Papa Eftim (Efthymios Karahissaridis), the metropolid of Keskin, was identified with an anti-Phanar movement and succeeded in gaining the support of the Turkish speaking Greeks in the interior of Anatolia. However, his movement could not find support on a broader front, and the Phanar remained unchallenged in terms of its influence among the Greeks of Asia Minor, regardless of linguistic differences. For the Turkish government, Lausanne was the best occasion to bring up and finalize this issue.[79]

As the negotiations continued at Lausanne, İsmet Paşa prompted the government to facilitate the establishment of the new Patriarchate. On December 10, 1922, İsmet Paşa received a telegram from Ankara stating that the Turkish Orthodox Church had constituted a synod of the metropolits and one of these Meltyos had been appointed as the archbishop to Konya and Prokopius to Kayseri and Papa Konstantin to Ankara.[80] In the course of the Lausanne discussions, İsmet Paşa received several other notes in which the appointment procedure of the metropolits was clarified.[81] All these developments followed the line of Turkish diplomacy at Lausanne concerning the removal of the Patriarch from Istanbul, and the Greek populations of the city. Once the negotiations concerning these issues were retracted in favor of the Greek side, the issue of the Turkish Orthodox Patriarchate became marginalized in the agenda of the Turkish delegation at Lausanne as well as that of the Grand National Assembly.

One of the other options in regard to the fate of the Greek Patriarch in Istanbul was that it would be moved to Mount Athos (Aynaroz), an option about which Riza Nur writes in his memoirs. "If we expel the Patriarch, he will move to Mount Athos, from where he will continue to spill his wrath at his own volition and then it [the Patriarchate] may become more of a danger than what it already is."[82] The discussions in the Grand National Assembly were characterized by an utterly anti-Greek sentiment in that the deputies argued that the insistence of the Greeks in keeping the Patriarchate in Istanbul was prompted by a long-term plan to seize the leadership in the Orthodox world. Since the Russian Patriarchate, which had recently taken over this leadership, was stripped of its power by the revolutionary government.[83] Given all these concerns, the Turkish side insisted that the Patriarch must be removed from Istanbul no matter what, which was rejected by the conference on January 4, 1923. Only five days later, in the face of American and British pressure, the Turkish side, having made all the calculations, agreed that the Patriarch would continue to stay in Istanbul.[84] Accordingly, İsmet Paşa asked the government to stop taking any actions on the project of an Anatolian Patriarch since the Turkish position for the removal of the Patriarch had become no longer arguable. Furthermore, Venizelos ensured the Turkish delegation that the Patriarchate of Constantinople would stay as a spiritual institution and deal only with ceremonial needs of the Greek community.[85] Following this remark, İsmet Paşa seems to have withdrawn his early proposal. This shift affected the Turkish position on the situation of the Karamanlides, that is, the Turkish-speaking Orthodox Greeks. These people were to be included in the coverage of the Exchange Convention. Ironically, in the aftermath of the Exchange, the Turkish government had to issue a special resolution to exempt the ex-Patriarch Papa Eftim and his family from the Exchange.[86]

END OF NEGOTIATIONS, BEGINNING OF REACTIONS

Once the thorny question of Constantinople Greeks was resolved, the conference changed gears to discuss the conditions for providing the safe removal of the remaining people as well as the formulation of principles to which the remaining minorities would be subject after the peace settlement. The top concern in this respect was the military obligations of the minorities, whether or not, for example, exemption from military service in return for payment (*bedel-i askeri*) or complete exemption would continue to be practiced.[87] Rıza Nur eventually imposed the Turkish position of mandatory military obligations on the remaining minorities.[88]

The Allies persistently asked for a "general amnesty" to be declared so that those who remained in Turkey could get out and those who had escaped could be repatriated. The Independence Tribunals (*İstiklal Mahkemeleri*), which were aimed among other things at the punishment of those who cooperated with the Greeks and other occupying forces, constituted a stumbling block before the declaration of a general amnesty.[89] On December 5, the Allies allowed the Turks to take over the passport control and thus relinquished all rights over Constantinopolitan Christians, whether Greeks or Armenians. The Turks demanded that every Ottoman subject who wished to leave Turkey had to obtain a Turkish passport.[90] As the Turks continued to chase the people who had earlier cooperated with the Allies or the Greeks, similar activities were taking place in the Greek territories as well. With the charges that "they are involved in practices and attempts against the security of the state," twenty-two persons, of whom two were Greeks and one Bulgarian, the rest being Turks, were arrested by the Police force in Salonica on December 31, 1922.[91] During the discussions over the declaration of a general amnesty in Turkey, as mentioned earlier, the Greek side expressed concern as to the exemption of pro-Gounaris persons and those of anti-government sentiment, to which the Turkish side responded with a similar concern that those who were against the national movement in Turkey should also be exempted from this amnesty.[92] The list of the Turkish side included many Circassians who had cooperated with the Greeks during the war and also the individuals with obvious attachment to the Sultanate.

In addition, the properties of the Greeks of Istanbul in Anatolia were to be expropriated in return for their assessed values. The issue of the Greek cemeteries was also resolved and it was decided that the proprietorship of these areas was to be transferred to the Turkish state.[93] Having agreed on the general contours of the exchange, the Turkish side pointed out that the properties and lands of the Turks in Greece had been confiscated by the Greek government and this issue must be taken into consideration in the elaboration of the details.[94] They expressed concern over the Greek mismanagement of the situation in regard to the assessment of the values of the properties left behind by the Turks in Greece.[95] The Turkish side also

expressed concern over the application of the Greek *"istimlak"* (expropriation) laws on the Muslim property in Greece after 1912.

In Turkey, on the other hand, the Turkish government had already
established an *ad hoc* commission, made up of finance and cadastre officials, and police agents. This commission was charged with the registration
of the abandoned movable and immovable properties of the Greeks and
the assessment of their values. The commission seized not only the properties abandoned by the Greeks but also those which had been transferred to
foreigners.[96] The Greek representative in Istanbul tried through the Spanish Embassy in the city to stop the Turkish measures of confiscation but it
failed. The French and Italian authorities in Istanbul refused to mediate on
the issue while the British openly indicated that they did not want to get
involved in a conflict with the Turks on any matter. The Greek representative
who sought the intervention of these countries in stopping the confiscation
attempt admitted that it could not be prevented.[97] This issue was harshly
criticized by the Greek delegates and remained uncertain but the other issues
were resolved during the forthcoming sessions. The news reached Ankara
on January 25, 1923 that both sides had reached agreement on the exchange
and there were only a few slight details regarding the situation of the prisoners, which needed to be cleared up before it could be signed.[98]

As the exchange negotiations came to an end, the emerging agreement
created great repercussions in Turkey and Greece. Major settlements along
the shores of the Black Sea witnessed the quick evacuation of the remaining Greek populations. Both Greeks and Armenians, who had already been
driven from the interior cities of Gümüşhane, Amasya and Tokat, were
gathered in harbors to be picked up by ships. Since the beginning of January, the Greek government had announced that its local offices in charge
of refugee affairs were "no longer able to cope with the situation owing
to the lack of funds and accommodation."[99] The Turkish authorities, on
the other hand, turned a deaf ear to such calls and continued to send the
refugees in bulk numbers to Istanbul. Alexander Pallis, who was a member of the Hellenic Delegation in Istanbul, informed the acting British High
Commissioner Henderson that "The Turkish local authorities are sending
refugees by the thousands to Constantinople, mostly by Turkish Government ships, forcing the refugees to pay for their passage. According to the
credible information, these ships are sometimes boarded, between Trebizond (Trabzon) and Kerasun (Giresun), by the notorious Osman Agha,
who robs the refugees of their last farthing."[100] The early days of February
saw many Turkish newspapers publishing notices ordering all the Greeks to
leave within a fortnight. As in the case of Trebizond, for example, the local
paper *İstikbal* had such a notice on January 2 and the next day all the local

officials including the Governor of the city were forcing the inhabitants of Trebizond to leave, in many cases without even allowing them to take their personal effects.[101] In the face of local banditry and mounting public pressure, some Greeks of the Anatolian interior had in fact begun depopulating their settlements earlier.

In Greece, the Turkish populations presented a mixed reaction to the exchange agreement. While there were those who asked the Greek government to grant them enough time so that they could sell their properties for a fair price, there were also many others who persistently appealed to the Greek government to be allowed to stay.[102] The Greek Ministry of Foreign Affairs received many letters and petitions from the Moslem Muftis of northern Greece requesting that they be granted permission to stay as they had no willingness to "return to the bad Turkish administration" (*Η Τουρκηκη Κακοδιοικιση*). Representing the voice of their communities, as they claimed in these letters, the religious leaders, called *müfti*s, expressed content with the "religious and ethnic freedom" in Greece and they were happy under the Greek government.[103] Although they were not to be included in the exchange, the Muslim populations in the Western Thracian town of Komitini organized public protests against the compulsory nature of the exchange. The representatives of many villages expressed their discontent over the decision of the Greek authorities and indicated they were willing to remain under the protection of the Greek state as long as "they are not uprooted from the land where they were born and the graves of their ancestors are located."[104] On several occasions, the arriving Greek refugees and would-be Muslim refugees conjoined to protest the Lausanne meetings. The People's Committee (*Επιτροπη Λαου*), which was comprised of the leading members of the local community in Pravia—mainly *müfti*s and *dimogerente*—sent a petition to the consulates of England, the United States, France, Italy, Belgium, Romania, and Serbia to protest the Lausanne decisions.[105] These were the refugees from Asia Minor and the local Muslims, numbering 10,000 each who were to be subjected to the exchange. Such appeals failed to affect the course of negotiations and the Exchange Convention was signed on January 30, 1923.

Chapter Four
Conclusion

Both Greeks and Turks came to Lausanne with a firm commitment to the idea of a compulsory exchange of their respective minorities. Where Greece was concerned, the ensuing socio-economic and political problems after the war, which were galvanized by the influx of refugees, forced the new government to "want a settlement at the earliest moment possible." To this effect, the new government not only devised effective mechanisms to provide quick removal of the Greek populations of Asia Minor, but also established new institutions and practices that would facilitate the settlement of the refugees in Greece. The stumbling block before the finalization of the process was the status of the Greeks of Constantinople, which conflicted with the plans of the contending Turks. While the Greek side was determined to exclude the Greeks of Constantinople from the exchange due to several major concerns, the Turkish side sought to achieve an unconditional exchange of all the Greeks except for some 150,000 Greeks of the Anatolian interior (i.e., Karamanlides). The Turkish determination was embedded in the commitment to the ideals of national sovereignty, which had been defined in a manner that excluded all non-Muslim and non-Turkish elements from participation. The envisioned or "imagined' socio-political future was without 'undesirable' elements. The situation of the Karamanlides was reconciled on linguistic as well as ethnic foundations, and the State had already taken effective steps to mould their religious leadership into the structure of the Turkish State apparatus. Had it not been for the intervention of Venizelos on December 16, the Ankara government had in fact already completed a major part of the work towards accomplishing this project. The agreement on the exemption of the Greeks of Constantinople from the exchange during the same week moved the negotiations to a platform on which the two sides had reciprocal interests to pursue.

As a turning point in the negotiations, the agreement on the exemption of the Greeks of Constantinople in return for the Muslim population of Western Thrace was achieved as much by the diplomatic skills of Venizelos as by the unexpected entanglement of the Turkish view on a variety of issues. The persistent pondering of the Allies on the subject of an Armenian Homeland played the most crucial role in the reassessment and eventual revision of the Turkish position. The question of an Armenian homeland not only distanced the discussion on the minorities from the orbit of the Turkish argument, namely the exchange, but also affected the Turkish concerns over the American factor, which was important during and after the conference. The majority of the conference agenda including the territorial issues, the Straits, and the capitulations was still pending, and the alienation of the Americans from their side would certainly leave them alone in the negotiations. In addition, given their reserved relationship with the British, French and Italians, the prospects of American aid in the reconstruction of the country during the post-conference era were deemed rather crucial. By declaring their strict attachment to the principle of the National Pact on the minorities, which entailed their adherence to the League's overall policies over the minorities, the Turks were able to appease the conference participants, especially the Americans on the situation of the remaining Armenians in Turkey. This position reduced the question of the Armenian Homeland to a territorial matter, which seemed less challenging to deal with than otherwise. By conceding to the Greek view on the status of the Greeks of Constantinople, the Turkish delegates were able to reset the focus of the discussions solely on the exchange. Thus, the reversal of the Turkish view on the status of the Greeks of Constantinople was a maneuver devised as a weapon to ward off the Allied offence on the one hand, and to cultivate the American position on the other issues on the other. The acceptance of the major demand of the Greek side prevented the negotiation of the exchange from reaching a deadlock and the road to the Convention was paved. The later stage of negotiations focused primarily on the other related aspects of the problem. Excepting several maneuvers by Venizelos on such issues as the future status of the Patriarchate in Turkey, there was minimal friction between the two sides.

By and large, the signing of the Convention for the population exchange between Turkey and Greece struck a major blow to most international trends that had taken shape since the beginning of the nineteenth century and had become more challenging in the aftermath of the Young Turk Revolution. First and foremost, this development made the infamous Eastern Question, which aimed at the disintegration of the Ottoman Empire from within, obsolete. Once military victory was achieved, the Turkish military leadership adopted a determined position so as to define the national sovereignty in a manner that was essentially against foreign intervention of any kind. The Greeks, on the other hand, having been exposed to military defeat in Asia Minor and having experienced the sudden disengagement of historic ties with the West, adopted a new policy of containment. The two sides were in fact going through a litmus test whereby, as one authority points out, "for the first time in a century they were left very much to their own devices in fashioning independent foreign policies."[1]

Diplomatic negotiations at Lausanne for an exchange were intended from the beginning to canonize a *de facto* situation. Many refugees, who had moved between Turkey and Greece during the war, continued to nourish hopes for repatriation during the Lausanne negotiations. In fact, such a development had taken place in the aftermath of WWI. Many Asia Minor Greeks who had moved away from the Black Sea and Aegean coasts following the Balkan Wars had returned to their homes. But this time, chances for the renewal of the situation were slim. When the Lausanne Conference opened, nearly five-sixths of all the Greeks from Anatolia and eastern Thrace were already in Greece, crammed into tents, army barracks, warehouses and theatres. The Moslem Turks of Greece, however, were, with the exception of those living in the borderlands, awaiting the decision of the treaty makers. These people inevitably "received notice to leave their homes and lands and the orders of transportation to unknown parts of Turkey."[2]

Nansen in his opening speech over the issue of the exchange had remarked that "I do not wish to be understood to say that I believe that any treaty which may be made for the exchange of the Greek and Turkish minorities will give entirely satisfactory results. On the contrary, I believe that any exchange of populations, however well it were carried out, must impose very considerable hardships, perhaps very considerable impoverishment, upon great numbers of individual citizens of the two countries who are exchanged."[3] In the same speech, he also drew attention to the complexity of the current issue, which involved registration of the refugees, recording and liquidating their immovable and movable properties, as well as compensation for their losses. Given the difficult conditions under which the exchange was deemed inevitable, Nansen pointed out that these problems could be overcome. This remark was in fact the last call for a possible retreat from the plan by both sides. Nevertheless, the members of the Turkish and Greek diplomatic teams proceeded with the endorsement of the plan as they were convinced that this was the last and perhaps the only solution. The immediate aftermath of the Lausanne negotiations demonstrated that most of the issues associated with the exchange were not to be so easily settled due to the nature of the Exchange Convention.

Lastly, the famous question of "who initiated the exchange plan," finds its answer in the postscript of the editor of the Forum to Nansen's article that "This plan was not, as some have said, suggested by Dr. Nansen. It is in fact a Greek and Turkish proposition. Nor is it a new plan foisted upon the world, but one which was discussed years ago (referring to the 1914 Agreement), both in Turkey and in Greece."[4] Now that both sides had finally accomplished their principal goal, the real litmus test was just about to start in the form of the implementation of the provisions of the Convention, which presented major potential to confirm the warning of the head of American Red Cross, Colonel Haskell "this [Exchange] is an unnatural solution and its execution will be subject to abuse and much graft."[5]

Part Two
Displacement

Chapter Five

Introduction

Ολοι οί Ελληνες στην Ελλάδα, όλοι οί Τούρκοι στήν Τουρκιά!. . Θρηνος
σηκώθηκε μέσα στό χωριό . . . Δύσκολα, δύσκολα πολύ, μαθές, ξεκολνάει
η ψυχή από τά γνώριμα της νερά κι από τα χώματα . . . Μας ξεριζώμουν!
Ανάθεμα στούς αίτιους! Ανάθεμα στούς αίτιους! Ανάθεμα στούς αίτιους!
Σήκωσε ο λαός τά χέρια στόν ουρανό, σήκωσε βουή μεγάλη:—Ανάθεμα
στούς αίτιους! Κυλίστηκαν όλοι χάμω, φιλουσαν μαλακωμένο από τή βροχή
χωμα, το 'τριβαν στήν κορφή του κεφαλιου τους στά μάγουλα, στό λαιμό,
έσκυβαν, τό ξαναφιλουσαν.[1]

The signing of the Convention of the Exchange of Populations between
Turkey and Greece at Lausanne on January 30, 1923 formalized an
already unfolding process that transformed minorities into refugees in
both countries. As the outcome of hasty diplomatic negotiations, the
Convention marked for the two parties the culmination of a pre-existing
refugee problem on the domestic scene.[2] In the course of the decade that
followed, the refugees of the Turco-Greek War, who were hailed as agents
of national unity at the outset, began to represent a source of a multi-
faceted national challenge, never absent from the agendas of parliamentary sessions and general public opinion in Greece and Turkey. After the
abolition of the principal institution in charge of implementing the Convention, namely the Mixed Commission, on December 28, 1933,[3] the
refugees on both sides, with their pending social, economic, and political
problems, were pushed to the background of history, a development that
found its expression in the political rhetoric of the ruling elite and the
historical discourse of the newly fashioned national biographies of both
countries.

GEOGRAPHY AND DEMOGRAPHY

The Turco-Greek War of 1920–1922 not only marked the last phase of the historical confrontation between the two parties[4] but also ended the long history of significant territorial adjustments and large-scale demographic movements in the region. Where Greece was concerned, the decade of 1912 to 1922 brought about its territorial and demographic expansion at the expense largely of the Ottoman Empire and, to a lesser extent, of Bulgaria. The two Balkan Wars (1912 and 1913) enabled her to annex the majority of Macedonia, and the whole of Southern Epirus and Crete.[5] The population of the country, which stood around 2,530,000 at the beginning of the first Balkan War, was nearly doubled at the end of the second, reaching 4,730,000. With the absorption of Western Thrace by the Treaty of Neuilly on November 27, 1919[6] and eastern Thrace by the defunct Treaty of Sèvres on April 10, 1920, the population of Greece, excluding the population of the Vilayet of Aydın and that of the Dodecanese Islands, which were then under Italian occupation, had reached 5,531,474 by the end of 1920. During the same period, in addition to a large number of Greek refugees from Bulgaria, fresh waves of immigrants from the Caucasus, Romania, and Russia swept into Greece, as well. From the Balkan Wars to the year 1920, the total number of refugees who arrived in Greece, was reported to be about 535,000 [Table 1].

A certain portion of the refugees from eastern Thrace and Asia Minor were repatriated after the Mudros Armistice, but those from the other regions remained largely in Greece. Therefore the above figure should be considered as the ceiling for the size of the refugee population in Greece on the eve of the Asia Minor Catastrophe. These numbers were readjusted during the last phase of the Turco-Greek War when nearly 900,000 Greek

Table 1. Number of Refugees Who Arrived in Greece by Place of Origin, 1912–1920

Asia Minor	190,000
Thrace	200,000
Bulgaria and Serbia	10,000
Russia	50,000
Constantinople	40,000
Dodecanese Islands	30,000
Macedonia	15,000
Total	535,000

Source: AYE, "Facts Relating to the Refugee(s) Situation in Greece," A/5, VI (10).

and Armenian refugees from various parts of Anatolia and eastern Thrace poured into the Aegean Islands and mainland Greece.

As for the Ottoman Empire, the territorial and demographic expansion of Greece implied for the most part a contraction on both fronts throughout the decade of the 1910s. Since the late nineteenth century, with the shrinking borders of the Empire, there had been a continuous outpouring of refugees from different sections of the formerly subject territories in the Balkans, and especially from Eastern Rumelian provinces (e.g., Bulgaria) due to the Turco-Russian War of 1877–78 and Greece following the Turco-Greek War of 1897.[7] However, it was the Balkan Wars that dealt the major blow to the largest segment of Muslim populations in the Balkans, quickly turning most of them into refugees.[8] The number of people who migrated from Western Thrace and Macedonia to Istanbul and Anatolia between the Balkan Wars and World War I (WWI) amounted to somewhere between 413,922 and 640,000.[9] It was reported by the Director of the Department of Tribes and Refugees, Hamid Bey, on March 12, 1917 that the number of refugees in the Ottoman-held areas had reached 700,000 since the outbreak of WWI.[10] Thenceforward, sporadic waves of migrants from Western Thrace and other parts of Greece and Bulgaria continued to bring further treks of refugees to Anatolia and eastern Thrace, which were what remained of the Ottoman Empire after WWI. In addition, Anatolia, having lost a great portion of its Armenian populations, witnessed a constant wave of internal migrations sometimes due to the war and often due to the search on the part of the local populations for more favorable economic conditions [Table 2]. After the Greek troops occupied the Vilayet of Aydın and began to take administrative and political measures for the full annexation of this area to the mainland, this district became yet another source of refugees for the rest of Anatolia proper.

Where the immediate effects of the Turco-Greek War on the human geography of the region, now claimed by Turkish nationalists, were concerned, they took the form of large-scale internal displacements rather than a new massive wave of refugees from outside. Approximately 900,000 Muslim refugees and immigrants were reported to have been in motion in Anatolia and Istanbul around 1920. During the same period, there were minor migrations across the eastern borders. Some 10,000 refugees from Azerbaijan, for instance, migrated to the eastern provinces of Ottoman Anatolia in 1920. It is suggested that a total of 243,744 Muslim refugees came to Kars and its environs from Armenia, Georgia, and Azerbaijan.[11] The country also provided temporary shelter to refugees from other countries. Following the Bolshevik Revolution, a number of White Russians, for example, arrived in Istanbul.[12] By the time of the signing of the Convention,

Table 2. Number of Muslim Refugees Who Arrived in Anatolia and Istanbul by
Place of Origin, 1912–1920

Periods	From All Territories Lost in the Balkan Wars	From Territories Lost to Greece in the Balkan Wars
1912–1913	177,352	68,947
1914–1915	120,566	53,718
1916–1917	18,912	1,252
1918–1919	22,244	6,736
1919–1920	74,848	12,536
Total	413,922	143,189

Source: Arnold J. Toynbee, *The Western Question in Greece and Turkey: A Study in the Contact of Civilisations* (Boston and New York: Houghton Mifflin Company, 1922) 138.

Anatolia and Istanbul were awash with external and internal refugees. In the case of some 132,550 and 145,868 refugees from Macedonia and Western Thrace who had moved respectively to eastern Thrace and Aydın between 1912 and 1920, the dislocation occurred many times.[13] While a significant segment of the population of these areas (in the case of Aydın, for example, nearly 80,000 people)[14] migrated to other parts of Anatolia, 64,500 Greeks, Armenians, and Circassians from the interior sections of Anatolia applied to the Greek High Commissioner in Izmir to be resettled in the Greek-administered areas.[15]

Greece lost all the territorial gains of the post-WWI period during its war with Turkey, which ended with the Mudanya Armistice of October 11, 1922. It is reported that some 900,000 Greeks were turned into refugees in Anatolia and eastern Thrace during the four-month period from August 27 to the end of the year.[16] During the initial stages of this movement, the hardships of the trek were further compounded by disease; a great number of Greek refugees perished. It is reported that "the death rate among children at first was as high as one in five and there was also a high mortality rate among the older refugees."[17] From September 1922 to July 1923, up to 70,000 Greek refugees died of disease and malnutrition.[18] During the same period, nearly 50,000 refugees, who had come to Greece with the first wave of refugees, emigrated to Egypt, France or the United States.[19] After the ratification of the Lausanne Treaty, Greece received 192,356 more refugees from Anatolia from the summer of 1923 to the end of 1924. The same period also saw the Greek refugees emmigrating in massive numbers to countries, especially the United States and Australia, where there were already established Greek communities and no restrictions on the acceptance of further immigrants. In 1924, however, when the emigration of Greek refugees sharply increased, new immigration laws in the United States closed the door to Greek refugees,[20] and the Australian government also introduced certain quotas to the admission of further Greek refugees.[21] Thus, with the completion of the transfer of the remaining Greeks in Anatolia in December 1924[22], the population of Greece leveled off to somewhere between 5,500,000 and 6,000,000 with a refugee segment of one quarter of the total population.[23] According to the 1928 census, Greece's population was 6,204,684, of which 1,221,849 were of refugee background [Table 3].

Table 3. Number of Greek Refugees by Place of Origin (1928)

Place of Origin	Refugees	
Asia Minor and Thrace (Including Pontus and Constantinople)	1,104,216	(90.3%)
Bulgaria	49,027	(4%)
Russia	58,526	(4.7%)
Other Regions	10,080	(1%)
Total	1,221,849	

Source: Α. Α. Παλλης, *Συλλογη των Κυριωτερων Στατιστικων των Αποροσων τη Ανταλλαγην των Πληθυσμων και Προσφυγικων Αποκαταστασιν μετα Αναλυσεως και Επεχηγησεως* (Athens, 1929) 4.

Table 4. Number of Muslim Refugees by Place of Origin

Place of Origin	Refugees
Macedonia	329,098
Thrace	-
Old Greece	5,910
Epirus	1,133
Crete	23,021
Nea Aigaiou	9,184
Other	19,800
Total	388,146

Source: Πελαγιδης, *Προσφυγικη Ελλαδα*,132.[26]

Table 5. Number of Muslim Refugees in Turkey by Years

Years	Males	Females	Total
1921	5,488	5,591	11,079
1922	5,189	4,904	10,093
1923	25,553	25,136	50,689
1924	120,322	115,092	235,414
1925	28,353	28,170	56,523
1926	18,481	16,570	35,051
1927	15,557	16,658	32,213
1928	15,573	16,689	32,442
1929	7,485	6,989	14,454
Total	242,001	235,957	577,958

Source: *İstatistik Yıllığı 1930*, vol. 3, (Ankara: T.C. Başvekalet İstatistik Umum Müdürlüğü, 1930) 99.[27]

DEFINING THE REFUGEE PROBLEM

As for reading the above geographical and demographical facts and figures into the post-Lausanne situation of Greece and Turkey, prominent scholars of the population exchange have been prompted to conclude "on the whole the problem of the settlement of the Moslem immigrants was much simpler in Turkey than the similar problem in Greece and Bulgaria"[28] because "the larger pool of abandoned Greek farmsteads for a smaller number of settlers meant that these Turkish immigrants had a larger portion of land per capita than their Greek counterparts."[29] Based on this presumptuous opinion, the leading scholars of the population exchange have assumed that the problem of the resettlement of incoming refugees was solved automatically in Turkey since the lands vacated by Greek evacuees in Anatolia and eastern Thrace were earmarked for the incoming Muslim populations from Greece.[30]

This cursory reading of the official figures and a bald interpretation of the land/population ratio of the two countries have remained the salient feature of historical writings on the situation of refugees in post-Lausanne Turkey. As discussed briefly in the Introduction of this book, certain domestic trends in Turkish historiography ranging from direct state intervention in the writing of the period's history to the neglect of archival research had left the population exchange out of the agenda of Turkish historiography, resulting in turn in the blind acceptance of the above views about the implications of this event for Turkey. All these factors have combined to constitute the conventional wisdom that the Turkish side confronted no serious challenge as far as the resettlement of refugees who came under the Exchange Convention was concerned.

We contest this conventional view concerning the Turkish case of resettlement on both theoretical and factual grounds.[31] To begin with, all the well-documented cases of the massive refugee movements, including the Greek one, suggest that the resettlement of refugees constituted only one aspect of the broad refugee problem. The latter involved both micro and macro aspects, ranging from the transfer of the refugees to their economic integration into the existing national framework. At the macro level, the problem required wider political and economic action on the part of the governments to coordinate the integration of the refugees and the economic reconstruction of the country. Real integration could not be achieved without planning and executing wide-scale development projects in agriculture, industry, social services and education.[32]

Against this background, the Turkish case requires a closer and more careful analysis. First, Turkey was neither politically nor economically united at the time and its landscape was almost entirely war-ravaged, unlike that of Greece. Second, the majority of the country's financial and professional men were among the thousands of Greek and Armenian refugees, who had moved to Greece, and in return the country got half a million impoverished Muslim peasants from Greece, most of whom had left their agricultural implements behind. Third, and perhaps even more importantly, the larger refugee problem in Turkey involved not only the problems of the relatively small number of refugees from Macedonia, Crete, Thessaly and other regions of Greece who came through the Exchange Convention, but also those of the already existing "refugee" populations, who had come from multiple directions since the Balkan Wars and even before. A great majority of these people had been subjected to temporary settlement (*İskân-i adi* or *tali İskân*) with a view to being repatriated to their homelands once these lands were recaptured and therefore not compensated properly for the properties they had left behind.[33] In fact, an overview of the pre-Lausanne refugee movements towards Anatolia shows that all the earlier refugees had been practically self-settled and widely dispersed, making their impact probably less dramatic than that of their counterparts in Greece and Bulgaria during the same period. The Ottoman government had provided these refugees with some emergency relief and established some primitive programs to support organized rural settlements and urban refugees, but most refugees had had to fend for themselves.[34]

Among the pending problems of the existing refugees in Turkey proper, compensation for their lost properties appeared to be the most dramatic, giving them a "legitimate claim" to take advantage of any available opportunity to minimize their losses. Given the fact that "Turkey had been a country of refugees and emigrants for practically a whole century"[35] and the decade of 1912–1922 marked the apogee of the refugee influx, the size of the population with its unsettled claims over abandoned properties must have been considerable.[36] The gravity of this problem can be further illustrated by the fact that a rough estimate of one quarter of the Anatolia and Thrace total population may have undergone some form of refugee experience from the start of the Balkan Wars to the dawn of the Lausanne Conference. Not the least of the problems was that the country had been undergoing a major agricultural crisis prior to the arrival of some half a million new refugees through the Exchange Convention.[37]

The proportions of the refugee problem in Turkey were further accentuated by certain other domestic developments. Especially since the beginning of the 1920s, the population of Anatolia had entered a new phase of mobility, for the early years, due to the war taking place on multiple fronts, and for the later years, owing to the developments in the Eastern provinces.[38] The nascent Turkish State adopted unchanged the displacement and sedentarization policies of the Ottomans concerning the tribal populations of Eastern Anatolia, namely the Kurds, and even intensified them in the latter half of the decade. Many Kurdish groups were systematically uprooted for security reasons with a view to being resettled in the western and southern sections of the country.[39] Most of these displaced populations actually ended up in the western provinces of the country, bringing yet another pressure on the lands and buildings abandoned by the Greeks and presumably earmarked for the refugees.

Furthermore, immediately upon the departure of the Greeks and Armenians, a large number of people, who had seen their houses burned (*harikzedeler*) during the retreat of the Greek army or had moved from the interior sections of Anatolia, as well as members of the Turkish army,[40] imposed themselves on the available properties in major cities. To cite one example, the newspapers report that following the departure of the Greeks and Armenians from the most populous and prosperous districts of Karşıyaka and Bornova in Izmir, there was not a single house available for the settlement of the incoming Muslim refugees from Greece.[41] The fact of the matter was that properties hastily and informally vacated by Greeks and Armenians were not reserved for those refugees from Greece, but used for the accommodation and settlement of all the local populations with a "legitimate" claim.[42] Some people, for example, claimed that they could not secure their debts from their Greek clients; therefore, they seized the properties vacated by their debtors instead.[43] In the parliamentary discussions a certain Ragıb Bey brought up the issue that the great number of people who plundered the abandoned properties belonged to the local Jewish community in Izmir.[44] This view cannot be verified, but what can be verified is that among the plunderers were members of the local refugee resettlement commission, which was made up of leading local government officials such as "Head Treasurer of Izmir (*Izmir Defterdarı*), Members of the Inspection Commission (*Müfettiş Komisyon Azaları*) and Scribes of the Inspection Commission (*Komisyon Katipleri*)."[45] But perhaps more ironically was that in this property rush, which continued during the implementation phase of the Convention, were included certain members of the Turkish Grand National Assembly. For instance, the Deputy of Balıkesir, Hulusi Bey, was accused of seizing two houses (one for each of his sons), a soap factory, and thousands of olive trees, all of which had been abandoned by the Greeks and earmarked for the incoming refugees.[46]

During the intensive telegram communication between the Ankara government and the Turkish delegation at Lausanne, it was indicated at some point that the precise scope of Greek refugees who had moved from eastern Thrace could not be determined due to the lack of registers.[47] Of 260,000 abandoned houses, 60,000 in Western Anatolia could be used for the resettlement of the refugees.[48] On January 23, 1923, only one week before the signing of the Convention, it became apparent that those houses considered for the refugees from Greece had already been assigned to the Muslim refugees who had been temporarily encamped in Istanbul.[49] On the other hand, the parliamentary proceedings reveal that the Anatolian landscape was concurrently undergoing an intensive struggle among members of local communities over the abandoned properties, during which time it was a common occurrence for some of the lands and buildings of the local populations to be taken over by other members of local communities.[50] Prompted by populist concerns, the government passed a major resolution in early 1923 with a view to satisfying the demands of the public: those who seized the abandoned properties could hold onto them in return for an insignificant amount of rent.[51]

In light of the above facts it can be said that where Turkey was concerned, the nature of the refugee problem involved as many qualitative aspects as quantitative. And the prevalent view among the scholars of the population exchange that Turkey had an abundance of the dispossessed property of all kinds certainly fails to take into account the deplorable conditions of the country at the time the Convention was signed at Lausanne. This view, which has thus far clouded scholarly research on the subject, will be completely abandoned in the near future especially when the newly discovered archives of the Provincial Bureaus of Village Affairs

(*Köy Hizmetleri İl Müdürlükleri*) in various cities of the country–most of which are now transferred to the Republican Archives in Ankara–are studied more extensively.

It was shown in Chapter Two that the rationale concerning the relation between the properties of the evacuees and the scope of Muslim refugees had surfaced originally in the speeches of Venizelos during the early phase of the negotiations at Lausanne when he labored to persuade the Turkish side for the swift settlement of the Convention. It was noted in Chapter Three that once the Turkish delegates consented to a draft convention,[52] the quantitative aspects of the population exchange became marginal in the negotiations. As a result, the diplomatic negotiations on the population exchange turned out to be limited merely to the technical principles of the process, leaving much room for interpretation by the governments of Turkey and Greece.

In retrospect, the success of the governments in managing the resettlement of refugees hinged from the beginning on their ability to secure financial assistance from the major parties at Lausanne. On the Greek side, the representatives, who recognized the grave nature of the problem at the outset, immediately began to negotiate for turning the temporal relief activities provided by international relief organizations such as the League of Nations High Commission for Refugees, the American Red Cross and the Near East Relief into a systematic plan under a permanent organization. Their laborious efforts bore fruit in the later stages of the Lausanne Conference when the Greek government and the Council of the League of Nations agreed upon the flotation of a loan and the establishment of an autonomous institution, namely the Refugee Settlement Commission. These developments were later interpreted by critics as infringements on national sovereignty and channels by which Greek economy was brought under heavy constraints. But to the extent that the Greek government was successful in its resettlement and rehabilitation efforts, these attempts proved of vital importance.

The Turkish delegates, on the other hand, tended to move the issue away from the diplomatic table and make it an internal issue. In complete contradiction to the Greeks, the Turks, refusing even "international commissions of various sorts to supervise matters as minor as the sanitary regime of the Straits,"[53] opposed the idea of an autonomous commission that would supervise minority affairs. Since a commission of this kind would be apt to interfere in the affairs of the Turkish government, it was consequently quite incompatible with the national sovereignty of the country. Against the background of similar concerns, the Turkish side never raised the issue of a comprehensive loan package similar to that of Greece to be used for the resettlement of the refugees. As a matter of fact, an overview of the Turkish government's early policies concerning the population exchange suggests that there were certain plans and projects at hand, the proper application of which would have greatly alleviated the burdens of the resettlement.[54] The ensuing developments, however, demonstrated that the authorities in charge implemented the population exchange in an *ad hoc* manner primarily through trial and error. Moreover, it soon became obvious that the inventories of the properties abandoned by Greeks, which had been prepared by the local administrations, were used as security against the war reparations to be demanded from Greece rather than providing the groundwork for the incoming refugees.[55] In a nutshell, it can be argued that from the beginning of the transfer of the refugees to the completion of the population exchange in the early 1930s, refugee affairs in Turkey became an arena for mismanagement and much graft on the part of government officials as anticipated by an international mediator, the head of the American Red Cross Colonel Haskell, who labored to undo the population exchange during and in the immediate aftermath of the Convention.[56]

Given this background, it was not so much the absence of plans and projects, as assumed by the traditional scholarship,[57] but the lack of effective machinery to conduct and supervise the whole process that exacerbated the refugee problem in Turkey. By the time the population exchange negotiations were completed, both governments had long been considering the establishment of permanent institutions and practices with which to handle the problems of refugees. In the midst of the catastrophic developments, however, neither of the two parties were sure as to the possible domestic mechanisms and policies that could be devised to provide for the permanent settlement of the refugees "on a productive basis and in a manner that would provide for the cultivation of the lands left vacant by the Greek [and Muslim] refugees and for the replacement of the latter in productive work and professional occupations."[58]

In Greece, the recent population exchange with Bulgaria had led to the creation of the Commission for Relief and Settlement of Refugees (*Επιτροπή Περιθαλψεως και Ευκαταστασεως Προσφυγων*) with its center in Salonica.[59] Thus, with the help of this institution, a certain percentage of early refugees was immediately resettled in northern Greece before the Exchange Convention began to operate formally. During the war and its immediate aftermath, certain domestic institutions, such as the Refugee Relief Fund, and some international relief organizations, such as the Red Cross and the Near East Relief, provided the mechanism by means of which the Greek government brought some order to the disorganized and panic-stricken trek of refugees. As soon as the Convention was signed, the Greek government entered into negotiations with the Council of the League of Nations for a refugee loan to turn the resettlement scheme into a large scale development program. The floatation of such a loan brought with it the establishment of the Refugee Settlement Commission in the later months of 1923, with which the Greek governments, notwithstanding the ongoing political turmoil, were able to implement many of the provisions stipulated by the Convention. The 1923–1930 period witnessed the efforts of governments in Greece to make a virtue out of necessity and to convert the obviously unavoidable tragedy of massive refugee flight into a state-directed instrument for the economic development of the country. There had been, it is true, some serious impediments along the way particularly with regard to the social and economic integration of the refugees, but the presence of the Refugee Settlement Commission offers a piecemeal explanation as to "how the military defeat was transformed into a peaceful success" in the specific case of the rehabilitation and partial "assimilation" of the Greek refugees during the first decade of the population exchange.[60]

In Turkey, on the other hand, the only organizational structures that existed to deal with the resettlement and rehabilitation of refugees were the Ottoman refugee bureaus (*muhacirin müdüriyetleri*), which were either defunct or lacked the means for transferring the refugees, let alone systematically turning them into producers in a short period of time.[61] That the new government in Ankara had virtually no institutional arrangement to oversee the transitive phase and regiment the implementation of the Convention created a great vacuum as far as the fate of abandoned properties was concerned. The latter issue not only constituted a source of endless heated debates in the Turkish parliament but also became a popular topic of concern in the newspapers and journals of the period. Needless to say, it created a major source of discontent among the incoming refugees, as will be shown in the following chapters.

The discussions in the Turkish parliament focused largely on the establishment of a permanent institution to handle the problems of the existing refugees and the protection of abandoned properties rather than preparing the background for the effective implementation of the Convention. The Commission of Abandoned Properties (*Emval-i Metruke Komisyonu*), which was established with a view to preparing the inventories of the abandoned properties, turned out to be involved more with the resettlement of existing refugees than its primary task.[62] In the face of growing problems concerning the abandoned properties, the Turkish government experimented with two more institutional innovations. It first tried to bring the previously Greek administered areas or war-ravaged regions under the administration of a specially designed ministry, namely, the Ministry of Liberated Provinces (*Memalik-i Müstahlasa Vekâleti*). Then, it tried to create (as part of this ministry) temporary local bodies, namely Commissions of Spoils and Social Assistance (*Menhubat ve Muavenet-i İçtimaiye Komisyonları*), to deal with the administration of the properties abandoned by Greeks and Armenians.[63] This attempt failed as a whole. Moreover, the three institutions that were in charge of the execution of the Convention––namely the Department of Refugee Affairs in the Ministry of Finance, the Red Crescent (*Hilal-i Ahmer*), and the Association for the Protection of Orphans (*Himaye-i Etfal Cemiyeti*)—lacked coordination, as became evident in their failure to meet the urgent needs of refugees upon their arrival.

Since late 1922, the necessity of effective machinery to facilitate the transfer of the Muslim populations from the Greek territories had become a widely recognized fact among certain members of the Turkish Parliament.[64] On October 25, 1922, a deputy, Tunalı Hilmi, urged the government to establish such a ministry to deal with the mounting problems of existing refugees before the arrival of new refugees.[65] When the Lausanne Conference was coming to a close, similar calls began to surface amongst various popular journalists of the period, both liberal and socialist. On July 3, 1923, Hüseyin Yalçın, drawing attention to the continuing onslaught on the abandoned properties, wrote that "since these properties have been earmarked for the refugees from Greece, they must be protected until their arrival."[66] A stronger statement was published on September 10, 1923 in *Vazife*, an unofficial mouthpiece of Turkish socialists. Şefik Hüsnü wrote that "hundreds of reasons and motives are currently being put forward to justify the impediments in the current state of affairs, but the relaxed attitude and negligence in the question of population exchange can by no means be explained. We neither face a problem of immediate occurrence nor are we in a situation to waste time by further delay."[67] Ahmet Emin, on the other hand, wrote that a successful resettlement policy would encourage the non-exchangeable Turks in Western Thrace to move to Turkey and accordingly the country would develop demographically.[68] Another recommendation came from a local newspaper in Izmir, namely *Ahenk*. The author of the article, Şevket Turgut, proposed that once the Ministry is created, the resettlement of the country should start from Edirne and the Red Crescent should immediately begin collecting donations to facilitate this process.[69]

By way of incorporating all existing Ottoman institutions concerning refugees, the political leadership eventually consented to the creation on October 13, 1923 of the Ministry of Exchange, Reconstruction and Resettlement (*Mübadele, İmar ve İskân Vekâleti*; MERR) a colossal bureaucratic body. The establishment of this ministry was delayed due to the long discussions concerning judicial and administrative principles. This government body, which will be discussed at length in Chapter Eight, also proved abortive, and the previous methods and institutions were more or less restored within a short period. Against the background of all these developments, it seems rather timely to assert that where the Turkish stance on the population exchange was concerned, the objective realities of the situation were not taken into account, neither in the plans and projects prepared on this matter prior to Lausanne nor in the decision-making process at Lausanne.[70]

The troubled nature of the Turkish stance on the population exchange was nowhere more apparent than in its economic aspects. Where Greece was concerned, it has been convincingly argued that Venizelos considered the arrival of refugees as the opportunity to push forward a project of economic development.[71] A similar concern was actually mirrored in the heated public speeches of the leaders of the new Turkish state who continued to uphold the rhetoric of "economic nationalism." However, there was no hint in their discourse as to the ways they anticipated the integration of the existing and incoming refugees into the national economic program, the details of which had been drafted in the Izmir Economic Congress only a month after the Convention was signed at Lausanne. The press had already published articles drawing attention to the economic aspects of the population exchange. A local newspaper, *Yenigün*, reported on November 25, 1922, when the Lausanne talks were underway, that the local governor of Çeşme was complaining about the unplanned settlement of the refugees in his region since most of the refugees, directed to this location by government officials, were unsuitable for the region's specific conditions and uninformed about the vineyards. Therefore, refugees who were suitable for the region and knowledgeable about grapes were needed.[72]

Taking the above facts into consideration, the Economic Congress in Izmir, which focused largely on macro-economic development and industrialization, made specific recommendations to the government concerning the settlement of the refugees. A telegram from Kazım Karabekir, the head of the Congress, only a few weeks after the signing of the Convention, stated that incoming refugees ought to be resettled in areas in relation to their skills (*kabiliyet*), physical capacities (*bünyelerine*), properties (*mülk*), specializations (*ihtisasat*) and natures (*mahiyyetlerine*), so a commission should be urgently established to this effect. The Congress also suggested that the government should take advance measures by way of renting, not simply granting, the abandoned properties and lands to the existing populations in order to prevent the refugees from becoming homeless and jobless.[73] In this way, it would also be possible to retain some funds for the refugees. As the following sections will demonstrate, neither the advice of the Congress nor the visibly mounting problems of the refugees prompted the government to take up refugee affairs in a systematic manner.

Scholars specializing in the Greek side of the population exchange have already illustrated the multi-faceted nature of the refugee problem in Greece. As the above discussion suggests, the Turkish case, with its additional disadvantages, seems to have presented more or less similar complexities. Therefore, it is our contention that the refugee problem came to pose as much of a challenge to Turkey as it did in Greece. This might have given the Turkish political leadership sufficient reason to mobilize all available means and mechanisms to settle the problem during the rest of the 1920s and the first part of the following decade. In fact, on November 10, 1923, İsmet Paşa himself announced in the Grand Assembly that "the exchange problem is a matter of life for us. It is the most urgent and greatest problem of our state. It is a matter that our politics cannot neglect and it has put us in great need and sorrow."[74] Caught between this political rhetoric and the irrepressible realities of the actual situation, Turkish refugees spent a whole decade moving from one location to another in the country. Theirs' was a problem that was of interest neither to politicians nor to local populations. It is this very problematic situation that this portion of the book sets out to investigate in juxtaposition with its well-documented Greek counterpart.

THEMES, METHOD, AND SOURCES

The chapters that follow counterpoise the refugee policies of both Turkey and Greece and the material conditions of the population exchange with a view to configuring the refugee presence in both countries throughout the first decade of the population exchange. In Greece, where the majority of the refugees had already been moved during the war and in its immediate aftermath, the government had taken certain measures in close cooperation with international relief organizations to alleviate the burden of the refugees upon their arrival. The government of the nascent Turkish State, though heavily preoccupied with the problems of existing refugees,[75] waited for the settlement of the population exchange negotiations at Lausanne to address the specific conditions of incoming refugees from Greece. Thus, its early approach to the refugee problem was characterized by a vague attitude, which set the tone for the later stages of the process, when the numerical scope of the displaced people grew steadily. As might be expected, the later stages were also dominated by the display of an indifferent attitude on the part of the political leadership to the incoming refugees as clearly manifested in the resettlement and rehabilitation policies. The properties which survived the property rush were redistributed on the basis of the first come-first serve principal, creating a vacuum for the existing populations and refugees.

In complete contrast to Greece, where refugee affairs were entrusted to the autonomous administration of the Refugee Settlement Commission shortly after the ratification of the Lausanne Treaty, the Turkish government made the refugees and all the problems connected with them the exclusive concern of the central authorities. Thus, a highly bureaucratic, yet unsystematic, approach in the form of a ministry was devised to resolve the refugee problem, which in turn not only accentuated the deplorable conditions of the refugees but also prolonged their integration into the ongoing process of national reconstruction. Given this background, it would not be too far-fetched to argue that the problem of resettling and integrating refugees in Turkey along a sound policy of economic reconstruction posed itself in similar, if not stronger, terms. Unlike Greece, where the problem took the form of transforming the refugees into economically self-supporting and politically well-integrated citizens, the Turkish case was characterized from its inception by a lack of necessary attention on the part of political authorities and ambiguities ranging from the transportation and settlement of the refugees to their integration. Moreover, the age-old practice, one that had doomed the Ottoman resettlement policies to failure, of settling refugees where there was room but not necessarily adequate resources and employment opportunities, persisted in the new Turkey.

The following chapters proceed at three levels of historical inquiry. Chapter Six offers an overview of the principles of the Convention, and pinpoints some of the deficiencies and flaws of the text. Chapter Seven traces the situation of refugees from the beginning of their trek to their landing in their destined countries against the background of the preparations undertaken by the governments of Greece and Turkey. Having mapped out the early nature of the refugee problem in the two countries, Chapter Eight proceeds to examine the structure and operation of major domestic and foreign institutions mobilized to deal with refugee affairs. In the concluding chapter, a preliminary comparison and contrast of the social, political and economic aspects of the refugee settlement vis-à-vis the reconstruction policies of the two governments will be attempted.

In terms of the periodization of the refugee problem, we follow earlier studies and see it through two consecutive diplomatic phases, each playing a special role in the refugee problem. The first stage refers roughly to the first three years, starting with the Lausanne negotiations, proceeding through the Ankara Convention of June 21, 1925,[76] and eventually ending with the Athens Convention of December 1, 1926. The early stage of this process was characterized by the respective governments' pragmatic interpretation and application of the first three articles of the Convention on the one hand, and their early confrontation with the social and economic problems associated with the refugees on the other. This period, which also witnessed the transformation of the regimes to a republican form of government, tested the abilities of Turkish and Greek governments in carrying out the reconstruction of their respective countries while incorporating, in the form of rehabilitation and assimilation, the large masses of displaced, disoriented and, perhaps more importantly, unemployed individuals into their evolving political systems.

The first three years proved that the population exchange was not to be tackled easily through the articulately stated provisions of the Convention and that it was in fact a multi-faceted issue, requiring further action on many fronts. During this period, the most basic principles of the Convention proved to be ineffectual in addressing the actual conditions of the issue at stake, including the fundamental questions of who were the exchangeables and what terms of residence were sought. First and foremost was the fact that the population exchange was not limited simply to the transferring, sheltering, clothing, and feeding of the refugees. Secondly, the liquidation of refugee properties and their proper indemnification had been under the authority of a Mixed Commission, whose work was from the beginning plagued by the absence of cooperation between the governments of the two countries. The emergence of these facts, in turn, resulted in the modification of some of the earlier principles laid out in the Convention in regard to the governmentality of the population exchange. These facts were integrated into the population exchange process through several diplomatic documents signed in Athens and Ankara after tortuous negotiations. With these new documents, both governments tried to redress the deficiencies of the Convention, especially on issues concerning the liquidation of properties and the terms of residence (*établi*).

The second phase refers to the period from the signing of the Athens Convention in 1926 to the Ankara Agreement of June 10, 1930, which marked to a great extent the diplomatic completion of the population exchange process. During this phase, the importance of the roles of the individual governments replaced that of diplomatic mechanisms. The Mixed Commission, which had already become a passive institution, was totally marginalized in the population exchange process and soon the major institutions devised to handle refugee affairs in both countries were abolished. With the Ankara Convention of 1930, both governments retained rights for the removal and disposal of refugees' movable property, envisaging the establishment of a joint governmental agency to supervise the execution of agreements, on which the two sides would enjoy equal representation. The last phase was characterized by the activities of the Mixed Commission on the perennial problems of refugees, such as liquidation and indemnification, caused by the deficiencies of the Convention, which ended with the signing of a bilateral agreement for the abolition of this institution on December 28, 1933, due to take effect three months later.

As for the sources, we rely heavily on the documents obtained from the Historical Archives of the Greek Ministry of Foreign Affairs, the Turkish Republican Archives, proceedings of the Turkish Grand National Assembly, oral testimonies of Turkish and Greek refugees, secondary literature specializing in the Greek side of the events and finally local and national newspapers in Turkey. As was emphasized in the earlier sections of this book, the principal concern of the present author is to bring to light the previously neglected story of the Turkish refugees and make a case in the final analysis that their precarious situation presented a great many characteristics commensurate with their Greek counterparts, whose plight has been covered by a large body of literature. It is our contention that only when the tales of Turkish refugees are incorporated into the existing story of the population exchange that an impartial picture of this tragic episode in Turkish and Greek relations can be (re)constructed, a mammoth task, indeed, for the accomplishment of which the current study should be considered only a preliminary step.

Chapter Six
The Convention:
The Beginning of the End

Turkish and Greek delegates signed "the Convention concerning the Exchange of Turkish nationals of the Greek orthodox religion established in Turkish territory and of Greek nationals of the Moslem religion established in Greek territory" on January 30, 1923, with effect from May 1, 1923.[1] But this plan was first delayed due to the unexpected suspension of negotiations on February 4. After the talks were resumed on April 23, the anticipated duration of the conference was further extended due to the diplomatic maneuvering of conference participants over the issues of war reparations, the judicial regime for foreigners, and economic clauses. While the second round of the Lausanne talks was underway, both sides commissioned the review and evaluation of the Convention to legal teams made up of internationally reputed lawyers and local legal advisors.[2] Meanwhile, the League of Nations, having considered a proposal by the Greek Foreign Minister N. Politis for a loan to be used in the resettlement of the refugees, referred the matter to the Financial Committee of the League for evaluation and later established a sub-committee (known as the Greek Committee) for this special task.[3] Thus, the study of certain legal and fiscal aspects of the Convention brought yet another delay.

The conference ended on July 23, 1923, but the ratification of the Lausanne Treaty and its annexed documents by the respective countries took place a month later.[4] Both sides had agreed earlier that the enforcement of the Convention would begin after the establishment of the Mixed Commission and the completion of domestic preparations necessary before the landing of the refugees.[5] Meanwhile, the exchange of war prisoners, which was laid down by Article 4 of the Convention as a prerequisite to the beginning of the actual transfer of civilians,[6] was not completed by late August 1923, another development that contributed to prolonging the implementation of the Convention. Under these circumstances, the transportation of Muslim refugees from the Greek ports could not begin until the end of 1923, while the Turkish government did not allow for security reasons the immediate evacuation of the remaining Greek and other non-Muslim refugees from the Turkish ports. The Turkish authorities made their only exception for the Greek refugees in Istanbul,[7] who had languished in camps throughout the city. Organized and coordinated evacuations of the remaining populations on both sides started in late December 1923. The transfer of Muslim and Greek refugees was complete as of December 1924.

REACTIONS: TOO LITTLE TOO LATE!

The year 1923 was in its entirety a time of uncertainty for all those whose fates were dependent upon the Convention. The early attempts of people to prevent the Greek and Turkish diplomats from signing this agreement were covered briefly in Chapter Three. Although these efforts yielded no results on the whole, collective refugee appeals to the Greek and Turkish governments as well as to the international public continued at full speed. Of these appeals, the most detailed one was drafted by the Central Committee of Constantinople Greeks (*Κεντρική Επιτροπή Κωνσταντινοπόλεως*) and sent to the Greek Ministry of Foreign Affairs. Having explained at length the effects of this covenant upon the future prospects of Hellenism in Istanbul, the Committee drew attention, on behalf of all the people—Greeks, other Christians, Jews, and Turks—to the pain and suffering this arrangement entailed.[8] Like all other calls for the reversion of the process, this one proved fruitless.[9] Having realized that the decision for the population exchange was irreversible, collective pleas were abandoned in favor of personal ones. Helpless as they were, many individuals sought to justify to the authorities in Ankara and Athens why they should be exempted from the application of the Convention.

In Turkey, many individual appeals for exemption were registered during the first several years of the population exchange. Having reviewed these applications, the government seems to have stubbornly turned most of them down as manifested in a series of resolutions found in the Republican Archives in Ankara. The only time exemptions were granted to individuals was when the assistance of the applying person to the Turkish forces during the Turco-Greek War was documented or supported by witnesses. A Konstantion Portil of Söke was granted exemption for his "good deeds" and "service to the Turks" during the Greek occupation of this region.[10]

A Perikli Efendi, doctor by profession, was excluded from the population exchange on the ground that "he had saved the lives of many people during the Greek occupation of Söke."[11] A more general reason was sometimes quoted as in the case of a İstamat Zihni of Bodrum, whose "service to law" was considered sufficient reason for exemption.[12] In the case of Papa Eftim, once beloved figure of the Ankara government, who was included among the exchangeables according to the Convention, the government had to issue a special resolution to exempt him and his family from the population exchange for the obvious reason that their lives would be endangered (*duçar-ı felaket)* in Greece.[13] There were also cases in which people brought up such reasons as "training someone to take their place" that were considered unacceptable and rejected by the government.[14]

In addition to these cases, would-be refugees in Turkey resorted to other tactics to avoid the population exchange. In this regard, one of the major methods devised by the local Greek populations was to change their faith rather than their home.[15] Apparently conversion took place in massive numbers during the Lausanne negotiations. The Ankara government passed a resolution through which "the applications of the non-Muslims to convert to Islam were halted until the agreement of peace and returning [of the conditions] to the normal," referring precisely to the Lausanne talks over the population exchange.[16] In the meantime, some non-Muslim women married Muslims, a development that attracted the attention of the Ankara government, issuing in turn another resolution prohibiting the official endorsement of such marriages.[17] Shortly afterwards, due perhaps to the declining number of such marriages, the government revised its policy and allowed official approval of such marriages.[18] Even so, there was apparently an increase in the number of marriages between exchangeable women and non-exchangeable men, which did not escape the attention of the government. Thus, the latter introduced another provision to the existing law: "the Orthodox women who were to be exempted from the population exchange included only those who had married the non-exchangeable men and registered their marriage with the census bureaus (*sicil-i nüfus*) before the signing of the Convention."[19] Perhaps the only people who were granted temporal delay of departure were the people with disabilities and health problems. This decision was taken nearly two years after the ratification of the Convention. Thus, there is no reason to assume that by this date most of the disabled and sick were not included among the early refugee wave.[20] By and large, restrictive governmental measures left no loophole for the evasion of the population exchange. Having exhausted all available options, Greek populations throughout Anatolia eventually had to give in to the provisions of the Convention. Those who managed to escape the attention of government authorities by way of hiding and did not possess *établi* documents were to be registered as *"Rum Ortodoks"* (Greek Orthodox) at the local census bureaus and granted Turkish citizenship in the mid-1930s.[21]

When the Greeks in Turkey realized that there was no other way apart from selling all their belongings and leaving, they rushed to sell their properties at a fair price to local Muslims. Greek businessmen, as in the case of the Vayanos Brothers in Selçuk, hurried to obtain a copy of the "text of the agreement signed between Greece and Turkey regarding the exchange of property in Turkey and Greece."[22] In the meantime, the Turkish government took action on property matters and issued a series of resolutions concerning the sale conditions. An earlier decree that had temporarily prohibited the selling of properties belonging to non-Muslims, with the exception of the Greeks who had come after November 30, 1918, was modified and all non-Muslims, except Greeks, were granted the right to sell their immovable properties.[23] This decision, which prohibited the Greeks from selling their immovable properties, was later repudiated by another decree.[24] The same was true of the movable properties of the Greeks. Although certain orders were passed allowing Greek refugees to take with them all their movable property, except bulk merchandise, it was very difficult to enforce these orders.

As for the Muslim populations in Greece, there is little information available about their last minute reactions to the Convention.[25] The few official documents located in the Historical Archives of the Ministry of Foreign Affairs in Athens provide meager evidence to argue that the Greek government pursued a policy similar to that of the Turkish government described above.[26] More concrete evidence is gleaned from oral sources. These sources suggest certain patterns of behavior common to Muslims when they were first notified by local government officials of the population exchange decision. For example, local Muslim notables in the region of Florina seem to have frequented the municipal building in the city in order to secure permission for stay but they were turned down.[27] Similarly, some descendants of refugees interviewed for a project speak of the laborious efforts of their fathers and grandfathers to stop the population exchange process during the 1923–1924 period.[28] They seem to have been advised by Greek government officials to return to their homes and prepare for evacuation in compliance with the terms of the Convention.

Not all of the Muslims learned of the decision for the population exchange from Greek authorities. Representatives of the Turkish Red Crescent (*Hilal-i Ahmer*) visited settlements with a Muslim majority and informed the religious leaders (*müftüs*) of the decision. Those who wanted to secretly remain could not do so because of rumors of conversion to Christianity.[29] It should be remarked, however, that there were instances when local Muslim populations were forcibly evicted from their homes before the Convention was actually implemented. Testimonies of Turkish refugees reveal that the first wave of Greek refugees from Anatolia and eastern Thrace during the second half of 1922 was hosted, sometimes with the intervention of local Greek authorities and sometimes voluntarily in the houses of local Muslim populations. This, some Muslim refugees testify, played an important role in their consent to the population exchange.[30] By and large, it can be argued on the basis of this brief discussion that the Turkish Muslim population did not wholeheartedly embrace the population exchange decision as assumed by traditional scholarship.[31]

REPORTED FACT AND REALITY[32]

"As from the 1 May, 1923, there shall take place a compulsory exchange of Turkish nationals of the Greek orthodox religion established in Turkish territory, and of Greek nationals of the Moslem religion established in Greek territory. These persons shall not return to live in Turkey or Greece respectively without the authorization of the Turkish government or of the Greek government respectively."[33]

Thus did the first article of the Convention stipulate. As the outcome of hasty negotiations, the official document contained nineteen provisions, describing a wide range of issues from the identity of the exchangeables to the methods to be pursued in the liquidation of their properties. This document was pregnant with many complications owing to the very fact that while crafting the provisions, the decision-makers in Athens and Ankara did not take into account the actual dynamics (e.g., the situation of the abandoned properties, the issue of liquidation, the financial cost of indemnification, the confessional differences among the people subject to the Convention, the status of the people with Greek nationality in Turkey) and the possible consequences of the issues at stake. Hence, the waverings, inconsistencies and contradictions that went into the making of this document proved to have the effect of obstructing the implementation of these provisions from the beginning, a fact that was attested to by numerous meetings between the Turkish and Greek diplomatic teams at various levels within the first decade of the Convention. Out of the deliberations and tortuous discussions in these meetings, a number of new documents (e.g., the Conventions of Ankara and Athens) cropped up to address the deficiencies and flaws of the original document, brought about by the obstinate attitude of both sides during the negotiations in Lausanne.

The major drawback of the Convention was related to the principal criterion adopted by the conference in designating the minorities, thus the exchangeables, which was closely associated with the definition of national identity by the two sides. During the tireless negotiations in the Sub-Commission on Minorities at Lausanne, the notion of minority as understood by the Turks and the contending parties had shown much discrepancy. In referring to the minorities under question, the discourse of both sides reflected more the ideal notions of national identity than actual realities. The Greeks spoke of a combined identity of ethnicity and religion for the Greek minority in Turkey, while the Turks, who came to Lausanne with a notion of "minority" based essentially on faith, persisted in using religion as the primary denominator. Therefore, the Turkish diplomats, İsmet Pasha and Rıza Nur, used the broad term "non-Muslims" *(gayri-Müslim)* to refer to the Greeks. As for the Muslim population in Greece, they used the term "people of Islam" *(ahali-i islamiye)* and "Turkish" *(Türk)* interchangeably from the beginning of the negotiations. Especially in the sessions of the Minority Commission, the members of the Turkish delegation, chiefly Rıza Nur, insisted on using the term "non-Muslims" to refer to the minorities.[34] The same tendency was concurrently prevalent in the open and secret meetings of the Turkish Grand National Assembly.[35] Thus, for the Turks, the concept of minority meant non-Muslims *(gayri Müslim)* and no such criterion as race or language could be accepted to redefine it.[36] On December 22, 1922, the Sub-Commission on Minorities agreed, in parallel to the view of the Turkish side, to the use of the term "non-Muslim" to designate the minorities in Turkey. In the meantime, the use of the term "Turkish Orthodox" for the Greeks living in the interior sections of Anatolia (Karamanlides) by the Turkish delegates, which reflected an unfolding political project in Turkey concerning the integration of these people as such within the national framework, astounded the conference participants, especially the Greeks.[37] In the final analysis, the Turkish definition of minority was adopted by the conference and the criterion to determine whether a person was exchangeable became "one of religion and not race."[38]

The underlying motives of the Turkish delegation for insisting on the use of a broad definition of the term "non-Muslim" throughout the conference appeared to have emanated from two principal concerns.[39] If the first one was to prevent the entanglement of Muslim groups (e.g., Kurds, Circassians[40] etc.) in Turkey in the discussions over the minorities and thereby barring the creation in the long run of national minorities out of Muslim populations based on ethnicity or language, the second one was to confirm the *de facto* status of the Armenians who had fled during the war, an issue discussed at length in Chapter Three. The adoption of this definition had the potential to complicate the application of the first clause of the Convention as it left the identity, status and other features of the people to be covered by this convention ambiguous.

Contrary to the established paradigm that the Convention came to be implemented strictly on the basis of religion, the actual process indicates that both Turks and Greeks interpreted this criterion pragmatically and in tandem with their notions of "Turkishness" or "Greekness." This interpretation took its toll on two groups of people: the first group of people included those who were ethnically of the same stock but different from the majority in terms of culture, language, and history; the second group consisted of people who were ethnically distinct but religiously associated with the target groups.[41] Thus the largely Turkish speaking communities of Cappadocia, namely the Karamanlides who were referred to as the Turkish Orthodox throughout the Lausanne negotiations, were eventually included among the exchangeables, despite their considerable efforts to avoid the population exchange.[42] These people had certain affinities of racial origin with other Greeks, but it would be a big mistake and a pitfall to assume that these communities were alike. In fact, later developments showed that the points of difference between them far outnumbered the points of resemblance.[43]

As for the second group of people who were religiously associated with Greeks and Muslims and therefore unjustifiably affected by the Convention, they belonged to different ethnic origins. Amongst them were the Armenians, Albanians, Circassians, Assyrians, and Bulgarians. There was another group religiously affiliated with one of the target groups, namely the *dönme* population of Salonica, who were affected by the population exchange. As the members of a Ladino-speaking Muslim sect, descendants of seventeenth century Jewish converts to Islam, these people were evicted by the Greek government and were entangled with the exchangeable Muslims.[44] During the same period, some 300 Orthodox Mesopotamians (Assyrians) from Baghdad and Mosul were reported to have been among the refugees quartered at the Camp of Makronissos in Baghdad and transferred to Greece along with the Greek refugees.[45]

The use of religion as the principal denominator produced further ambiguities, especially for two other groups, during the implementation of the Convention. These were the Albanian Muslims (who spoke only Albanian and Turkish) and the Gagavuz Turkmens, a Turkish tribe of Christian faith, who had settled in Thrace well before the Ottomans (who spoke only Turkish). At the outset, both groups were viewed as subject to the Convention.[46]

The situation of the Albanians living in Greece best illustrates the confusion associated with the first article of the Convention. These people were divided among themselves in terms of religious affiliation. While some of them were Muslims (belonging to various Sufi orders such as Bektashi), others were Christians (mainly Orthodox and Catholic).[47] While the latter were categorically exempted from the Convention, Muslim Albanians, who had originally been considered exchangeable, were granted special status through bilateral agreements between the Greek and Turkish delegates during the second phase of the Lausanne meetings. According to Alexander Pallis, it was thanks to a special declaration made by one of the members of the Greek delegation, Kaklamanos (the Greek Minister to London), that "the compulsory exchange shall not be applicable to her Moslem subjects of Albanian origin."[48] The following incident best illustrates the situation of the Albanians. On August 24, 1923, a delegation from Paramythia filed a complaint to the Dutch Legation in Athens that they had opted to stay in Greece but they had since been subjected to discriminative attitude of the local Greek authorities. They were not granted the right to vote but were asked to report to the local military bureau for conscription. They further explained their situation that when they decided to stay, they thought they could maintain their status as Ottoman subjects, a status conferred upon them through the Treaty of Athens in 1914.[49]

It is unknown how many Muslim Albanians were eventually relocated through the Convention. A. Pallis mentions that many Muslim Albanians had the desire to immigrate to Turkey.[50] As we learn from Rıza Nur's memoirs, the Anatolian section of Istanbul, especially the districts from Erenköy to Kartal, which had been populated by the wealthiest of the Greek minority, was subjected to the invasion of the Albanian refugees from Janina, who spoke only Greek.[51]

A few years after the Convention was put into practice, the Albanians maintained their precarious situation. For example, a Turkish government decree dated May 6, 1925 reveals that "some 240 persons of Albanian race who came to Turkey together with the exchangeable people from Greece are allowed to move to a foreign destination of their own choice."[52] The great majority of Muslim Albanians who decided to stay in Greece after the Convention were to migrate to Turkey in the immediate aftermath of WWII. Most of these latecomers would be resettled in various towns of Bursa (especially Mudanya) in 1948.

Thus, the religious affiliation adopted as the yardstick in defining the status of many Greek-Orthodox Christians and Muslims failed to effectively differentiate certain groups from the exchangeables. Due to the loose definition of the criterion, many Pomaks, who were Slavik-speaking Muslim peoples,[53] and Cretan Muslims, who spoke Greek but no Turkish at all, came to be subjected to the principles of the Convention. A Halis Turgut Bey in the Turkish Grand National Assembly spoke of a large group of non-Turkish *kıptı*s (Roma) being resettled in Sivas.[54] It was reported that a group of some 290 Roma families were resettled around Bursa.[55]

There was also some confusion regarding the situation of Bulgarians. In one particular case, the Turkish government ordered that the residents of the village of Kurfalli in the region of Çatalca who had declared that they were Bulgarians were suspected of being Greeks and should be investigated to determine if they are exchangeables.[56] The Bulgarian government intervened in time to exempt this community from the Convention.[57]

In the same vein, in Greece, a community of around one thousand people, consisting of the local residents of Parga and some immigrants from Koniçe (in the district of Çamlık) was first thought to be non-Turkish, but later it was discovered through the intervention of the Mixed Commission that they were Turkish and considered exchangeables.[58] On the other hand, there were cases where the Turkish government allowed other refugees who were not eligible for resettlement to be subjected to the clauses of the Convention and to resettle in Turkey. In the case of refugees from Cyprus who had come and resettled in Konya, the government approved their settlement "in accordance with conscience" (*zaruret-i vicdaniye*).[59]

The fog and mist that shrouded "non-exchangeable" Christian communities throughout the Turkish territories persisted for many years to come. And the term "Greek Orthodox religion" which was interpreted loosely as a yardstick to denote all the populations of Orthodox faith, continued to create problems as late as 1928 when local authorities referred to the Convention in their attempt to deport a group of Orthodox Arabs, who had been resettled in Mersin and the surrounding country on the basis of their faith.[60] It was with the intervention of the Mixed Commission, which argued that "this problem should be settled along common-sense lines" that these people were spared from the Convention. The decision stated that the Orthodox Christians who were associated with various churches (e.g., the churches of Cyprus, Serbia, Romania, Albania and Bulgaria) and Patriarchates other than the Greek Orthodox Patriarchate at Phanar (the Patriarchates of Antioch, Jerusalem, and Alexandria) were not to be subjected to the Convention. This was especially important for the Greek Protestants and Catholics who thereby obtained the right to stay in Turkey on the condition that they live in Istanbul.

The second article of the Convention states that "the Greek inhabitants of Constantinople" who were defined as those who were "already established before October 30, 1918, within the areas under the Prefecture of Constantinople as defined by the law of 1912" and "the Moslem inhabitants of Western Thrace" who were "established in the region to the east of the frontier line laid down in 1913 by the Treaty of Bucharest" shall not be included in the population exchange.[61] This article became the source of a major diplomatic crisis between the two sides. What is called the *établi* problem, which first erupted in the immediate aftermath of the ratification of the Lausanne Treaty, was to turn into a major source of conflict in mid-October 1924, during which time the transfer of the refugees on both sides was still underway.[62]

As a matter of fact, the problems associated with this article had begun to appear shortly after the signing of the Convention, as the two sides sought to reduce the number of their respective minorities in the areas, the populations of which were excluded from the Convention.[63] Upon the departure of the Allied forces from Istanbul, N. Politis met with Adnan Bey in November 1923 and expressed his concerns as to the violation of the Lausanne principles concerning the properties of the city's Greek residents (*établis*). In his correspondence with the ministry's headquarters in Athens, Politis mentioned that violations were continuing at full speed as a way of intimidating the unexchangeable Greeks and that he had received news of three new incidents after his meeting with Adnan Bey: "Turkish authorities had seized considerable stocks of tobacco that belonged to the Jordanoglou Brothers, the house of a Madame Papadopoulos had been requisitioned, and the furniture of the Hotel Pera Palace, which belonged to an exchangeable Greek, had been sequestered on the grounds that the owner had not paid the taxes."[64] In response to increasing complaints, the Turkish government ordered that the Greek Orthodox people residing within the limits of the Istanbul municipality and not exchangeables should be distinguished from the others.[65] Even then, complaints continued to pour into the Mixed Commission.

Although a great majority of the Greek population of Istanbul has been residing in the European section of the city, there were many Greeks settled across the Bosphorus, living in the quarters from Kadıköy to Pendik. Prior to the Convention, the latter were major centers of Greek families who had also large estates in these districts. When the Turkish government began to resettle Muslim refugees in these locations (e.g., Pendik, Kartal, Maltepe),[66] the Greek residents appealed to the Mixed Commission on the grounds that their districts were included in the prefecture of the city of Constantinople as defined by the Convention.[67] Nevertheless, government officials informed them that they had to evacuate these areas by September 15, 1924, no matter how long they had been living there. They were not considered "non-exchangeables."[68] Some 4500 Greeks were detained by the Turkish authorities and placed in camps for evacuation.

In the meantime,[69] the local Turks, instigated by government authorities and the press, seized the properties of some *établi* Greeks in the European sections of the city in retaliation for similar acts of the Greek government in Western Thrace. On behalf of these people, the Greek government appealed to the League of Nations on the grounds that the Turkish authorities were violating the principle of *établi* as mentioned in the Convention. The explanation offered in defense by the latter was that Turkish law should determine who were the *établis*, an issue that had in fact been left unclear by the Convention. The Greek government argued, on the contrary, that there was no specific reference in the Convention to local legal regulations and the issue should be taken up by the League of Nations for re-evaluation. Thus the implementation of the Convention was plagued by the fact that it adopted general categories for regions (e.g., Western Thrace and the Prefecture of the city of Constantinople) whose populations were exempted from the Convention instead of specifying the names of towns, villages, and even quarters in these locations.

In Greece, on the other hand, the government had ordered the evacuation of the Muslim populations from the border settlements, especially along the Maritsa River in Western Thrace. As early as the autumn of 1922, many Muslims in Western Thrace had been forced by the incoming Greek refugees and the soldiers of the Fourth Army to evacuate these areas. Some of these people had migrated to Turkey while others moved to the other parts of the region. These developments continued well up to the end of 1923 and even afterwards. The sessions of the Turkish Grand National Assembly often witnessed the heated speeches of deputies who accused the ruling government of not taking any action on the continuing violations by the Greek authorities of the related article of the Convention.[70] Concurrently, the newspapers called on the populace to organize large rallies to protest against the Greek "atrocities" committed against the Turks in Western Thrace.[71] In his speech before the Turkish Parliament on November 10, 1923, İsmet Paşa openly criticized the Greek government and stated in a threatening manner that "those who were responsible for a great number of damages during the War of Independence will be held accountable for the new incidents as well."[72] In response, the Turkish government appealed to British, French, and Italian authorities, saying that the Greek government was systematically violating the principles of the Convention.

A letter sent by Adnan Bey to the Dutch Legation in Athens describes in detail the violations of the Convention and the Lausanne Treaty by the Greeks.[73] As a follow-up, on November 27, 1923, the Dutch legation in Athens informed the Greek Ministry of Foreign Affairs that the Muslim inhabitants of the villages, Küçükkonak (Kouchi-Konak), Çaycuma

(Cheich-Cuma), and Darıdere (Dari-Dere) in the region of Dimotiko were being pressured by local Greek bands and military forces to immigrate to Turkey although these people were considered "non-exchangeables" according to the Convention.[74]

It is unknown what steps the Greek government undertook, but it is documented that the number of Greeks in Western Thrace increased from 64,000 (35.6% of the region's total population) in 1920 to 189,000 (62.1% of the region's total population) in 1924. Approximately 100,000 refugees accounted for more than half of this population.[75] After the Mixed Commission began to function, the Greek government transferred 40% of these refugees to other parts of the country, while allowing the permanent settlement of the rest in Western Thrace after having liquidated the Muslim properties that they had seized. The size of the occupied Muslim lands declined from 100,153 stremmata (one stremma is equivalent to a quarter of an acre) to 22,159.[76] The 1928 census shows that that there were 107,607 Greek refugees in Western Thrace and a total population of 303,171 in the region.

The conflict over the situation of the Greeks of Constantinople and the Muslims of Western Thrace soon came to a deadlock. In 1925, the Mixed Commission submitted a request to the Permanent Court of International Justice of the League of Nations for an advisory opinion in regard to article 2 of the Convention. On January 16, 1925, the Court was summoned to hear the arguments of the two parties involved.[77] The question before the Court was "What meaning and scope should be attributed to the word *établi* in Article 2 of the Convention of Lausanne of January 30, 1923, regarding the exchange of Greek and Turkish populations, in regard to which discussions have arisen and arguments have been put forward which are contained in the documents communicated by the Mixed Commission? And what conditions must the persons who are described in Article 2 of the Convention of Lausanne under the name of 'Greek inhabitants of Constantinople' fulfill in order that they may be considered as "established" and exempt from compulsory exchange?"[78]

These questions brought the two sides to the negotiating table, first in Ankara and then in Athens. In these meetings, both sides tried to clarify the content of the article and make the implementation of the other principles of the Convention practicable. The interpretation and translation of the term *établi* by the Turkish government was a constant item on the agendas of these meetings.[79] The two sides also convened in Ankara to work on these issues and the meetings revealed greater differences of opinion. After tortuous negotiations, the two parties reached an agreement on June 21, 1925 and signed the Ankara Agreement, which not only affirmed the terms of *établi* in line with the Greek view but also set the guidelines for proper indemnification and liquidation of the properties of the *établis* in Istanbul and Western Thrace which had been seized by the two governments. However, the application of this agreement could not be carried out due to the stiff position of the Pangalos government in Athens. After the overthrow of this government, the two sides came to the negotiation table once again in Athens in 1926.[80]

The Athens Convention was signed on December 1, 1926 and stipulated that the Turkish and Greek states would take the possession of the abandoned properties. This document granted the exchangeable persons with the right to file their cases with the Mixed Commission in order to receive compensation for the value of their properties from the respective governments. In Turkey, these cases seem to have produced on the whole no favorable consequences for the Greek claimants. A dozen of the files examined by the author in the Republican Archives in Ankara revealed that almost all the cases brought before the court of the Mixed Commission had been finalized, with the exception of a few cases, in favor of the Turkish government.[81]

Thus, with this new agreement, the problem of *établis* was for the time being resolved, but issues concerning the liquidation of their properties remained pending until the early 1930s when the two sides finalized the diplomatic phase of negotiations of the Convention for the Exchange populations. By the terms of the Ankara Convention on October 30, 1930, the exchange of populations was officially completed and the ownership of all the abandoned properties of the exchangeables and non-exchangeables was legally transferred to the respective governments. One of the most important consequences of the Ankara agreement for Greece was that many refugees who were disappointed by the terms of this Treaty gradually moved away from Venizelism to more radical political ideologies such as Communism. The most obvious indication of this shift appeared in the national elections of 1932, when the Greek Communists almost tripled their votes in certain locations such as Mytilene, "where half the inhabitants were refugees."[82]

Another problem that stemmed from the subjective interpretation of this particular article was related to the status of the Greek residents of Istanbul who had left the city before the Convention was put into effect. This article stipulated that Greeks who were established in Istanbul before October 30, 1918 but had departed from the city since then would be allowed to return to their homes. It turned out that the Turkish government issued a resolution to the effect that passports issued by the Ottoman regime were to be annulled and people in possession of these passports were not to be permitted to return. In other words, the only Greeks who could return were those who had departed after the Turkish Republic became established (October 29, 1923) and were in possession of Turkish passports. The number of Greeks who held Ottoman passports (*Σουλτανικα Διαβατιρια*) and were in Greece at the time numbered around 30,000. It was only after the Ankara Convention of 1930 that the properties of these people were considered for indemnification, but to no avail.[83]

Article 3 stipulated that "those Greeks and Moslems who have already, and since the 18th October 1912, left the territories of the Greek and Turkish inhabitants of which are to be respectively exchanged, shall be considered as included in the exchange provided in Article 1."[84] Taken as such, this is a clear appraisal of the fact that both governments were aware of the implications of leaving out the refugees who had come earlier. When read against the background of the fact that the great majority of the Greek refugees in Greece lacked their title deeds let alone proper certificates of exchange, we can safely assume that many locals presented themselves as refugees before the Mixed Commission.

In the same vein, Turkey was full of people of refugee background. The conditions in Turkey were perhaps more favorable for them for the obvious reason that the war ravaged areas had been inundated by people from other areas. By the time the implementation of the Convention began, the great majority of the existing refugees had been granted compensation for the properties they had lost before and during the Balkan Wars. In the region of Bursa, for example, the "ninety-three refugees," people who had migrated to Anatolia from the Eastern Rumelian provinces during the Turco-Russian War of 1877–78 (H. 1293), and the refugees who had come from the eastern Anatolian provinces occupied by the Russians during WWI seized a great portion of the abandoned Greek and Armenian properties, and the Turkish government recognized their claims as legitimate. Before the transfer of Muslim refugees was completed, the Turkish government passed a resolution stating that "if the refugees who had moved to Turkey before 1912 from Greece could produce a good case, they would be considered as beneficiaries (bona fide) of the Convention in terms of getting their abandoned properties, both movable and immovable, compensated."[85] Although the Mixed Commission intervened to stop this process, it was too little too late. The great majority of existing refugees had already seized the opportunity to reclaim their "losses."

As a matter of fact, the populist policies of the Turkish government had resulted in the promulgation of a similar resolution while the Lausanne negotiations were underway. Correspondingly, many soldiers and government officials, along with the local populations, had already occupied the great majority of Greek houses and business. The only measure the government took to stop this process was a resolution stipulating that these people had to pay a certain amount of rent until they were granted title deeds.[86] Later on, the government enforced various legislative measures in an attempt to create order out of chaos concerning the treatment of abandoned properties. However, much of this emergency legislation was inadequate and the government tried one provisional policy after another.

While Article 4 laid out the principle concerning the status of war prisoners, as mentioned earlier, Article 6 described the technicalities concerning the status of indicted criminals. Articles 5 and 7, on the other hand, ensured that there would be no reversal of the decision for the exchange as the people who were subjected to the Convention were to be automatically stripped of their nationality upon the ratification of the Convention and those who had left prior to the Convention were ensured of their rights in regards to the resettlement and liquidation processes. The fifth article was perhaps the only clause of the Convention that the two sides honored from the moment the Convention was signed. As for Articles 6 and 7, concerning the proper liquidation of refugee properties and the resettlement of refugees, the discussion on the resettlement of the refugees later on in Chapter Seven will show that the reality was far from what these clauses stipulated and a great majority of the refugees on both sides faced severe impediments in obtaining the actual value of their properties through indemnification.

The most important provisions of the Convention, which are at the same time the most confusing, are in Articles 8 through 10, all of which deal with property issues. Article 8 ensures that the refugees will be allowed to carry all their transportable properties with them, and the remaining properties including the immovables, will be registered with the local authorities under the supervision of the Mixed Commission. This provision not only failed to specify the nature of movables but also neglected to address properly the conditions of the formerly abandoned properties. The transport of the annual harvest of most refugees, which included, among others, the tobacco stocks of the Muslim refugees from Macedonia[87], the currants of the Greeks in the Western provinces of Turkey[88], and the silk-cocoons of the Greeks in Anatolia, was not allowed. The Turkish government had already passed a resolution declaring that the sacks and boxes that contained the silk cocoons of the departed Greeks were to be sold and the revenues to be transferred to the coffers of the Ministry of Finance.[89]

The new protocol in 1925 also proposed additional measures to provide for the fulfillment of Article 9 in the Convention. This protocol gave directions concerning the liquidation of immovable properties abandoned by Greek and Turkish refugees in their country of origin. It prescribed, among other things, that a person appointed by the claimant as custodian would be joined by a government official who would go to the location of this property and assess its value. If there was a discrepancy between the earlier declared value and the newly assessed one, the difference would be compensated by the "host" government under the supervision of the Mixed Commission (*Derhal peşin ve bakiyesi için hükümet obligasyonu*). This government "obligation" was to be fulfilled by an advance payment to to the claimant of 50% of the new valuation into the *Ziraat Bankası* (Turkish Agricultural Bank) and the National Bank of Greece. By this arrangement, it was hoped that the abandoned properties of refugees which indigenous populations or the incoming refugees might have occupied or the government might have confiscated would be properly liquidated and its value paid in full to the claimant.[90] The information available does not allow for a clear cut assessment to be made as to the application of this plan, but the conditions of the abandoned properties in Turkey, which will be examined in detail in the subsequent sections, suggest that the Anatolian landscape was certainly far from making such a plan practicable.

Almost all the articles on the property issues are vague in the sense that the Mixed Commission seems to be vested with extensive authority in the registration and liquidation process. For the Greeks who had been transferred to Greece during the war, the problem was perhaps more dramatic, since most of them were without title deeds or other certificates of ownership, which were required at the time of registration with the Mixed Commission. The same was true for the Muslim refugees, who arrived in Anatolia in the last months of 1922. A Turkish member of the Mixed Commission mentions in his memoirs that the valuation of properties previously owned by Muslims was not conducted at the point of departure but upon their arrival in Turkey. Moreover, most refugees filled out the documents of ownership (*tasarruf senetleri*) by themselves at the points of registration in Greece. Officials at the points of arrival in Turkey, however, carried out the valuation, and subsequently the refugees proceeded for allotment (*tevfiz*).[91] Whatever the size of their registered properties, the Turkish refugees faced a *fait accompli* on this issue. The government passed a resolution on February 13, 1924 stipulating that the exchangeables who had come before and will be coming in the near future will be granted 17.5% of the abandoned properties (*emval-i metruke*) declared on their documents of ownership.[92] It was later decided that this rate could be increased to 50–60% upon the completion of the population exchange process.[93] Later on, as the official publications confirm the testimonies of refugees, the distribution of the property values did not take place during the implementation process as stated in the Convention.[94]

The people who held Greek citizenship and were not considered exchangeables according to the Athens Agreement also suffered from the *ad hoc* implementation of the Convention concerning the liquidation and indemnification of immovables. The Turkish Agricultural Bank was responsible for the administration of their properties and in turn exacted a series of taxes from them and pledged to return to the owners only a small amount of the actual value of these properties after the Ankara Convention of 1930.[95]

A major impediment for the refugees stemmed from the inconsistencies in the taxation policies of the respective governments concerning movable properties. Although the Convention ensured that the refugees could take with them their properties and would be exempted from various taxes, the actual situation soon proved the opposite. Both Turkish and Greek customs officials stationed at the points of arrival proceeded with the exaction of certain customs dues from the *bona fide* refugees. On the other hand, bulk merchandise could not be transported from one country to another. In Greece, for example, the tobacco producers in Drama and Kavala had four and a half million kilos of tobacco that they could not transport to Turkey. Realizing that these goods could be purchased at a minimum price, Greek merchants pressured the Greek government not to allow them to be transported. The Turkish government intervened through the mediation of Hamdi Bey, a member of the Mixed Commission in Greece, and the Ministry of Finance was ordered to extend one million liras to the tobacco producers prior to their departure, purchase their stocks and transport them to the depots in Samsun and Izmir.[96]

While the Turkish authorities appealed to their Greek counterparts for the exemption of the goods of Muslim refugees from customs dues, they themselves taxed these goods (*rıhtım vergisi*) upon the registration of the refugees at the ports. A refugee from Rethymno, who brought 17 barrels of *ispirto* (alcohol) was asked to pay the custom dues on his merchandise appealed to the authorities for exemption of from payment of custom fees. His appeal was approved on the basis of Article 8 of the Convention.[97] Available documentation also suggests that the Turkish government charged refugees according to the kinds of livestock they brought with them.[98] Once the refugees arrived at the points of resettlement, local government officials seem to have demanded a housing tax (*meskufat*). The refugees opposed this tax and tried to evade it by moving from one location to another.[99] It is also documented that the tax officials hunted them wherever they went. Once the refugees decided to resettle in a certain area, they were asked to pay the municipal taxes in cities, and different kinds of taxes (*köy sandığına karşı vergi, harç* etc.) in rural areas. The refugees were asked to pay the taxes according to the Law of Inheritance and Transfer (*Veraset ve Intikal Kanunu*).[100] On December 9, 1931, the government issued a decree with a view to exempting the refugees (both exchangeables and non-exchangeables) from the tax on their title deeds (*tapu harcından istismarı*).[101] It seems that this situation lasted until 1934 when the government passed a resolution exempting refugees from such taxes on a one time basis. Another major exemption was the military services. Periodically the government issued resolutions exempting refugees from this obligation.

A CASE IN POINT: GREEK DEPOSITS IN FOREIGN BANKS IN IZMIR

Besides the movable and immovable property left behind by the panic-stricken Greek refugees, there were considerable amounts of cash and money deposited with local banks in Turkey. The situation of the banks in Izmir provides a good case in point. The Greek community of Izmir was regarded as one of the most prosperous communities of the Ottoman Empire, and the city had many banking institutions with both domestic and foreign capital. Upon their recapture of Izmir, the Turkish soldiers looted many safes in these banks and the government confiscated the ones that were untouched. The government later issued a series of proclamations for the return of the contents of the looted safes to the Ministry of Finance. Some of the contents were returned to the Ministry and sealed in accordance with the Law of Abandoned Properties.[102]

In protest of the Turkish action concerning the banks in Izmir, the Greek Ministry of Foreign Affairs invited the governments of various states to intervene. After this attempt proved inconclusive, the Greek government immediately sent separate letters to provoke action on the part of the British and French governments in regard to the status of all the banks, including the Bank of Athens, Banque d'Orient, Credit Foncier d'Algerie et Tunisie and the Bank of Salonica, which were said to contain the deposits of Greek subjects. According to the report of the Greek government "an approximate amount of one billion francs is deposited in these banks, besides considerable amounts of stocks, securities and valuables belonging to Greeks or other European nationals. The Kemalist authorities have already issued proclamations inviting the customers of these banks to submit regular notices of their deposits which leads one to the conclusion that the aforesaid measure was imminent."[103] When the issue was brought to the attention of the Greek authorities on April 6, 1923, by a note from a Lancelot Oliphant, a member of the British legation in Istanbul, indicating that the Turkish authorities had the intention of confiscating the deposits of Greeks and foreigners at various banks in Smyrna, it was too little too late. The British High Commissioner in Constantinople, Sir H. Rumbold with his French and Italian colleagues had made a joint protest to Adnan Bey regarding this issue on March 19. Subsequently, the Allied High Commissioners learned that certain safes in an Italian bank in Smyrna had been opened and were now considering what further action to take.[104] Prompted by the above developments, the Ottoman Bank in Istanbul seems to have transferred, in the meantime, a large sum of its holdings to its headquarters in Paris.[105]

A note-verbal from the Greek Legation in Paris to the French Foreign Ministry shows that the situation had not been resolved by the end of 1923. Having obtained further information about the issue, the Greek Legation contacted the French Foreign Ministry and informed them that the French Banks (e.g., Credit Lyonnais, Banque Française d'Orient, Crédit Foncier d'Algérie et de Tunisie) in Izmir contained a considerable amount of valuables deposited by the Greek subjects before the evacuation of Asia Minor. The Legation learned from reliable sources that these valuables had been transferred on a warship to France before the entry of Turks to the city. After the Ankara government declared that these deposits were "frozen," the French banks refused to return them to their Greek clients, thereby violating not only the Convention but also certain Articles (65 and 66) of the Lausanne Treaty. Accordingly, the Greek authorities argued that now that the Mixed Commission had begun its work for the liquidation of the immovable and movable properties of the refugees, the French banks should comply with the terms of the Convention and release the deposits of the Greek clients.[106]

Although it had been agreed that five days after the signature of the Lausanne Treaty, the bank accounts would be freed from governmental control,[107] it was not until June 20, 1924 that the Turkish authorities took any action on this matter. Then the only action taken was concerned with the release of the deposits of the non-exchangeable Greeks in the Bank of Athens. The Turkish government resolution stated that "the deposits of the non-exchangeables in the Bank of Athens be returned on the provision that the non-exchangeable Muslims in Greece would be subject to the same procedure."[108] A review of negotiations between the Turks and Greeks in Athens in 1926[109] shows that this issue was included in the agenda and the representatives of both sides reached agreement on the principle of unfreezing on a basis of equal and reciprocal compensation. The agreement granted the people the right to bring their cases before the Mixed Commission. The majority of these applications were dismissed on the grounds that there was not enough documentation.

Articles 11 through 17 deal essentially with the establishment of a Mixed Commission and its functions in overseeing the proper execution of the Convention on both sides. This commission, the activities of which will be covered in Chapter Eight, was charged with a wide range of duties from the registration and valuation of movable and immovable property to the liquidation of these properties. The governments were ordered to work in close coordination with the Commission and were supposed to furnish it with funds whenever necessary. Article 18 of the Convention furnished the High Contracting Parties with the right to "introduce in their respective laws such modification as maybe necessary with a view to ensuring the execution of the present Convention," a provision which left much room for reinterpretation.

In a speech to the Grand Assembly, in which he tried to defend the Convention against the rising critical voices concerning the situation of Western Thrace, Ismet Paşa pointed out that "the Exchange Convention included all the principles that would alleviate the suffering involved in the transfer of the people from place to another."[110] The above survey suggests that the contents of the Convention, which looked good on paper, primarily defined the technicalities of the population exchange. Many technical issues proved to have been poorly defined. Thus, a number of issues, from the description of the prefecture of the city of Istanbul to the status of abandoned properties, had to be clarified in the course of time. During bilateral talks in Athens and Ankara, certain changes were inserted to make the implementation of the Convention more practicable. However, the real concern in these negotiations was never directly related to the increasingly worsening plight of the refugee populations in the respective countries. The governments of the two states labored intensively during the Lausanne negotiations to alleviate their burdens. Accordingly, no measures were taken beforehand for the protection of the rights, property, and interests of the refugees. The legal steps to provide for the proper liquidation and indemnification of refugee properties were undertaken with a view to appeasing international public opinion. In none of these diplomatic documents was the question of political and juridical protection of the refugees mentioned or alluded to. For the Greek government, these steps were taken to ensure the inflow of foreign loans and assistance to facilitate the continuing economic recovery. As for the Turkish officials, they aimed to prevent direct foreign involvement in the internal affairs of the country. Both sides accomplished their goals. In the background were the refugees whose plight had been growing worse since late 1922.

Chapter Seven
The Refugee Plight

This chapter concentrates on the experiences of the Greek and Turkish refugees from their transfer to resettlement and economic integration in their destined countries. The movement of the refugees began with the flight of the Greek communities from Asia Minor during the later phases of the Turco-Greek War and ended with the organized evacuation of Muslim and Greek refugees through the hand of the Mixed Commission in the last days of December 1924. The displacement of such a massive number of people underscored the unfolding of a humanitarian crisis in both countries. The scope of the crisis was further exacerbated by the inability of the two governments, along with the inefficiency of the international organizations, to properly address the issues of resettlement and indemnification. Furthermore, upon their arrival in their new countries, the refugees encountered serious discrimination and exploitation by government officials and native populations, hampering their integration with the physical and human environment. All these developments constitute the episodes of a tragic saga that is the focus of the present chapter.

TRANSFER

Since the intensification of the war in the mid-summer of 1922, hundreds of thousands of Greeks from the western sections of Asia Minor had been continuously pouring into the Aegean Islands under Greek or Italian jurisdiction (e.g., the Dodecanese Islands), where various foreign relief agencies were soon to station themselves.[1] While most of these refugees relied on the support of the charitable organizations on these islands, those who could pay their passage moved to mainland Greece.[2] Those who safely arrived in Piraeus were sheltered in all the available buildings in Athens and some were transferred to other major cities.

The Mudanya Armistice of October 11, 1922 sealed the fate of the Greek populations in eastern Thrace. Despite objections raised by the Greek government to the terms of the Armistice concerning the duration of evacuation, many of these people were removed from the region within a month. A great number of eastern Thracian refugees were transferred to Macedonian towns such as Kozani, Kastoria, Grevena, Florina, Drama, and Kavala where the Muslim populations were still in place.[3] While some of these people were placed in the houses and schools of Muslims in these cities, others ended up in Western Thrace, where the Greek government had been vigorously involved in a campaign to create room for them by forcing the local Muslim population to leave.[4]

In mid-December 1922, Greeks from the Black Sea area began to arrive in Istanbul (then under the Allied Administration) and were placed in refugee camps throughout the city. In the face of escalating pressure from Turkish local authorities, the movement of Pontine refugees from places like Trabzon and Samsun gained momentum when the negotiations for the population exchange were nearly complete. From February 1923 onwards, Greek refugees from the Aegean Islands and Istanbul began to arrive in mainland Greece in large numbers. By the conclusion of the Lausanne meetings in mid-summer, the principal Greek ports had already been engulfed by the influx of refugees, and Athens had become a refugee city.

The first group of Muslim refugees from Greece came in small numbers from Western Thrace to Istanbul during the last phase of the Turco-Greek War. As soon as the war was over, they scattered throughout Anatolia and availed themselves of the post-war situation by joining the local populations in seizing the properties abandoned by Greeks and Armenians. The majority of the Muslim exchangeables in Macedonia, however, waited until the very last minute for the conclusion of the Lausanne talks; their transfer to Turkey took place long after the signing of the Lausanne Treaty. The refugees from Western Thrace who had already found their way to Anatolia prior to and during the Lausanne discussions resettled themselves throughout the coastal areas. Like many Greeks, they had moved by their own means and passed unregistered by the authorities due to the war conditions. This created a serious problem during the liquidation of property and indemnification of refugees by respective states after the Mixed Commission began to function following the ratification of the Lausanne Treaty in August 1923. While the number of refugees from Asia Minor, including Greeks and Armenians who arrived unregistered before the initial stages of the implementation of the Convention, were slightly more than 1,000,000, the number of Muslim refugees who arrived without proper papers was, according to İsmet Paşa in a speech before the Grand Assembly on November 10, 1923, was a modest 14,000.[5]

The great majority of exchangeable Muslims in Greece, especially those gathered in Macedonian towns, and nearly the entirety of the Karamanlides in the central part of Turkey, however, were awaiting the conclusion of negotiations at Lausanne. Although the Convention was signed in the latter days of January 1923, it did not kill the efforts of certain international mediators such as the head of the American Red Cross, Colonel Haskell, for the reversion of the process. Correspondingly, those Turkish and Greek refugees who had left during the war in fact nourished the hope that they would be allowed to return to their homes once the war was over.[6] The ratification of the Lausanne Treaty and the Convention by both sides in August proved this dream to be illusory. Although the ratification did not necessarily mean the beginning of an organized transportation of the refugees, both governments began to take effective measures for the removal of the remaining populations in their territories. The majority of Muslim refugees in Macedonia were directed to the principal ports of northern Greece, namely Salonica and Kavala, while the Greek refugees in Asia Minor, dispersed throughout the country, were rounded up and gathered by Turkish troops in major port cities such as Samsun and Mersin.[7] From this point on, the exchangeable Greeks, who were driven away from territories subject to the Convention, were strictly prohibited from entering these areas.[8] The controls were so tight that the Turkish government even prohibited foreign ships with Greek crews from approaching these areas; this prohibition was repudiated by a decree on February 13, 1924.[9] The last group of refugees who were transferred without any recourse to the clauses of the Convention consisted of 8,000 Muslims from Mytilene who were brought to Ayvalık and nearly the same number of Greeks from Samsun to Salonica in October 1923.[10] Organized and coordinated evacuation of the remaining Greek and Armenian refugees in Anatolia and nearly the entirety of the exchangeable Muslims in Greece started under the supervision of the Mixed Commission in December 1923. The position then was that approximately 200,000 Greeks (including the Pontines stranded in refugee camps in Istanbul) were in Turkey, awaiting evacuation, and about 360,000 Muslims in Greece had to be brought over to Turkey.

As far as the situation of the Greek refugees was concerned, the period from the Mudanya Armistice through the end of the Lausanne negotiations was the most decisive. The Greek government, which had been vehemently engaged in their transferal from the Anatolian littoral since the Smyrna disaster, exhausted its available food stocks and money resources for the relief efforts. As of February 24, 1923, lack of accommodation and food shortages forced the Greek government to temporarily suspend the admission of further refugees. A wave of violent epidemics seems also to have played a significant role in this decision.[11] Many refugees who had been languishing in camps throughout the islands broke down under the strain of malaria. Similarly, the refugees who were being brought to Istanbul from port cities such as Samsun and Trabzon faced the most appalling conditions in the refugee camps in which they were literally dumped.

On March 27, 1923, the representatives of the Greek government in Istanbul, Pallis and Anninos, informed the Ministry of Public Health in Athens that the conditions were worsening every day and the director of the hospital, one Kontopoulos, who was dealing with the Greek refugees, had died of typhus recently. They also stated that other personnel of the hospital had similar problems and the Greek government should take measures, such as establishing a new hospital with 500 beds and providing further funds to this cause. Based on this dispatch, the Minister of Public Health appealed to the League of Nations and stated that "the Greek government can no longer take care of the subsistence and health problems of the refugees without the assistance of foreign philanthropic organizations. The situation of the Greek refugees in Istanbul, especially those encamped in the barracks of Selimiye, has deteriorated to the point where epidemics can no longer be prevented. At least 100,000 liras are required to meet their subsistence needs and to establish a hospital for their growing health problems."[12] The available information does not offer any evidence as to whether or not these demands were ever met. It is reported, however, that of some 67,312 Greek refugees in Istanbul during the period of March 1–22, 1923, 1,434 people were not able to keep body and soul together until the end of the month.[13]

The situation was no better in Greek port cities such as Piraeus and Salonica where the Greek cargo ships disembarked refugees from the islands and Istanbul. As Alexis Alexandris mentions, "the health hazards posed by these refugees are illustrated by the cargo of a ship, which arrived in the port of Piraeus from Samsun (Amisos) in early January 1923. Out of a total of 2,000 refugees 1,600 were stricken with typhus, smallpox and cholera, with two out of three doctors on board were seriously ill."[14] This dismal picture was echoed in Salonica, as reported by Henry Morgenthau, who was in the city at the time. Observing the situation of the refugees upon their landing in the port of Salonica, he wrote:

> [S]even thousand people crowded in a ship that would have been taxed
> to normal capacity with two thousand. They were packed like sardines
> upon the deck, a squirming, writhing mass of human misery. They had

been at sea for four days. There had not been space to permit them to lie down to sleep; there had not been no food to eat; there was no access to any toilet facilities. For those four days and nights many had stood upon the open deck, drenched by an autumn rain, pierced by the cold night wind, and blistered by the noonday sun. They came ashore in rags, hungry, sick, covered with vermin, hollow-eyed, exhaling the horrible odor of human filth- bowed with despair.[15]

It is documented that the transportation of the Greek refugees continued unceasingly under the aforementioned circumstances until the Mixed Commission began to operate. Although the conditions gradually improved in the course of time, nearly the entirety of the Greek refugees arrived in their new homeland under most desperate conditions, as the Greek expression goes "με την ψυχη στο στομα." Perhaps the only group of Greek refugees evacuated in compliance with the terms of the Convention was those who came to Greece during the eight month period, May-December 1924. These included 150,000 refugees (94,000 from Asia Minor; 18,000 from eastern Thrace; and 38,000 from Istanbul and its environs).[16]

As for the Muslim refugees, with the exception of those from Western Thrace who were evicted from their homes by the Greek troops, they were boarded on ships from various ports of Greece (Candia, Hania, Kavala, and Salonica)[17] in a less tense environment and under relatively better conditions.[18] This is not to suggest that their treks from their places of origin to these port cities took place in a peaceful manner. On the contrary, many Greek army irregulars as well as the newly formed bands of refugees did not lag behind their Turkish Muslim counterparts in Anatolia in terrorizing these people prior to and during their passage.

The transfer of Muslim refugees was delayed due to the prolonged discussions in the Turkish parliament over the question of which ships would be used to evacuate them from the Greek ports. The government organized a competition to determine the lowest bidder (*münakasa*) in which many transportation companies (interestingly enough, among them was a Greek Company) participated. An Italian enterprise named Lloyd Triestino Company made the lowest bid to win the competition.[19] A deputy in the Turkish parliament, namely Mustafa Necati, carried the issue to the parliament and vehemently argued that this was against the interests of the Turkish nation. Further arguments were put forward in favor of the view that the commissioning of this task to a foreign company would result in the flow of the limited national resources to the foreign coffers and the job should be vested in a Turkish company.[20] Only two weeks after the parliamentary discussions on this issue, the same Mustafa Necati was elected as head of the newly founded Ministry of Exchange, Reconstruction and Resettlement (*Mübadele, İmar ve İskân Vekâleti*; MERR) and the result of the auction was repudiated in favor of a domestic freight company, namely the Turkish Maritime Company (*Türk Vapurcular Birliği*), which would cooperate with the Administration of Navigation (*Seyr-i Sefain İdaresi*). The most decisive role was played by the lobbying efforts of the head of this company, Sufizade Sudi, who also gave interviews to the leading newspapers and journals.[21] The nationalist rhetoric eventually prevailed; but the fact of the matter was that the majority of the 17 boats in the fleet of this company were either too-aged or below the capacity of the boats of the Lloyd Triestino Company.[22] Not the least of the problems was the higher freight rates of the Turkish Maritime Company, which were to be paid in full by the refugees themselves. It was soon decided that the government should provide the Administration of Navigation with 600,000 liras for the purchase of six new ships. This they did. In the meantime, Muslims refugees, a great majority of whom had been housed in the staple-houses (for which they had to pay) in the port cities of Salonica, Kavala, Candia and Hania were desparately awaiting the arrival of Turkish ships. In the early 1930s, a critic of the Turkish government policy wrote the following on this matter:

> The owners of ships under the foreign banner offered more favorable conditions for the transportation of the Exchangeable Turkish Muslims. They even offered to lower the freight rate to two thirds and agreed to purchase coal from Turkey. However, the Turkish government, considering the inadequacy of the ships under the Turkish banner, extended financial assistance to the Turkish ship owners. Certain other permissions and protections have also been provided to these ship owners.[23]

Prior to the beginning of the organized transportation, the government in Ankara adopted certain resolutions to expedite the transfer of refugees. In this regard, certain tax exemptions were introduced. The Turkish boats that were to transport the refugees were exempted from the "health tax" (*sağlık vergisi*).[24] The period following the arrival of first refugee boat was divided into segments and for each segment arrangements were made for evacuation by ship. This gave the Muslim refugees, especially in western Macedonian towns, some time to sell their properties and make preparations before they left their homes. The first boat departed from the port of Salonica on December 19, 1923. Within two weeks, about 26,691 refugees were brought to Turkey from the ports of Salonica, Kavala, Candia and Hania. According to a national newspaper, *Hâkimiyet-i Milliye*, the number of refugees who had come to Turkey by the end of 1923 reached 60,318.[25] The ships went back and forth between port cities in Greece and Turkey, but there was apparently no knowledge on the part of refugees about the transportation arrangements. A refugee named Zehra Kosova says that when they were waiting their turn in Salonica, they heard that the people from Kavala were gathered in one ship (*Reşadiye vapuru*) and sent directly to Samsun.[26] From October 1923 through November 1924, the number of Muslim refugees from Greece reached 348,000. Those refugees who arrived by ship numbered 279,900. The transportation conditions seem to have improved in the course of time. In 1924, around 9,493 refugees who took the boat from Salonica to Izmir are recorded to have brought with them their livestock such as cows, asses, oxen, camels, goats, sheep and even dogs.[27] A certain number of refugees traveled by train or on foot. It was reported on March 21, 1924 that some 3,236 refugees from Drama traveled through Dedeağaç-Burgaz to Thrace by train.[28] The actual working of the transfer by boat from Salonica and other port cities in Greece in the following months can be seen from the following table [Table 6]:

Table 6. Number of Muslim Refugees Transferred to Turkey by Boat, 1923–1924

Months	Number of Refugees
December	26,691
January	15,117
February[29]	19,973
March	20,904
April[30]	56,979
May	42,270
June	27,673
July	30,192
August	21,065
September	4,322
December	2,935
Total	268,121

Source: Mehmet Çanlı, "Yunanistan'daki Türklerin Anadolu'ya Nakledilmesi, II," *Tarih ve Toplum*, 130 (1994) 51–59. (Figures are based on the documents from the archives of the Turkish Red Crescent, file no: 252)

Table 7. Muslim Refugees Transferred from Crete to Turkey by Boat, December 15, 1923–March 31, 1924

Date	Number of Refugees	From-To
December 15, 1923	3,072	Candia-Mudanya
December 31, 1923	716	Hierapatra-Erdek
January 1, 1924	1,012	Candia-Mudanya
January 15, 1924	1,244	Candia-Erdek
January 21, 1924	631	Lassithie-Darıdja
February 11, 1924	3,244	Candia-Mersin
March 3, 1924	1,860	Candia-Çeşme (702), Ourla (759), Izmir (399)
Total	11,779	

Source: AYE, "Report to the President of the Mixed Commission, K. M. Widding, Candia, April 8, 1924," KTE/29.

Refugees from Crete are not included in this list. A report submitted to the president of the Mixed Commission by a member of this Commission's office in Candia provides the following information on the transportation of Muslim refugees from the Cretan ports [Table 7].

The last ship, named Ampazia, carrying Greek refugees took off from Mersin on December 17, 1924, while the one carrying the Turkish refugees which was named Tsar Ferdinand, took off from Salonica on December 26, 1924.[31]

RELIEF EFFORTS

From the very beginning, Greek political authorities tried their utmost to secure help and support from the international public. They pledged their readiness to cooperate with the League of Nations, which had already recognized the urgency of the Greek refugee problem and taken certain steps to alleviate their destitute conditions by mobilizing private relief agencies.[32] However, the decision for the population exchange had aroused deep apprehension in Western capitals. In response to this situation, many relief organizations mobilized their resources to supply food provisions and medical care to the Greek refugees during the early phase of their plight.

The principal organizations involved in the relief operations were the American Red Cross and the Near East Relief. There were also other private relief agencies, rendering service to the refugees throughout Anatolia and the neighboring Greek Islands. These organizations included, among others, All British Appeal, The British Red Cross Society, Save the Children Fund, American Women's Hospitals, Friends of Greece, Fatherless Children of Greece Committee; the last two organizations were united with the Near East Relief.[33]

A critic of these relief organizations commented at the time that "a large proportion of the wholesale evacuation of the Christian (mostly Greek and Armenian) population from Turkey was unnecessary and was carried out under the influence of panic fostered by well-meaning but hasty foreign organizations prejudiced against the Turks for personal and religious reasons."[34] No matter what their motives were, it is certain that the early problems concerning the Greek refugees were alleviated to a certain extent by the work of these international organizations. The Near East Relief took urgent steps to provide relief for the refugees in the islands, especially after September 1922, and in Istanbul, Mersin and Samsun. In Chios and Mytilene, designated as the first stopping points for the Greek soldiers and the panic-stricken refugees from Asia Minor, the Near East Relief secured its food and clothing stocks partially from the local residents of the islands and from its offices in Istanbul and established distribution centers that played a crucial role in the refugee relief.[35] The first Near East Relief supplies arrived on the islands from Istanbul on October 7, 1922. The Near East Relief Committee in Istanbul shipped 425 tons of flour within two weeks. Apparently 175,000 refugees benefited from the relief efforts of the Near East Relief and there were at the time 75,000 refugees dependent on its supplies.[36] In the beginning, the relief operation concentrated upon the essential distribution of basic rations (e.g., loaves of bread, hard biscuits, milk, rice) in order to fend off starvation. Gradually the work in the field changed to a broad range of activities such as providing health services in hospitals and clinics. The efforts of the Near East Relief were not limited to the distribution of food, clothing and medicine to the refugees but also dissemination of information to the international public on the progress of the refugee relief.[37] The initial success of the Near East Relief encouraged other organizations to start or speed up their relief work in various areas designated for the arrival of refugees.

Dr. Nansen, who served as the High Commissioner of the League of Nations for Russian refugees in Istanbul, had long been pursuing a campaign to draw the attention of the world to the plight of the Greek refugees by using the press as a means to disseminate the story of their plight. The publicity they received enabled him to obtain humanitarian help from private agencies and individuals. As discussed earlier, the most outstanding of his early achievements was to entrust foreign relief agencies with funds donated by many governments to the Nansen Refugee Relief Fund. It is thanks to these funds that organizations like the Near East Relief were able to continue their relief operation longer than the anticipated duration. The funds that were donated directly to the Greek government were sometimes not publicized for fear that the relief organizations would stop their operations.[38] The evidence also suggests that the Greek government closely watched the relief efforts of the Italian organizations especially after a month-long occupation of Corfu by Mussolini in August 1923.[39] The following document provides a glimpse of the Greek government's motives:

> Moussolini voulant atténuer sentiment répronation universel produit par extorsion 50 millions de la Grèce fut une offre de dix millions en faveur des réfugiés. Il fallait sauf autres, ne pas oublier qu'ordre militaire de Malta qu'il charge distribuer argent est un ordre catholique qui veut aser (?) de notre argent pour faire de la propagande italienne et catholique chez nous et introduire à Corfou une forme d'occupation morale presque aussi dangereuse que l'occupation militaire.[40]

After a series of letters between the General Administration of Macedonia in Salonica and the Ministry of Foreign Affairs from mid-summer of 1924 to the end of the following year, the Greek government prohibited the operation of a Malta-based missionary group, called "the Knights of Melitis" in the region of Salonica. This was clearly the Catholic Order mentioned in the above telegram. The group was accused of conducting propaganda among the refugees on behalf of the Italian government and its activities were suspended.[41]

The relief work within the interior of Anatolia was handicapped because of restrictions the Ankara government placed on communication and transportation.[42] The refugees who were gathered in Istanbul, Samsun, Trabzon, and Mersin and awaiting the decision from Lausanne were forced by the Turkish authorities to vacate these cities as soon as possible.[43] The latter resorted to various measures to accomplish this.[44] In the case of Istanbul, the most notable method was the "refusal . . . to allow any further consignments of food stuffs etc. intended for the refugees at Constantinople to be imported duty-free."[45] Hikmet Bey, who was in charge of refugee affairs, mentioned in his conversation with George White of the Near East Relief that the object of this measure was to force the removal of 21,000 refugees from Constantinople. The Greek representatives in Istanbul, such as Alexander Pallis, asked the American government in the person of the American High Commissioner in Constantinople, Admiral Bristol, for help by drawing attention to the acute suffering of Greek refugees. He demanded support on their behalf and asked him to persuade the Turkish authorities to alter their decisions concerning the refugees on matters such as the imposition of multiple duties on foodstuffs. On the other hand, the French Government was pressing for the removal of Greek refugees gathered in Syrian and Lebanese cities. On May 31, 1923, the president of the Committee of Greek refugees in Aleppo cabled the Ministry of Foreign Affairs in Athens that the refugees in Asia Minor should be prohibited from coming to Aleppo where "it has become impossible to admit further refugees."[46] On July 11, a letter, dispatched from the Greek Legation in Paris, informed the Ministry of Foreign Affairs in Athens that the French government demanded the quick removal of between 1,500 and 2,000 Greek refugees in Beirut.[47]

Relief for Greek refugees, torn between the deteriorating situation in their native settlements and the pressure of local authorities in port cities, took an important turn in mid-summer of 1923 and their tragic and precarious condition was fully revealed. The position then was that there were 23,000 refugees in Istanbul; 20,000 in Black Sea Ports; 4,000 in Mersin; and about 17,000 in various Syrian cities. In addition to these 64,000, there were approximately 150,000 refugees still in the interior of Anatolia ready to leave for the ports as soon as those in the ports were moved.[48] The limited food supplies that the relief organizations had provided were by then exhausted, and the threat of starvation for thousands of men, women, and children became very real. The relief agencies, owing to diminishing funds and the economic problems of their own countries, gradually reduced their activities in the field of operation. Most of these organizations soon began to pull out their personnel. The American Red Cross, despite the persistent calls of the Greek government and its lobbyists in Washington, terminated its relief to Greek refugees in Istanbul on August 1, 1923.[49] This organization had been active in the field since October 1922 and had spent nearly $2,605,696.09 for the relief of 500,000 to 850,000 refugees during its nine months of work.[50] The withdrawal of the Red Cross created great discontent not only among the Greek authorities but also among those who were acting on behalf of the Greek government in the United States. A letter from a Brainerd Salmon criticized the Red Cross:

> No large portion of the personnel of the American Red Cross went to Greece out of either humanitarian motives or of love for Greece, and many of them have shown plainly enough by their actions that they were devoid of either of these sentiments. I do not want to place myself in the position of speaking in a criticizing manner of any American institution, but in several ways, the American Red Cross, in spite of

what they did in Greece, have complicated rather than helped the general situation.[51]

On June 1, 1923, the British Red Cross informed the Greek government through the mediation of British authorities that it would stop its operations in August due to "the fact that it has been unable to collect sufficient funds to carry on its work any longer."[52] Furthermore, the Near East Relief revealed its intention to terminate its activities in September. They were unable to assist some 9,000 refugees from Pontus (6,000 from Samsun and 3,000 from Trabzon) and the food provisions for these people had to be provided by the Greek government.[53] Although the Greek government immediately appealed to the Near East Relief and requested that these refugees be fed and shipped to Greece, where they would be granted financial aid (1.5 Turkish liras per head) sufficient for their survival,[54] the organization did not recede from its early position. In the meantime, the Minister of Public Health urged the Minister of Foreign Affairs to persuade both relief agencies to continue their activities, since his ministry was not in a situation to deal with the needs of the refugees on its own.[55] These efforts proved inconclusive. All the foreign relief agencies withdrew from the field by the end of the summer of 1923.

Many Greeks, who were unable to move to Greece during the Lausanne negotiations or nourished hope for the reversion of the population exchange decision, spent almost all of 1923 in refugee camps established in pre-designated areas of Istanbul such as St. Stephano. Istanbul provided shelter not only to the outgoing Greek and Armenian refugees but also to those Muslim refugees from Greece who were housed temporarily before they were assigned to their new homes. Many Europeans and Americans visited the refugee camps in the city and prepared reports, based on their impressions. The observations of these visitors about the camps reflected for the most part the political stance of their governments towards Turkey and Greece.[56] While the French often praised the Turks for their handling of the refugee affairs as manifested partially in those camps, the British and Americans often expressed opposite concerns. Dr. Vidal, a representative of the "Corps d'Occupation Francais de Constantinople," along with several other figures (Mr. Childs, Major Hobson, and Dr. Pabis), visited the refugee camp in St. Stephano on May 17, 1923 and wrote his observations in a report later submitted to the "Commission of Greek Refugees." This report is very much illustrative of the French discourse skewed towards the Turkish side. In this camp, there were 4,000 refugees crammed in tents and barracks.

Ceux arrivant au camp sont épouille: douchés; ont leurs cheveux coupés; leurs effets, leurs bagages, leur linge de corps sont désinfestés, et ils ne sont installés avec les autres émigrés qu'apres ces opérations. Le local des douches et de désinfection est à l'entrée du camp. A proximité du pavillon de désinfection est une infirmerie pour malades ordinaires, les malades contagieux ne sont pas gardés au camp et sont évacués immédiatement sur l'hôpital grec de Yedikule . . . [L]e autorités turques y donnent sous réserve un concours très effectif, et on a l'impression qu'il est dirigé avec fermeté et intelligence.[57]

The refugee camps, praised by the French authorities, were providing shelter mainly to the Pontines and Karamanlides. On April 28, 1923, a group of around 400 Karamanli women and children from Kayseri, Nigde and Konya with recourse to the reinstated law of "freedom of travel" took the train and arrived in Haydarpasha.[58] Immediately upon the arrival of those refugees whose adult male members had been left behind, the Turkish authorities detained them and herded them to refugee camps. The conditions in these camps were far from the picture drawn above, as alluded to many times in Pallis' correspondence with the Greek government and the Allied representatives.[59] The efforts of Pallis to improve the situation in the camps through the hand of the High Commissioner in Istanbul proved fruitless.[60] The plight of the Greek refugees in these camps dragged on almost to the end of the year. The organized evacuation of these people began under the supervision of the Mixed Commission in December 1923 and continued unceasingly until the end of the next year.

As for the Muslim refugees, the initial phase of their plight remains for the most part a mystery due to the absence of related documentation and especially owing to the policy of the archives of the Ministry of Foreign Affairs in Ankara, which is still closed to researchers. The oral evidence on hand does not suggest any involvement of foreign organizations in the relief of Muslim refugees in Greece.[61] When they began to arrive in large numbers in Turkey, it is clear that there was no foreign relief agency active in the field of operation. Those who were involved in the relief of Greek and Armenian refugees had already ceased their operations. The reserved position of the Turkish government on the issue of foreign involvement in the country's internal affairs, which had found its most concrete manifestation during the Lausanne negotiations, offers an explanation for the absence of any foreign relief organization assisting Muslim refugees at any point in their plight. This is an issue that will certainly become elucidated once the archives of the Ministry of Foreign Affairs is open to researchers.

The relief of Muslim refugees, at the points of departure and arrival, was provided by the Turkish Red Crescent (*Hilal-i Ahmer*), the archives of which is currently located in Ankara but came too late to the attention of the author.[62] Official sources reveal that the Turkish government signed a protocol with the Red Crescent on September 5, 1923 with a view to extending relief to Muslim refugees in Greece. With a budget of 616,857 liras at its disposal, this institution set out to respond to the food and medical needs of the refugees.[63] The first team of the Red Crescent departed from Istanbul to Salonica on October 18, 1923. Concomitantly, a telegram by A. Anninos, a member of the Greek legation in Istanbul, was dispatched to inform the authorities in Athens that "among the 18 people sent to Salonica in order to assist the refugees were included some agents who were coming to communicate with the Muslims in Western Thrace."[64] The Ministry of Foreign Affairs transmitted the information to the General Administration of Macedonia in Salonica asking it to take the necessary measures for the prevention of such contacts.[65] The nature of these measures cannot be traced through the available documents. It is known, however, that the first team of the Red Crescent was followed by other groups, dispatched to various Greek cities (e.g., Candia, Hania, Salonica, Kavala, Kayalar, Kozani, and Drama). These teams apparently set up medical stations at points of departure and assisted the local branches of the Mixed Commission in registering the refugees. The most important tasks of the Red Crescent were the registration of refugees arriving in Turkish ports, recording their health conditions, and temporarily detaining them in the quarantine stations. Once released, the refugees, who had been greeted with music and an air of official celebration in these ports, were taken on ships to the designated ports where they were literally left at the mercy of the local government officials who distributed them in an arbitrary fashion throughout the country.

RESETTLEMENT

One of the principal tenets of the literature on the population exchange is the portentous space devoted to the documentation and analysis of the resettlement program in Greece with special emphasis on the activities of the Greek Refugee Settlement Commission, which came as part of the loan package negotiated at Lausanne. This literature has doggedly argued that given the enormity of the refugee influx and the economic and political instability of the country, the resettlement of refugees was on the whole a success story as the great portion of the destitute refugees was not only resettled but also turned into producers in the short run. The literature also holds that the success of the resettlement program under the aegis of the Refugee Settlement Commission brought in turn the integration of the refugees within the national framework. Although recent scholarship has brought under question the validity of this success paradigm by looking at the social and economic ramifications of the resettlement and integration from the point of view of the refugees, the fact that the resettlement of such a massive displaced population, notwithstanding certain impediments it created for the refugees, was carried out resourcefully by the Refugee Settlement Commission remains uncontested.

As far as the Turkish side of the resettlement story is concerned, the general literature on the population exchange has ignored it, based on the assumption that refugees posed no significant challenge to Turkey, as they were resettled in the abandoned homes of Greeks and Armenians and were granted cultivable fields which existed in abundance throughout Turkey proper. The historical and historiographical aspects of this discussion have already been laid out in Chapter Five. Against this background, we firstly probe into the objective conditions against which the resettlement of the refugees was carried out in Turkey with a view to arguing that the above-stated conventional view suffers from a chronic misconception of the Turkish side of the refugee problem and resettlement in the immediate aftermath of the population exchange. Secondly, we review the highlights of the process by which the refugees were resettled in Greece with a special reference to the factors that impaired or fostered this process.

Before the Lausanne Conference was convened, preparations had been made by the Ankara government to take stock of the social, economic and sanitary conditions of the country, and many reports had already been completed for the internal sections of Anatolia.[66] It was decided in Ankara on November 12, 1922 that "eight scientific committees (*fen heyetleri*) were to be established during a period of three years to prepare the maps and plans for resettlement and reconstruction of the areas recaptured from the Greek army."[67] Such plans were made for various parts of Anatolia but not for eastern Thrace, where skirmishes between the Turkish troops and Greek irregulars were continuing.[68] As for the administration of refugee affairs, the government tended to adopt with certain modifications the existing Ottoman legislative documents, such as the Regulations for the Resettlement of Refugees (*İskân-i Muhacirin Nizamnamesi*), and the Ottoman institutions such as the Refugee Directory (*Muhacirin Müdüriyyeti*) and its local organs, placed within the structure of the Ministry of Health and Social Assistance (*Sıhhiye ve Muavenet-ı İçtimaiye Vekâleti*).[69] After the Convention was signed and more concrete information about the numerical scope of the refugees was obtained, the Turkish government was compelled to take up the refugee problem and the resettlement issue more seriously, to the effect of which it formulated a number of protocols and established a number of institutions, soon to be brought under the Ministry of Exchange, Reconstruction and Resettlement (*Mübadele, İmar ve İskân Vekâleti*). The ever-deteriorating situation of the abandoned properties also played a significant role in these developments.

On July 17, 1923, only one week before the conclusion of the Lausanne Conference, the first comprehensive protocol "Regulations Prepared by Way of Amendment in Conformity with the High Decision of the Committee of Ministers (*Encümen-i Vükela Karar-ı Aliyesine Tevfiken Tadilen Tanzim Olunan Talimatname*), which consisted of thirty-two articles categorized under several headings, was issued.[70] This official document defined the terms and conditions for the reception of refugees and their transfer to the locations of resettlement (*Mübadeleten Türkiye Hududlarına Gelecek Ahalinin Suret-i Kabulleri ve Menatik-i İskâniyelerine Suret-i Sevkleri*) as well as the duties of commissions in charge and other administrative matters (*Komisyonlar ve Malumat-ı İdariye*). The document also alluded to certain conditions, such as the attributes of refugees, namely, their climatic characteristics, professional specializations and skills (*gelecek ahalinin yaşadıkları iklim, ma'luf oldukları san'at ve meziyetleri ve her türdeki kabiliyet*), to be taken into account during the resettlement. Although the protocol hinted at many institutional and practical measures for the implementation of the Convention, it generally offered no clues as to how the attributes of refugees would be incorporated into the resettlement project. Furthermore, the Resettlement Scheme (*İskân Cetveli*),[71] which was annexed to this document, does not have any indication that the architects of the plan had paid attention to the aforementioned attributes of refugees [Table 8].

Despite the warnings of contemporary prominent journalists, the recommendations of the Economic Congress (*İktisat Kongresi*), and the instructions included in the protocol, the government authorities classified the refugees according to their places of origin and divided them into three broad categories: 1) tobacconists (*tütüncü*), 2) agriculturalists (*çiftçi*), and 3) grape-growers and dealers in olives (*bağcı ve zeytinci*). In other words, instead of classifying the refugees according to their urban or rural origins, as was the case in Greece, the Turkish government, by adopting broad categories, considered most refugees as being of rural background and involved exclusively with agricultural pursuits. While many Muslim refugees were affiliated with various sectors of agriculture, the government did not take into account the fact that each category also consisted of people who specialized in a particular aspect of agricultural economy such as manufacturing, commerce etc.

Moreover, the category of agriculturalists (*çiftçi*) comprised both people who held large estates and often lived in cities as absentee landlords (usually engaged with credit) and others who lived either as sharecroppers (*rençber*) or ordinary peasants (*köylü*) with a small plot of land

Table 8. Resettlement Scheme (*İskan Cetveli*)

Places of Origin	Tütüncü (Tobacconists)	Çiftçi (Agriculturalists)	Bağcı-Zeytinci (Grape-growers and Dealers in Olives	Total	Regions of Resettlement
Drama and Kavala	30,000			30,000	Samsun
Seres	20,000	15,000	5,000	40,000	Adana
Kozani, Nasiliç, Kesriye, Grevena	2,500	15,000	5,000	22,500	Malatya
Kayalar, Vudine, Katrin, Alasony, Langada, Demirci	3,500	25,000	15,000	43,500	Amasya, Tokat, Sivas
Drama, Kavala, Salonica	4,000	20,000	40,000	64,000	Manisa, Izmir, Menteşe, Denizli
Kesendi, Sarisa, Avrathi, Nevroko	20,000	55,000	15,000	90,000	Çatalca, Tekirdağ
Preveze, Janina	15,000	40,000		55,000	Antalya, Silifke
Mytilene, Crete and Others		30,000	20,000	50,000	Ayvalık, Edremid, Mersin, Adalar
Total	95,000	200,000	100,000	395,000	

Source: *İskân Tarihçesi*, (Istanbul: Hamit Matbaası, 1932) 18.

and a pair of oxen. Similarly, people who were referred to as "dealers in olives" (*zeytinci*) included people specializing in the cultivation of olives, merchants, and manufacturers who were engaged in the production of olive oil, soap and other olive-related products. Certain individuals might have fulfilled all these tasks, but the assumption that all the people listed under the same category were similar in socio-economic terms or of similar social status indicates nothing but the blatant indifference of the Turkish government to the actual dynamics of the question at stake.

This issue becomes even more complicated in light of the information that the documents for the refugees had not been properly and truthfully prepared by the Mixed Commission. A deputy in the Turkish Grand National Assembly later testified to this fact in his speech: "The Committees of the Mixed Commission asked the refugees to write the movable and immovable properties that they were to abandon on a piece of paper and have it sealed by the Commission. As a result of this arbitrary behavior, many refugees came to Turkey with documents in their possession, the genuineness of which should be doubted."[72] Last but not least, the most dramatic fact was that all the refugees, regardless of their background, were entitled to 17.5% of the value of their abandoned properties upon their arrival in Turkey.

The most critical voice drawing attention to this problem came from a non-governmental refugee organization, namely the Resettlement Assistance Association (*İskân Teavün Cemiyeti*), which, having reviewed the government's resettlement scheme, drafted its own plan on the basis of the refugees' backgrounds. Their proposed plan divided the refugees into the two broad categories, urban and rural; while the former included the merchants (*eşraf*), manufacturers (*esnaf*), and urban workers (*işçiler*), the latter consisted of villagers (*köylüler*) and farmers (*çiftçiler*), and those involved with animal husbandry. The plan of the Association also contained certain information as to the magnitude of the refugee populations in each category. The following table is derived from the narrative plan and shows roughly the resettlement scheme proposed by this organization [Table 9].

According to the Association, refugees from Salonica were largely of urban background and therefore should be considered for resettlement in highly urbanized areas in Anatolia and Thrace. Similarly, refugees from Seres and Drama contained a good number of urban refugees, while those from Manastır were largely of agricultural background. Against the backdrop of these facts, the Association also pointed to the deficiency of the government's resettlement scheme on the grounds that it showed the number of tobacconist refugees lower than that of the people engaged in viticulture and olive-growing. The resettlement scheme showed the number of

Table 9. Resettlement of Muslim Refugees According to Place of Origin

Places of Origin	Number of Refugees	Places of Resettlement
Drama and Serez	200,000	40,000: Edirne 60,000: Samsun and Bafra 70,000: Manisa, Akhisar, Muğla, Milas, Kuşadası, Torbalı, Söke, Ödemiş, Izmir
Salonica	130,000	40,000: Bursa 50,000: Izmir, Bergama, Alaşehir, Nazilli, Isparta, Burdur 40,000: Izmir, Çatalca, Istanbul
Manastır	150,000	150,000: Amasya, Tokat
Total	480,000	450,000

Source: İskan ve Teavün Cemiyeti, *Umumi Kongre Mübadele Encümeni Mazbatası, İskân ve Teavün Cemiyeti Mübadele Rehberi*, Izmir: Ahenk Matbaası, 1339 [1923].

refugees from Janina and Preveze as 55,000 and the total number of refugees considered tobacconists as 95,000. The contention of the Association was that there were only 6,000 people in these locations. Also the total number of tobacconist refugees far exceeded the given figure of 200,000. In their view, the resettlement scheme of the government required substantial revision before it could be adopted for implementation.[73]

The government turned a resolutely deaf ear to the recommendations and warnings of organizations and individuals. It began to transfer the refugees according to its own plans, which became sanctioned with the establishment of the Ministry of Exchange, Reconstruction and Resettlement.[74] The Ministry adopted the already drafted plan as its own.[75] In compliance with the adopted regulations, the refugees were shipped to the ports nearest to the regions specified for them on the resettlement scheme.

The steps followed in the reception of the refugees can be traced through various registers found in the Archives of the Village Bureau in Samsun. The collection contains more than 40 registers. Of these registers, the most important ones are undoubtedly the Principal Registers of Refugees (*Muhacir Kaydına Mahsus Esas Defter*)—which include information about the refugees such as their names, ages, places of origin, dates of arrival, professional specializations, and the place of resettlement. These registers have been organized according to the years the refugees arrived. Another group of registers consists of multiple volumes of Granted Property (*Tevzi Defteri*) which contain detailed information about the properties distributed to the refugees. These registers do not provide any information as to whether or not the refugees eventually retained ownership of these properties. Such information can be found in another group of registers called Registers of Allotment Decisions (*Tefviz Karar Defteri*). Perhaps the last group of registers that should be mentioned is the Registers of Greek Buildings (*Rum Bina Defteri*). Some of these registers were also called the Registers of Greek Abandoned Properties (*Rum Emval-i Metruke Defteri*). These registers show the names of these buildings' former Greek owners, their addresses, detailed descriptions of each building as well as the names of the Muslim refugees to whom they were granted. Due to the physical conditions of these registers, the present author was not able to make extensive use of these sources but a Samsun-based scholar has made a preliminary attempt in this direction.[76]

A few words are in order about the most striking features of these sources. The most interesting, in this respect, is the organization of the Registers of Allotment Decisions. A cursory view reveals that among the refugees who registered for the allotment of abandoned property were many refugees who had come after the Balkan Wars, but were recorded together with the refugees who were subject to the Convention. Tülay Alim-Baran notes the same tendency in similar sources in the Provincial Bureau of Village Affairs in Izmir.[77] Another observation that sheds light on the nature of the Turkish policy of resettlement concerns the Principal Registers of Refugees. The official procedure shows that the government took into consideration the professional qualifications of refugees once these people arrived at their destinations rather than at their points of departure. This caused a major problem for the newcomers. Despite the fact that there were many refugees who declared that they used to practice a craft in their former locations, they were directed to the countryside due to the absence of proper premises for practicing such pursuits. These problems, among many others, certainly determined the success of the resettlement program. At this point it can only be suggested that the Turkish case of resettlement was characterized from the beginning by an arbitrariness in conduct and the absence of a coordinated plan for the economic integration of refugees.

The above point can be substantiated by examining the process by which the refugees were registered in Samsun. When refugees arrived at the local offices of the the Ministry of Exchange, Reconstruction and Resettlement

(*Mübadele, İmar ve İskân Vekâleti*; MERR), they held either a certificate of ownership (*tasarruf senedi*) issued by the office of the Mixed Commission in the location from which they originated, or, if they lacked such a certificate, an official document for the liquidation of property (*tasfiye talebnamesi*), which they secured from the offices of the Mixed Commission in Istanbul. The former document, the accuracy of which had been subjected to much criticism by the press and certain deputies in Parliament, contained a detailed statement about the number of dependent individuals in the family and the size of the property the family left behind. When the head of a family proceeded to the office of the MERR, he would submit his certificate together with his title deed to the Value Assessment Commission (*Takdir Kıymet Komisyonu*) which then carried out the valuation of the abandoned properties. Then he was forwarded to another commission (*Tefviz Komisyonu*), which assigned him abandoned Greek properties matching in value 17.5% (raised to 20% in 1924) of the properties that he had left behind.[78]

Refugees who were considered for resettlement in a different area were subjected to a random selection through a lottery in the MERR office. As in the case of 80 families from Kavala, they were selected by a lottery and sent to Tokat.[79] If it was decided to resettle a refugee in the city where the registration took place, the officials decided on the basis of submitted documents whether the refugee was to be resettled in the urban center or directed to the surrounding countryside. On the basis of these certificates, the head of each refugee family, if considered for resettlement in an urban center, was granted housing and business premises abandoned by the Greeks. If the family was considered for resettlement in a rural area, the officials assigned to it abandoned fields. In some instances, refugees were assigned housing and business premises in the city as well as agricultural fields.

The duration of this process (*tefviz*) varied from region to region. A refugee named Zehra Kosova, for example, states that the official process was completed in Samsun within two to six days. Her recollections also provide a glimpse of the problems involved in the process of allotment. Coming from a family specializing in tobacco cultivation, she says, "my father was granted two fields and a vineyard. But we were unable to sow (*ekip-biçmek*) the fields. Because half of the vine stock was of black grapes (*kara üzüm*) while the other half was of golden red grapes."[80]

The real problem started when the refugees began to claim the lands and buildings to which they had been assigned. Here the problem was not so much the incompatibility of the refugees' attributes with the kinds of fields and buildings they were assigned as with the conditions in which these properties were found. Many urban refugees, especially in cities such as Izmir and Samsun, found their assigned homes either occupied by the local populations or in the most dismal of conditions. The former not only led to a continuous friction between the refugees and natives but also created many homeless refugees, who waived their rights to the given properties by moving to a different area where they had to rent homes.[81] In the case of Izmir, as late as 1928 to 1930, there were many refugees who declared that they were staying as guests in the houses of their relatives or paying rent for their houses.[82] As for the latter situation, the government had no program to extend loans to the refugees for the repair of these houses. The following examples, which were mentioned only in one of the sessions of the Grand National Assembly, are selected, among many others, to illustrate the various difficulties experienced by the refugees during the resettlement process.

In Kayseri, for example, the refugees who were brought to this location consisted mainly of agriculturalists, and they were granted houses and business premises but no fields for cultivation. Those who had brought their livestock (e.g., cows and mules) were sharing these houses with their animals. Certain deputies argued vehemently in the Grand National Assembly that Kayseri required refugees of urban background who were familiar with commerce.[83]

The frequent movement of refugees from one place to another led some deputies in the Grand National Assembly to liken them to dominoes (*dama taşı*). A group of refugees who came from the villages of Dospat and Zagos were first sent to Balıkesir for resettlement, then they were distributed to Akçaabat, Şiran, and Kelkit. For the third time they were transferred to İnebolu and some of them unpacked on the way in Kastamonu. A few others from this group eventually ended up in Keskin.[84]

Refugees who were sent to Çirkince, near Ephesus, for resettlement found all the properties assigned to them already occupied. They asked to be transferred to another location.[85] In the same fashion, refugees who were sent to Gürün, near Malatya, found no land suitable for agriculture and asked for relocation to a different area. The government interpreted this as a violation of the official order and cut off their provisions. According to a deputy, "they were crammed into the old government building in the town and condemned to starvation and misery."[86]

Resettlement was less of a problem when politicians acted on behalf of the refugees. Rıza Nur made a case in the National Assembly that the refugees to be resettled in the region of Sinop had to be either tobacco growers or fishermen.[87] In the same vein, Celal Bayar also intervened to change the status of a group of refugees who had come from Mytilene to Ayvalık, from temporary settlement (*İskân-i adi*) to permanent settlement (*İskân-ı kati*) without notifying government officials.[88] Lastly, it should be also mentioned that certain people who had come from Greece long before the Convention and had not been able to liquidate their properties, tried to solve their problem by using their government connections. A certain Ahmed Bey, who had served as the governor of Sivas, sent a letter to a minister in the cabinet stating that he owned large tracts of land in Salonica but he was unable to receive any compensation for them from the Greek government. In Izmir, he had recently seized a flour mill formerly owned by a Greek family, namely, Tozanoglou, and asked whether he would be able to register this property as the compensation for his lost properties in Salonica. The government discussed the matter and approved his request before the population exchange negotiations were over.[89]

The most significant problem that hampered the proper resettlement of incoming refugees was the state of abandoned properties. As was covered briefly at the outset of Chapter Five, the problems associated with the occupation of abandoned properties by the local populations constituted one of the much debated issues of the contemporary press. Many houses and business premises abandoned by Greeks and Armenians and earmarked for the refugees had been occupied by a diverse group of people prior to the arrival of the newcomers. In the case of Izmir, for example, those who seized the abandoned Greek properties included the people who suffered from the great fire in Izmir (*harikzedeler*), the people (*felaketzedeler*) who moved to Izmir from previously Greek-occupied territories (e.g., Aydın, Alaşehir, Manisa, Salihli, Kasaba, and Nazilli), the people who had fled from the Russian occupation (*vilayet-i şarkiyye muhacirleri*) during WWI and army officials, soldiers and state servants.[90]

Also there was the group of non-exchangeables (*gayri mübadiller*), refugees from Western Thrace or other places in the Balkans who had come during the war and imposed themselves on the abandoned properties. This situation constituted a stumbling block in the face of the efficient functioning of property assignments to incoming refugees.[91] The government tried to institute a special commission, made up of representatives of the Health and Social Ministry and the Ministry of Finance and Economic Affairs, in order to look after the problems of the people who were categorically labeled as "*harikzedeler*" or "*felaketzedeler.*"[92]

This decision was taken in early August 1923 but newspapers continued to report similar incidents more intensively thereafter. The Grand Assembly passed a law requiring everyone to reside for at least five years in their designated location in order to be eligible to move to a different location.[93] These efforts seem to have failed on the whole owing to the fact that the government, instead of anticipating developments and preparing a constructive scheme for channeling the refugees, persisted in satisfying the demands of the existing populations from the very beginning.[94]

Without any doubt, the indifferent attitude on the part of local government authorities towards the incoming refugees accentuated the tendency among the local populations to seize abandoned properties.[95] While the government took certain legal steps such as the Expropriation Law (*İstimlak Kanunu*) to regulate, among other things, the transfer of full ownership of the abandoned properties to the State, it also asked the occupiers to relinquish the buildings and suspended all the procedures of settlement and property allotment on October 4, 1922.[96] Moreover, the properties that had earlier been left to the administration of the Ministry of Finance and abandoned by the Greeks and Armenians[97] were now entrusted to government officials.

These developments not only failed to remedy the situation but actually accentuated it. The newspaper *Tanin* reported on November 1922 that a Hulusi Efendi, a vice police chief in the district of Karataş, who was appointed to supervise and oversee the abandoned properties, had been involved in a great fraud. The officials found in his house abandoned goods valued at 26,000 lira, and he was exiled to interior Anatolia.[98] The same day, another newspaper reported that "officials of low ranking were behaving as they wished without taking into account the misery and suffering of the needy." According to the paper, "this behavior emanated from the very fact that the officials did not grasp the nature of the new administrative system. If officials have the understanding that they represent a government of the people, neither would such confusions be faced nor would the people be nagging the government offices, and come face to face with the legacy of the old regime. These affairs should be entrusted to the people who are specialized in them."[99]

The grave nature of the problem was pronounced in the Grand National Assembly, and it was acknowledged that there was extensive theft of abandoned properties and that all the schemes failed to be realized owing mainly to the fact that those who did it were actually state officials themselves.[100] Whether the government ever succeeded in stopping the officials from seizing abandoned properties is hard to say.[101] But this tendency on the part of local notables continued at full speed. The leading local newspaper of Izmir, *Ahenk,* reported on August 30, 1923 that "some of the abandoned property in Izmir was occupied unnecessarily (*fuzulen işgal*) by people who were natives of Izmir and owned large properties and wealth or power (*aslen Izmirli ve mesken ve akar veya iktidar sahibi*), who in fact had occupied one house for each member of the household."[102]

An investigation of the issue was apparently launched and the government tried to evict the occupiers and demanded a lump sum rent for the period of their occupation.[103] Despite all the investigations and other measures, the general situation in Izmir deteriorated from day to day, the local adminis-tration became paralyzed and government offices ceased to function, which made the city the most popular area for illegal settlement.[104] The newspa-per *Ahenk* reported again on October 14, 1923 that some of the people who had illegally occupied abandoned houses actually began to rent them out.[105] The housing crisis reached enormous dimensions. The rents nearly quadrupled, jumping from 400 to 1,500 liras.[106]

The tenants who were distressed by the developments had formerly organized themselves into an association, namely the Association for the Protection of Tenants (*Müstecerin Müdafaa Cemiyeti*), to defend their rights and pressure the government into issuing laws to regulate the rent conditions.[107] The government not only ignored such calls but also abol-ished the Law of Habitation (*Sükna/Sekene Kanunu*), which could have prevented rent hikes if properly implemented.[108] Moreover, the government policy to evacuate the refugees from the houses they had occupied and to auction them for rent was postponed, thanks to the intervention of certain politicians.[109] A year later, the situation was the same and such laws had not been issued.[110] There were many individuals who had occupied more than one house.[111] The original plan of the government was to resettle well above 50,000 refugees in Izmir. The survey of the National Statistical Office in 1930 shows that there were 32,000 people of refugee background in Izmir and its environs.[112]

One of the ways in which the Turkish government tried to address the influx of refugees was by the adoption of a program for creating new villages. This program operated on the principle that "the proportion of refugees, settled in a town or village, whose language and traditions are of a race other than Turkish will not exceed 20 per cent."[113] The Otto-man governments had also tried to solve the settlement problem of refu-gees by the creation of new villages (*numune köyler*) during the previous decade (1910s).[114] The new government decided to construct houses for the refugees on its own account (*emanet*).[115] The Minister of Exchange, Recon-struction and Resettlement, Necati Bey, proposed to the Grand Assembly the construction of 42 villages: 15 in the region of Samsun and 27 in the rest of the country. Although the government adopted his proposal, finan-cial resources were not sufficient to construct that many villages.[116] The total number of villages built throughout the country was limited to 14. The distribution of these villages was as follows: 2 each in Samsun, Izmir, and Bursa, and 1 each in İzmit, Adana, and Antalya. Each village consisted of 50 houses and a mosque.[117] Even then, the contract for the construc-tion of villages (e.g., Ökse, Çırakman, Canik, Asarağac, Örnek) had to be extended due to insufficient funds.[118] As the campaign for the construction of new villages failed, the government resorted to a new housing project, called "economic houses" (*iktisadi evler*) in the villages. Through this project, an attempt was made to build compact buildings that contained multiple homes. But the evidence suggests that this project was limited to only a few locations and could not be extended nationwide.[119]

A final word is in order concerning the relations between refugees and locals. The fact that there was a limit to the number of refugees that would be absorbed into a particular location not only failed to mitigate local opposition but was also a determinant in producing tension between locals and newcomers. Samsun provides a good case in point. Here great strife occurred between the local populations and incoming refugees as soon as the latter began to arrive in great numbers. Local government officials in the city established an association called "Union of Natives and Refugees" (*Yerli ve Muhacir Birliği*) to end the friction but it failed.[120] There is ample evidence showing that the tension between the refugees and locals in this area continued well into the later years of the 1930s. To cite one example, as late as 1937, a refugee petitioned the government that he was unable to obtain the title deed to the field that he had been granted through the Convention. He explained that certain people from the local populations had been persistently claiming that this field belonged to them and they even took their case to the Council of State (*Şuray-ı Devlet*).[121] How this case was resolved is unknown to the present author. There are many documents of similar content available in the Republic Archives dated from the 1930s.[122]

In light of the above discussion, it can be argued that the Turkish case of resettlement was plagued from the beginning by the populist policies of the ruling government and the absence of a genuine interest on the part of the political authority in the plight of the refugees. While the populist policies created a major vacuum for the fate of the abandoned properties presumably earmarked for the refugees on the one hand, the arbitrary attitude of the government officials towards the resettlement of refugees engendered a situation hardly conducive to transforming the refugees into economically self-sufficient citizens on the other. These two facts prompt us to conclude that the ruling elite tended to move beyond the Exchange as quickly as possible and concentrate its efforts on the draconian task of building the new State, the first major step of which, the declaration of the Republic, had been taken only a few weeks before the actual transfer of the refugees began.

Insofar as the Greek side of the resettlement is concerned, the story of Greek refugees is well documented and has been examined in great deal by two separate scholarly traditions. On the one hand, a descriptive tradition, dominated by the writings of people affiliated with the Refugee Settlement Commission (RSC)[123] and those of the representatives of Greek nationalist scholarship,[124] has addressed the subject with emphasis on the role of their adopted unit of analysis, that is, the League of Nations and the Greek State. This genre has been characterized on the one hand by a tendency to depict the whole process of resettlement as a success story without alluding to the predicaments experienced by the refugees. On the other hand, a critical scholarship, started recently amongst political scientists, economic historians and anthropologists, has examined resettlement and integration from the viewpoint of the refugees with an emphasis on the short-term and long-term political, social, and economic ramifications of these processes. Casting serious doubts on the success paradigm of mainstream scholarship, the research of representatives of the latter tradition offers significant insights into the early years of resettlement and related problems of refugees based on previously neglected oral sources and certain national and local archival collections in Greece.[125]

Anastasia Karakasidou's research, for example, sheds significant light on the fate of Muslim properties in Greek Macedonia in the immediate aftermath of the Convention. The movable and immovable properties previously owned by the Muslims in this region apparently witnessed developments commensurate with the Greek abandoned properties in Anatolia.[126] Upon the departure of Muslims from the region, local powerful notables (*tsorbadjides*) and other members of the local communities, rich and poor alike, seized their fields and buildings. These properties could only be expropriated by the government in the late 1920s with a view to being redistributed to the refugees.[127]

Thus, the occupation of abandoned properties by local populations, especially in the northern sections of the country, obstructed at the outset the implementation of resettlement programs in these areas. Another factor that played a significant role in this respect was, as argued by Elisabeth Kontogiorgi, the "delays in the departure of Muslims from most villages of Macedonia and Crete [which] worsened the problem of the shortage of land."[128] As it was shown above, the transfer of a great majority of Muslims took place in the first half of 1924. Conventional wisdom suggests, however, that delays in the departure of the Muslims might have prevented the local populations from "squatting" on more lands than they had already occupied illegally.[129]

Not much is known about the fate of homes and commercial properties of Muslims in cities with substantial Muslim communities such as Florina, Drama, Salonica and Kavala.[130] Limited information about the conditions of Greek refugees during the first years of their arrival, however, is available in the accounts of the foreign observers of the situation.

It is established that the RSC was not able to start its permanent settlement projects in most places until the summer of 1924 owing to the delays in the placement of land and funds at the disposal of this institution.[131] Once launched, the implementation of urban and rural resettlement projects through the offices of this institution took several years in some locations and longer in others.[132] Until then, most refugees remained encamped on the fringes of big port cities such as Piraeus, Athens, Patras, and Salonica. Mears reports that "at Salonika, abandoned army barracks a hundred feet long were each used by twenty or more families."[133] On account of the housing shortage, conditions in most of the industrial buildings had become desolate. As Mears vividly describes, "many bakeries and chocolate factories, for instance, are located in basements with bare ground for floor, and the work tables upon which food is made in the daytime are used as beds by the employees at night."[134] The same was true of Piraeus,[135] Athens, and Patras. [136] As Hirschon documents, in the case of Kokkina, the housing projects took many years to complete and many refugees spent the first years of their arrival sheltered in the warehouses and basements of factories in Piraeus.[137] An actual observer of the situation mentions that "in the two years after their arrival in Greece, the refugees have been living . . . in the suburbs and in the country districts they have maintained a fox-like existence in tents, wooden barracks, shelters of twigs or of turfs, even in caves."[138] The gravity of this situation is attested to by the fact that when the transfer of Greek refugees was completed in late 1924, the population of Athens had more than doubled, jumping from 300,000 to 700,000, and Salonica's population had risen from 174,000 to 334,000.

Under these circumstances, turning the refugees into self-sufficient and productive individuals was probably less of a concern—both for the Greek government and the RSC—than providing necessary shelter and sustenance for the survival of these people. The early phase of resettlement, following this line of logic, resulted in the progress of permanent settlement in urban areas at a slower pace. [139] In rural areas of northern Greece, the resettlement of which constituted a priority for the Greek government and the RSC due to the strategic and economic importance of these areas, the work proceeded at a much quicker pace.[140]

Even then, the refugees seem to have been irked by the progress of the resettlement work. Accordingly, organizations representing the refugees, particularly those in northern Greece urged the government to speed up the process of land distribution and resettlement as well as to facilitate the work of the RSC. As the research of Kontogiorgi documents, these organizations "sent telegrams to the Prime Minister, the Mixed Commission for the Exchange of Populations and the Assembly, protesting against, first, the order to prohibit agricultural resettlement before the appraisal of the value of Muslim properties by the Mixed Commission and second, the delay in the departure of Muslims."[141] During the first three years after the Convention was signed, the number of refugees permanently resettled in rural sections of Greek Macedonia numbered nearly half of the total refugee population of 550,635. The number of urban refugees remained at a low level of 72, 230.[142]

A general assessment of the resettlement work carried out by the RSC will be provided in Chapter Eight. It is important, however, to pinpoint two areas in which the resettlement related experiences of the refugees complemented their predicaments during the uprooting and impaired their integration within the wider Greek society. Here the research of two prominent scholars, Reneé Hirschon and George Mavrogordatos, should be appraised for addressing the issue effectively at both the factual and analytical level. While Hirschon was concerned with the process by which the refugees, specifically urban ones, developed a separate identity from the larger Greek society, Mavrogordatos sought to chart the dynamics of the process by which the political behavior of the refugees was shaped and came to play an arbiter role in Greek political life during the interwar period.

Having conducted her fieldwork in an urban refugee community in Kokkinia, Piraeus, Hirschon shows that the impediments associated with the resettlement and housing projects contributed to the creation of physical and mental barriers between refugees and natives. The continued exposure of the former to the physical and economic hardships (e.g., housing and employment constraints) within contained spaces brought about a growing attachment to their cultural heritage, which they considered on the whole superior to the one that surrounded them.[143] Her contention is that the rural-bias of the resettlement projects[144] was one among many other factors that played a significant role in prolonging the plight of urban refugees, contributing in turn to their social segregation and the development of a sense of identity separate from that of the larger Greek society. These two developments combined to affect the political orientation of refugees in the years to come, a subject that constitutes the focus of George Mavrogordatos.[145] Mavrogordatos, who examined the conditions of refugees in terms of economic deprivation, downward social mobility, status deprivation, and discrimination, considers the resettlement, more specifically, the land, as a major and permanent source of conflict between the natives and refugees, especially in the rural areas of northern Greece. He states:

> The implementation of the land reform and the massive departure of exchanged Turks and Bulgarians released enormous amounts of vacant agricultural land, which the local peasants expected to get and which they often seized without waiting. Native expectations were brutally

frustrated when rural refugee settlement perforce received first priority with respect to this land. The whole process should be seen in the context of poor records, inadequate control by the authorities, great haste, and concomitantly great confusion. Evictions, quarrels over disputed land, and the manifest native aspiration to drive the refugees away and seize their fields produced continuous clashes in the countryside, throughout the interwar period.[146]

The author makes a similar argument for the urban areas as a setting that witnessed significant rivalries between natives and refugees over properties.[147] This factor, among many other problems of social and economic nature, caused the economic deprivation of refugees, rural and urban alike, and determined the orientation of their political behaviors. In the face of emergent reactionary attitude on the part of the natives (politically represented in the Antivenizelist Populist Party) towards the refugees, the latter, guided largely by refugee associations, threw their support on Venizelism and remained loyal to its cause until the early years of the 1930s. Later a growing alienation of the refugees from Venizelism was observed in reaction to the rapprochement with Turkey, which was sanctioned by the Ankara Convention of 1930, ending the hopes of the refugees for compensation for the actual values of their properties. In his assessment of the consequences of this Convention, Mavrogordatos states: "The property of exchanged Turks . . . to be used expressly for the settlement of the refugees, never adequately benefited them, because of its disastrous mismanagement and its extremely slow and unprofitable liquidation, a problem which has continued well into the postwar period."[148]

Undoubtedly, the predicaments involved in the reception and accommodation of Greek refugees, as documented by the above-mentioned scholars, shed significant doubt on the success paradigm championed by mainstream scholarship on the resettlement and integration of refugees. But it should be noted that, including the most ardent critics of the subject, all the scholars of the population exchange invariably underline the importance of the presence of the RSC as a factor that not only prevented such a high number of refugees from becoming entrenched in "chaos, extreme physical hardship and staggering mortality" for a longer period, but also anticipated a wholesale national reconstruction for a country that had been politically and economically in disarray for more than a decade.[149]

In the final analysis, as far as the resettlement dimension of the population exchange was concerned, it is quite clear that the resettlement of nearly one and a half million refugees was a challenge of immense of proportions to Greece, the engagement with which was naturally bound to create many problems for the refugees. Here, the presence of the RSC was a factor that prevented these problems reaching a point of disarray, leading ultimately to national disaster. The RSC, the presence of which was linked to foreign loans, helped the refugees voice their concerns more effectively. Perhaps, more importantly, it enabled these concerns to be given a fair consideration during the process of resettlement. While the refugees in Turkey seemed not to pose as much of a challenge quantitatively, the above discussion reveals that the adoption by the Turkish government authorities of a blatantly indifferent attitude toward the whole question of resettlement was bound to create a problem of immense proportions from the very outset. Their belated realization of the gravity of the problem could not save the plight of the refugees from turning into an epic tragedy commensurate with that of their Greek counterparts due to the fact that their capabilities and efforts were overwhelmed by the realities of the situation.

Unlike their Greek counterparts, the refugees in Turkey had no institutional agency to appeal to when government officials overlooked their problems. Given these conditions, when the transfer of refugees from Greece was halfway complete and the resettlement of arrivals began to pose significant challenges, the leading politicians in Turkey were still using the "repatriation" discourse as part of their political rhetoric. This discourse, which found its best expression in one of the speeches of İsmet Paşa to the refugees in Manisa, is indicative of the indifferent attitude on the part of the Turkish government to the plight of the refugees.

> There is no doubt that the country is in dire need and suffering. Nevertheless, it is our responsibility to make the newcomers not feel strangers to this environment and give them utmost assistance. We encourage the desires of our friends abroad who want to come to their motherland. The empty building is doomed to perish and [therefore] it will be filled. We will do all in our capacity and use all means in our power to bring to our country all our citizens and brothers abroad in addition to the refugees who are coming now.[150]

What is perhaps more interesting in this regard, despite all kinds of problems associated with the refugees, the country continued to receive further floods of refugees from various countries in the Balkans during the latter part of 1920s and the entire decade of the 1930s.

Chapter Eight
Regimenting the Exchange: Institutions

Upon the signing of the Lausanne Treaty, several institutions were created at national and international levels to implement the clauses of the Convention as well as to manage the whole process of implementation. The Mixed Commission (*Muhtelit Mübadele Komisyonu/Η Μικτη Επιτροπη*) which was established according to Article 11 of the Exchange Convention began to function nearly one month after the ratification of the Lausanne Treaty by the parliaments of Turkey and Greece. Of the 19 articles in the Convention, Articles 11 to 17 deal specifically with the organization and functions of the Mixed Commission. Two domestic institutions specializing in refugee affairs, namely the Refugee Settlement Commission (from now on RSC) (*Επιτροπη Αποκαταστασεως Προσφυγων*) in Greece and the Ministry of Exchange, Reconstruction, and Resettlement (from now on MERR) (*Mübadele, İmar ve İskân Vekâleti*) in Turkey were established in the last months of 1923. Undoubtedly, the successful progress of the regimentation of the population exchange hinged on the level of coordination between these three institutions. However, an overview of their foundation principles and early operations shows that each institution was exclusively concerned with its specifically designed duties and, even in cases where their obligations overlapped, there was a lack of cooperation between them, a significant factor that hampered the efficient regimentation of the population exchange process and prolonged the transfer and resettlement of the refugees.

The Mixed Commission was established with a view to providing the proper registration and evacuation of the refugees as well as the arbitration of the differences between the two governments that might arise during the implementation of the Convention. The Convention authorized the

Mixed Commission to intervene when it deemed necessary and create sub-commissions at the expense of the country where the sub-commission was established. The RSC and the Turkish Ministry of Exchange, Reconstruction and Resettlement were responsible for refugee-related matters, especially concerning resettlement, in their respective countries. The RSC and the MERR differed from one another in terms of judicial status. The former, whose presence was linked to a series of agreements between Greece and the League of Nations for a broad financial loan scheme, was intended mainly as autonomous machinery and had more responsibilities towards the League of Nations than to the Greek government. Its operation was contingent on the floatation of financial loans and the constant reassessments of the League. Thus, it was in fact more of an international agency than a national one. In complete contradistinction to the RSC, the MERR was established as a strictly governmental organization with a view to taking over the responsibilities of all the existing refugee-related institutions in Turkey. With limited funds at its disposal, the MERR was charged with a wide range of responsibilities from the transfer and provisioning of the refugees to their resettlement. Unlike the RSC, which continued its operation for nearly a decade, the MERR had a very short lifespan due to its inability to cope with a challenge of such nature and magnitude as well as certain political reasons to be covered below. What follows is a very brief description and discussion of the operations of these institutions from the moment of their inception to their abolition.

THE MIXED COMMISSION

The continued factional deadlock amongst the Greek and Turkish leaders in the immediate aftermath of the Convention increased the role of the League of Nations and placed it in a predominant position as regards the whole conflict. At the center of this conflict stood the Mixed Commission, which had been constituted on September 17, 1923 with a view to arbitrating the implementation of the Convention and supervising the liquidation of movable and immovable properties of the refugees as well as the indemnification of the latter.[1] The Commission consisted of four members from Greece[2] and four from Turkey.[3] There were also three members representing countries that had not participated in WWI.[4] It had two separate bodies stationed in Istanbul and Salonica. Although the Turkish side insisted on designating Salonica as the seat of the Commission, the Council of the League of Nations selected Athens as the location where the principal offices of the Commission were situated.[5] The first meeting of the Commission took place in Athens on October 8, 1923.

Due to increasing pressure from the Turks, the seat of the Commission was moved from Athens to Istanbul after the meeting on June 21, 1924.[6]

As the principal agency responsible for settling all questions concerning the population exchange, the Mixed Commission was furnished with full authority to deal with a set of administrative, legislative, and judicial matters.[7] The principal administrative function of this Commission was related to the transfer of both Greek and Muslim populations, who had not yet been removed from the territories of Turkey and Greece. Although the Commission was furnished with full responsibility to conduct the transfer of the refugees, the fact that it had undertaken no preparatory work to this effect caused long delays in transferring the majority of the refugees from one country to the other. The transfer of Greek refugees, gathered in principal Turkish port cities, as well as Muslim refugees, already congregated in Greek port cities, started in mid-December under the supervision of the Mixed Commission. Later on, the Commission extended its field of operation to the interior sections of both countries. For example, roughly half of the 3,000 Greek refugees who had come to Ankara from Akdağ, Keskin, Haymana and Yozgat and were being pressured by local Turkish authorities were to be evacuated with the direct intervention of the Mixed Commission.[8] The work of the Commission also included collecting and transporting to Turkey the official Ottoman archives and registers from all parts of Greece, especially Crete.[9] There is also evidence that the Commission was involved in the same task for the archives of the Greek institutions in Istanbul and other parts of Turkey. For example, the Metropolitan of Kayseri, Yervasios, managed to salvage from destruction the library holdings of several churches and monasteries and transferred them through the mediation of the Mixed Commission to Greece to be added in due course to the collections of the Byzantine Museum and the Benaki Museum in Athens.[10] However, not all the Greek libraries and archives were as fortunate. In the case of the library and archives of the Literary Society of Constantinople, for instance, the official Turkish documents suggest that the Turkish authorities transferred them from Istanbul to a local library in Ankara.[11] The whereabouts of these library and archival collections are presently unknown.

The most important obligations of the Mixed Commission were in the realms of legislative and judicial affairs such as the appraisal of immovable and movable properties, the determination of the methods of appraisal and the adoption of measures required by the Convention. In order to address these issues, the Commission created at the outset three sub-commissions in Athens.[12] The first one was intended for the determination of the methods of the population exchange while the second was established for the adoption of the bases for the liquidation of refugee properties. The last one aimed to study the measures to be taken in each country for putting the legislation in harmony with the Convention. Later on, several other sub-commissions were created to address the financial and juristic matters.[13] All these institutions remained in operation until July 1928. They were abolished because of increasing expenditures in maintaining the Commission; their duties were transferred to certain bureaus at the seat of the Commission. A compilation of documents in Turkish offers detailed information about the organizational aspects of the Mixed Commission and the functions of each sub-commission.[14] The following is a brief discussion of the issues that have been hardly mentioned in the population exchange literature.

As part of its judicial task, the Commission was involved in determining who would be exempt from the population exchange.[15] The thorniest question in this regard was related to the situation of the Albanians. Earlier, when the Albanian government expressed its concerns as to the situation of the Albanians in Greece and Turkey, the President of the Section of Minorities in Lausanne had given assurances to the Albanian representative, Mehdi Frashëri, that the Albanian minorities in these two countries, regardless of their religious beliefs, were certainly exempted from the population exchange.[16] On August 6, 1923, Venizelos himself sent a letter to the Secretary of the League of Nations stating that the Greek government had no desire to force the Albanian Muslims to leave the country.[17]

Although the Greek representatives gave yet another set of assurances at a meeting of the sub-commission of Epirus (*Epir Tali Komisyonu*) on June 17, 1924,[18] certain developments proved the opposite to be true. Five thousand Albanian Muslims from the district of Chamouria in Epirus, for example, were considered for exchange with the same number of Greeks who had already been removed from Istanbul. The Albanian government appealed to the Mixed Commission to stop the violation of the Convention by the Greeks. The Albanian representatives, Mehdi Frashëri and Viscount Ishii, presented detailed reports at the Council of League of Nations during the first weeks of December 1925.[19] An investigation was launched and the Mixed Commission was asked to present its views before the Council. After the Mixed Commission conducted proper investigations, the issue was resolved in favor of the Albanian government the following year.[20] Similarly, in 1928, when the Turkish government attempted to deport a group of Orthodox Arabs from Mersin on account of their exchangeability, the Commission intervened to stop the process.[21] As mentioned previously, there were a few minor cases of similar nature where the Commission acted on behalf of the people concerned. But on the whole, Commission members seem to have adopted a passive attitude on issues concerning individual cases of this sort and complied with the decisions of their respective governments regarding this matter.

The Commission started to fulfill its primary responsibilities when the differences of opinion between the Turkish and Greek members surfaced and the two governments began to accuse each other of violating the principles of the Convention. The most important of these disputes had to do with the situation of the Greeks of Constantinople and the Muslims of Western Thrace. While the Greeks accused the Turks of not observing the second article of the Convention concerning the Greek inhabitants of Constantinople, the Turks, referring to the same article, held the Greeks accountable for using excessive force to expel the Muslims of Western Thrace from their lands. This dispute focused for the most part on the situation of the Greeks of Constantinople and took the form of a chronic conflict over the *établi* problem between the Greek and Turkish members of the Mixed Commission.[22]

Having failed to reconcile the differences of opinion between the two sides, which focused on the real "intentions" of the Greeks pertaining to their presence in Istanbul on October 18, 1918 and thereafter, the neutral members of the Commission took the matter to the Permanent Court of International Justice in the Hague. The proceedings of the Court concerning this matter have been extensively quoted in the literature on the population exchange.[23] What is important for the purpose of the current discussion is that the Mixed Commission, having adopted the proposal of the Court, issued a decision in which the principal criteria for exempting the Greeks of Constantinople and the Muslims of Western Thrace were established. According to this decision, which was taken on March 19, 1927, all Greeks, regardless of their intentions, who were present in the city on October 18, 1918 and at the time (March 19, 1927) the decision was taken, were considered not subject to the Convention.

Correspondingly, the Muslim Turkish populations of Western Thrace were to be subjected to the same principles. The Mixed Commission was supposed to observe that both governments comply with this decision. Although the Commission established a sub-commission to this end, the ultimate decisions seem to have rested for the most part with the governments. The arbitrary conduct of this decision by the Turkish government can be seen in the numbers of Greeks whose exchangeability had been established and who were transferred from Constantinople to Greece from January 1, 1924 to December 31, 1928. Their numbers reached 99,730.[24] Analogously, the number of Muslims who moved from Western Thrace to Turkey steadily increased during the period concerned.[25]

Table 10. A Sample List of Decisions of the Mixed Commission

No. de la requite	Date d'en-registr.	Objet	Démarches faites	Date	Résultat obtenu
2443	5/1/25	Hadji-Ilia Tocouroglou, propriétaire de 3 magasins et 3 maisons à Kadikeuy nous informe qu'il a reçu ordre d'évacuer ses immeubles	Vali de Stamboul	7/1/25	nul
1855	Oct. 8	Stavro et Hellène Palandjo-glou demandent restitution de leurs immeubles saisis, consi-dérés comme bien abandonnés	Vali de Stamboul	9/12/24	nul
673	Avr. 22	Saisie de la maison de Hadjétoglou, sise à Scutari et considérée comme bien abandonné	Verbale-ment par Riza Bey	–	nul
3046 2508	Janv. 9 Janv. 15	Yordan Didonakis, muni d'une fische rouge de notre S.C. nous informe que les autorités de Scutari ont requsitionné sa maison et y ont installé de réfugiés turcs	Au Vali de Stamboul Lettre de rappel	19/2/25	– (nul)

Source: AYE, 1925, A.A.K./3.

Yet another example of the incompetence of the Mixed Commission can be seen in its decisions concerning the applications of the Greeks of Constantinople for compensation for their properties or restitution. Of those applicants, the great majority consisted of people who had left the city either of their own will or had been forced to leave the city by the Turk-ish local authorities (e.g., governors etc.) on the grounds that they had been collaborating with the Greek occupation forces. Considered "fugitives" (*fuyard*), many of these people submitted their claims to the local branches of the Mixed Commission with files that contained the notarized copies of title deeds for their properties. These files were sent to the Sub-Commission of the Mixed Commission in Istanbul for evaluation. The following table is excerpted from a list of decisions taken by the office of the Mixed Commis-sion in Istanbul [Table 10]. As the obtained results show, these applications were on the whole rejected.

As for the question of the liquidation and indemnification of proper-ties of the exchangeable Greeks and Muslims, the issue was discussed at length in Chapter Six. The evidence suggests that neither side honored the related articles of the Convention.[26] The fact that the appraisal of the properties and the transfer of populations had not taken place concomitantly, especially in the case of the Greeks, prevented the proper valuation and liquidation of these properties by the Mixed Commission.[27] Considered against the background of the fate of the abandoned properties belonging to the Greeks in Turkey, the preposterousness of such a task becomes evident. As for the properties of the Muslims, a certain portion of which had been exposed to a similar *kismet*, the Mixed Commission failed to arbitrate the differences between the Turks and Greeks. The Turks persisted in the view that the properties (especially immovables) of Muslims outnumbered those of Greeks. Where the method of appraisal was concerned, they refrained from adopting an individual appraisal of the properties of refugees.[28] The latter view was in fact in line with that of the Greek side for the obvious reason that its ongoing land reform and the resettlement of Greek refugees by the RSC would certainly be obstructed, should they have observed a systematic individual appraisal of the Muslim properties. Due to the reciprocating interests of the two parties, this whole question could not be addressed until the early 1930s.

In the meantime, the Turkish and Greek government representatives convened to discuss this matter several times in Ankara and Athens under the aegis of the Mixed Commission. At these meetings, however, the discussions concerning property issues focused largely on the related problems of the non-exchangeables (*établis*). In the Ankara Convention of June 21, 1925, both sides sanctioned the decision. They agreed, after tortuous negotiations and deliberations, that Greek and Muslim refugees who had moved from Istanbul and Western Thrace respectively prior to Lausanne were to be entitled to compensation for the unregistered movable and immovable property which they had left behind.[29] In the face of ongoing violations, the same issue was made part of the agenda of a new meeting in Athens and was concluded with the Convention of Athens in which the early decision was reinstated.[30] The Mixed Commission failed to bring about an agreement between the two sides on a method for the valuation of properties including the properties of the non-exchangeables,[31] and on a plan to indemnify the refugees. Thus, the two governments agreed that the only solution to indemnification was by direct negotiation to the effect of which they met in Ankara and signed a convention on June 10, 1930.

With this agreement, a general balancing of property claims was made and all refugee properties were transferred to the ownership of the respective governments.[32] The governments, in turn, issued bonds to the refugees for partial indemnification of the certified value of their properties. From

June 10, 1930 until its official abolition on October 19, 1934, the Commission focused its work on the individual cases of refugees, a development that turned this institution into a channel whereby refugee complaints were forwarded to the respective governments.[33] My many years of research on the subject in Turkey and Greece have not revealed a single case where a refugee, Greek or Turkish, received an actual cash payment on account of his or her abandoned property. All the bonds issued to this effect by the Turkish and Greek governments remained in the hands of refugees as concrete proof and a reminder of the injustices they faced during the implementation of the Convention.

In light of the above discussion, it can be said that the only accomplishment of the Commission took place at the outset in regards to the issue of evacuating the remaining Greeks and Turks from their respective countries. A partial success was achieved in clarifying the situation of certain communities, such as the Albanian Muslims, with respect to the Convention. Other than that, the Commission did very little until its abolition in 1934.

REFUGEE SETTLEMENT COMMISSION

As was discussed at length above, the relief of incoming refugees in Greece was provided through coordinated action between the Greek government and many international relief agencies from the end of the Turco-Greek War to mid-1923. The Greek government, which had been unremittingly engaged with the transfer and relief of refugees since the latter part of 1922, soon found itself overwhelmed by the ever-increasing number of refugees. In early 1923, when the Lausanne negotiations over the population exchange were in progress, Greek representatives in the Council of the League of Nations appealed to the Council for a loan and asked for its "moral and technical support."[34] In response, the Council referred the matter to the Financial Committee which, in return, sent two representatives to Athens; the first one to look into the material securities that Greece could offer for a loan and the second to inspect the conditions for the resettlement of the refugees. On July 9, 1923, the Financial Committee of the League approved a comprehensive resettlement plan that included the provision of "financial resources to be supplied by a loan and the execution of the [resettlement] scheme to be entrusted to the Refugee Settlement Commission (RSC)."[35] This plan was sanctioned by a protocol between the Council of the League of Nations and the Greek government on September 29, 1923 in Geneva. With this agreement, the League of Nations took full charge of the resettlement and stood as the guarantor of loans contracted from foreign agencies for this purpose.

The establishment of the RSC signified the transfer of emergency relief work conducted by international relief organizations, like the American Red Cross and the Near East Relief, from a temporary to permanent base.[36] As a matter of fact, most of these organizations stopped their operations as soon as the agreement between the Council and the Greek authorities was reached in July 1923. The Commission not only assumed the groundwork of the international organizations but also took over the responsibilities, and in some cases the staff, of Greek official institutions, such as the Refugee Assistance Fund and the Directorate of Colonization of Macedonia,[37] which were engaged in the relief and resettlement of refugees. In this regard, the pending settlement of refugees who had come from Bulgaria through the Treaty of Neuilly (1919) and those who had arrived from Russia before 1922 was also inherited by the RSC.

The RSC was officially established in November, 1923 and provided with full legal capacity to formulate and oversee the settlement program. Having taken up the responsibility to resettle all the refugees, including those from Bulgaria and Russia, it began its work with the clarification of the objective conditions that would hinder or facilitate its operation, especially in the rural sections of northern Greece. In this respect, the Commission sought to secure from the Greek government, in concordance with the Geneva Protocol, a sizeable amount of land in this region for the settlement of refugees. The work of the Commission was in fact greatly enhanced at the outset by the cooperation of the Greek government, particularly in regards to the issue of land. With its commitment to a comprehensive land reform, the Greek government adopted a stiff position on the remaining large estates of Muslim notables and the departing Bulgarians, as well as on the holdings of the Monasteries of Mount Athos, breaking up the latter into small holdings for peasants, whether natives or refugees.[38] Although a great portion of these lands wound up in the hands of native peasants,[39] the government granted the RSC all rights of ownership to 500,000 hectares of cultivatable and uncultivatable land, especially in the northern parts of the country, with a view to being used only for the resettlement of the refugees.[40] As some historians argued later, the resettlement program of the RSC was designed to run as a long-term project for economic development particularly of the rural sections of Greek Macedonia and Western Thrace,[41] which in turn would bring political stability to these regions where skirmishes between Greek villagers and Bulgarian *comitadjis* were frequent, especially along the bordering settlements.[42] Insofar as the settlement of refugees in urban areas was concerned, the RSC and the Greek government focused their attention on Piraeus, Athens and Salonica where they carried out limited work of construction and promoted small-scale businesses among the refugees.[43]

Unlike the rural settlement scheme, the progress of urban settlement projects was strictly contingent upon incoming foreign loans, the use of which was subject to rigid principles of the protocols signed between the Greek government and the Council of the League of Nations.[44] The rural bias of the RSC's work, coupled with the tumultuous negotiations over foreign loans, caused the slow progress of urban resettlement which in turn pushed many refugees of urban background into rural areas[45], a process which was to be reversed later when the Great Depression shook the yoke of the Greek economy, not to mention the whole world economy, at the turn of the decade.

The flotation of loans abroad was a *conditio sine qua non* to the execution of the resettlement scheme. From the beginning, the Council of the League of Nations had several reservations about extending guarantees to the Greek government for loans. If the first one was the near bankrupt state of the country's economy, the second had to do with the fear that the Greek government would divert the funds for military purposes. The placement of funds at the disposal of the RSC ensured creditors that the loans would not be used for purposes–including charity and temporary relief—not authorized by the RSC. Therefore, while drafting the terms of the protocol for the establishment of the RSC, the Council paid particular attention to the fact that the Greek government would have no right to either supervise or interfere with the operation of this institution, even in cases where the activities of the Commission were considered inappropriate or inadequate.[46] In other words, the establishment of such an institution signified that the practical administration of refugee resettlement was to take place independent, as underlined by John Campbell, "of the defective machinery of [the] Greek government."[47] It is against the backdrop of such concerns that the League of Nations appointed a non-Greek as chairman of the Commission and a member from its own ranks as vice-chairman in addition to a few Greek members to be appointed by the Greek government.[48]

Special mention should be made here of Henry Morgenthau, the first president of the RSC, whose skillful loan diplomacy greatly enhanced the work of the Commission from the very beginning. As soon as he entered office, he launched negotiations with various European governments and banking institutions for loans to finance the work of the RSC. However, due to the absence of a stable government in Greece, his early attempts to this end were met with little success.[49] Morgenthau was convinced that "it was necessary to obtain about eight million pounds to solve the whole problem. With that sum, the whole question could be settled within two years, and that [he] considered it highly probable that at the expiration of that period, Greece would be self-supporting."[50] Having conducted and eventually secured on behalf of the Greek government two consecutive loans of one million pounds each (August 1923 and May 1924) in England, Morgenthau eventually managed to secure a guarantee from the Council of the League of Nations to raise a loan of up to ten million pounds on September 12, 1924, which was then added to the Protocol and Statutes of the Greek RSC of September 29, 1923.[51] This was followed by a series of agreements between the Greek government and several financial agencies in London and New York. In due course, Greece secured a loan of 12,300 million pounds (10 million pounds in net amount) to be placed at the disposal of the RSC:

> [S]olely for permanent and productive uses as provided in the Protocol, and none of it from temporary charity or temporary relief. These moneys must be used to restore the refugees to self-support and economic usefulness. They must provide farmers with seed, plows, and work animals, so that Greece might become productive. They must provide artisans with tools, industrial enterprises with equipment, and working people with permanent homes. These uses of money would restore Greece to a permanent earning power that would be a blessing to the refugees and that would provide funds to repay the loan.[52]

Further details on these loans will be provided in the last pages of the present chapter. It is important, however, to underline here the role that Venizelos played in Morgenthau's loan diplomacy. Venizelos, who had directed the pre-Lausanne diplomatic negotiations of Greece behind the scenes, adopted a similar diplomatic role in securing foreign assistance. Morgenthau, who met with Venizelos on multiple occasions in Paris, makes it clear in a private letter to his family, dated November 17, 1923, "Venizelos realizes that Greece must cater to [the] "Big Powers" so that she can have a successful bond issue, which would enable her to solve her refugee problem."[53]

It was not only in matters concerning foreign loans but also in formulating and conducting the resettlement projects of the RSC that Venizelos worked closely with Morgenthau. The latter kept a close eye on the progress of refugee resettlement in Salonica upon the recommendations of Venizelos and even at some point went to see the Vardar and Struma valleys which "Venizelos thought should be drained and cured of malaria, thereby redeeming hundreds of thousands of acres which are now uncultivated."[54] The cooperation between Morgenthau and Venizelos, especially during the period of the American diplomat's presidency of the RSC from September 1923 to December 1924, which overlapped with Venizelos' short-term government in January 1924, was crucial to the initial organization of the RSC and its later operations.

Another factor of similar importance to the functioning of the RSC was its relations with the Greek government. Although the general work of this institution was greatly enhanced by the cooperation of the Greek government, especially through the Land Distribution Program (*Διανομή*),[55] the friction between the two parties was also a common occurrence. This tension stemmed primarily from the greater autonomy of the RSC and its persistent desire to safeguard its total independence. Disputes arose especially over the administration of the funds allocated for the resettlement of refugees. While the RSC tended to fully control the administration of incoming loans, the Greek government persisted in claiming that "the funds of the Commission were funds of the government" therefore should be subjected to the close supervision of the former.[56] Such disputes became most overtly pronounced during the conclusion of large-scale housing contracts involving the expenditure of these funds.[57] The controversy took the form of accusations by local Greek government officials directed at the field administrators, who were mainly Greeks. The latter were accused of corruption and many failings. Whether such accusations were prompted by the influence of private persons on ministers and high officials to obtain concessions and agreements in the housing projects cannot be verified on the basis of available documents. But the summer of 1925 attested to the proliferation of such attacks against the RSC on the ground that the Greek officials of the RSC had favored some of the contracting companies. What was then called the "Malama Affair," which almost brought to an end the RSC's operations, provides a good case in point.

Konstantinos Malamas, a private contractor, was hired to build a housing project of 3500–5000 houses for the refugees in Salonica. The houses built by this company became a major source of complaint among the refugees due to the inferior construction and the absence of basic sanitary facilities.[58] In response to complaints from the refugees, an inspector was immediately dispatched to oversee the situation in the mid-summer of 1925. Having conducted interviews with the refugees[59] the inspector reported that the project was useless in its entirety and that Malamas apparently obtained this contract through his connections in the RSC. The President of the Military Council, Pangalos, sent a telegraph to the Governor General of Salonica, stating that "this affair is related to the high interests of the state and the refugees. If there are any criminals, they will certainly be mercilessly punished by the application of very severe penalties which will be decided by pertinent decrees."[60] Some individuals and a high-ranking official of the RSC, namely Karamanos, who mediated between *Εταιρια*

Μαλαμα Εμμανουηλ and the RSC, were accused of bypassing the auction process and granting the contract to Malamas.

Four functionaries of the RSC, including Karamanos, were detained in August 1925 on charges of misuse and misappropriation of state funds allocated for the resettlement of the refugees. Two Greek members of the RSC subsequently resigned. The RSC raised the issue with the Council of the League of Nations, where the chairman of the RSC argued that such charges were motivated by the influence of people who were uncomfortable with the autonomous position of the RSC. After long discussions and deliberations, the Council not only issued a decision in favor of the RSC but also affirmed the autonomous status of this institution.[61] Thus the issue, which was covered widely in the leading newspapers of Europe at the time,[62] was finally settled by the Council of the League of Nations.[63] Eventually, two of the four detainees were acquitted and the other two were arrested. The most important result of this incident was that the work of the RSC was suspended for the period of the dispute and the vigor and dynamism that had characterized its resettlement efforts until then was replaced by caution and lethargy, causing, in turn, the slow progress of the resettlement process.

Despite accusations of fraud and cheating in the housing projects, the RSC had succeeded in settling 622,865 refugees (550,635 rural; 72,230 urban) by the middle of 1926.[64] The following year, it reported that 175,000 houses for the refugees had already been built or repaired and that it was planning to build an additional 42,000 houses although there was urgent need of almost 100,000 more in 1927. From 1928 to 1929, the RSC planned to build 3,398 additional rural dwellings for refugees mostly in Macedonia and 1,235 urban dwellings in 28 different cities and towns. By 1929, the RSC had succeeded in settling over half a million refugees primarily in the northern sections of the country.

The plight of the refugees could have plunged Greece into both political and economic chaos. This was prevented by the RSC and the methods it used to resettle the refugees. For the purpose of the current discussion, suffice it to mention the three major principles that underlined the workings of this institution during the process of resettlement. The first was the arrangement of the resettlement of refugees according to their urban and rural backgrounds;[65] the second was the resettlement of refugees from the same place of origin in the same area;[66] and the third was allowing the refugees "to establish themselves in three different communities on a trial basis before they were required to make a decision on where to settle permanently."[67] These three principles, which were absent in the Turkish case of resettlement, enabled at least a certain percentage of refugees to establish themselves in areas that suited their attributes. The first two were particularly important in terms of enabling the refugees to implant their communal organizations in various parts of Greece. Here the RSC's recognition of the powerful bond of religious association among the refugees, which was certainly existent among the Muslim refugees but ignored, played a significant role. As many studies have pointed out, many refugees, soon after their arrival, sought to locate their village priest before searching for their relatives. As Mears states, "many of the new towns in Macedonia, Thessaly, and Crete [became] merely transplanted replicas of the old Turkish communities, bearing the same name, and fathered by the same priest whom they had in Turkey."[68]

The farming villages of Asia Minor successfully reactivated their traditional dynamics and, preserving their old village name, came to reconstitute viable communities in a short period of time. In the same vein, refugees of urban background, who were resettled in the outskirts of Athens, renamed their districts such as Philadelphia (Akhisar), Nea Smyrni (Izmir) and Nea Amissos (Samsun). The same story holds true for northern Greece.[69] A glance at the map of Greece and more specifically the plans of Athens and Salonica suffices to confirm the point that Greece was, toponymically speaking, on the way to becoming a copy of Asia Minor.

The resettlement efforts of the RSC, when considered simply as the physical accommodation of the refugees, were a success story since the RSC managed to construct many settlement areas and resettle nearly the entirety of the refugee populations within a period of seven years. Nonetheless, it would be wrong to assume that the RSC achieved complete success in turning the refugees into producers during this period. By the time the first signs of the Great Depression appeared, these people had not yet built a foundation of human and material resources with which they could face the economic crisis. Many refugees in the countryside, who were unable to pay their remittances, began to migrate to the towns to "work as laborers, or if they were lucky, to set up a shop with the money they had gained from selling off land and farming equipment."[70] As the depression hit the urban centers, natives and the great majority of refugees, whether rural or urban, bowed to the price fluctuations and declining demand. Perhaps the most severely affected in this environment were the self-employed traders, peddlers and shopkeepers. Many in this group were refugees from Asia Minor, whose hopes for compensation for their abandoned properties were dashed with the conclusion of the Ankara Convention with Turkey. The signing of the Ankara Convention coincided with the abolition of the RSC and, thereafter, the Greek Ministry of Agriculture and the new Agricultural Bank took over its functions. The pending problems of the refugees became henceforward responsibility solely of the Greek government.[71]

MINISTRY OF EXCHANGE, RECONSTRUCTION AND RESETTLEMENT

The new Turkish state adopted without much modification most of the Ottoman institutions and practices that had been created in order to handle the refugee problem, which had existed since the last decades of the nineteenth century.[72] After the establishment of the provisional government in Ankara in 1920, the political leadership brought all these institutions and practices under a general directorate (*Muhacirin Müdüriyeti*) as a branch of the Ministry of Health and Social Welfare (*Sıhhıye ve Muavenet-i İçtimaiye Vekâleti*).[73] With the ratification of the Lausanne Treaty in August 1923, refugee affairs were entrusted to this general directorate that was to implement the provisions of the Convention through district refugee departments in all the major provincial centers.[74] However, before this directorate embarked on the creation of its offices, it was abolished, and a detailed plan was submitted by 134 deputies to the Turkish Grand National Assembly, envisaging the formation of a special ministry to administer and coordinate the transfer and relief of refugees, while entrusting provisioning and health-related services to the Red Crescent.[75]

The Ministry of Exchange, Reconstruction and Resettlement (*Mübadele, İmar ve İskân Vekâleti*), a highly bureaucratic body, was created on October 13, 1923 and the Law of Exchange, Reconstruction and Resettlement (*Mübadele İmar and İskân Kanunu*), which outlined the program of the ministry, was adopted by the Grand National Assembly on November 8, 1923.[76] The new ministry was charged with the transfer, shelter, provisioning, and resettlement of all existing and incoming refugees and other issues pertinent to the refugee problem, including the reconstruction of the country.[77] With a budget of 6,095,183 liras at its disposal,[78] the ministry initiated the establishment of local branches, called Commissions of Exchange, Reconstruction and Resettlement (*Mübadele, İmar ve İskân Komisyonları*). Each commission consisted of five officials: the highest administrative official (governor or *kaymakam*) to chair the commission, two officials to be appointed directly from the center and the other two to be appointed by the local administration.[79]

As soon as the decision to establish the ministry was made, certain newspapers drew attention to the belated realization of such a necessity by the government and stated that "while the refugees were flooding in bulk numbers, we do not believe that this ministry which will reconstitute itself, establish its machinery, elect its officials and organize its offices will succeed in dealing with such thorny and complicated issues as resettlement and reconstruction."[80] Other papers, however, published articles in support of the decision to establish such a ministry.[81] Amidst this controversy, Mustafa Necati [Uğural] Bey[82] was appointed as the first minister. He stayed in this position for four and a half months. Mustafa Celal [Bayar] Bey succeeded him, but held this office for only a few months (March 06, 1924—July 07,1924).[83] The last minister was Refet [Canıtez] Bey, whose term (July 07,1924—November 05,1924) witnessed the most heated debates about the poor performance of the ministry. At some point, the minister himself acknowledged the inefficiency of the work the ministry undertook. Refet Bey testified in one of his speeches before the Grand National Assembly that the frequent replacement of ministers certainly hampered the efficient working of this ministry.[84]

In October 1924, the deputy of Menteşe, Esat Bey, posed a question to the presidency of the Grand National Assembly on three major issues regarding the handling of the refugee affairs. These issues were: how many refugees have already arrived? how many of the refugees have already been resettled? and how much and in which regions has reconstruction been undertaken?[85] These questions, which were obviously intended to intimidate the government, were warded off by feeble explanations. In yet another session of Parliament, an Ali Şuuri Bey stated that the MERR had been involved more with the provisioning of local populations than in dealing with the resettlement of the "guests" (refugees).[86] Certain deputies argued that the MERR had been sending officials to regions that were not included in the resettlement plans and where there were, in fact, no refugees. In their view, the ministry had turned into a nursing home (*Vekâlet darülacezedir*).[87] As for the Red Crescent, which had been designated as the operational body of the MERR, the argument was that it was operating only in certain locations and where it was most needed; it had failed to establish its offices, and many refugees died of diseases.[88]

Attacks on the MERR intensified during the latter part of 1924. Abuses and misuses of authority associated with local branches of the ministry, especially in cities like Izmir and Samsun, were all too common a news item to contemporaries.[89] Government officials in charge of the distribution of abandoned properties, whether movable or immovable, were accused of favoritism, fraud, and embezzlement, which in turn contributed to the growing discontent among the refugees.[90] Especially in Izmir, the dimensions of the corruption can be traced through the press as well as through government orders that were issued one after another. There, the incoming refugees had found most of the houses assigned to them already occupied.[91] This discontent among the refugees sometimes manifested itself in acts of violence directed at officials in the short run[92] and, as will be discussed later, in the long run it was transformed into political opposition that found its expression in the quick rise of an opposition party, Free Republican Party (*Serbest Cumhuriyet Fırkası*), within the first decade of the population exchange.

During the first year of its existence, the MERR seems to have devoted most of its efforts and resources to the transfer of refugees at the expense of many other issues such as the control of abandoned properties and the proper allocation of these properties. As for the resettlement of the newcomers, the lack of coordination between the different government institutions made it quite difficult for the ministry to engage in prolonged, large scale operations that required planning, precision, and above all money. The problems associated with the working of the MERR provided certain members of the Grand National Assembly with ammunition to attack the government. A foreign observer of the situation, who was in Istanbul at the time, namely Maxwell H.H. Macartney, states that "as the immediate peril of war was over, the unity of front was quickly broken and an attack was launched against the cabinet. This attack took mainly the form of an onslaught upon the Ministry of Exchange and Reconstruction, and it was apparently regarded as a piece of superior parliamentary tactics that Ismet Pasha diverted the opposition from a series of attacks piecemeal against certain of the more unpopular ministries."[93]

When the MERR became the focus of attacks in Parliament,[94] the government resolved the problem by abolishing the whole institution, which had turned out to be a clerical rather than an executive body. It was abolished through a government resolution on November 3, 1924, and its functions were transferred to a directorate (*İskân Umum Müdürlüğü*) within the Ministry of Interior.[95] With the abolition of the MERR, the refugees gradually disappeared from the agenda of the Grand National Assembly and also as a subject of discussion in national newspapers. In 1930, the directorate was abolished and a small office was established under the General Directorate of Population Affairs (*Nüfus İşleri Genel Müdürlüğü*).[96] On February 1, 1931, the Turkish government issued a resolution for the abolition of all the practices concerning the exchange of populations and property allotment (*mübadele ve tevfiz muamelerinin intacı ve kati tasfiyesi*).[97] Thereafter, the government forwarded the petitions of refugees to the relevant ministries while certain refugees tried to use, without success, the mediation of the nearly defunct Mixed Commission to solve their problems.[98]

THE ISSUE OF FOREIGN LOANS

Preparing for war, waging it, and salvaging the resulting human and property wreckage absorbed an undue proportion of the available wealth of both the Ottoman Empire and Greece for a full decade. After the Balkan Wars, Greece faced its financial burdens by obtaining international loans and by issuing an abnormal amount of paper money, thus reducing the exchange value of the drachma and increasing the cost of living. Although Greece incurred little external debt after 1914, the internal debt of the country had increased enormously. The external debt of Greece at the end of 1923 was 1,641,407,532 drachmas ($316,792,000), while the internal debt amounted to about 2,863,000 gold drachmas plus 7,715,683,000 paper drachmas.[99] Under these circumstances, the economy of Greece was certainly not capable of handling, let alone absorbing, such vast numbers of penniless and destitute refugees.[100]

It was against this background that the Greek representatives in Lausanne, who recognized the heavy costs of both short-term and long-term resettlement, set out to secure a loan to facilitate the resettlement of the refugees as soon as the Convention was signed.[101] After long negotiations and inspections, and on condition that it would be used for the resettlement of refugees, Greece was granted a guarantee for the flotation of a loan by virtue of the Geneva Protocols, the related decisions of the League of Nations of September 29, 1923 and September 19, 1924, and the resolutions of the Hellenic Constituent Assembly of June 7, 1924 and October 24, 1924.[102] In this context, Greece secured a loan, which was called the "Seven Per Cent Greek Government Refugee Loan," amounting to 12,300,000 pounds to be distributed as follows: 7,500,00 pounds in London by English banks; 2,3000,000 pounds in New York by American banks; 2,500,000 pounds in Greece by Greek banks. A net amount of 10,000,000 pounds was immediately available.[103] As was previously mentioned, this loan played a crucial role in facilitating the work of the RSC and financing its large-scale resettlement projects.

Be that as it may, whether this loan was designated for humanitarian purposes has long been debated among Greek scholars.[104] That it was secured at an extremely high interest rate has prompted certain scholars to argue that this loan brought about the increasing domination of the Greek economy by foreign interests.[105] As early as 1929, criticizing the unfavorable terms of the loan, Stephen Ladas argued that Greece could have probably raised such a loan without the assistance of the League of Nations.[106] A relatively more recent study lists the concerns of the League of Nations behind its agreement to such a large loan. According to this list, the loan was floated with a view to putting an end to a potential ethnic conflict in the region by providing for the permanent settlement of the displaced populations. It is also stated that had Greece been left on its own, it would have faced a great economic disaster thereby endangering the prospects of a stable and lasting peace in the Balkans.[107] In this regard, the

Communists were prepared to take advantage of the vacuum. In the final analysis, this loan prevented Greece from plunging into further social and economic chaos while allowing Britain and the United States to establish their commercial interests in the area.[108]

Much like Greece, Bulgaria, which was also involved with large-scale refugee resettlement at the time, secured a loan of 3,325,000 pounds through the League of Nations for the purpose of resettling incoming refugees from Greece and Turkey. As for the Turkish side of the story, the question of foreign aid in the form of direct assistance or financial borrowing remains an enigma. The principal tendency among scholars of the early Republic is that the Turkish political leadership refrained from seeking foreign aid as it would run contrary to its fundamental principle of absolute independence.[109]

The new Turkish state inherited the legacy of the Ottoman Empire in the realms of financial capitulations and foreign debts. The newly established revolutionary government succeeded in defraying some of the debts in Lausanne but failed in most of its attempts to secure foreign aid or loans. Two missions which went to Paris and London in the aftermath of the Lausanne Conference to negotiate a loan were unsuccessful and Hamdullah Suphi, the Minister of Finance, reported in January 1924 that "there was very little chance of securing any loan either in Europe or in the United States, but that a substantial loan might be secured in South America, provided Turkey was willing to pay from 18 to 20% interest."[110]

In light of this information, Robert Gates, the former president of Robert College, argued at the time that no one considered the new state "economically viable" and that western public opinion was not convinced that Kemalist Turkey was a lasting phenomenon. The kinds of contacts Turkey established with the European states for a loan for the resettlement of refugees cannot be elucidated at least until the archives of the Turkish Ministry of Foreign Affairs are open to researchers. However, it is known that the estimated cost of the refugee settlement was about 20,000,000 liras for the year 1923 and that the government earmarked only 6,000,000 liras for such a draconian task. It may be concluded that the Turkish state relied solely on its own sources for the resettlement of refugees.[111] Under these conditions, having recognized the urgency of the situation, Mustafa Kemal issued a public proclamation in late 1923 calling on Muslim populations of the world to aid their Muslim brethren in Turkey. Having described the details of the situation, Mustafa Kemal stated in a highly religious tone,

> It is a great challenge to enable our Muslim brothers to reach the Turkish land, give an end to the suffering and misery of our brothers who

have families like we do and whose total numbers exceed 600,000. Brothers! Whatever means the Turkish government has at its disposal, these means are not sufficient enough. Anatolia proper, upon which the Greeks landed during the war, has been destroyed. The lands of our brothers, who have been victimized by the Greek passion of crime, have turned into ruins. Our brothers in religion! In order to reconstruct these places, to resettle these locations with the Muslims under the Greek administration who have to be urgently recovered from the deprivation and misery which they have suffered, to give bread to 600,000 people, the Turks appeal to the generosity of the world of Islam not to allow their brothers to perish owing to misery.[112]

This proclamation was followed by the dispatch of representatives of the Turkish Red Crescent to the capitals of various East Asian states in order to secure assistance for the refugees. The evidence suggests that the limited assistance that came from these locations was mainly in the form of food and clothes rather than money, which was certainly more needed than anything else at the time.

From the foregoing discussion on the institutional mechanisms involved in the implementation of the Convention, it can be concluded that the institutional arrangements at national and international levels were hardly conducive to the execution of the agreement. Where the Mixed Commission was concerned, this institution focused a major part of its work on registering refugees and issuing certificates verifying their refugee status. When the question of *établis* brought the process of population exchange nearly to a halt during late 1923, the Commission refocused its work on the resolution of this issue to the neglect of many other issues. Moreover, the Commission's decisions concerning such issues as the proper liquidation or restitution of the properties of non-exchangeable Greeks and Turks, who had vacated their settlements prior to the Convention, remained bound for the most part by the views of the respective governments. The Commission seems to have conducted no proper investigation of such issues. As many students of the population exchange argued later on, the Mixed Commission was, on the whole, a failure.

A similar story applied to the MERR. Its failure manifested itself concretely in its abolition within the first two years of its existence. This ministry envisaged at the outset an institutional set-up that required the integration of numerous existing refugee-related institutions and the establishment of new offices in the capital city and provinces. The prolongation of the structuring process, combined with the inefficiency of the officials and the absence of coordination between various institutions, resulted in the *ad hoc* implementation of the Convention and related official plans and projects for resettlement.

The RSC, on the other hand, whose work was plagued at the outset by the inability of the Greek government to expropriate large estates and to put them at the disposal of this institution, manipulated—thanks to the terms of the financial agreements—the support of the Greek government and succeeded in fully controlling the resettlement project. Although its work was occasionally handicapped by differences of opinion within the Greek government and the pressure from the refugees, the RSC managed to resettle nearly the entirety of the Greek refugees, rural and urban alike, before its abolition in 1930. Thus, the RSC appears to have been the only success story, albeit an ambiguous one, as far as the regimentation of the population exchange was concerned. It is this ambiguous success that has prompted many students of the population exchange to consider this event as a full-fledged success story and recite it as a precedent-setting event for resolving future conflicts of a similar nature.

Chapter Nine
Conclusion

The Convention of the Exchange of Populations was adopted with a view to removing minorities from their native lands with no concern on the part of the decision-makers as to the practical implications of such an arrangement. During the population exchange negotiations in Lausanne and their immediate aftermath, the efforts of the minority populations on both sides to evade the exchange proved unsuccessful on the whole. While it is true that a great number of Greeks in Asia Minor had already fled to Greece during the war, given the conditions under which they left their homes, these people were probably less concerned with the outcome of the diplomatic negotiations at Lausanne than with developing survival strategies or finding a way to move to the mainland. The importance of the population exchange negotiations was greater especially for the remaining Greeks and Muslims who had been either crammed in major port cities or stuck in the interior sections of Turkey and Greece, nourishing hopes for the reversal of the process; they were disillusioned with the final decision at Lausanne. Once the Convention was signed, the absence of concrete institutional and practical measures to provide for the transfer, relief and resettlement of the refugees enhanced the uncertainty of the situation and further contributed to the plight of the people subject to the agreement. Complicating this situation was also the vague language of the Convention that was used by the respective governments concerned with entangling "unwanted" minority groups, such as the Albanians in Greece and the Armenians and Assyrians in Turkey, with this agreement. Thus, this hastily formulated and adopted historical document not only engendered a difficult situation for the minority populations whose fates were at stake but also for the people who had no known relation to the decade-long military conflict that came to an end with the formulation and adoption of such a radical solution.

The majority of the Greek refugees, who had been uprooted from various parts of Asia Minor during the war, spent the whole year in refugee camps on the islands off the coast of Asia Minor and on the edges of major Greek cities. Many of those who lacked minimum means of subsistence remained dependent on relief agencies stationed in these locations where many perished owing to bad sanitary conditions. The conditions of reception and accommodation were certainly not better for the Greek refugees who were transferred according to the terms of the Convention. They too ended up in refugee camps on the outskirts of major Greek port cities where they were to stay for many months to come. As for the Muslim refugees, the great majority of whom had not yet been removed from their settlements when the Convention was signed, they were, relatively speaking, in a better situation as their transfer took place in accordance with the conditions prescribed by the Convention. Although their transfer was delayed due to prolonged transportation arrangements, the Turkish government eventually adopted a systematic program to provide for the efficient removal of these people from their locations. However, unlike the Greek refugees, whose relief was provided by a number of foreign agencies, the Muslim refugees were left for the most part on their own in meeting their basic needs. The Turkish Red Crescent, the only institutional arrangement in charge of Muslim refugee relief, was impeded in its effort by the limited funds at its disposal. Within a year, the remaining Greek and Muslim minority populations were uprooted from their respective home countries with a view to being resettled in their new countries.

The conditions of Greek refugees, whose plight was initially characterized by the most appalling war conditions, gradually improved during the process of resettlement due to the presence of an efficient institutional mechanism, namely the Refugee Settlement Commission. The pressure of this international institution on the Greek government for the reclamation of Muslim properties seized by the native populations and the implementation of the Land Redistribution Program combined with incoming foreign loans to facilitate the resettlement of Greek refugees. However, in the face of political instability in the country, the RSC acted in haste and prioritized the resettlement of refugees in a way that paid little attention to the social and economic aspects of the resettlement process. The ways in which the refugees were resettled both in urban and rural areas brought about their social isolation from established Greek society, a factor that would contribute to the growing hostilities between the natives and refugees.

The Muslim refugees, on the other hand, were greeted upon arrival in the ports with an air of official celebration but were soon left at the mercy of the age-old refugee bureaus which had recently been brought under the umbrella of a colossal administrative structure, namely, the Ministry of Exchange, Reconstruction and Resettlement. The continued onslaught by the local populations and, in some cases, by the government itself upon the abandoned properties of the Greeks, which had been presumably earmarked for the refugees, created an environment inconvenient for the implementation of the terms of the Convention, not to mention those of the plans and projects designed to resettle the refugee populations. Unlike the Greek case in which the enormity of the task in resettling the refugees by the RSC was caused primarily by the sheer size of the refugee population, the work of the MERR was plagued at the outset by the indifference of the Turkish government and later on by its inability to bring under control the abandoned properties upon which all the resettlement plans and projects were based. The Mixed Commission, in the meantime, failed to address the question of liquidating the properties left behind by the refugees and did not cooperate with Turkey and Greece for the proper indemnification of the refugees. All in all, the implementation of the Convention in Greece and Turkey did not take place in the manner anticipated by the decision-makers in Lausanne. Accordingly, the refugee problem in both cases turned out to be not really one problem, but literally scores of problems, each one having an importance and urgency of its own.

Nowhere was the inefficiency of the Convention more visibly marked than in the economic realm. During the opening speech of the discussions of the population exchange at Lausanne, Nansen had remarked that "such an exchange will provide Turkey immediately and in the best possible conditions with the population necessary to continue the exploitation of the cultivated lands which the departed Greek populations have abandoned."[1] He continued, "the departure from Greece of its Muslim citizens would create the possibility of rendering self-supporting a great portion of the refugees now concentrated in the towns and in different parts of Greece."[2] When the implementation of the Convention began, it became apparent that the majority of these lands had already been occupied by the local populations in both countries and the produce to benefit the displaced populations had already been harvested by the native populations in Greece and confiscated by the government in Turkey. The Muslim refugees were left for the most part with houses that had been destroyed and fields that had been burned. The immediate aftermath of the Convention was thus disastrous for both the Greek and Muslim refugees who were directed to these fields, which proved that the causation of Nansen was only a rhetorical device to facilitate the progress of the decision-making process.

Thanks to incoming foreign loans in the following years, the RSC took preliminary steps to turn the refugees in urban and rural areas into self-sufficient individuals by extending to them various kinds of loans. But the rural bias of this institution prevented a great number of refugees in urban areas from permanently resettling in these areas and caused them to move in bulk numbers to rural areas, a process soon to be reversed due to the changing world economic conjuncture. Many Greek refugees who went to the countryside with a view to benefiting from the Land Redistribution Program returned, in the face of diminishing future prospects, to the major Greek cities, becoming lumpen-proletariat or, at best, a source of cheap labor. The refugees who had been resettled originally in the rural sections of northern Greece seemed at the beginning to have benefited from the work of the RSC. The high interest rates on their debts (for housing) and their failure to pay their remittances gradually brought about their destitution as well.

In the meantime, diplomatic negotiations on the liquidation of the properties of these people in their country of origin proceeded at a slow pace, turning gradually into a zero sum game in which the governments of the two countries eventually agreed to waive the rights of the refugees to their properties. This development perhaps struck more dramatically the Muslim refugees, whose resettlement was subjected to the arbitrary policies of the government and undertaken with no recourse to a systematic economic plan or program. Many of the Muslim refugees who had secured a house and perhaps a plot of land waived their rights to their abandoned properties in Greece. In the final analysis, the Convention, which converted nearly two million people from minorities into refugees, scarcely turned these people into economically self-supporting individuals, as the decision-makers had anticipated, and numerous problems, mainly of socio-economic nature, cropped up and thwarted their integration into their new countries.

As for the social aspects of the exchange of populations in Greece and Turkey, at the beginning of the process there were no sharp social differences distinguishing the refugees from the native inhabitants of the areas where they were resettled. But the conflicting interests over the (re)allocation of limited resources soon led to the resurfacing of differences. Recent anthropological and political research in Greece on this particular issue has demonstrated that these differences between the local Greek population and incoming refugees took the form of social and cultural grievances. In the same vein, in Turkey, the limited information at our disposal reveals that the local populations received incoming refugees with much contempt and resentment especially in areas where the abandoned properties of the departed Greeks and Muslims were in abundance. The oral evidence suggests that the natives ridiculed their language, attire, and manners, and subjected the newcomers to a certain degree of discrimination. Under these circumstances, the predicaments of orientation and adaptation which originated as much from the refugees themselves as from the native residents of the areas where the former were resettled brought about the socio-economic marginalization of the refugee populations both in Greece and Turkey.

The misery and poverty that became so familiar to them from the early days of their arrival prevented Greek and Muslim refugees from nurturing the will to partake in the social and economic lives of their new countries. Accordingly, the refugees did not feel at home within the first decade of the population exchange and the majority of these people, whether Greeks or Turks, entertained hopes of returning to their former homes.[3] In the case of the Greeks, their hope of repatriation became manifested concretely in their petitions to the RSC in which they repeatedly brought up the question of "whether they would be permitted to reestablish themselves in their native soil."[4] As for the refugees in Turkey, the situation was apparently not much different, an issue that has only recently been documented on the basis of oral evidence.[5] Many Muslim refugees who were unable to obtain a piece of property and a suitable job or failed to adapt to the physical conditions of their new environment continued to frequent the local government offices in vain. The political leadership, preoccupied with a structural reform program, ignored such material problems of the refugees and even took measures to prevent them from organizing themselves in cultural associations where they could take refuge and redress piecemeal their psychological problems.[6]

Given this background, the political behavior and orientation of the refugees emerges as a crucial variable in the post-Lausanne era in Turkey and Greece, both of which experienced significant developments in their political systems after the population exchange. Both countries witnessed the transformation of their political regimes from a monarchy to a republic. The historical details of this process in which refugees came to play a significant role have been the subject of numerous studies in Greece. These studies have also addressed refugee participation in mass politics with due attention paid to the social and economic grievances between natives and refugees. As for Turkey, the political history of the Early Republican period has been one of the most studied subjects of modern Turkish history, but the refugees have been categorically left outside the scope of this historiography. The absence of relevant documentation, among other factors, has certainly prevented scholars from incorporating the refugees into the picture. But recently, some information obtained from local newspapers and oral sources has revealed that the refugees were also involved in politics upon their arrival and even came to play a significant role in the political life of the country during the late 1920s. The following discussion is intended to counterpoise the participation of refugees in the political life of Greece and Turkey for the period 1923–1933.

The refugees in Greece were involved with politics from the very beginning and their arrival significantly changed the political complexion of the country. Here, two major facts determined the political orientation of the refugees. If the first one was their resentment towards the political leadership, that is, the monarchy, the second was their uncourteous reception by the native populations, which soon led to an all-out conflict that manifested itself in the cultural, economic, and social realms. As Campbell and Sherrard argue, the great majority of refugees were convinced that King Constantine and the Populists were responsible for uprooting them from their homelands and their destitute situation since their landing in Greece.[7] Thus, most refugees supported Venizelos and his Liberal Party and hence Republicanism at least until the early 1930s when the Venizelist-Liberal policies succumbed to the effects of the Great Depression.[8] During this period, interrupted by several military coups, the refugees who succeeded in forming powerful pressure groups, thanks to the preservation of their communal ties, appeared as arbiters not only in the declaration of the Republic but also in the triumph of the Venizelist Liberal Party over the conservative Populist Party in several nationwide elections. In the short run, this support was recompensed in the form of benefits from the land redistribution program together with foreign loans[9]. When the Greek economy suffered a major setback in the late 1920s and the refugees were impeded by fiscal burdens, their support for Venizelos began to falter especially during the 1928–1932 period. In the general election of August 1928, the Venizelists received an overwhelming majority of the refugee votes despite their failure to cope with the effects of the Depression. The prime motive behind this support had, however, less to do with sympathy towards Venizelos than with the fear that the overtly anti-refugee Populist Party would have an opportunity to reclaim power.

Where the refugees were concerned, the only significant alternative political movement to the Liberal Party of Venizelos was the Greek Communist Party (KKE). From the very beginning, the refugees were exposed to the activities of the Greek Communists, who at the time focused their attention on the urban areas. As Angelos Elefantis points out, the Communists failed to attract a larger group of adherents, especially among the refugees, to their cause at the beginning due largely to the internal dissension within the Party.[10] The painstaking process that the refugees underwent during the first several years of the resettlement resulted in the drawing of a certain segment of the refugee electorate in rural sections of Greece to the KKE. Despite the overtly anti-Communist attitude of the official state, the

KKE succeeded in organizing itself in the refugee communities, especially in northern Greece. The tobacco fields provided the KKE with a large number of the supporters because the tobacco sector was the most underpaid sector and most suitable for organized reaction due to the nature of the work. The elections of 1926 introduced ten Communist deputies to the Greek Parliament, eight of whom were from refugee-dominated provinces.[11]

It would be wrong to assume, however, that the KKE established a solid stronghold among the refugees during the decade of the 1920s. According to Philip Carabott, "the adoption of a slogan for an independent Macedonia and Thrace in late 1924 severely damaged the KKE's public image and hindered its influence in inter-war politics and was largely responsible for the introduction of emergency legislative measure (*Ιδώνυμο*)—apart from claiming heavy casualties among its members."[12] A significant portion of the refugee electorate remained voters for the bourgeois parties of the Liberals and Republicans throughout the 1920s. It was only after 1930, when Venizelos adopted a more peaceful stance (rapprochement) towards Turkey and agreed to a diplomatic document transferring the rights of the refugees to their properties to the Turkish government, the refugee vote changed direction, largely towards the leftist track represented by the KKE, and to a limited extent, to the Populist Party which by then had begun to stand for the right of refugees to compensation. After the anti-Venizelists came to power in 1933, they adopted a hostile attitude toward the refugees especially in northern Greece, culminating in an open war against them after 1935.

Where the Turkish case is concerned, the political realm was under the monopoly of a single party that did not allow any alternative political movement to emerge and flourish. When the Convention was signed in Lausanne, the character of the Turkish regime was still blurry. According to Henry Morgenthau, who was carried away at the time by the intensive relations between Turkey and the Soviet Union, it appeared to be of a leftist orientation.[13] Be that as it may, once the Republic was declared, the ruling elite set out to carry on with a "national project" that aimed to mold the country's population, whether natives or refugees, into a socio-political framework that would support the ideals of the new nation-state. The implementation of this project took the form of (re)constructing a national identity based on a sense of territorial belonging rather than regional, communal, religious, linguistic, ethnic, or class affiliations. In this respect, the political leadership tended to pursue from the beginning a deliberate policy to suppress tendencies with a potential to threaten this project. Where the refugees were concerned, the leadership did not to allow those from the same place of origin to be resettled in the same area.[14]

Unlike the Greek refugees, the resettlement pattern of refugees in Turkey could not mirror their communal ties. Had it been otherwise, the refugees might have been able to act collectively in the face of rising predicaments. In times when the refugees felt the need to join forces and organize themselves into certain institutions[15], the government suppressed these tendencies either by restricting them from doing so from the beginning or by banishing them later when their voices became associated with opposition to the policies of the government. The Minister of Interior, Recep Bey, who also served as the acting minister of the MERR, made it clear in a speech to the Grand National Assembly on November 5, 1924 that "the organizations established by the refugees have been involved with political activities that harmed the image of the government and caused the rise of an anti-government sentiment throughout the country. These organizations have all been banned and abolished by the local government offices while their leaders have been forwarded to the pertinent courts."[16] He concluded his speech by remarking that he had "already prepared a document to totally ban such tendencies which aim [at] nothing but the polarization of the country."[17] Given the fact that the political elite in the country was not concerned with the electoral constituency, the refugees, much like the great majority of the population, were to remain passive observers of the political life in the so-called National Assembly for a long time to come. As a matter of fact, my own research over the years has not uncovered any traces of a politically active refugee organization in Turkey from 1924 to 1933.

Thus, in complete contradistinction to Greece, the political framework in Turkey, dominated by the Republican People's Party, did not permit the establishment of opposition parties, with the exception of the short-lived Progressive Republican Party (*Terakkiperver Cumhuriyet Fırkası*) in 1924–25,[18] and all channels for political representation (including the MERR) were closed to incoming refugees. This policy prevented the refugees from carrying their discontent onto the political platform. The very scanty information on hand suggests that some of the labor-intensive agricultural sectors, such as tobacco production, witnessed growing organizational efforts on the part of agricultural and factory workers of refugee background to join various unions in cities such as Samsun, where a sizeable refugee population existed. In this city, the great majority of refugees had come from northern Greece and more specifically from Kavala, where strikes and organized labor protests had been a common occurrence during the 1910s. Here, refugees seem to have led tobacco workers in the unionization movement.

However, collective attempts among the workers seem to have been prompted not so much by political concerns as by certain practical reasons, such as low wages and unfavorable working conditions. For example,

Zehra Kosova, a veteran socialist, mentions that after a tobacco-processing factory in Samsun was shut down by the government, the workers (most of whom were from Kavala) appealed to the local administration for the resumption of tobacco labor in Tokat. On another occasion, the tobacco workers went on strike due to low wages. Kosova also mentions that "the factory was closed for two days and the third day the overseer went to the coffeehouse frequented primarily by refugees and offered the workers a wage of 15 *kurush* per day. The workers accepted this offer and resumed work."[19]

The active involvement of the refugees in politics began with the establishment of the Free Republican Party (*Serbest Cumhuriyet Fırkası*; FRP) in the early months of 1930. The discussions at the time about the foundation of the FRP can be found in many publications,[20] but these studies hardly touch upon the composition of the populace that supported this party. A recent study argues that the FRP received mass support, especially in areas where the majority of the population was of refugee background.[21] This is not at all surprising as many refugees were still frequenting the doors of local government offices for the definite title deeds to their properties. Those who had secured title deeds faced significant challenges posed, if not by the worsening economic conditions, by the claims of the local populations.[22]

Around the turn of the decade, many refugees who were hit hard by the Great Depression and still lacked the title deeds to their lands expressed their resentment by registering in the lists of the local branches of the FRP.[23] Among them were many peasants, whether of refugee background or otherwise, whose credit applications had been turned down by the state-owned Agricultural Bank (*Ziraat Bankası*) and who began to feel that the government had abandoned them. Needless to say, western Anatolia became the stronghold of the party, especially Izmir where the party branches were opened one after another in the districts of Karşıyaka, Bornova, Seydiköy, Değirmendere, and Cumaovası.[24]

Public discontent with the policies of the ruling government was echoed particularly in the speeches of Fethi Okyar, the founder of the FRP. When he arrived in Izmir before the municipal elections of September 1930, the people received him in large numbers with slogans like "*Kahrolsun mutemetler, yaşasın serbest ülke!*" (To hell with the officials, long live the free country!).[25] The FRP participated in the municipal elections of 1930 in 37 provinces and emerged victorious in three major cities with large refugee populations, namely, Izmir, Aydın and Samsun.[26] In addition, the FRP triumphed in the refugee-settled regions of Thrace and Marmara. But much like the earlier PRP, the FRP, turned out to be an abortive development as it was closed down by the orders "from above." The seed of opposition implanted in the country's population, especially among the refugees, resurfaced in the course of time as the Turkish experience with multi-party system was reinstituted in late 1946. The majority of agricultural producers, among whom were people of refugee background, supported the Democratic Party.[27]

In the final analysis, it is our contention that the Exchange Convention was equally a landmark event in the modern histories of Turkey and Greece. As an arrangement that was unplanned on the part of political leadership, unwanted on the part of minorities, and merely tolerated on the part of the League of Nations, this diplomatic agreement, which was unprecedented in terms of its compulsory character, sanctioned the uprooting of nearly two million people from their native lands. The inefficiency of the hastily formulated and adopted diplomatic document was bound to create numerous predicaments that would impede the processes of reception, resettlement, rehabilitation, and integration of these people in their receiving states and societies during the post-Lausanne era. In Greece, the relative flexibility of the political system enabled the refugees to voice their concerns more effectively and negotiate the terms of their integration into the national framework. In Turkey, the fact that the populism of the Republican People's Party was embedded in the rationale of "for the people" and never "by the people" turned the refugees into a silent crowd to be integrated into the system according to the terms of the political leadership.[28] It is this particular fact that suppressed the voices of Muslim refugees in Turkey and distinguished their trajectory from that of their counterparts in Greece.

Epilogue

From the moment it was signed at Lausanne on January 30, 1923, the Convention concerning the Exchange of Greek and Turkish Populations has been the subject of much rhetorical explanation and misinterpretation. Characterized primarily by the disregard of the actual effects of this arrangement upon the people and the absence or on-behalf representation of the Turkish component in the whole discussion, these tendencies generated a conventional view of this event that is blatantly unbalanced if not altogether misrepresentative. As was discussed in the opening sections of this book, these tendencies were associated largely with two distinct strands of scholarship that appropriated this historical event in accordance with their driving motives. On the one hand, a policy-oriented scholarship that emerged and flourished in Europe and the United States during the inter-war era attempted to sanction the exchange of populations as an instrument for solving inter-state disputes and settling minority problems under the aegis of an international organization (i.e., the League of Nations). On the other hand, a highly politicized, not to say markedly nationalistic-minded, Greek scholarship hastened to read this tragic occurrence into the existing narrative of the Greek nation. Whereas these two strings of thought remolded the subject into their working agendas and engendered the conventional view of this event, the nascent Turkish national historiography indifferently left the subject outside the scope of the newly written biography of the Turkish nation-state. The conspicuous absence of the subject in the general framework of Turkish national history should also be interpreted as yet another form of representation, especially in view of the recently emerged interest, both popular and academic, in the subject.[1] These observations upon the representation of the Exchange in various scholarly traditions provided the historiographical background against which this book was conceived and the established view of this event was exposed to a critical assessment on factual and theoretical grounds.

The principal point of convergence in the international and Greek scholarly traditions has been the tendency to represent the Turco-Greek Exchange of Populations as an abstraction in which this event is treated simply as a reported fact with little or no concern on the part of scholars with its actual ramifications on the ground. As early as the first decade of the Exchange, international students of the subject vehemently argued that such an agreement enabled the principal parties, namely Turkey and Greece, to settle their grievances by way of eradicating their respective minorities as a major potential for conflict. The removal of the minority populations on both sides not only drastically improved the conditions of national security but also brought about the ethnic homogenization of the countries concerned. These two goals were then deemed crucial to the fulfillment of a universal objective, namely the promotion of the nation-state as the ultimate unit of political organization. Furthermore, in the attainment of these goals, these studies tended to emphasize the role of the international community, represented then by the supranational organization of the League of Nations, and neglect the role of the Turkish and Greek states.

The direct involvement of the League of Nations in the regimentation of the Exchange through a Mixed Commission, and the resettlement of the Greek refugees through the establishment of an autonomous institution, namely, the Greek Refugee Commission, and the floatation of various foreign loans to finance the large-scale resettlement projects of the Greek state were all underlined with a view to serving two major purposes. If the first one was to depict the Turco-Greek Exchange with an emphasis on its compulsory character and provisions of resettlement as a workable solution to be applied to minority problems elsewhere, the second had to do with the forging of a history to sanctify the emergence of an international refugee regime.

The first goal was served several times during the interwar period. The method of exchange, as internationally sanctioned by the success story of the Turco-Greek experience, was adopted as a legitimate instrument to get rid of unwanted minorities and achieve ethnic homogeneity either by political regimes that had severed their ties with the international community or by political organizations such as the Zionist Jewish Agency that attempted to consolidate the territorial and demographic foundations of a National Jewish Home. Ironically, in none of these cases did the League of Nations or its refugee-related body seem to have been directly involved. It was only at the end of WWII that the peacemakers at Postdam cast their eyes back to the successful (i.e., internationally sanctioned) precedents of 'ethnic unmixing' and applied their derivatives upon the war-torn sections of Europe, more particularly the formerly German-occupied areas.

Although ethnic motives behind territorial disputes were replaced by ideological ones during the post-WWII era, international scholarship retained the Turco-Greek Exchange of Populations in its agenda and continued to quote it as a successful precedent for settling territorial conflicts involving minority problems. The most influential text on the Turco-Greek Exchange of Populations, Pentzopoulos' dissertation[2], was written in the early 1960s, when a border crisis involving minority problems emerged between Greece and Yugoslavia, on the one hand, while the Turco-Greek dispute over the island of Cyprus gained a serious dimension, on the other.

Fortunately, neither of the above crises necessitated the implementation of large-scale population displacements through the exchange. Nor did any other dispute of the next three decades, perhaps with the exception of the Turco-Greek agreement on the divided Cyprus, furnish the decision-makers with the grounds to appeal to such a solution with appalling consequences for the people. The vigorous debut of the subject in the agenda of world diplomacy, however, took place in the early 1990s when ideological friction was substituted once again by ethnic and religious cleavages *à la mode Européenne* in the Balkans and the Middle East. Then the success paradigm associated with the Turco-Greek experience and identified by the term the "Lausanne principle" resurfaced in the political rhetoric and the discourse of policy-oriented scholarships. Strangely enough, the international community, represented by the post-WWII organizations of the United Nations and its refugee-related body, UNHCR, which had once championed the option of exchange as a viable policy to handle ethnic or religious conflicts, now moved on to condemn such practices.[3]

Although the resistance of the international community to partition and ethnic unmixing, especially in Croatia, Bosnia, and Kosova, took its toll on tens of thousands of people, the decisive stand taken by the international community has prevented the return of the exchange as a legitimate instrument to redress conflicts of ethnic and religious nature. One may argue that the adoption of such a measure might have prevented mass killings and deportations in the Balkans, (in the Caucasus, for that matter) and, more specifically, it might have saved the lives of 7000 Muslims near the town of Srebrenica in July 1995 or thwarted the human and material losses of hundreds of Serbs who were driven from their homes during two days of rioting in Kosova in spring 2004. That might have been the case. But one should never forget that the temptation of using a legitimate instrument, such as the Turco-Greek Exchange Convention, to get rid of unwanted peoples is an integral part of the mental make-up of many policy makers around the globe. After all what the Turkish and Greek diplomats did at Lausanne under international tutelage was to opt for the easy way out and solve an intractable dispute over territory by partitioning the disputed area and compelling everybody on the "wrong side" of the newly drawn line to move, until boundaries and ethnic groups coincided perfectly. Only a simple glance at the unfolding of the events in different regions of the world from Kashmir to Palestine and the Caucasus to Sri Lanka, not to mention Modern Turkey, would suffice to show that such an instrument has already much appeal to power-mongers, be they military or civilian.

As the recent history of the Balkans shows, the reaffirmation of the principles of the Helsinki agreements is an imperative: that countries must respect the human and cultural rights of their citizens, including minorities; and at the same time states must respect each other's borders or at least avoid imposing boundary changes by force. Accordingly the decision-makers should dispel the phantom of the Turco-Greek Exchange Convention once and for all.[4] This is at least what many scholars, studying the past occurrences of ethnic conflicts and refugee generating phenomena, have been laboring to attain by drawing their attention away from the interests of the nation-state (e.g., security) to the human rights dimension of such historical occurrences.[5] It would not be wrong to state that thanks to the arduous efforts of these scholars, earlier tendency to abstract the Turco-Greek Exchange of Populations from its actual context and portray it as a diplomatic instrument has been recently replaced by a more realistic conception of this phenomenon. Admittedly, there is a long way to go before this notion becomes firmly entrenched in international scholarship. That aspiration is probably more applicable to the representation of this event at domestic level.

From the moment of its signature, the representation of the Exchange in the Greek scholarship has been the subject of a double-edged interpretation. While its occurrence was considered as a tragedy to be endured by the Greek society, the successful handling of this draconian challenge by the Greek state was regarded as a testimony to the vitality of Greek statecraft. The tragic dimension of the story was effectively incorporated into the political rhetoric and historical discourse with a view to being "remembered" in pertinence to the ideological goals of the political leadership. More often than not, it was the success paradigm attributed to the role of the Greek state in the handling of such a huge influx of refugees in a short period of time that became largely identified with the Exchange in historical writings.

Under the dictating effects of these tendencies, the study of the Exchange with its causes and consequences has been the subject of much distortion. Where the genesis of this phenomenon was concerned, it was resonated as the inevitable outcome of a failed military campaign, namely the Asia Minor Catastrophe, due mainly to the withdrawal of the Great Powers' support, with no reference to the irredentist and expansionist ambitions of Greek political leadership behind this assault. A compulsory exchange of populations was dictated by the Turks and accepted by the Greeks at Lausanne since such an agreement befitted the then prevalent conditions, not to mention the long-term interests of the Greek state. After all, this decision meant but the formalization of a *de facto* situation. A great number of Greek populations in Anatolia and eastern Thrace had moved to Greece during the last stages of the war (especially during the Turkish recapture of Izmir) and the Turkish nationalists under the leadership of Mustafa Kemal would not permit the repatriation of displaced Greek populations.

This verdict of the Exchange deliberately neglects to recount the Greek position at Lausanne which, as Chapter Two of this study showed, was characterized from the very outset by a tendency to conclude a compulsory agreement owing to certain concerns of Greek political leadership over domestic and foreign affairs of the country. Some of those concerns were certainly embedded in the consequences of the recently concluded war with Turkey. They also included, among others, the urgency of the long-neglected economic and social problems of the country as well as the ever-growing schism between the Venizelists (Liberals) and anti-Venizelists (Royalists) on the political arena, not to mention the increasing leverage of the communists. Furthermore, as Petropoulos has effectively argued, the political leadership had realized the long-term importance of foreign assistance to be secured for the resettlement of refugees.[6] Such a financial scheme could be used as part of a broader project to reconstruct economically and demographically the war-torn country.

At a more specific level and closely linked with the consequences of the war, there were certain "accomplished facts" from the Greek point of view that laid down the foundations of a compulsory exchange. Of those facts, the irreversible character of the efforts of the Greek government to evacuate the Greek populations from Anatolia and eastern Thrace prior to and during the Lausanne negotiations should be given a fair consideration. By the time the Lausanne talks began, most of the Greek populations had already been removed from their locations and some of them had even been herded to the heavily Muslim-populated northern sections of the country for resettlement. Given the conditions under which these people left their homes, the option of repatriation, so emphasized by the traditional scholarship, was merely a rhetorical device used by the Greek diplomats to increase their negotiating strength at Lausanne.

The Greek position at Lausanne should also be evaluated against the backdrop of the activities of the Greek populations, whether natives or refugees, and the army towards the Muslim populations and properties in northern Greece, including Western Thrace, during the period of the Lausanne negotiations. As recent research has ably demonstrated, the conditions of Muslim populations and properties in these regions certainly did not lag behind those of their Greek counterparts in Turkey during the war and after. The last critical point on the representation of the role of the Greek decision-makers at Lausanne is related with the entanglement of Karamanlides, the last group of Greeks to be evacuated from Turkey, in the whole scheme of the Exchange. Even a cursory reading of the Lausanne minutes suffices to show that the Turkish diplomats were inclined to leave this community of nearly 200,000 people out of an exchange agreement. It was with the intervention of the head of Greek plenipotentiaries, namely Venizelos, that the Karamanlides were incorporated, first into the draft treaty and then in the final agreement.

The representation of the Exchange in Greek scholarship is even more problematic in explaining the aftermath of the phenomenon. It is doggedly argued that the execution of the Exchange Convention was carried out successfully by the Greek state. Although refugees suffered numerous predicaments along the way, the long-term advantages of such an arrangement were praised to have far outweighed its short-term disadvantages. After all, such an arrangement brought in its wake the safety of the northern borders of the country, on the one hand, and accounted for its ethnic and national homogenization, on the other. Furthermore, the refugee input into the Greek economy in the form of industrial workforce and the expansion of the domestic market was coupled with foreign loans floated at the time to boost the country's economy. Thus, in the final analysis, the standard Greek explanation on the consequences of the Exchange reciprocated that of the international scholarship on the subject.

Needless to say, the emphasis of domestic scholarship on various aspects of the event showed some slight variations. In this regard, certain scholars of refugee backgrounds moved the attention away from the virtues of the Greek state to the contributions of refugees to the wholesale reconstruction and economic development of Greece. Others of anti-Western opinion focused their attention on the genesis of the Exchange and accused the Great Powers of withdrawing their support during the war with Turkey and even lending support to the latter, causing the Greeks to lose the war, thus paving the way to the Exchange. Notwithstanding these slight differences in opinion, the double-edged tendency to identify the source of the Exchange with the Turkish political leadership as well as to underscore in a highly selective fashion the consequences of this event for the Greek state, society, and economy held its sway over eighty years of Greek historiography on the Exchange.

In recent years, the topic of the Exchange, like many other subjects of modern Greek history, has taken its share from the emerging revisionist trends in Greek historiography. The biases and deficiencies in the conventional representation of the Exchange by mainstream Greek scholarship have been promptly attacked and in some cases significantly revised by new waves of scholarship. Several scholars have dealt with the consequences of the Exchange upon the political, social and economic conditions in Greece and, more particularly, concerned themselves with the people, namely the refugees, whose lives were radically altered due to this event. They have documented and analyzed the life-worlds of refugees and amply demonstrated that a major segment of refugee populations was hardly integrated to the established Greek society and the quandary of refugees lasted in the face of native reactions at least until the aftermath of WWII (i.e., the Civil War), if not later. As for the contributions of refugees to the economic development of the country, it was argued that many refugees became a source of cheap labor to be widely exploited upon their arrival by the industrialists and even by the Greek state. The resettlement projects, highly appraised by international and national scholarships, not only failed to accommodate most of the Greek refugees according to their social and economic traits but also came to foster their differences with the larger Greek society. These settlements, both urban and rural, quickly turned into isolated locations where a great portion of the refugees failed to relate themselves to the rest of Greek society and economy. These circumstances led to the social and economic marginalization of most refugees, a process to be precipitated further under the effects of the Great Depression. In addition, certain scholars have also demonstrated that there were major differences amongst the refugees themselves that was reflected in the political process during the inter-war era and even during the Greek Civil War.[7]

With all the points recounted above, the revisionist scholarship modified the standardized account of the Exchange and its consequences upon Greece. The twin myths of ethnic and national homogeneity, which had dominated the existing Greek view of the Exchange, have thus come under severe criticism and revision. Despite all these developments, however, it would be wrong to conclude that the conventional view of the Exchange has been totally discredited in Greece. Like many other historical events of modern Greek history, which have been politicized through the combined efforts of politicians and historians, the unbalanced representation of the

Exchange continues to dominate many historical writings and its political and national use to vilify Turkey remains in effect.

In the midst of an utterly generalizing international scholarship and highly involved and parochialist Greek domestic scholarship, the Turkish dimension of the Exchange has been rendered nearly obsolete in the conventional narratives of the subject. This monolithic tendency was buttressed from the very outset by the indifferent approach of the Turkish national historiography to the event. Like many historical developments behind the making of the Turkish nation-state, the Exchange could not secure itself a place in the newly written biography of the Turkish nation. The new political leadership tended to "forget" many historical occurrences that they considered irrelevant or potentially threatening to their national project. The adoption of religion as the principal criterion for the exchange might have been considered quite incompatible with the secular vision of the political leadership. In addition, the differences between the incoming refugees and the native populations were not so easily reconcilable given the fact that religion–upheld as a unifying device during the war—was discredited as a baseline for national unity. Perhaps more importantly, the revolutionary leadership adopted a commanding attitude on the 'imagination' and imposition of a national identity that would unify the populations on the basis of common ethnicity and territorial belonging. These concerns figured prominently in the identity politics of the ruling elite and underscored the template of national history. Needless to say, such concerns brought about the exclusion of historical occurrences, such as the Exchange, from the newly reconstructed "History of the Turkish Revolution." The silence of the Turkish historiography on the Exchange has in turn contributed to the reinforcement of the unbalanced representation of this event recounted above, in which the Turkish role in the decision-making process as well as the implementation of the Exchange Convention, more particularly in the resettlement of the incoming refugees, have been subjected to overt generalizations and unfounded assumptions.

Regrettably, the recently emerged domestic interest in the Exchange that attempted to document and examine the Turkish side of the decision-making process and the state of Turkish refugees has tended to adopt the traditional views of the subject.[8] As far as the decision making process goes, Turkish scholars have reciprocated the mainstream Greek view and taken pride in the imposition of such an arrangement upon Greece or depicted this arrangement, in line with the conventional view of this event, as a way to prevent the involvement of the 'foreign finger' in the internal affairs of Turkey. The very nationalism of Turkish political leadership, held accountable for the creation of conditions that necessitated the adoption of the

Exchange, turned into a source of pride. These scholars amply brought to the fore the Greek motives behind the expansion into and annexation of certain parts of Anatolia and the atrocities committed by the Greek army but deliberately ruled out the reciprocating tendencies on the part of Turkish leadership and populations towards the native Greek populations of Anatolia and Thrace.

This study has not been concerned so much with these highly politicized issues as they require a more in-depth analysis of the social, economic, political and military conditions of the respective geographies and the contents of the respective ideologies prior to the Lausanne Peace Settlement. It has been generally argued, however, that the century-long Greek nationalism took on a new, this time, irredentist turn after the Balkan Wars. On the other hand, the full-fledged demise of Ottomanism in the wake of the Balkan Wars paved the way for the genesis of Turkish nationalism. These two competing nationalisms inadvertently nurtured one another over the following decade. As the respective minorities were effectively integrated with the nationalist agendas on both sides, the fate of these populations was made strictly contingent upon the working-out of the rivalry between these two nationalisms. It is true that the realization of the Exchange Project owes much to the mediation of the Great Powers and such a development was part and parcel of a long historical process on a world scale, namely the ascendancy of nationalism and the nation-state. However, the creation of the conditions behind this project cannot be fully understood without a thorough and unbiased examination of the agendas and activities of the Greek and Turkish nationalisms.

Nowhere has the conventional representation of the Exchange been more problematic than in the assessment of the consequences of this event for the Turkish refugees and the role attributed to the Turkish state in the resettlement of the displaced populations. In the absence of a related-Turkish historiography and in the light of the quantitative dimensions of this event, the resettlement of Turkish refugees was considered to have posed, on the whole, no challenge to the Turkish side as the abandoned properties of the Greeks and other minorities were supposed to have been sufficient for the resettlement of a relatively small number of incoming Turkish refugees. This assumption has been effectively integrated into the success paradigm associated with the aftermath of the Exchange. We contended this particular dimension of the success paradigm and showed that the Turkish political leadership addressed the question from the very beginning in an *ad hoc* manner, and the arbitrary policies of the ruling government on the abandoned properties and the resettlement of refugees caused the Turkish refugees to experience enormous difficulties. Therefore, the explanation for the omission of the Exchange from the general framework of Turkish official history should not only be sought in the identity politics of the nascent Turkish state but also in the concrete historical developments surrounding the implementation of the Exchange Convention in Turkey. This major correction to the conventional view of the Exchange as a successful undertaking complements the emergent critical view of this event in Greek scholarship. Undoubtedly, the grounding in general historiography of a more realistic conception of this event along the above lines hinges on the deconstruction of the underlying motives behind the representation of the Exchange as an abstract phenomenon. Perhaps only when the Exchange is viewed not only as a reported fact but also as a multi-faceted historical reality, diplomats as "the predilect agents of history"[9] will not turn a resolutely deaf ear to the voices of the displaced.

Notes

NOTES TO THE NOTE ON DATES

1. Greece officially shifted from the Julian calendar to the Gregorian calendar on March 1, 1923. For a brief overview of the political debate on the calendar shift in Greece see, Αλκης Ρηγος, *Η Β' Ελληνικη Δημοκρατια, 1924–1935, Κοινωνικες Διαστασεις της Πολιτικης Εκηνης*, 2nd Edition, (Athens: ΘΕΜΕΛΙΟ, 1992) 215–216.
2. The Ottoman Empire integrated the monthly aspects of the Gregorian (*Miladi*) calendar to the fiscal calendar on February 13, 1917 to take effect on March 1, 1917 while the new Turkish state fully adopted the Gregorian system on December 26, 1925 to be implemented from January 1, 1926.
3. Two reference works were used throughout this study for conversion between various calendar systems in Ottoman and Turkish documents: Faik Reşit Unat, *Hicri Tarihleri Miladi Tarihe Çevirme Kılavuzu* (Ankara: Türk Tarih Kurumu Basımevi, 1988); Gazi Ahmet Paşa, *Takvimü's Sinin*, eds. Y. Dağlı and H. Pehlivanlı (Ankara: Genelkurmay Başkanlığı, 1993) (originally published in 1331 [1915])

NOTES TO THE INTRODUCTION

1. This date must have been written according to the 'old' (i.e., Julian) calendar, which corresponds in the 'new' (i.e., Gregorian) calendar to September 03, 1922, a Sunday. This date also coincides with the military developments that led to the recapture of Izmir by the Turkish forces. See Gotthard Jaeschke, *Türk Kurtuluş Savaşı Kronolojisi, Mondros'tan Mudanya'ya Kadar (30 Ekim 1918–11 Ekim 1922)* (Ankara: T.T.K. Basımevi, 1989) 190–192.
2. This incident is reconstructed on the basis of data from my interviews with local villagers in and around Izmir. Those which were particularly valuable were my interviews with the old time residents of the villages within the municipal borders of Menemen and Yeni Foça. I visited the Archives of the Center for Asia Minor Studies in Athens to crosscheck the information about this specific incident. But this location, which contains thousands of

files of interviews conducted with people from almost all the settlements in Asia Minor, did not have any file under the heading of Κοζμβεϊλη. See the catalogue of the Center's archival collections, Κεντρο Μικρασιατικων Σπουδων, *Ο Τελευταιος Ελληνισμος της Μικρας Ασιας, Εκθεση του Εργου του Κεντρου Μικρασιατικων Σπουδων (1930–1973), Καταλογος* (Athens: Εκδοσεις του Κεντρου Μικρασιατικων Σπουδων, 1974). The only information concerning this small village is found in the Historical Archives of the Greek Ministry of Foreign Affairs (from now on AYE which stands for Ιστορικο Αρχειο του Υπουργειου Εξωτερικων της Ελλαδας), 1925-B/40, I. See the table "Στατιστικος Πιναξ των Εκκλησιων και Σχολων της Επαρχιας Εφεσου Εξηγμενος εκ των μεχρι του Ετους 1914." In this table, the population of the village is given as 145 before the year 1914.

3. The tellers of the latter story were two sisters who have been living together since they moved to Turkey with their family due to the population exchange. Both were school age at the time of the Exchange. They both died shortly after my interview. The narration of their experiences exemplifies at its best the endurance of historical memory and the length of time which individuals associate themselves with events which occurred during their childhood. In this specific case, the duration covers approximately 70 years. See Tamara Hareven, "The Search for Generational Memory," in *Oral History, An Interdisciplinary Anthology*, eds. David K. Dunaway and Willa K. Baum, 2nd Edition (Walnut Creek, London and New Delhi: Altamira Press, 1996) 241–256.

4. For a comprehensive survey of the political developments in the Balkans during the first decades of the century, see Lord Courtney Penwith, *Nationalism and War in the Near East* (Oxford: Clarendon Press, 1915) 251–291; R. W. Seton-Watson, *The Rise of Nationality in the Balkans* (New York: E. Dutton and Company, 1918) passim. Fikret Adanır gives a summary of the nationalist movements in the Balkans with emphasis on the role of the élites in his "The Macedonians in the Ottoman Empire, 1878–1912," in *The Formation of National Elites: Comparative Studies on Governments and Non-Dominant Ethnic Groups in Europe, 1850–1940*, ed. A. Kappeler (in collaboration with F. Adanır and Alan O'Day), vol. 6 (Dartmouth: New York University Press) 161–191, especially 170–181.

5. A. A. Pallis, "The Exchange of Populations in the Balkans," *The Nineteenth Century and After*, 47:576 (February 1925) 2. For the broader implications of this policy upon the Ottoman minorities, especially Armenians, see Fikret Adanır and Hilmar Kaiser, "Migration, Deportation, and Nation-Building: The Case of the Ottoman Empire," in *Migrations et Migrants dans une Perspective Historique. Permanences et Innovations*, ed. René Leboutte (Brussels: Peter Lang, 2000) passim.

6. Enver Paşa openly said this to Henry Wood, staff correspondent for the United Press Association in Istanbul. "When Turkey last September abolished the capitulations which had been imposed on her for years past principally by the very powers who say that they are now fighting to establish an independent government for each people, we were for the first time in years in complete control of the administration of our own affairs and our

own government. It is as much for that independence as it is for our continued existence as a nation that we are now fighting and shall continue fighting to the end. We want *a Turkish Empire for the Turks and by the Turks* [my italics]. That is our idea of independence." "Interview With His Excellency, Enver Pasha, Minister of War and Vice-Generallissime of the Ottoman Army and Navy," The Library of Congress, the Papers of Henry Morgenthau, Reel 39/41, 3.

7. Ahmed Emin [Yalman], *Turkey in the World War* (New Haven: Yale University Press, 1930) 189–193. Hüseyin Cahit [Yalçın], *Siyasal Anılar* (Istanbul: İş Bankası Kültür Yayınları, 1976) 43–44. An ardent supporter of Ottomanism, Abdullah Cevdet, admitted the failure of this ideology during this period. See Şükrü M. Hanioğlu, *Bir Siyasal Düşünür Olarak Doktor Abdullah Cevdet ve Dönemi* ([Istanbul]: Üçdal Neşriyat, 1981) 216–219. For the political developments that underlined the failure of Ottomanism, see Adanır and Kaiser, "Migration, Deportation, and Nation-Building," 273–292.

8. Şükrü Hanioğlu has thoroughly examined the ideological course of the Young Turk movement and its political offshoot, namely the Committee of Union and Progress (CUP). See his *The Young Turks in Opposition* (New York: Oxford University Press, 1995) 213–216. Also by the same author *Preparation for a Revolution: The Young Turks, 1902–1908* (New York: Oxford University Press, 2000) 34–46. Cf. Kemal Karpat, *The Politicization of Islam: Reconstructing Identity, Faith and Community in the Late Ottoman State* (New York: Oxford University Press, 2001) 353–373.

9. For a general idea of the composition of the Ottoman Parliament during this era, see Feroz Ahmad and D. A. Rustow, "İkinci Meşrutiyet Döneminde Meclisler, 1908–1918," *Güney Doğu Avrupa Araştırmaları Dergisi*, 4/5 (1976) 250–283. For the Greek representatives in the Ottoman Parliament, see Katherina Boura, "The Greek Millet in Turkish Politics: Greeks in the Ottoman Parliament (1908–1918)," in *Ottoman Greeks in the Age of Nationalism: Politics, Economy and Society in the Nineteenth Century*, eds. D. Gondicas and C. Issawi (Princeton: The Darwin Press, Inc., 1999) 193–206.

10. See the speech of Emanuel Emanuelidi Efendi, the deputy of Aydın, in the Ottoman Assembly of Deputies (*Meclis-i Mebusan*), who comments on the boycotts and recent deportations of the Greeks from the Vilayet of Aydın. *Meclis-i Mebusan Zabıt Ceridesi* (İçtima-i Fevkalade), Devre: III, İçtima Senesi: 1, Cilt: 1, 1 Mayıs 1330 [May 1914]—23 Haziran 1330 [June 1914] (Ankara: T.B.M.M. Basımevi, 1991) 606–614.

11. See the booklet (*risale*) of Hüseyin Kazım, *Rum Patrikhanesine Açık Mektub; Boykot Müslümanların Hakkı Değil mi?* (Istanbul: Yeni Turan Matbaası, 1330 [1914/1915]). This booklet is a response to a recent *Mazbata* (petition) of the Greek Patriarch to the Ministry of Justice, which had appeared in some of the Greek dailies of Istanbul.

12. There were 528,000 Greeks and 465,000 Muslims in the newly captured territories. The total non-Greek population is estimated to have been somewhere

around 750,000. Douglas Dakin, *The Unification of Greece, 1770–1923* (London: Ernest Benn, 1972) 202. For the administrative and other community aspects of the Muslims in Greece, see Ν. Π. Ελευθεριαδου, *Μελεται Μουσουλμανικου Δικαιου Οθωμανικης Νομοθεσιας και Δικαιων των εν Τουρκια Χριστιανων* (Mytilene: Τυποις Σαλπιγγος, 1912); idem, *Οι Μουσουλμανοι εν Ελλαδη* (Athens: εκ του Τυπογραφειου Π. Α. Πετρακου, 1913). For the religious affairs of Muslim population and their pious foundations in Greece, see Γ. Α. Ροδοπουλου, *Περι Θρησκευτικης Ανεξαρτησιας των Μουσουλμανων και περι Διοικησεως και Διαχειρισεως των Οθωμανικων Βακουφιων εν Ελλαδη* (Athens: Τυπογραφειον Δ. Γ. Ευστρατιου και Δ. Δελη, 1913).

13. The interview with Nafia and Zeliha Bilge, October 21, 1994. Reşat D. Tesal, in his memoirs, provides extensive information on these developments in Volos. See his "Yunanistan'da Azınlık Olarak Nasıl Yaşardık," *Tarih ve Toplum*, 48 (1991) 179. Also Turkish Military Chief of Staff Archives (from now on ATASE which stands for *Askeri Tarih ve Stratejik Etüd Başkanlığı*), 1. Cihan Harbi, Box No: 2088, File No: 58–3.

14. Mark Mazower, *Salonica, City of Ghosts: Christians, Muslims and Jews, 1430–1950* (New York: Knopf, 2005) passim.

15. Adanır and Kaiser, "Migration, Deportation, and Nation-Building," 284.

16. An accord was signed between Bulgaria and the Ottoman Empire on November 15, 1913, as a result of which the two sides agreed to "facilitate the optional reciprocal exchange of the Bulgarian and Muslim populations and of their properties in a zone of 15 kilometers at the maximum along their entire common frontier." For details of the Convention and its application see, Séfériadès, *L'Échange des Populations*, 46–48. Ladas, *The Exchange of Minorities*, 18–20.

17. Little is known of the diplomatic details of the Convention between the C.U. P. government and Greece, which took place in the form of *note-verbaux*. This convention aimed at the exchange of "the Hellenic rural population of the Smyrna region against the Muslim minority of Macedonia." For the outline of the Convention see Séfériadès, *L'Echange des Populations*, 48–59; for the full text see *Atina Konvensiyonu (1913)*, Türkiye Büyük Millet Meclisi Kütüphanesi. Also Ν. Π. Ελευθεριαδου, *Τα Μετα την Συνθηκην Αθηνων περι των εν ταις Νεαις Χωραις Εγκαταλειμμενων Κτηματων* (Athens: Τυπογραφειον της Αυλης Α. Ραφτανη, 1915). For a preliminary analysis, see Pentzopoulos, *The Balkan Exchange of Minorities*, 54–57. Ladas, *The Exchange of Minorities*, 20–23. Also Yannis G. Mourelos, "The 1914 Persecutions and the First Attempt at an Exchange of Minorities between Greece and Turkey," *Balkan Studies*, 26:2 (1985) 389–413.

18. Pallis, "Exchange of Populations," 3. According to Cemal Pasha, the offer for the exchange came from Talat Pasha. See, Djemal Pasha, *Memoires of a Turkish Statesman, 1913–1919* (New York: George H. Doran Company, 1922) 71–73. Galip Kemali [Söylemezoğlu], *Hatıraları, Canlı Tarihler 5* (Istanbul: Türkiye Yayınevi, 1946) 102.

19. Hilmi Uran, *Hatıralarım* (Ankara: H. Uran, 1959) 69–71.

20. *Ahenk*, 7 Temmuz 1330 [July 1914].

21. During WWI, many Greeks were expelled from the settlements along the Black Sea and the Sea of Marmara. ATASE, 1. Cihan Harbi, Box No: 500, Files No: 777–1955. These files contain documents for the period 17–18 Aralık 1330 [December 1914] and 30 Kasım 1332 [November 1916]. The documents provide detailed lists of locations, households and the number of Greek populations considered for expulsions. After the war, Said Halim Paşa, who was then the head of the government, was questioned before he was brought to the Higher Court of Justice (*Divan-ı Âli*) for charges that his government was responsible for the expulsions. In his defense, Said Paşa pleaded that the expulsions were carried out as a military necessity since the Greek populations of these areas were assisting the Russian Navy and the naval forces of other adversaries. He also added that he spared the Greek population of Istanbul from facing the same fate as he indicated in his recommendations to the Ministry of War that such an action was not necessary from military point of view. For the details of this report see, *Meclis-i Mebusan, Encümen Mazbataları ve Tekalif-i Kanuniyye ile Said Halim ve Talat Paşa Kabineleri Azalarının Divan-ı Aliye Sevkleri Hakkında Beşinci Şubece İcra Kılınan Tahkikat*, No. 503–523, Vol. 1, sene: 1334 [1918] (Ankara: T.B.M.M. Basımevi 1993) 97. Documents from ATASE reveal that the expulsions were not limited to the coastal settlements along the Black Sea (*Bahr-i Siyah*) and the Marmara Sea. Many Greeks in the interior sections of Anatolia (e.g., Isparta, Konya etc.) and the Mediterranean (*Bahr-i Sefid*) coast of Anatolia were also subjected to expulsions. The expulsions did not necessarily imply the deportation of the Greeks outside of Anatolia. Many Greeks in the coastal settlements were expelled to a location within Anatolia which was not considered as a military zone and 6 hours away from the coast. It should also be mentioned that many Greeks from the Black Sea coast fled to Russia only to return after the Mudros Armistice. See below footnote 23.

22. "Memorandum Presented by the Greek Members of the Turkish Parliament to the American Commission on Mandates over Turkey," Published by the American Hellenic Society, Inc. (Columbia University, New York, 1919) 3. The appeal of the Greek deputies includes such claims as "1- We demand the total abolition of the Turkish rule over the Greeks, 2- We desire to be united to the Greek Kingdom, thus forming one national state under a democratic government." Cf. "Meclis-i Osmani Rum Azasının Siyasi Programı." This undated document can be dated roughly to the period 1909–1912. It contains 9 sections. The second article of the first section entitled *Kavaid-i Esasiye* (Principal Rules) states the goal of the Greek deputies as "to preserve the territorial unification of the Ottoman State and to spread and provide for the idea of the political oneness of various communities in the country" (*Tamamiyet-i mülkiye-i Devlet-i Osmaniyenin muhafazası ve memleketki akvam-ı muhtelifenin vahdet-i siyasiyeleri fikrinin neşr ve temini*).

23. Among others, the testimony of Κωνσταντίνου Σιδηρόπουλου of Αλιμπέη (Alimbeğ) in Samsun (Αμισο) provides valuable information on incidents of expulsion during 1916–1922 period. See File 259, Καδίκοι, the Archives

of the Centre for Asia Minor Studies (from now on KMS which stands for Κεντρο Μικρασιατικων Σπουδων), Athens.

24. Fuad Dündar, *İttihad ve Terakki'nin Müslümanları İskan Politikası (1913–1918)* (Istanbul: İletişim Yayınları, 2001) 57–62; Nedim İpek, *Rumeli'den Anadolu'ya Türk Göçleri* (Ankara: T.T.K. Basımevi, 1994) 155–239.

25. For a survey of the origins and objectives of the 'Great Idea,' see Richard Clogg, "The Byzantine Legacy in the Modern Greek World: The Megali Idea," in *The Byzantine Legacy in Eastern Europe*, ed. Lowell Clucas (Boulder: East European Monographs, 1988) 253–281. Also Stephen G. Xydis, "Modern Greek Nationalism," in *Nationalism in Eastern Europe*, eds. Peter F. Sugar and Ivo J. Lederer (Seattle: University of Washington Press, 1969) 235–243. Finally John S. Koliopoulos and Thanos M. Veremis, *Greece: The Modern Sequel from 1821 to the Present* (New York: New York University Press, 2002) 227–235.

26. *Matbuat* (Der Saadet [Istanbul]: Matbaa-i Askeriye, 1335 [1919]). This is a compilation of news clippings from the newspaper 'Sabah' about the Greek occupation of Izmir. For a detailed documentation of the political developments that led to this incident, see Engin Berber, *Sancılı Yıllar: Izmir 1918–1922, Mütareke ve İşgal Döneminde Izmir Sancağı* (Ankara: Ayraç Yayınevi, 1997) 209–230.

27. H. W. V. Temperley, ed. *A History of the Peace Conference of Paris*, vol. 6 (London: Oxford University Press, 1924) 115.

28. M. S. Anderson, *The Eastern Question, 1774–1923, A Study in International Relations* (Reprint of 1966 edition) (London: Macmillan, 1991) 376; George Lenczowski, *The Middle East in World Affairs* (Ithaca, New York: Cornell University Press, 1953) 110; Harry N. Howard, *The Partition of Turkey* (Norman: University of Oklahoma Press, 1931) 301–304; Briton Cooper Busch, *Mudros to Lausanne: Britain's Frontier in West Asia, 1918–1923* (Albany, N.Y.: SUNY Press, 1976) 359; L. Carl Brown, *International Politics and the Middle East, Old Rules, Dangerous Games* (Princeton: Princeton University Press, 1984) 35 and 86. Also M. E. Yapp, *The Making of the Modern Near East, 1792–1923* (London and New York: Longman, 1987) 320–321.

29. Such an orientation has also been very typical of many academic and non-academic meetings as well as anniversaries commemorating the Lausanne Treaty. Most of these meetings are dominated by redundant historical discussions and political rhetoric of the worst parochialism. See, for example, the proceedings of the conference organized by the İnönü Vakfı (İnönü Foundation) and published under the title *70. Yılında Lozan Barış Antlaşması, Uluslararası Seminer, 1993*, 25–26 October, 1993, The Marmara Oteli, Istanbul. In this meeting, there was hardly any discussion of the other aspects of the Treaty, such as the Exchange, by the conference participants, which included prominent diplomats and historians. Also see the slim volume with the transcribed speeches of diplomats from various countries, presented to the Turkish Grand Assembly on July 24, 1993. *Lozan Barış Antlaşması'nın 70. Yıldönümü* (Ankara: T. C. Dışişleri Bakanlığı, 1993). In his very brief speech, the then Greek Ambassador

to Turkey, Alexander Philon made a passing remark, perhaps in order to draw attention to the recent situation of the Greek minority in Istanbul, that "the clauses of the Lausanne Treaty concerning the exchange of populations created great problems during their implementation." *Lozan Barış Antlaşması'nın 70. Yıldönümü*, 28.

30. Stephen Ladas, *The Exchange of Minorities, Bulgaria, Greece, and Turkey* (New York: The MacMillan Company, 1932). Ladas undertook his research under the patronage of the Bureau of International Research of Harvard University and Radcliffe College in the early 1930s.

31. Sir John H. Simpson, *The Refugee Problem: Report of a Survey* (London: Oxford University Press, 1939) 11–28. The author carried out his research under the auspices of the Royal Institute of International Affairs. He presented the preliminary findings of his research on the subject to the Institute in the mid-1930s which then published it as *Refugees, Preliminary Report of a Survey* (London: The Royal Institute of International Affairs, 1938).

32. C. A. Macartney, *National States and National Minorities* (New York: Russell & Russell, 1968) (first published in 1934) 255–258. The information, gleaned from the preface to the first edition, suggests that the author served as secretary to the Minorities Committee of the League of Nations and his book was published under the auspices of the Royal Institute of International Affairs, London.

33. Joseph B. Schechtman, *European Population Transfers, 1939–1945* (New York: Russell & Russell, 1946) 16–22. This book drew upon a research project on European post-war reconstruction, conducted under the auspices of the Institute of World Affairs and sponsored by the Rockefeller Foundation. Before the Institute of World Affairs, the support for the research of this book was provided by the Institute of Jewish Affairs. See also his *Population Transfers in Asia* (New York: Hallsby Press, 1949) 101 and *Postwar Population Transfers in Europe*, 1944–55 (Philadelphia: University of Pennsylvania Press, 1962). Although Schechtman published his books after WWII, he conducted most of his research on population transfers in 1941. See his remarks in the Introduction to *European Population Transfers*, x.

34. Ladas, *The Exchange of Minorities*, 703; Macartney, *National States*, 450.

35. Yossi Katz, "Transfer of Population as a Solution to International Disputes, Population Exchanges between Greece and Turkey as a Model for Plans to Solve the Jewish-Arab Dispute in Palestine during the 1930s," *Political Geography*, 11:1 (January 1992) 55–56.

36. Rogers Brubaker, *Nationalism Reframed: Nationhood and the National Question in the New Europe* (Cambridge: Cambridge University Press, 1996) 107–178.

37. Schechtman, *European Population Transfers*, 22. The South Tyrol was part of the Austrian royal domain until 1919, when the treaty of St. Germain gave it to Italy. The latter launched a systematic Italianization of the region after 1923 to the detriment of the German elements. For a full discussion of the issue, see Stefan Wolff, *Disputed Territories: The Transnational Dynamics of Ethnic Conflict Settlement* (New York: Berghahn Books, 2003) 114–150.

38. Dariusz Stola, "Forced Migrations in Central European History," *International Migration Review*, 26:2 (1992) 336–337.

39. Schechtman, *Postwar Population Transfers*, 364. See also Norman M. Naimark, *Fires of Hatred: Ethnic Cleansing in Twentieth-Century Europe* (Cambridge, MA and London: Harvard University Press, 2002) 110–111.

40. Simpson, *The Refugee Problem*, 1. Sir John H. Simpson had served as the Vice President of the Refugee Settlement Commission in Athens from 1926 to 1930 and was then dispatched to Palestine by the British Government to investigate possibilities of immigration, land settlement and development in the region.

41. For a detailed account of the activities and negotiations related with the exchange project, see Rony E. Gabbay, *A Political Study of the Arab-Jewish Conflict: The Arab Refugee Problem (A Case Study)* (Geneve: Librairie E. Droz, 1959) especially 113–219. On the same issue also see Yossi Katz, *Partner to Partition: The Jewish Agency's Partition Plan in the Mandate Era* (London, Portland, Or.: Frank Cass, 1998) 85–109.

42. Schechtman, *Population Transfers in Asia*, 87. The summaries of the reports prepared by the Royal Commission can be found in Katz, "Transfer of Population," 59–62. Katz quotes the following from the original of the principal report of the Commission: "But the courage of the Greek and Turkish statesmen concerned has been justified by the result. Before the operation, the Greek and Turkish minorities had been a constant irritant. Now the ulcer has been clean cut out, and Greco-Turkish relations, we understand, are friendlier than they have ever been before." Palestine Royal Commission, Report. Cmnd. 5479, London: HMSO, 1937, 390, quoted by Katz, "Transfer of Population," 61.

43. Katz, "Transfer of Population," 62.

44. Schechtman, *Population Transfers in Asia*, 1–50.

45. Ibid, 37.

46. Dimitri Pentzopoulos, *The Balkan Exchange of Minorities and its Impact upon Greece* (Paris: Mouton & Co., 1962) 18.

47. Push factors are defined as various disruptive conditions, such as conflict, political instability, social inequalities, poor economic opportunities, that "push out" individuals from their home countries. Pull factors are generally positive conditions, such as higher standards of living, jobs or freer communities in the country of destination, that "pull" or attract people to them. For a detailed description of push and pull factors, see Gil Loescher, *Beyond Charity, International Cooperation and the Global Refugee Crisis* (New York and Oxford: Oxford University Press, 1993) 16.

48. The only exception to this generalization is provided by an agreement for a "voluntary regrouping of populations" between the Turks and Greeks after the Turkish intervention in Cyprus. After this event, Turkish and Greek diplomats met several times to discuss an exchange between the Greek and Turkish residents of the divided island. Both sides agreed to a voluntary exchange at the third round of negotiations which took place in Vienna during the summer of 1975. See Clement H. Dodd, *The Cyprus Imbroglio* (Cambridgeshire: The Eothen Press, 1998) 31–32.

49. For a detailed account of negotiations over the idea of population exchange among the leaders of the former Yugoslavian states (i.e., Bosnia-Herce-govina, Croatia and Serbia), see the observations of a Serbian journalist at http://www.cdsneu.edu/info/students/marko/vreme/vreme. Prime Minister Meciar of Slovakia, during a meeting with Hungarian Prime Minister Gyula Horn, suggested a possible population exchange of minorities between Hungary and Slovakia. See Michael Roddy, "Horn Angrily Rejects Slovak Plan to Move Hungarians," Reuters, Sept. 9, 1997. See http://www.house.gov/csce/slovakia97.htm.

The term 'exchange' is frequently encountered in the writings of Israeli journalists. Don Fedder says that "The only business we have left with you is to arrange an exchange of populations. We will take the 200,000 Jewish settlers living on the West Bank, and you will take the Arabs living in what's left of Israel." See Don Fedder, "Israel Should Prepare for Armageddon"; http://www.townhall.com/columnists/donfeder. Another article, published in the *Jerusalem Post* states that "Beit Iksa next to Jerusalem (a nest of criminal activities) could be exchanged with Netzarim in the Gaza Strip, or Kadim near Jenin. Exchange of populations, cruel as it may sound, is basically a wise policy in a protracted ethno-national conflict, such as the one between the Jewish and Arab communities in the Land of Israel." See http://www.jpost.com/com/Archive/01.Jun.1998/Opinion/Article-1.html. Turkish Minister of State, Şükrü S. Gürel offered in a speech at the Washington Institute for Near East Policy the option of exchange as a viable solution to the conflict between Azerbaijan and Armenia over the disputed region of Karabagh. For the transcription of this speech, see http://www.washingtoninstitute.org/media/turkish.htm. The United Nations denounced the idea of population exchange as a solution to inter-ethnic conflicts, see http://www.unhchr.ch/Huridocda/Huridoca.nsf/TestFrame/ee7

50. Chaim D. Kaufmann, "When All Else Fails: Ethnic Population Transfers and Partitions in the Twentieth Century," *International Security*, 23:2 (Fall 1998) 120–156. Idem, "Possible and Impossible Solutions to Ethnic Civil Wars," *International Security*, 20:4 (Spring 1996) 136–175. Also see Triadafilos Triadafilopoulos' lecture "Debating 'Engineered Unmixing': Partition and Transfers of Populations in 20th Century," in a series on "Minorities and Minority Conflicts in Transition: Central and Eastern Europe in the Era of Post Socialism," Humboldt University, Berlin, 24 October 2000. Triandafilopoulos treats population transfers as a specific case of 'ethnic cleansing,' i.e. the forced homogenization of territories. For a similar view see, Andrew Bell-Fialkoff, *Ethnic Cleansing* (New York: St. Martin Press, 1996) 24–27. Finally, see Naimark, *Fires of Hatred*, 42–56.

51. In his celebrated 1976 article, John Petropoulos asked without researching the details of the case "why was there no concerted challenge from the Greek refugees to the notion of compulsory exchange?" John A. Petropoulos, "The Compulsory Exchange of Populations: Greek-Turkish Peacemaking, 1922–1930," *Byzantine and Modern Greek Studies*, 2 (1976) 136. The impossibility of coordinating a collective action on such an issue during the catastrophic post-war conditions needs not be commented. But the

fact of the matter was that many refugees appealed to the Greek and Turkish governments as well as the international community for the reversal of the decision for a compulsory exchange. This issue is discussed at length in Chapter Six of this book.

52. For a brief historical survey of the development of the field of Refugee Studies, see Richard Black, "Fifty Years of Refugee Studies: From Theory to Policy," *International Migration Review*, 35:1 (Spring 2001) 57–78.

53. Michael R. Marrus, *The Unwanted, European Refugees in the Twentieth Century* (New York and Oxford: Oxford University Press, 1985) 3–13. Aristide Zolberg, Astri Suhrke and Sergio Aguayo, *Escape from Violence: Conflict and the Refugee Crisis in the Developing World* (New York and Oxford: Oxford University Press, 1989) 14–15. Claudena M. Skran, *Refugees in Inter-War Europe, the Emergence of a Regime* (Oxford: Clarendon Press, 1995) 1–10, 41–48. See also Naimark, *Ethnic Cleansing*, 1–16.

54. Marrus, *The Unwanted, European Refugees*, 96–106; Zolberg et al. *Escape from Violence*, 4.

55. "International regimes are defined as principles, norms, rules and decision-making procedures around which actor expectations converge in a given issue area." Stephen D. Krasner, "Structural Causes and Regime Consequences: Regimes as Intervening Variables," *International Organization*, 36:2 (Spring 1982) 185. The formation of the "international refugee regime" involved the creation of the International Refugee Organization (1949) and the United Nations High Commissioner for Refugees (1951). For a comprehensive analysis of the developments associated with the formation of the international refugee regime, see Loescher, *Beyond Charity*, 32–54.

56. Nevzat Soğuk, *States and Strangers, Refugees and Displacements of State-craft* (Minneapolis and London: University of Minnesota Press, 1999) 57–100. Also see E. Valentine Daniel and John Chr. Knudsen, eds, *Mistrusting Refugees* (Berkeley: University of California Press, 1995) 2–6.

57. Soğuk, *States and Strangers*, 57–100.

58. Daniel and Knudsen, eds., *Mistrusting Refugees*, viii.

59. Renée Hirschon, *Heirs of the Greek Catastrophe: The Social Life of Asia Minor Refugees in Piraeus* (Oxford: Clarendon Press, 1989) passim.

60. The term "twin myths of ethnic and national homogeneity" was originally coined by George Mavrogordatos to refer in a critical fashion to the attempts of the Greek nation-state to construct a national identity. See his "Party and Society in Modern Greece," *New Trends in Modern Greek Historiography*, eds. A. L. Macrakis and N. Diamandouros (Athens: The Modern Greek Studies Association in cooperation with Anatolia College, 1982) 105.

61. Jacques LeGoff, *History and Memory*, trans. S. Rendall and E. Claman (New York: Columbia University Press, 1992) 54. Cf. Giovanni Levi, "The Distant Past: On the Political Use of History," *Mediterranean Historical Review*, 16:1 (June 2001) 61–73.

62. For a historiographical survey of the literature on the Asia Minor Catastrophe, see Victoria Solomonidis, "Greece in Asia Minor 1919–1922, A

Historiographic Survey," *New Trends in Modern Greek Historiography*, Occasional Papers 1, eds. A Lily Macracis and Nikiforos Diamandouros (Athens: The Modern Greek Studies Association in Cooperation with Anatolia College, 1982) 121–128. For a thorough analysis of the intricate relationship between politics and history in Greece with special reference to the "strategic manipulation of nationalist feelings by politicians," see A. Triandafyllidou, M Calloni and A. Mikrakis, "New Greek Nationalism," *Sociological Research Online*, 2:1, http://www.socresonline.org.uk/socresonline/21/7/html.

63. For a periodization of modern Greek historiography, see Alexander Kitroeff, "Continuity and Change in Contemporary Greek Historiography," in *Modern Greece, Nationalism and Nationality*, eds. M. Blinkhorn and T. Veremis (London: Sage-ELIAMEP, 1990) 143–144.

64. Anastasia Karakasidou, *Fields of Wheat, Hills of Blood, Passages to Nationhood in Greek Macedonia, 1870–1990* (Chicago: The University of Chicago Press, 1997) 147. The author notes "the refugees are still enshrined in much Greek historiography as exemplary victims of the persecution suffered by the Greek nation at the hands of its eternal enemy, the Turks." Karakasidou, *Fields of Wheat,* 150. For an in-depth psychological analysis of the Greek view of the Turks and vice versa, see Vamik Volkan and Norman Itzkowitz, *Turks and Greeks: Neighbours in Conflict* (Cambridgeshire: The Eothen Press, 1994) 10–12.

65. This discourse is represented by a vast literature written in Greek and French by Greek authors of varying backgrounds. For practical purposes, only the five most representative studies are cited here. Alexandre Devedji, *L'échange obligatoire des minorités grecquès et turques* (Paris: Imprimerie du Montparnasse et de Persan-Beaumont, 1929); Stelio Séfériadès, *L'Échange des Populations* (Paris: Librairie Hachette, 1929); Th. Kiosséoglou, *L'echange forcé des minorités d'après le traite de Lausanne* (Nancy: Imprimerie Nancéinne, 1926); C. G. Ténékidès, "Le statut de minorités et l'échange obligatoire des populations Gréco-Turques," *Revue Générale de Droit International Public*, 31 (1924) 72–88; Αθανασιου Πρωτονοταριου, *Το Προσφυγικον Προβλημα απο Ιστορικης, Νομικης και Καρατικης Αποψεως* (Athens: Τυποις Πυρσου Ανων. Εταιριας, 1929). A few foreign observers of the situation who also participated in the official undertaking of the Exchange shared the same discourse. See Charles Eddy, *Greece and the Greek Refugees* (London: George Allen & Unwin LTD., 1931); Henry Morgenthau (in Colloboration with French Strother), *I Was Sent to Athens* (Garden City, NewYork: Doubleday, Doran & Company, Inc., 1929); Eliot Grinnell Mears, *Greece Today: The Aftermath of the Refugee Impact* (Stanford University, California: Stanford University Press, 1929).

66. Pentzopoulos, *The Balkan Exchange of Minorities*; Ευστρατιου Χρ. Ζαμπατα, "Οι εκ Μικρας Ασιας Ελληνορθοδοξοι Προσφυγες," Ph.D. Dissertation (University of Athens, 1969). Αγγελου Τσουλουφη, Η Ανταλλαγη Ελληνικων & Τουρκικων Πληθυσμων και η Εκτιμηση των Εκατερωθεν Εγκαταλειφθεισων Περιουσιων (Athens: Εκδοσεις Ενωσεως Σμυρναιων, 1989) (first edition appeared in 1982); Κωνσταντινου Σβολοπουλου, *Η Αποφαση*

για την Υποχρεωτικη Ανταλλαγη των Πληθυσμων μεταξυ Ελλαδος και Τουρκιας (Salonica: Εθνικη Βιβλιοθηκη, 1981); Γιωργου Ν. Λαμψιδη, *Οι Προσφυγες του 1922, Η Προσφορα τους στην Αναπτυξη της Χωρας* (3rd Edition) (Salonica: Εκδοτικος Οικος Αδελφων Κυριακιδη, 1992). A more comprehensive list of such publications for the 1923–1978 period can be found in Παυλος Χατζημωυσης, *Βιβλιογραφια 1919–1978, Μικρασιατικη Εκστρατεια-Ηττα Προσφυγια* (Athens: ΕΡΜΗΣ, 1981). For the publications after 1980, see Γιοργος Α. Γιαννακοπουλος, "Οι Μικρασιατες Προσφυγες στην Ελλαδα, Βιβλιογραφικο Δοκιμιο," *ΔΕΛΤΙΟ ΚΜΣ*, 9 (1992) 283–291.

67. Ευσταθιος Πελαγιδης, *Προσφυγικη Ελλαδα (1913–1930), Ο Πονος και Η Δοξα* (Salonica: Εκδοτικος Οικος Αδελφων Κυριακιδη Α. Ε., 1997); also by the same author *Η Αποκατασταση των Προσφυγων στη Δυτικη Μακεδονια (1923–1930)* (Salonica: Εκδοτικος Οικος Αδελφων Κυριακιδη Α. Ε., 1994). These two studies present a fairly rich documentation of the refugee resettlement in Greece, but in terms of their approach to and analysis of the Exchange, they are also characterized by a parochial view of the subject. For some insightful comments on the parochial orientation of Modern Greek historiography, see Thomas W. Gallant, "Greek Exceptionalism and Contemporary Historiography: New Pitfalls and Old Debates," *Journal of Modern Greek Studies*, 15:2 (1997) 209–216.

68. M. Cemil (Bilsel) *Lozan*, Reprint of 1933 Edition (Istanbul: Sosyal Yayınlar, 1998); Yusuf Hikmet Bayur, *Yeni Türkiye Devletinin Harici Siyaseti* (Istanbul: Burhaneddin, 1935); Yusuf Hikmet Bayur, *Türk İnkilabı Tarihi* (Istanbul: T.T.K., 1940); Enver Ziya Karal, *Türkiye Cumhuriyeti Tarihi (1918–1944)* (Istanbul: Milli Eğitim, 1945). The findings and arguments of this early scholarship were adopted without modification by later scholars. See Hamza Eroğlu, *70. Yıldönümünde Lozan* ([Ankara]: T. C. Kültür Bakanlığı, 1993); Salahi Sonyel, *Türk Kurtuluş Savaşı ve Dış Politika*, 2 Vols. (Ankara: T.T.K. Basımevi, 1986); *Türkiye Dış Politikasıida 50 Yıl: Lozan (1922–1923)* (Ankara: T. C. Dışişleri Bakanlığı, 1973).

69. Prof. Sinop Saylavi [Yusuf Kemal Tengirşenk], *Türk İnkilabı Dersleri— Ekonomik Değişmeler* (Istanbul: Resimli Ay Matbaası, 1935) 34.

70. For a concise review of the early developments in Turkish national historiography see, İlber Ortaylı, "Atatürk Döneminde Türkiye'de Tarihçilik Üzerine Bazı Gözlemler," in his *Gelenekten Geleceğe* (Istanbul: Hil Yayınları, 1982) 72–79. Çağlar Keyder offers some explanations as to why certain historical events such as the Exchange were left outside the scope of Turkish national history in his "Whither the Project of Modernity? Turkey in the 1990s," in *Rethinking Modernity and National Identity in Turkey*, eds. Sibel Bozdoğan and Reşat Kasaba (Seattle and London: University of Washington Press, 1997) 44. Cf. Lucette Valensi, "Notes on Two Discordant Histories: Armenia during World War I," *Mediterranean Historical Review*, 16:1 (June 2001) 49–60. As for the reasons behind the under-representation of the refugees in Turkish national historiography, some insights can be gained from Kemal Karpat's "Historical Continuity and Identity Change or How to Be Modern Muslim, Ottoman, and Turk" in *Ottoman Past and Today's Turkey*, ed. K. Karpat (Leiden: E.J. Brill, 2000) 1–28.

71. L. S. Stavrianos, *The Balkans Since 1453* (New York: Holt, Rinehart and Winston, 1958) 589–591; Γρηγοριου Δαφνη, *Η Ελλας μεταξύ Δυο Πολεμων, 1923–1940*, Vol. 1 (Athens: Εκδοσεις Κακτος, 1997) 36–63. Harry J. Psomiades, *The Eastern Question: The Last Phase, A Study in Greek-Turkish Diplomacy* (Salonica: Institute for Balkan Studies, 1968) 60–68. Cf. Fahir Armaoğlu, *20. Yüzyıl Siyasi Tarihi (1914–1980)* (Ankara: T.T.K. Basımevi, 1988) 320–333; Oral Sander, *Siyasi Tarih, İlkçağlardan 1918'e* (Ankara: İmge Yayınevi, 2000) 368–377. A more recent study on the history of Turkish foreign policy acknowledges the importance of the Exchange for Turkey with the following words: " . . . the draconian exchange of populations, combined with the massacres and deportation of virtually all the former Armenian community of Anatolia during the great war. . . . had a transformatory effect on the cultural and political landscape of the country." See William Hale, *Turkish Foreign Policy, 1774–2000* (London: Frank Cass, 2000) 55–56. A similar tendency characterizes some recent general studies on the Balkans. See Misha Glenny, *The Balkans, 1804–1999, Nationalism, War and the Great Powers* (London: Granta Books, 1999) 392–396; and finally Mark Mazower, *The Balkans* (London: Weidenfeld & Nicolson, 2000) 101–102.

72. An assessment of the Exchange dimension of the Lausanne Treaty was made in a conference organized at the Oxford University with the participation of scholars from Greece, Turkey and other countries. The meeting was dedicated in its entirety to the discussion of the Exchange with special emphasis on its social, political, economic, and psychological impact on both Turkish and Greek refugees. *Turkey and Greece: Assessment of the Consequences of the Treaty of Lausanne Convention 1923 (75th Anniversary)*, hosted by the Refugee Studies Programme, Queen Elizabeth House, Oxford University, September 17–20, 1998 (Later published as *Crossing the Aegean: An Appraisal of the 1923 Compulsory Population Exchange Between Greece and Turkey*, ed. R. Hirschon (New York, Oxford: Berghahn Books, 2003). The Turkish counterpart of this conference took place five years later in Istanbul, organized by the Foundation of the Lausanne Refugees. The proceedings of this conference were later published. See Müfide Pekin ed., *Yeniden Kurulan Yaşamlar: 1923 Türk-Yunan Zorunlu Mübadelesi* (Istanbul: Bilgi Üniversitesi Yayınları, 2005). It is worth noting that in 1998, the Boğaziçi University of Istanbul and the Panteion University of Athens signed agreements for the exchange of students and scholars, and also organized conferences in Athens and Istanbul: "Socio-Political Sciences and Historiography in Turkey Today: Major Currents," 28–30 May, 1998, Panteion University, Athens and "The Greek–Turkish Workshop on Citizenship and the Nation-State," 8–9 January 1999, Boğaziçi University, Istanbul. These collective ventures focused largely on the current state of social sciences and specifically that of historical studies in both countries with special reference to historiographical problems. Another conference, organized by the Centre for the Study of South Eastern Europe, was entitled "Intersecting Times, The Work of Memory in Southeastern Europe" and had a special workshop devoted to the Turco-Greek Exchange

of Populations, 25–28 June 2000, Prifysgol Cymru University of Wales, Clyne Castle, Swansea, Wales, UK. The proceedings of this workshop were published in *Balkanologie*, 5:1–2 (2001) 143–289.

73. Michael Herzfeld, *A Place in History, Social and Monumental Time in a Cretan Town* (Princeton: Princeton University Press, 1991) 65–66. Also see by the same author, *The Poetics of Manhood, Contest and Identity in a Cretan Village* (Princeton: Princeton University Press, 1985) 31–32. Also see his review essay on Hirschon's book "Displaced: The Spaces of the Refugee Identity in Greece," *Anthropological Quarterly*, 64:2 (1991) 92–95.

74. Hirschon, *Heirs of the Greek Catastrophe*, 2.

75. Μαρια Βεργετη, "Η Ποντιακη Ταυτοτητα της Τριτης Γενιας," *ΔΕΛΤΙΟ ΚΜΣ*, 9 (1992) 80–96.

76. Karakasidou, *Fields of Wheat*, particularly 146–161.

77. For an anthropological study that places the Exchange dimension of the Lausanne Treaty within the general literature on forced migrations and juxtaposes the stories of Greek and Turkish refugees with the other victims of ethnic-unmixing policies during the late Ottoman period, see Peter Loizos, "Ottoman Half-lives: Long term Perspectives on Particular Forced Migrations," *Journal of Refugee Studies*, 12:3 (1999) 237–263. This article is an expanded version of the Colson Lecture that the author has given at the invitation of the Refugee Studies Program at Oxford University, 12 May 1999. For a study that compares the case of Greek refugees with that of other refugees (e.g., White Russians) in Europe during the inter-war era, see Eftihia Voutira, "Population Transfers and Resettlement Policies in Inter-War Europe: The Case of Asia Minor Refugees in Macedonia from an International and National Perspective," in *Ourselves and Others, the Development of a Greek Macedonian Cultural Identity Since 1912*, eds. Mackridge and E. Yannakis (Oxford, New York: Berg, 1997) 111–131. Voutira acknowledges that "most Greek research and scholarship on the Asia Minor refugee resettlement and assistance polices" are characterized by the "exilic bias" which her study "seeks to redress." See 111.

78. George Th. Mavrogordatos, *Stillborn Republic, Social Coalitions and Party Strategies in Greece, 1922–1936* (Berkeley: University of California Press, 1983); Mark Mazower, *Greece and the Inter-War Economic Crisis* (Oxford: Clarendon Press, 1991) 73–100; also his "The Refugees, the Economic Crisis and the Collapse of Venizelist Hegemony, 1929–1932," *ΔΕΛΤΙΟ ΚΜΣ*, 9 (1992) 120. See in the same volume, Κωστας Κωστης, "Η Ιδεολογια της Οικονομικης Αναπτυξης, Οι Προσφυγες στο Μεσοπολεμο," *ΔΕΛΤΙΟ ΚΜΣ*, 9 (1992) 31–46.

79. Recent developments in the Balkans prove that the coexistence of different ethnic and religious groups within a nation-state framework continues to be an artificial construction translating easily into inter-communal strife. The case of the ex-Yugoslavian republics, Bosnia-Herzegovina, Croatia, Serbia and more recently Kosova, demonstrated at best the failure of such attempts. Worldwide examples range from Lebanon and Ireland to the ex-Soviet states. In particular, the appearance of old-style ethnic cleansing techniques in the Balkans during the early part of the 1990s increased

interest in the demographic and ethnographic history of the region, of which Greece and Turkey are integral parts with sizable minorities. The Bosnian case, and more recently Kosova brought about further interest in the Ottoman past, which is held accountable on the whole for the developments currently unfolding in the region. Greece and Turkey are viewed as potential arenas for such incidents and therefore attract the attention of individual scholars as well as that of international organizations, such as the European Union and the United Nations. Under the auspices of those institutions, certain projects and scholarly meetings were organized in both countries to promote dialogue between Turkish and Greek scholarly circles. See, for example, the proceedings of the Second International History Congress (8–10 June 1995, Istanbul) devoted to the topic of History Education and the Problem of "the Other" in History. The majority of the presentations were on the contents of history textbooks in Greece and Turkey. *Tarih Eğitimi ve Tarihte "Öteki" Sorunu* (Istanbul: Tarih Vakfı Yurt Yayınları, 1998). A similar meeting on the contents of history textbooks had been held in Istanbul some thirty years ago. Felsefe Kurumu Seminerleri, November13–15, 1975, Istanbul. In May 1986, a similar colloquium was convened in Paris under the title of "Le Differend Greco-Turc." The proceedings of the latter were published as *Türk-Yunan Uyuşmazlığı*, ed. Semih Vaner (Istanbul: Metis Yayınları, 1990). Lastly, one should mention the activities of a Salonica-based NGO, the Center for Democracy and Reconciliation in Southeast Europe. The Center has been pursuing multiple joint-history projects about history teaching in the region. The preliminary results of one of these projects were published in 2001. See Christina Koulouri, ed., *Teaching the History of Southeastern Europe* (Salonica: Center for Democracy and Reconciliation in Southeast Europe, 2001).

80. The recent waves of attacks on the policies of the early Republic originated from two extremist sides, namely Islamic fundamentalists and Kurdish nationalists. Both movements claim anonymously that early Republican efforts to transform the country into a secular one and to mold different ethnic groups into one homogenous nation have thus far proven unsuccessful. Since both movements are inclined to legitimize their ideologies by blaming the policies of the early state authorities for producing a false account of the Early Republican history, they tend to reread this particular phase of contemporary Turkish history in a manner exclusive to their "adherents." These tendencies are not without their advocates among the leading journalists and intellectuals of the country. With their liberal views, they are pejoratively referred to as "*İkinci Cumhuriyetçiler*" (Second Republicanists). This somewhat alternative re-reading of history has certainly stimulated interest in the origins and growth of Turkish nationalism and played a major role in bringing the social foundations of the Turkish Republic under the magnifying glass. It will awaken further interest in the essence and early manifestations of Turkish nationalism and thus in the hitherto neglected aspects of the early Turkish history, such as the Turco-Greek population exchange. Interestingly enough, most of the publications

and television documentaries on the Exchange continue to be undertaken by intellectuals and organizations closely associated with these views.

81. For example, some political scientists who were concerned about the educational policies of the current government studied the foundations of the educational system. See İsmail Kaplan, *Türkiye'de Milli Eğitim İdeolojisi* (Istanbul: İletişim Yayınları, 2000). Some other political scientists who were prompted by the revival of the nationalist movement, attempted to examine the institutional foundations of this movement. See Füsün Üstel, *İmparatorluktan Ulus-Devlete Türk Milliyetçiliği, Türk Ocakları (1912–1931)* (Istanbul: İletişim Yayınları, 1997). An urban planner who was intrigued by the relationship between ideology and architecture looked at the early manifestations of this relationship in the example of *Halkevleri*. See Neşe Gürallar Yeşilkaya, *Halkevleri: İdeoloji ve Mimarlık* (Istanbul: İletişim Yayınları, 1999). Finally, a few anthropologists who were prompted by the current orientation of anthropological research, looked at the early institutional developments and the work of leading anthropologists. See Arzu Öztürkmen, *Türkiye'de Folklor ve Milliyetçilik* (Istanbul: İletişim Yayınları, 1998). A few other studies on the topics of political opposition and minorities also appeared during the 1990s. For the political opposition see Ahmet Demirel, *Birinci Meclis'te Muhalefet, İkinci Grup* (Istanbul: İletişim Yayınları, 1994) and Faruk Alpkaya, *Türkiye Cumhuriyeti'nin Kuruluşu (1923–1924)* (Istanbul: İletişim Yayınları, 1999). As for the minorities see Rıfat Bali, *Cumhuriyet Yıllarında Türkiye Yahudileri, Bir Türkleştirme Serüveni (1923–1945)* (Istanbul: İletişim Yayınları, 1999). A good foreign representative of the newly emerging revisionist scholarship on the early Republican period of Turkish history is Eric J. Zürcher. See his *Turkey: A Modern History* (London: I. B. Tauris & Co Ltd., 1993) 170–172. Also "Young Turks, Ottoman Muslims and Turkish Nationalists: Identity Politics, 1908–1938," in *Ottoman Past and Today's Turkey*, ed. Kemal Karpat (Leiden: Brill, 2000) 150–179.

82. Kemal Arı, *Büyük Mübadele, Türkiye'ye Zorunlu Göç (1923–1925)* (Istanbul: Tarih Vakfı Yurt Yayınları, 1995) 1–5. Tülay Alim Baran, *Bir Kentin Yeniden Yapılanması İzmir, 1923–1938* (Istanbul: ARMA, 2003); Nedim İpek, *Mübadele ve Samsun* (Ankara: T.T.K. Yayınevi, 2000); Ramazan Tosun, *Türk-Yunan İlişkileri ve Nüfus Mübadelesi* (Ankara: Berikan, 2002).

83. Ayhan Aktar attempts to assess critically the importance of the Exchange for the economic and social foundations of Modern Turkey. See his "Nüfusun Homojenleştirilmesinde ve Ekonominin Türkleştirilmesi Sürecinde Bir Aşama: Türk-Yunan Nüfus Mübadelesi, 1923–1924," in his *Varlık Vergisi ve 'Türkleştirme' Politikaları* (Istanbul: İletişim Yayınları, 2000) 17–69. For an attempt that places the Exchange in the historical context of the Ottoman collapse, see Adanır and Kaiser, "Migration, Deportation, and Nation-Building," 273–292. Fikret Adanır has also undertaken a survey of Turkish historiography on the Exchange. The findings of the author are on the whole in line with my findings but he seems to provide a more optimistic view of the current scholarship on the subject. A major novelty of

Adanır's article is found in his explanation of why the Exchange has become a popular topic of research in recent decades. He provides the following explanation: "The discourse on the history of the early Republic has undergone significant shifts during the last decades. To some extent, this had to with the growing international interest in the question of the Armenian genocide during World War I, which was articulated with special urgency in the aftermath of the Turkish intervention in Cyprus in 1974, when Armenians and Greeks succeeded in mobilizing Western public opinion against Turkey. In the 1980s, the U.S. Senate, the U.N. and the European Union began to pass resolutions which aimed at institutionalizing the remembrance of the victims of the Armenian genocide. The pressure upon Turkey to reconsider her stand in the Cyprus question and vis-à-vis Greece mounted. The Turkish nationalists' reaction was unequivocal and quite sharp. Some authors even spoke of a conspiracy, which had always striven for Turkey's destruction. One result of this political development for historical research was a renewed effort to collect evidence underlining the Turkishness of Asia Minor from times immemorial." See Fikret Adanır, "Lo Scambio Greco-Turco di Populazioni nella Storiografica Turca," in *Esodi: Transferimenti Forzati di Populazioni nel Novecento Europeo*, eds. M. Cattaruzza, M. Dogo and Raoul Pupo (Napoli: Edizioni Scientifiche Italiane, 2000) 89–101. I thank Fikret Adanır for sending me the English version of this article (The Greco-Turkish Exchange of Populations in Turkish Historiography) and Marco Dogo for providing me with a copy of the volume in which this article was originally published.

84. Barbara Tuchman, "Distinguishing the Significant from the Insignificant," in *Oral History, An Interdisciplinary Anthology*, eds. David K. Dunaway and Willa K. Baum, 2nd Edition (Walnut Creek, London and New Delhi: Altamira Press, 1996) 92.

85. George Kritikos makes extensive use of these sources to examine the situation of urban refugees. See his "State Policy and Urban Employment of Refugees: the Greek Case (1923–30)," in *European Review of History*, 7:2 (2000) 189–206. Also see his unpublished dissertation "Greek Orthodox Refugees and the Making of a New Greek Community (1923–193)," European University Institute, Florence, 2001.

86. Baran, *Bir Kentin Yeniden Yapılanması*; İpek, *Mübadele ve Samsun*. For the use of the Archives of the Turkish Red Crescent see Mesut Çapa, "Kızılay Hilal-i Ahmer Cemiyeti (1914–1925)," Unpublished Ph.D. Dissertation (Ankara, 1989).

87. See footnote 49 above.

88. Alexis Alexandris, *The Greek Minority of Istanbul and Greek-Turkish Relations, 1918–1974* (Athens: Centre for Asia Minor Studies, 1992) 234.

89. Fernand Braudel, *The Identity of France*, Volume One: *History and Environment*, trans. Sian Reynolds (New York: Harper & Row Publishers, 1988) 15.

90. Karakasidou, *Fields of Wheat*, xix.

91. Braudel, *The Identity of France*, 17.

92. David Lowenthal, *The Past is a Foreign Country* (Cambridge: Cambridge University Press, 1985).

93. Jan Vansina, "Oral Tradition and Historical Methodology," in *Oral History, An Interdisciplinary Anthology*, eds. David K. Dunaway and Willa K. Baum, 2nd Edition (Walnut Creek, London and New Delhi: Altamira Press, 1996) 125.

NOTES TO CHAPTER ONE

1. Henry Morgenthau, "Turk's Eyes on Europe Says Our Ex-Ambassador," *The New York Times*. undated newspaper clipping, The Library of Congress, the Papers of Henry Morgenthau, Containers 50–52, Reel 39/41.
2. Salahi R. Sonyel, *Turkish Diplomacy, Mustafa Kemal and the Turkish National Movement* (London: Sage Publications Ltd., 1975) 185.
3. Morgenthau's speech for the National Milk Producers' Federation at its opening session, see "Morgenthau says Turks are a Band of Marauders," *New York City Post*, November 9, 1922. The Library of Congress, the Papers of Henry Morgenthau, Containers 50–52, Reel 39/41.
4. *Hakimiyet-i Milliye*, 31 Teşrin-i Evvel 1338 [October 1922] and *Yeni Gün*, 1 Teşrin-i Sâni 1338 [November 1922]. *T.B.M.M. GCZ*, 6 Mart 1338 [March 1922]—27 Şubat 1338 [February 1923], vol. 3. (Istanbul: İş Bankası Kültür Yayınları, 1985) 956–969. Also see Ahmet Demirel, *Birinci Meclis'te Muhalefet, İkinci Grup* (Istanbul: İletişim Yayınları, 1994) 483–531. Also Rıdvan Akın, *TBMM Devleti (1920–1923), Birinci Meclis Döneminde Devlet Erkleri ve İdare* (Istanbul: İletişim Yayınları, 2001) 385–407. For the observations of a foreign journalist on the opposition movement after 1923, see Maxwell H. H. Macarthney, "The New Opposition in Turkey," in *The Fortnightly Review*, 117 (1925) 781–793.
5. On the Turco-Soviet alliance see Bülent Gökay, *A Clash of Empires, Turkey between Russian Imperialism and British Imperialism, 1918–1923* (London: I. B. Tauris, 1997) 92–112. For a concise review of the relations of the Ankara government with the French and the Italian governments prior to Lausanne, see William Hale, *Turkish Foreign Policy, 1774–2000* (London: Frank Cass, 2000) 44–56. Also Sonyel, *Turkish Diplomacy*, 161–184.
6. On the eve of Lausanne, speaking before the Unitarian Club in Boston, Morgenthau declared, "It is up to the United States to tell the European powers that we will stand behind England against the Turks." *Boston Mass. Herald*, November 9, 1922. The Library of Congress, the Papers of Henry Morgenthau, Containers 50–52, Reel 39/41. The conflicting interests of France and Italy prevented the two sides from agreeing for such a conference; which was reconciled by the mediation of Britain. "Despite all the differences the Allied powers came to Lausanne with an earlier agreement initiated by Lord Curzon and signed on November 18, 1922 on the fundamental principles that would guide the discussions at the conference." See Psomiades, *The Eastern Question*, 36. Also see Earl of Ronaldhay, *The Life of Lord Curzon, Being the Authorized Biography of George*

Nathaniel Marquess Curzon of Kedleston, K. G., vol. 3 (London: Ernest Benn Limited, 1928) 338.

7. The Allies extended an invitation to the Istanbul Government, which was protested by the Ankara Government. This event engendered a series of developments in Turkey which brought about the abolition of the Sultanate on November 1, 1922. Only three days before the Conference, the last Ottoman sultan, Vahdettin (Mehmed VI) and his son Ertuğrul were taken by a British warship from Istanbul and transferred to Malta. See the telegram "From Hüseyin Rauf to İsmet Paşa," 19 Teşrin-i Sâni 1338 [November 1922]. *Lozan Telgrafları (1922–1923)*, vol. 1, ed. Bilal Şimsir (Ankara: Türk Tarih Kurumu Basımevi, 1990) 108–109. (From now on *Lozan Telgrafları*) On November 18, 1922, the Grand National Assembly in Ankara voted for Abdülmecid bin Abdülaziz to assume the caliphate in the name of the Ottoman dynasty. "From Hüseyin Rauf to İsmet Paşa," 20 Teşrin-i Sâni 1338 [November 1922]. *Lozan Telgrafları*, 109–110. İsmet Paşa received an Indian delegation from London, which expressed great concern over the new status of the Caliphate. He tried to persuade the delegation that the abolition of the Sultanate was intended to enhance the position of the Caliphate. See *Lozan Telgrafları*, 126. See Muhammed Sadiq, *The Turkish Revolution and the Indian Freedom Movement* (Delhi: Macmillan India Limited, 1983) 92–93. A detailed documentation and analysis of this issue is found in a book by Azmi Özcan. See his *Pan-Islamism, Indian Muslims, the Ottomans and Britain (1877–1924)* (Leiden: E. J. Brill, 1997) 184–204. With the *de jure* abolition of the Sultanate, a great debate ensued concerning how to transfer all the rights of the Sultanate to the newly elected Caliph. "From Mustafa Kemal to İsmet Paşa, 26 Kânun-ı Evvel 1338 [December 1922]," in *Lozan Telgrafları*, 278–279. See Michael Martin Finefrock, "The Second Group in the First Grand National Assembly," *Journal of South Asian and Middle Eastern Studies*, 3 (Fall 1979) 3–20. Also see the classic study by Lewis V. Thomas, "The National and International Relations of Turkey," in *Near Eastern Culture and Society*, ed. T. Cuyler Young (Princeton, 1951) 167–187.

8. Harry Psomiades, "Thrace and the Armistice of Mudanya, October 3–11, 1922," *ΔΕΛΤΙΟ ΚΜΣ*, 12 (1997–1998) 227.

9. Richard Clogg, *Parties and Elections in Greece: The Search for Legitimacy* (London: C. Hurst & Co., 1987) 8–9. John Campbell and Philip Sherrard, *Modern Greece* (London: Ernest Benn Limited, 1968) 128–129. Also see Koliopoulos and Veremis, *Greece: The Modern Sequel*, 126–140.

10. Σβολοπουλου, *Η Αποφαση για την Υποχρεωτικη Ανταλλαγη*, 112.

11. Μαργαριτα Δριτσα, "Πολιτικες και Οικονομικες Οψεις του Προσφυγικου Προβληματος," *Συμποσιο για τον Ελευθεριο Βενιζελο, Πρακτικα*, December 3–5, 1986 (Athens: Εταιρεια Ελληνικου Λογοτεχνικου και Ιστορικου Αρχειου, Μουσειο Μπενακη, 1988) 133–144. In his recollections of the Lausanne Conference, the American diplomat, Joseph Grew, would speak of Venizelos and his personality as "so attractive and his manner so forceful and convincing that one is always impressed when he talks. He is undoubtedly

the outstanding figure in the conference." Joseph C. Grew, *Turbulent Era*; *A Diplomatic Era of Forty Years, 1904–1945*, vol. 1 (London: Hammond, Hammond & Co., 1953) 497.

12. A leading Greek historian, for example, argues that "Judged by Turkish maximal demands, the Lausanne settlement is a tribute to diplomacy's power to minimize the consequences of military defeat." See Petropoulos, "The Compulsory Exchange of Populations," 140.

13. Grew, *Turbulent Era*, 491.

14. *İsmet Paşa'nın Siyasi ve İçtimai Nutukları* (Ankara: Başvekalet Matbaası, 1933) 26–27.

15. Roderic Davison, "Turkish Diplomacy from Mudros to Lausanne," in *The Diplomats, 1919–1939*, eds. Gordon A. Craig and Felix Gilbert (Princeton: Princeton University Press, 1994) 200. Davison quotes these 'judgements' from the American observers of the conference, Richard Washburn Child and Joseph Clark Grew. The latter was to go to Turkey as ambassador in 1927.

16. *Turkey and the United Nations*, Prepared under the auspices of the Institute of International Relations of the Faculty of Political Science at Ankara University for the Carnegie Endowment for International Peace (New York: Manhattan Publication Company, 1961) 15.

17. *Lozan Barış Konferansı, Tutanaklar, Belgeler*, Takım 1, Cilt 1, Kitap 1, ed. Seha Meray (Ankara: Ankara Üniversitesi Siyasal Bilgiler Fakültesi Yayınları, 1969) 20, 33. (From now on *Lozan Konferansı*) Throughout the current chapter, the Turkish translation of the Lausanne proceedings will be used interchangeably with the English translation. Unless otherwise stated, all the references are to be made to the Turkish version, which contains extra details about the developments in the conference.

18. For the full English text of the National Pact, see "The text of the pact as translated from a French copy furnished by Yusuf Kemal Bey, the Nationalist Foreign Minister," The Library of Congress, the Papers of Henry Morgenthau, Containers 50–52, Reel 39/41.

19. *Lozan Konferansı*, 20–21.

20. "From İsmet to Hey'et-i Vekile Riyaseti, 22 Teşrin-i Sâni 1338 [November 1922]," in *Lozan Telgrafları*, 120–121.

21. "From Hüseyin Rauf to İsmet Paşa, 26–27 Teşrin-i Sâni 1338 [November 1922]," in *Lozan Telgrafları*, 133–134. "Your opinion concerning the liberation of Karaağaç and that it is difficult to obtain a decision in favor of a plebiscite in Western Thrace has been found appropriate by the Council of Ministers" (*Karaağaç'ın kurtarılması ve Garbi Trakya'daki re'y-i ammın te'mininin müşkil olduğu hakkındaki iş'arınız Hey'et-i Vekilece muvâfık görülmüştür Efendim*).

22. Psomiades, *The Eastern Question*, 48. The presence of a large Greek army on the Maritsa, which threatened to resume the war and advance to Istanbul, is considered as one of the major factors that affected the Turkish position on the Thracian border. See Douglas Dakin, "The Importance of the Greek Army in Thrace during the Conference of Lausanne, 1922–1923," in *Greece and Great Britain during World War I, First Symposium Organized*

in Salonica by the Institute for Balkan Studies and King's College (Salonica: Institute for Balkan Studies, 1985) 210–232.

23. Δαφνη, *Ελλας μεταξυ Δυο Πολεμων*, 34.

24. The Conference manual of the Turkish delegation consisted of 14 principles ranked according to their level of importance, and ordered in relation to one another. The ninth heading was the problem of minorities for which it states "the principal goal is the exchange" (*Esas Mübadeledir*). See the introductory remarks by Bilal Şimşir in *Lozan Telgrafları*, xiv. For a summary and analysis of the contents of this document, see chapter on the Turkish Case.

25. Towards the end of his speech Venizelos remarked that "in stating these facts he had no intention whatever of being disagreeable to the Turkish delegation, and by chance a hard word should escape him, he was ready to withdraw it." Great Britain, Foreign Office, Turkey, No. 1 (1923) *Lausanne Conference on Near Eastern Affairs, 1922–1923, Records of Proceeding and Draft Terms of Peace* (London: H. M. Stationary Office 1923) 24. (From now on, *Lausanne Conference*).

26. *Lausanne Conference*, 23.

27. Ibid, 20–22.

28. The Treaty of Neuilly on November 27, 1919 surrendered Western Thrace to the Allies with the provision that the latter would ensure the economic outlets of Bulgaria. The conditions of this guarantee would be finalized at a later date. The defunct Treaty of Sèvres stipulated that the rights over this region be transferred to Greece. Eddy, *Greece and the Greek Refugees*, 43.

29. *Lozan Konferansı*, 25.

30. *Lozan Konferansı*, 23.

31. *Lausanne Conference*, 27.

32. Campbell and Sherrard, *Modern Greece*, 129.

33. Harold Nicolson, *Curzon: The Last Phase, 1919–1925, A Study in Post War Diplomacy* (Boston and New York: Houghton Mifflin Company, 1934) 282–283. Also Hale, *Turkish Foreign Policy*, 54–55. For full coverage of Britain's position at Lausanne, see Briton Cooper Busch, *Mudros to Lausanne, Britain's Frontier in West Asia, 1918–1923* (Albany, N.Y.: State University of New York Press, 1976) 359–392.

34. Hamilton Fish Armstrong, "The Unredeemed Isles of Greece," *Foreign Affairs*, 4:1 (1925) 154–157. Italy occupied the Dodecanese Islands, then under Ottoman rule, in May 1912. The Treaty of London between the Entente Powers and Italy on April 26, 1915 gave the latter complete suzerainty over these islands. Although the Treaty of Sèvres on August 10, 1920 recognized the Italian sovereignty over these islands, Greece and Italy signed a special agreement during the Sèvres negotiations to the effect that Italy would renounce at a later time its control over these islands minus Rhodes in favor of Greece. Since neither the Sèvres nor any other agreement conducted there was implemented, the status of these islands became the subject of discussion at Lausanne as a result of which the Italian position in the Dodecanese Islands was to be officially endorsed. These Islands remained under Italian rule until February 15, 1947. For an interesting

study that provides a chronological survey of the political developments concerning the status of the Dodecanese Islands as well as an unconventional view, from the standpoint of islanders, of Italian colonial rule in these islands until the end of WWII, see Nicholas Doumanis, *Myth and Memory in the Mediterranean: Remembering Fascism's Empire* (London: Macmillan, 1998) passim. As for the diplomatic dimensions of the subject, certain insights can be gained from Psomiades, *The Eastern Question*, 53–55.

35. The head of the American delegation, Joseph Grew states that "Our present position is that of representatives of the United States, who in plenary and other sessions, including those of the Commissions and committees, will be entitled to be present and to be heard in equality with other members, but we are to have no right of voting nor obligations of taking office, presiding or otherwise, or of becoming signatories of agreement or reports." "From the Special Mission at Lausanne (Grew) to the Secretary of State (Hughes), November 21, 1922," in *Papers Relating to the Foreign Relations of the United States 1923*, vol. II (Washington, D. C. United States Government Printing Office, 1938) 900. (From now on F.R.U.S.)

36. "The High Commissioner at Constantinople (Bristol) to the Secretary of State (Hughes), Constantinople, October 5, 1922," in *F.R.U.S.*, 880–881.

37. For the "outline of American interests" see "From the Secretary of State (Hughes) to the Ambassador in France (Herrinck), Washington, October 27, 1922," *F.R.U.S.*, 886–888. A comprehensive survey of the American position at Lausanne with special reference to the status of the Straits and the Open Door policy in the Near East is available in Harry N. Howard, *Turkey, the Straits and U.S. Policy* (Baltimore: The Johns Hopkins University Press, 1974) 113–129.

38. *Lozan Konferansı*, 29–30.

39. Ibid, 46.

40. Ibid, 52.

41. Fridtjof Nansen was appointed as the High Commissioner for Russian Refugees, a post created by the League of Nations in 1919. His negotiating skills were recognized by the newly established League during his humanitarian work at the end of WWI, when he "arranged for prisoners-of-war repatriation and organized aid for victims of the Russian famine." Upon his appointment, Nansen appointed delegates in member countries of the League of Nations with a view to keeping the League in touch with the governments of these countries and the refugees. He organized conferences and made public speeches as well as acted as a mediator between the warring countries over issues of refugee assistance and protection. His office, known as the Nansen International Office, played a significant role in the relief of Russian refugees during the 1919–1923 period. A special certificate of identity for Russian refugees was created on July 5, 1922 at an intergovernmental conference called upon by Nansen. These certificates were later called "Nansen Passports." Nansen was also mandated to work on the situation of refugees during the Turco-Greek war, to the effect of which he initiated various fund drives and worked closely with the Allied Administration in Istanbul. He served the League until his death in 1930.

Nansen's role in the formation of an international refugee regime has been the subject of many studies. See, for example, Skran, *Refugees in Inter-War Europe*, 74–75, 104–109; Marrus, *The Unwanted*, 86–121. Marrus refers to the 1919–1930 period as "the Nansen Era." Also Guy S. Goodwin-Gil, *The Refugee in International Law*, 2nd Edition (Oxford: Clarendon Press, 1996) 207–209.

42. *Lozan Konferansı*, 29.
43. See for example, F. Nimet Beriker, "Negotiating Styles of the Minor Parties in Multilateral Peace Negotiations: Greece and Turkey at the Lausanne Peace Conference, 1922–1923," Ph.D. Dissertation (George Mason University, 1993).
44. Howard, *Turkey, the Straits and U.S. Policy*, 113–129.
45. In his discussion on the future status of the foreigners in Turkey, Busch notes that "there was a general amnesty for political acts committed between 1914 and 1922. Annexed to the draft was a separate Greco-Turkish agreement on the exchange of population, to take effect when both states ratified the larger treaty." Busch, *Mudros to Lausanne*, 382.
46. Davison, "Turkish Diplomacy," 172–209.
47. "İsmet Paşa'dan Büyük Millet Meclisi Riyasetine, 20 Teşrin-i Sâni 1338 [November 1922]," in *Lozan Telgrafları*, 111.
48. "İsmet Paşa'dan Hey'et-i Vekile Riyasetine, 10 Kânun-ı Sâni 1339 [January 1923]," in *Lozan Telgrafları*, 362. Joseph Grew quotes a conversation between Child and Curzon: "The French and Italians will not support with any zeal a demand for a cession of territory by Turkey as a refuge for minorities. Curzon, however, will take whatever position we [the United States] take and will appear in person to present his case." Grew, *Turbulent Era*, 495–496.
49. *Lozan Telgrafları*, xvii.
50. Ténékidès, "*Le Statut des Minorites*," 12. Γουναράκη, "Περι της Συνθηκης Λωζανης," 4; Δαφνη, *Η Ελλας μεταξυ Δυο Πολεμων*, 42; Séfériadès, *L'echange des populations*, 362; Pentzopoulos, *The Balkan Exchange of Minorities*, 66. Very few scholars neglect to mention the name Nansen in their studies. See Alexander Pallis, who, much like the early abortive agreement of 1914, cites Venizelos as the originator of the idea. Pallis, "The Exchange of Populations," 3. George Streit also believes that the first idea of an exchange of populations was suggested by Venizelos at the Conference of London after the First Balkan War and since then has remained in the agenda. M. G. Streit (Address before the Academy of Athens), *Messager d'Athènes*, February 7, 1930.
51. *Lozan Konferansı*, 206, 212, 220.
52. Arı, *Büyük Mübadele*, 16; Murat Hatipoğlu, *Yakın Tarihte Türkiye ve Yunanistan, 1923–1954* (Ankara: Siyasal Kitapevi, 1997) 46; Baskın Oran, *Türk-Yunan İlişkilerinde Batı Trakya Sorunu*, 2nd Edition (Ankara: Bilgi Yayınevi, 1991) 77. Oran provides a brief survey of the debate and ultimately points to Nansen as the originator of the idea of 'compulsion.' See also Ayhan Aktar, "Türk-Yunan Nüfus Mübadelesi'nin İlk Yılı: Eylül 1922-Eylül 1923," in *Yeniden Kurulan Yaşamlar, 1923 Türk-Yunan Zorunlu*

Nüfus Mübadelesi, ed. M. Pekin (Istanbul: Bilgi Üniversitesi Yayınevi, 2005) 57–62.

53. Eddy, *Greece and the Greek Refugees*, 51.

54. This plan was considered as part of a broader scheme that would enable Greece to enter the war on the side of the Allied Powers. Such an exchange would help Greece to obtain Bulgaria's cooperation in saving the Greek presence in Asia Minor and thereby paving the way for the realization of Greece's expansionist policy in Asia Minor. For a brief discussion of this plan, see Ladas, *The Exchange of Minorities*, 27–49.

55. N. Petsalis-Diomidis, *Greece at the Paris Peace Conference, 1919* (Salonica: Institute for Balkan Studies, 1978) 280–290. In compliance with the terms of this Convention, 92,000 Bulgarians were exchanged for 46,000 Greeks.

56. Eddy, *Greece and the Greek Refugees*, 50.

57. For biographical information on Fridtjof Nansen, see Kathleen E. Innes, *The Story of Nansen and the League of Nations* (London: Friends Peace Committee, 1931) passim; Marrus, *The Unwanted*, 51–121.

58. *Lausanne Conference*, 114.

59. Ladas, *The Exchange of Minorities*, 335–338; Σβολοπουλου, *Η Αποφαση για την Υποχρεωτικη Ανταλλαγη*, passim; Pentzopoulos, *The Balkan Exchange of Minorities*, 63–64.

60. See Petropoulos, "The Compulsory Exchange of Populations," 142–143. The inevitability of an exchange was foreseen by several leading figures of world diplomacy. On October 27, 1922, the Secratary of State, Hughes, writing to the Ambassador to France (Herrick) notes that "the most feasible solution of the [minority] problem might possibly be an exchange of Christian and Moslem minorities in Asia Minor and Greece." "The Secretary of State to the Ambassador in France (Herrick), October 27, 1922," in *F.R.U.S.*, 887.

61. *Açıksöz*, 4 Kânun-ı Evvel 1937 [December 1921].

62. *İkdam*, 16 Mart 1338 [March 1922], *Vakit*, 16 Mart 1338 [March 1922].

63. The League of Nations had signed several minorities treaties with European countries since 1919. For "the character and purpose" of these treaties see Macartney, *National States and National Minorities*, 212–294.

64. *Açıksöz*, for example, published 9 consecutive articles on this issue. These articles, transcribed into Latin characters, can be found in *İsmail Habib Sevük'ün Açıksöz'deki Yazıları, Makaleler, Fıkralar*, ed. Mustafa Eski (Ankara: Atatürk Kültür, Dil ve Tarih Yüksek Kurumu, Atatürk Araştırma Merkezi, 1998) 174–203.

65. *İkdam*, 5 Teşrin-i Evvel 1338 [October 1922]; *Sabah*, 5 Teşrin-i Evvel 1338 [October 1922].

66. *İkdam*, 14 Teşrin-i Evvel 1338 [October 1922].

67. Ladas, *The Exchange of Minorities*, 337.

68. *Sabah* 17 Teşrin-i Evvel 1338 [October 1922].

69. *Akşam*, 22 Teşrin-i Evvel 1338 [October 1922].

70. *İkdam*, 25 Teşrin-i Evvel 1338 [October 1922]. Nansen apparently received a telegram from Mustafa Kemal on October 23, which I could not trace, that says "the exchange proposed . . . is acceptable in principle." Quoted in Ladas, *The Exchange of Minorities*, 337.

71. *Sabah*, 31 Teşrin-i Evvel 1338 [October 1922].
72. CA, "From Refet to Hey'et-i Vekile Reisi Rauf Bey," 29 Teşrin-i Evvel 1338 [October 1922], Uncatalogued official document.
73. Ladas, *The Exchange of Minorities*, 337. Venizelos would later say in the conference that it was first Hamid Bey who proposed a compulsory exchange. See *Lozan Konferansı*, 229.
74. *İkdam*, 5 Teşrin-i Sâni 1338 [November 1922].
75. *Lausanne Conference*, 118.
76. Ibid, 119.
77. Ibid, 118.

NOTES TO CHAPTER TWO

1. Petropoulos, "The Compulsory Exchange of Populations," 142. Douglas Dakin, however, takes a different stand and argues that Venizelos was strongly opposed to the principle of compulsion and had to accept the proposal through the mediation of Lord Curzon. Dakin, *The Unification of Greece*, 243. For a comprehensive survey of Greek motives for a compulsory population exchange see Giorgos Kritikos, "Motives for Compulsory Population Exchange in the Aftermath of the Greek-Turkish War," *ΔΕΛΤΙΟ ΚΜΣ*, 13 (1999–2000) 209–224.
2. *Lausanne Conference*, 120.
3. Petropoulos, "The Compulsory Exchange of Populations," 141–148.
4. *Lausanne Conference*, 120.
5. Psomiades, "Thrace and the Armistice of Mudanya," 227.
6. *Lozan Konferansı*, 23.
7. Psomiades, "Thrace and the Armistice of Mudanya," 239–242. AYE, "Ragkavis to the Ministry of Foreign Affairs, 20/3/9, 1922," 1922, A/5 (VI). Also see Dakin, *The Unification of Greece*, 238. For Venizelos' intensive communication with the Ministry of Foreign Affairs during this period see, Σβολοπουλου, *Η Αποφαση για την Υποχρεωτικη Ανταλλαγη*, 12–18.
8. AYE, "[Venizelos] to Lord Curzon, October 13, 1922," A/5 (VI).
9. AYE, "Venizelos to the Ministry of Foreign Affairs, October 5/18, 1922," A/5 (VI).
10. Αλεξανδρου Μαζαρακη-Αινιανος, *Απομνημονευματα* (Athens: Ικαρος, 1948) 272–276. See also Dakin, "The Importance of the Greek Army in Thrace," 211–232.
11. Psomiades, "Thrace and the Armistice of Mudanya," 213. Also by the same author, *The Eastern Question*, 39–50.
12. Psomiades, "Thrace and the Armistice of Mudanya," 213.
13. AYE, "Memorandum of the British Legation to the Ministry of Foreign Affairs, October 2, 1922," 1923, A/5, VI (5).
14. *Lozan Konferansı*, 181.
15. AYE, "Note Verbale from [the] British Legation to the Royal Hellenic Ministry of Foreign Affairs, November 24, 1922," and "Note Verbale from Légation de la Republique Française en Grèce to the Ministry of Foreign Affairs, November 20, 1922," A/5, VI (5).

16. *Lozan Konferansı*, 52. He would raise this point very frequently throughout the conference, 225. See also Psomiades, "Thrace and the Mudanya Armistice," 246.

17. League of Nations 48/24441/24337, "Letter to M. Venizelos from Fridtjof Nansen, October 10, 1922." These two consecutive documents from the Archives of League of Nations are cited in detail by Michael Dark. I thank the author for providing me with a copy of his unpublished paper. Michael Dark, "The Comparative Politics of the Greco-Turkish Exchange," Unpublished paper presented at the conference *Turkey and Greece: Assessment of the Consequences of the Treaty of Lausanne Convention 1923 (75th Anniversary)*, hosted by the Refugee Studies Programme, Queen Elizabeth House, Oxford University, September 17–20, 1998.

18. League of Nations 48/24441/24337, "Letter to M. Venizelos from Fridtjof Nansen, October 10, 1922."

19. League of Nations C.729.M.441.1922, "Telegram attached to 'Exchange of Greek and Turkish populations and prisoners and civilian hostages.'"

20. Ladas, *The Exchange of Minorities*, 336.

21. League of Nations, 48/24441/24337, "Letter to Fridtjof Nansen from M. Venizelos, October 17, 1922."

22. Ladas, *The Exchange of Minorities*, 337. See the section "The Nansen Debate" in Chapter One of this book.

23. Pentzopoulos, *The Balkan Exchange of Minorities*, 64. Cf. Ladas, *The Exchange of Minorities*, 337.

24. For the details of Nansen's communication with the Greek government and Venizelos, see Pentzopoulos, *The Balkan Exchange of Minorities*, 64 and Ladas, *The Exchange of Minorities*, 337.

25. "From the British Ambassador (Geddes) to the Secretary of State (Hughes), November 7, 1922," in *F.R.U.S.*, 892.

26. This policy had been in effect since January 1, 1922, when the properties of all the Greeks in portions of the *Vilayet* of Aydın–recaptured by the Turkish forces–were seized and their rights were transferred to the Ministry of Finance. See CA, 554, 18 Kânun-ı Evvel 1338 [December 1922]. (From now on the uncatalogued resolutions will be cited only with their original number.)

27. The 'Independence Tribunals' were special courts, established in eight different districts (i.e., Ankara, Eskişehir, Konya, Isparta, Sivas, Kastamonu, Pozantı and Diyarbakır) in 1920 with a view to prosecuting war crimes, more particularly desertions from the army. They were abolished on February 17, 1921, to be reopened in three districts only three months later. During the war, these courts were also in charge of prosecuting those who failed to pay a newly instituted tax known as *Tekalif-i Milliye*. This tax was imposed upon the population of Anatolia, regardless of ethnic or religious affiliation, to contribute (up to 40% of individual wealth) to the financing of war efforts. In the post-war period, the Independence Tribunals were used by the government to serve a wide range of purposes from the purging of political opposition to the enforcement of reforms like the abolition of traditional headgear (e.g., *sarık, fez* etc.). Although these institutions

had always been in the center of a hot-heated political debate in the Turkish Grand National Assembly, they remained in operation until 1949. See Akın, *TBMM Devleti*, 164–180. For the debates in the Turkish Parliament on these institutions, see *T.B.M.M. GCZ*, 6 Mart 1338 [March 1922]—27 Şubat 1338 [February 1923], vol. 3. (Istanbul: İş Bankası Kültür Yayınları, 1985) 606–637. An English summary of the activities of these courts can be found in Eric J. Zürcher, *The Unionist Factor: The Role of the Committee of Union and Progress in the Turkish National Movement, 1905–1926* (Leiden: E. J. Brill, 1984) 146–148.

28. See for example *T.B.M.M. ZC*, 18 Teşrin-i Evvel 1338 [October 1922]—18 Teşrin-i Sâni 1338 [November 1922] Devre I, İçtima Senesi: 3, Cilt: 24, (Ankara: T.B.M.M. Matbaası, 1960) 263–264. Also see various resolutions of the Turkish government concerning the areas evacuated by the Greeks. CA, 2001, 16 Teşrin-i Sâni 1338 [November 1922]; 2146, 7 Kânun-ı Sâni 1339 [January 1923]; and (unnumbered) 23 Kânun-ı Sâni 1339 [January 1923].

29. CA, 1875, 1 Teşrin-i Evvel 1338 [October 1922]. Until quite recently these inventories remained in the possession of the archives of Provincial Bureaus of Village Affairs (*Köy Hizmetleri İl Müdürlükleri*). Most of them were transferred to the Republican Archives (*Cumhuriyet Arşivi*) in Ankara.

30. Mavrogordatos, *Stillborn Republic*, 202.

31. Ibid, 199–201.

32. John V. Kofas, *Authoritarianism in Greece, the Metaxas Regime* (Boulder, Colorado: East European Monographs, 1983) 32. Also Mazower, *Greece and the Inter-War Economic Crisis*, 51. On the early position of the Greek socialists concerning the situation of the Greeks in Asia Minor, see the pamphlet entitled "La Question d'Orient, Vue par les Socialistes Grecs" (Mémoire soumis par les Socialistes grecs a la Conférence Socialiste Interalliée de Londres, 1918).

33. See Philip Carabott, "The Greek Communists and the Asia Minor Campaign," *ΔΕΛΤΙΟ ΚΜΣ*, 9 (1992) 99–118. For the stance of the Greek socialists on a variety of domestic and foreign issues, see Αγγελος Γ. Ελεφαντης, *Η Επαγγελια της Αδυνατης Επαναστασης, Κ.Κ.Ε. και Αστισμος στον Μεσοπολεμο* (Athens: Εκδοσεις Ολκος, 1976) 23–55.

34. Γιαννης Κορδατος, "Οικονομικη Χρισις που Γεννηθηκε απο τον Πολεμο Γινεται καθε Μερα Μεγαλυθερη και Βαθυτερη," *Κομμουνιστικη Επιθεωρησις*, 1:1 (June 1921) 25.

35. Quoted in Alexandris, *The Greek Minority of Istanbul*, 84.

36. Θανος Βερεμης, *Οι Επεμβασεις του Στρατου στην Ελληνικη Πολιτικη, 1916–1936* (Athens: Εξαντας, 1977) 123–124.

37. Mavrogordatos, *Stillborn Republic*, 201.

38. The minutes of court proceedings were published in 1931 and reprinted recently. *Η Δικη των Εξ, Τα Εστεσογραφημενα Πρακτικα, 31 Οκτωβριου-15 Νοεμβριου 1922* (Athens: Δημιουργια, 1996).

39. Mavrogordatos, *Stillborn Republic*, 29.

40. Βερεμης, *Οι Επεμβασεις του Στρατου*, 133.

41. Ladas, *The Exchange of Minorities*, 3.

42. Pallis, "The Exchange of Populations," 4.
43. AYE *"Εκθεσεις Κατατεσεων Προσφυγων,"* A/5, VI (1). The document reports the ongoing relief efforts on various islands.
44. AYE, "Anonymous telegram, Raidestos, October 8/21, 1922," A/5. This telegram from Raidestos (Tekirdağ) informs Athens that 4,000 refugees were shipped and 600 tons of grain were accompanying them. Numbers: Nearly 600,000 refugees already in Athens, 130,000 in Mitylene, 60,000 in Chios, 70,000 in Salonica, 40,000 in Piraeus. Each refugee was accorded 2 francs, 52 centimes per day. AYE, "Exposé de Romanos, Ministre de Grèce sur la situation des réfugies d'Asie mineure, fait à l'Assemblée de la colonie Grecque, tenue à la Légation Hellénique le 18 Octobre 1922," A/2 (6).
45. AYE, "E. Carlile to His Excellency the Greek Minister, November 27, 1922," A/2 (6).
46. "From İsmet to Hey'et-i Vekile Riyasetine, 13 Kânun-ı Evvel 1338 [13 December 1922]," in *Lozan Telgrafları*, 213–214.
47. AYE, "Aide Memoire, October 9/22, 1922," A/5, VI (11).
48. AYE, "From the Greek Consulate in Rhodes to the [Greek] Ministry of Foreign Affairs, October 14, 1922," A/5, VI (11).
49. AYE, "Secrétariat Hellénique Permanent Auprès de la Société des Nations, Genève, le 13/26 Décembre 1922," A/5, VI (11).
50. AYE, "Letter from the Greek Embassy in Bern to [Greek] Ministry of Foreign Affairs, December 29, 1922," A/2 (6).
51. AYE, "Societe des Nations, Communiqué au Conseil et aux Members de la Société, C. 754.M.456.1922, Geneve, le 8 Décembre 1922," A/2 (6). This document is an official League of Nations document, blueprinted and forwarded to the Greek Ministry of Foreign Affairs.
52. AYE, "Exposé de Romanos," A/2 (6).
53. Henry Morgenthau was particularly effective in raising funds in the United States to give aid to Greece for the refugees. Many fund raising drives were organized through his initiative, the most effective of which was the Roll Call for the Red Cross, which operated through the clubs in major universities. "Nine university clubs expect a hundred per cent enrolment. They are Harvard, Yale, Army and Navy, Massachusetts Institute of Technology, Pennsylvania, Princeton and Williams clubs." *The New York City Times*, October 15, 1922. Morgenthau gave lectures all over the United States on what was happening in the Near East, speaking before the students of Columbia University, he says "Turks Strike Fear into Nations" *The New York City Times*, January 19, 1923. The Library of Congress, the Papers of Henry Morgenthau, Reel 39–41. For a brief review of Morgenthau's activities related with refugee relief see the pertaining section in Chapter Seven of this book.
54. AYE, "From Secretariat Hellénique Aupres de la Société des Nations to the [Greek] Ministry of Foreign Affairs, December 13/26, 1922," A/5, VI (11).
55. AYE, "Légation Royale Hellénique in Rio de Janeiro to the Ministry of Foreign Affairs, December 1/14, 1922," A/5, VI (1).
56. AYE, "Exposé de Romanos," A/2 (6).
57. Charles Howland, "Greece and Her Refugees," *Foreign Affairs*, 26:4 (1926) 622.

58. James L. Barton, *Story of Near East Relief (1915–1930), An Interpretation* (New York: The MacMillan Company, 1930). Barton provides a full picture of Athens for the time period concerned. For a list of public buildings which were turned into orphanages and dormitories for refugees, see 162–163.

59. AYE, "From the Legation of the Republic of Tchécoslovaque in Athens to the [Greek] Ministry of Foreign Affairs, January 4, 1923," A/5, VI (11).

60. Pallis, "The Exchange of Populations," 4.

61. *Lausanne Conference*, 121.

62. Ibid.

63. Ibid, 225.

64. Throughout the conference, Venizelos repeated his preference for a voluntary exchange. *Lozan Konferansı*, 212, 226. Also *Lozan Barış Konferansı*, Takım 1, Cilt 1, Kitap 2, ed. Seha Meray (Ankara: Ankara Üniversitesi Siyasal Bilgiler Fakültesi Yayınları, 1969) 5.

65. *Lozan Telgrafları*, 223.

66. Σβολοπουλου, *Η Αποφαση για την Υποχρεωτικη Ανταλλαγη*, 18–19.

67. *Lozan Konferansı*, 120.

68. Ibid, 123.

69. Pentzopoulos, *The Balkan Exchange of Minorities*, 63.

70. *Lausanne Conference*, 177.

71. *Lozan Konferansı*, 201.

72. *Lozan Telgrafları*, 212.

73. *Lozan Konferansı*, 201–202.

74. Ibid, 125.

75. Ibid, 200–207.

76. "From İsmet to Hey'et-i Vekile Riyasetine, 13 Kânun-ı Evvel 1338 [December 1922]," in *Lozan Telgrafları*, 211–212.

77. For the earlier version of Venizelos' speech in the Commission, see AYE, "From the Délégation Hellénique to the [Greek] Ministry of Foreign Affairs, January 17/30, 1923," A/5, VI (11).

78. Ladas, *Exchange of Minorities*, 344.

79. AYE, "Dépêche Télégraphique Chiffrée, Kaklamanos, Lausanne, January 30, 1923," A/5, VI (1).

80. Richard Clogg, "A Millet within a Millet: the Karamanlides," in *Ottoman Greeks in the Age of Nationalism, Politics, Economy, and Society in the Nineteenth Century*, eds. D. Gondicas and C. Issawi (Princeton: The Darwin Press, Inc., 1999) 115–142.

NOTES TO CHAPTER THREE

1. For the members of the Turkish delegation, see Ali Naci Karacan, *Lozan Konferansı ve İsmet Paşa (*İstanbul: Milliyet Yayınları, 1971) 95–113; M. Cemil Bilsel, *Lozan*, vol. 2, Reprint of 1932–1933 Edition (Istanbul: Sosyal Yayınlar, 1998) 2–12.

2. It should be remarked here that İsmet Paşa was the chief assistant to İzzet Paşa during the negotiations with İmam Yahya and took an active part in

drafting the covenant known as the Treaty of Da'an (October 1911) that granted partial autonomy to the mountainous part of Yemen inhabited by the Zaydis. He later conducted a similar negotiation with Sayyid İdrisi in Asır. The Treaty of Da'an stipulated the conditions for the division of Yemen into two administrative units according to the demographic figures pertaining to the Zaydis and Shafi'is. The same treaty also put down the legal framework for the treatment of remaining minorities in respective territories. Whether İsmet Paşa's experience in Yemen played any role in his appointment as the head of the Turkish delegation at Lausanne is an issue to be explored. I am grateful to Şükrü Hanioğlu for bringing this point to my attention. For the details of the Treaty of Da'an, see Manfred W. Wenner, *Modern Yemen, 1918–1966* (Baltimore: The Johns Hopkins Press, 1968) 47–48.

3. İsmet İnönü, *Hatıralar*, vol. 2 (Ankara: Bilgi Yayınevi, 1987) 87.

4. *Dr. Rıza Nur'un Lozan Hatıraları* (Istanbul: Boğaziçi Yayınları, 1992) 101–102.

5. İnönü, *Hatıralar*, 79; Cf. *Dr. Rıza Nur'un Lozan Hatıraları*, 99. Rıza Nur writes that he was surprised when the question of minorities and the prospect of an exchange were raised so soon in the conference. (*Bu mübadele benim Türkçülük noktasından ehass-ı emelim [en has emelim] idi; fakat böyle tarihte görülmemiş bir şeyi nasıl edeceğim diye öteden beri düşünüp duruyordum. Şimdi kendi kendine ortaya geldi. Yani gökten düşmüş "minkudretin" oldu.*) This statement contradicts the list of instructions that the Turkish delegation had been given in Ankara.

6. *Lausanne Conference*, 114. The emphasis is mine.

7. Ibid, 114.

8. "From İsmet Paşa to Hey'et-i Vekile Riyaseti, 22 Teşrin-i Sâni 1338 [22 November 1922]," Lozan Telgrafları, 120–121. "From İsmet Paşa to Hey'et-i Vekile Riyaseti, 23 Teşrin-i Sâni 1338 [23 November 1922]," *Lozan Telgrafları*, 122–123.

9. "From İsmet Paşa to Hey'et-i Vekile Riyaseti, 22 Teşrin-i Sâni 1338 [November 1922]," *Lozan Telgrafları*, 122–123; "From İsmet Paşa to Hey'et-i Vekile Riyaseti, 25 Teşrin-i Sâni 1338 [November 1922]," *Lozan Telgrafları*, 125; "From İsmet Paşa to Hey'et-i Vekile Riyaseti, 25 Teşrin-i Sâni 1338 [November 1922]," *Lozan Telgrafları*, 129.

10. "From İsmet Paşa to Hey'et-i Vekile Riyaseti, 23 Teşrin-i Sâni 1338 [November 1922]," *Lozan Telgrafları*, 122–123. The original text reads as "*Bir de Orta Anadolu'da bulunan Hıristiyanların nakli ve yetimlerin seyahatı asla lazım ve müstacel olmadığı halde bu esnada bize şiddetli zarar ve aleyhimize galeyan-ı efkar husule getireceğini arz ederim. Bu hususta da vazıhan tenvir buyurulmaklığımı istirham ederim. Ekalliyetler ve Hıristiyanlar gibi mesailde bihassa Amerikalıların iştiraki ile şiddetli müşkilat göreceğimizi tahmin ediyorum.*"

11. The Archives of the Turkish Ministry of Foreign Affairs still remains closed to researchers. The document has been published by Bilal Şimsir, one of the select few with unlimited access to this repository. See *Lozan Telgrafları*, xiv.

12. Ibid, xiv.
13. "From İsmet to Hey'et-i Vekile Riyasetine, 25 Teşrin-i Sâni 1338 [November 1922]," in *Lozan Telgrafları*, 124–125. The emphasis is mine.
14. İsmet Paşa refers here to the minorities treaties concluded recently between the Allies and the states of such countries as Romania. For the details of the minorities treaty signed with Romania after WWI, see Macartney, *National States and National Minorities*, 240–247.
15. "From İsmet Paşa to Hey'et-i Vekile Riyasetine, 28 Teşrin-i Sâni 1338 [November 1922]," in *Lozan Telgrafları*, 147. İsmet Paşa told this view to a member of the British diplomatic team on November 27.
16. *T.B.M.M. ZC*, Devre: I, İçtima Senesi: 3, Cilt: 24, 18 Teşrin-i Evvel 1338 [October 1922]—18 Teşrin-i Sâni 1338 [November], 340–376. Speaking of the religious minorities, a deputy, namely Mehmed Şükrü Bey, made the following remark: "These people have resorted to all kinds of violence and committed all sorts of crimes to destroy this [Turkish] nation. They no longer have a place in this country. There is one thing to be done for these [people]. Exchange, gentlemen, it is necessary to **exchange** these [people]." *T.B.M.M GZC*, 25 Kânun-ı Evvel 1338 [December 1922] vol. 3 (Ankara: Türkiye İş Bankası Kültür Yayınları, 1985) 1148–1155. Also *T.B.M.M. ZC*, Devre: I, İçtima Senesi: 4, Cilt: 29, 9 Nisan 1339 [April 1923]- 16 Nisan 1339 [April 1923], (Ankara: T.B.M.M. Matbaası, 1961) 173–174.
17. Tunalı Hilmi dominated most of the discussions. See for example, *T.B.M.M. ZC*, Devre: I, İçtima Senesi: 3, Cilt: 24, 18 Teşrin-i Evvel 1338 [October 1922]—18 Teşrin-i Sâni 1338 [November], 145.
18. *Tevhid-i Efkar*, 13 Kânun-ı Sâni 1339 [January 1923].
19. "From Hüseyin Rauf to İsmet Paşa, 27/28 Teşrin-i Sâni 1338 [November 1922]," in *Lozan Telgrafları*, 138.
20. "From Hüseyin Rauf to İsmet Paşa, 28 Teşrin-i Sâni, 1922 [November 1922]," in *Lozan Telgrafları*, 141. See also "From Hüseyin Rauf to İsmet Paşa, 13 Kânun-ı Evvel 1338 [December 1922]," in *Lozan Telgrafları*, 209.
21. AYE, "Το Υπουργειον των Στρατιωτικων προς Στρατιον Θρακης, September 21, 1922," A/5 (V) (VI) (VII).
22. AYE, "Διοικησις Χωροφυλακης Σαμου προς την Ανωτεραν Διοικησιν Χωροφυλακης Νησων Αιγαιου εις Μιτυληνη, January 30, 1923," 1923, A/5, VI (8). Also AYE, "Anonymous Letter to the [Greek] Ministry of Foreign Affairs, May 16, 1923, Κων/πολει," A/5 (V) (VI) (VII). The letter informs the Foreign Ministry of the complaints of the Turks concerning the activities of Greek bands.
23. AYE, "Memorandum, [the] British Legation, Athens, October 2, 1922," A/5 (V) (VI) (VII).
24. "From Hüseyin Rauf to İsmet Paşa, 10 Kânun-ı Sâni 1339 [10 January 1923]," in *Lozan Telgrafları*, 357.
25. "From Hüseyin Rauf to İsmet Paşa, 26 Kânun-u Evvel, 1338 [26 December 1922]," in *Lozan Telgrafları*, 279.
26. AYE, "Note du Secretariat General, Lausanne, le 23 Décembre 1922," A/5, VI (1). The letter seems to have been dispatched on November 26, 1922.

27. *Lozan Konferansı*, 122.

28. "From Hüseyin Rauf to İsmet Paşa, 26/27 Teşrin-i Sâni 1338 [26/27 November 1922]," in *Lozan Telgrafları*, 133–134. "From İsmet Paşa to Hey'et-i Vekile Riyasetine, 1 Kânun-ı Evvel 1338 [1 December 1922]," in *Lozan telgrafları*, 154. İsmet Paşa's concerns were well-taken by his government, meaning that he was allowed to withdraw his claim to a plebiscite. In the meantime, the issue had been complicated by the Bulgarian claims and eventually referred to a sub-commission.

29. "İsmet Paşa to Hey'et-i Vekile Riyasetine, 2 Kânun-ı Evvel 1338 [December 1922]," in *Lozan Telgrafları*, 156.

30. Roger Owen and Şevket Pamuk, *Middle East Economies in the Twentieth Century* (Cambridge, M.A.: Harvard University Press, 1999) 12. For a more comprehensive survey of the CUP's economic nationalism, see Zafer Toprak, *İttihad-Terakki ve Devletçilik* (Istanbul: Tarih Vakfı Yurt Yayınları, 1995), 72–87; idem, *Milli İktisat-Milli Burjuvazi* (Istanbul: Tarih Vakfı Yurt Yayınları, 1995) 10–22, 64–78.

31. Owen and Pamuk, *Middle East Economies*, 12.

32. Falih Rıfkı Atay, *Eski Saat, 1917–1933* (Istanbul: Akşam Matbaası, 1933) 90.

33. Tekin Alp, *The Turkish and Pan-Turkish Ideal*, Constantinople, Admiralty War Staff, Intelligence Division, March 1917, 22–24. Jacob M. Landau, *Tekinalp, Turkish Patriot, 1883–1961* (Istanbul: Nederlands Historisch Archaeologisch Instituut, 1984) 33–37. Also Çağlar Keyder, *State and Class in Turkey: A Study in Capitalist Development* (London: VERSO, 1987) 71–90.

34. Lord Curzon remarks that "He [İsmet] adopted a stiff attitude about capitulation(s)." See *Lozan Telgrafları*, 137.

35. Ziya Gökalp, *Türkçülüğün Esasları* (Istanbul: Varlık Yayınevi, 1973) 161–165.

36. Caleb F. Gates, "Kemalist Regime Doomed," in *The Lausanne Treaty and Kemalist Turkey*. The essay is presented with a brief forward saying that it "was written before the Lausanne Conference, when American nationals in Turkey, or those who have relations with Turkey, could still express themselves without intimidation and restraint," 21.

37. *Lausanne Conference*, 326.

38. Ibid, 207.

39. "Influence of Pan-Turkish Political Aims on Turkish Military Policy, 1914–1918" (official report prepared by the British Foreign Intelligence). The late Naim Turfan made a good case on this issue. See the epilogue in his *Rise of the Young Turks, Politics, the Military and Ottoman Collapse* (London: I. B. Tauris, 2000) 429–443.

40. *Lausanne Conference*, 312.

41. Ibid, 117. İnönü, *Hatıralar*, 79–86.

42. *Lozan Konferansı*, 178.

43. *Lausanne Conference*, 204.

44. Ibid, 203.

45. İnönü, *Hatıralar*, 79.

46. *Lausanne Conference*, 179.

47. Ibid, 203.

48. *Daily Telegraph*, December 8, 1922.

49. "From Hüseyin Rauf to İsmet Paşa, 7 Kânun-ı Evvel 1338 [December 1922]," in *Lozan Telgrafları*, 176.

50. *Lausanne Conference*, 207.

51. "Text of the National Pact," The Library of Congress, the Papers of Henry Morgenthau, Containers 50–52, Reel 39/41.

52. "From İsmet Paşa to Hey'et-i Vekile Riyaseti, 15 Kânun-ı Evvel 1338 [December 1922]," in *Lozan Telgrafları*, 220.

53. For a comprehensive survey of the Turkish concerns over the signature of a Minorities Treaty with the League of Nations, see Mim Kemal Öke, *The Armenian Question, 1914–1923* (Nicosia: K. Rüstem & Brother, 1988) 219–220. Turkey joined the League of Nations in 1932 and thereby accepted the mandate of the League over the minority affairs.

54. "From İsmet Paşa to İcra Vekilleri Riyasetine, 15 Kânun-ı Evvel 1338 [December 1922]," in *Lozan Telgrafları*, 224–225.

55. "From Hüseyin Rauf to İsmet Paşa, 17 Kânun-ı Evvel 1338 [December 1922]," in *Lozan Telgrafları*, 233.

56. *Lozan Telgrafları*, 123. America's pressure to partake in Lausanne relates very much to its failure to find welcome support among the Turks for a mandate. Although many people were attracted to the idea earlier, the developments reversed their opinions. See also Bilal Şimsir, *İngiliz Belgelerinde Atatürk (1919–1938)*, vol. 1 (Ankara: Türk Tarih Kurumu Basımevi, 1979) 171. On the terms for an American Mandate over the Ottoman Empire, see Henry Morgenthau's article, "Mandates or War?" *The New York Times*, November 9, 1919. Speaking in the opening session of the National Milk Producers' Convention, Morgenthau states that "We Americans must be ashamed that we did not see the necessity and the wisdom of accepting the mandate over Turkey when it was offered us," November 1922. The Library of Congress, the Papers of Henry Morgenthau, Reel 39/41.

57. "From İsmet to Hey'et-i Vekile Riyaseti, 23 Teşrin-i Sâni 1338 [November 1922]," in *Lozan Telgrafları*, 123.

58. Ibid, 122–124.

59. For a survey of the broader interests of Americans at Lausanne see Howard, *Turkey, the Straits and U.S. Foreign Policy*, 113–129.

60. "From İsmet to Hey'et-i Vekile Riyaseti, 25 Teşrin-i Sâni 1338 [November 1922], " in *Lozan Telgrafları*, 125–126. Also "From İsmet to Hey'et-i Vekile Riyaseti, 27 Teşrin-i Sâni 1338 [27 November 1922]," in *Lozan Telgrafları*, 137.

61. "From Hüseyin Rauf to İsmet Paşa, 28 Teşrin-i Sâni 1338 [November 1922]," in *Lozan Telgrafları*, 140.

62. "From İsmet Paşa to Hey'et-i Vekile Riyaseti, 23 Teşrin-i Sâni 1338 [November 1922]," in *Lozan Telgrafları*, 123.

63. "From İsmet Paşa to Hey'et-i Vekile Riyaseti, 25 Teşrin-i Sâni 1338 [November 1922]," in *Lozan Telgrafları*, 125.

64. "From İsmet Paşa to Hey'et-i Vekile Riyaseti, 23 Teşrin-i Sâni 1338 [November 1922]," in *Lozan Telgrafları*, 123.
65. "From İsmet Paşa to Hey'et-i Vekile Riyaseti, 13 Kânun-ı Evvel 1338 [December 1922]," in *Lozan Telgrafları*, 213.
66. Ibid, 214.
67. "From the Special Mission at Lausanne to Secretary of State [Hughes], December 7, 1922," in *F.R.U.S.*, 916. Also see "From Secretary of State to the Special Mission at Lausanne, December 22, 1922," in *F.R.U.S.*, 932. On December 13, the American delegation paid a visit to the Turkish delegation and expressed their concern over the minority problem. "From İsmet to Hey'et-i Vekile Riyaseti, 14 Kânun-ı Evvel 1338 [December 1922]," in *Lozan Telgrafları*, 215–216. This was the point at which the Turkish position on the League and the other provisions of the Allies became crystallized.
68. Grew, *The Turbulent Era*, 495–496.
69. A political adviser to the Turkish delegation, ex-Minister of Justice, Cela-leddin Arif Bey, seems to have been frequently visited by the members of the American delegation at Lausanne. After one of his conversations on the situation of Armenians with Joseph Grew, the latter wrote the following "territorial home for Armenians or other minorities impossible in view of public opinion and sentiment of National Assembly, but expressed willingness to give strongest possible guarantees provided outlook for gradual reduction of minorities should be carried out by emigration over a term of years." Grew, *The Turbulent Era*, 492. Secretary of State, Hughes, responded Grew's communication on Djelaleddin (Celaleddin) Bey with great interest, asking "to what guarantees would the Turks agree for the protection of minorities?" "From the Secretary of State [Hughes] to Joseph Grew, November 27, 1922," in *F.R.U.S.*, 907.
70. For a detailed analysis of the Chester concession, see John A. DeNovo, *American Interests and Policies in the Middle East, 1900–1939* (Minneapolis: University of Minnesota Press, 1963) especially chapters 3, 5–7. See also Bülent Bilmez Can, *Demiryolundan Petrole Chester Projesi (1908–1923)* (Istanbul: Tarih Vakfı Yurt Yayınları, 2000) passim.
71. Davison, "Turkish Diplomacy," 206. Also see "From İsmet Paşa to Hey'et-i Vekile Riyaseti, 22 Nisan 1338 [April 1923]," in *Lozan Telgrafları*, vol. 2, 205.
72. "From İsmet Paşa to Hey'et-i Vekile Riyaseti, 26 Teşrin-i Sâni 1338 [26 November 1922]," in *Lozan Telgrafları*, 131–32. Also see "From İsmet Paşa to Hey'et-i Vekile Riyaseti, 10 Kânun-ı Evvel 1338 [December 1922]," in *Lozan Telgrafları*, 192. Also İnönü, *Hatıralar*, 80–84.
73. Henry Morgenthau gave numerous interviews to the reporters of various U.S. and British newspapers on the situation of Armenians. See, for example, "An Independent Turkey!" *Philadelphia PA. Record*, November 28, 1922; "Morgenthau Asserts We Can Silence Turks," *Boston Mass. Herald*, November 9, 1922. The Library of Congress, the Papers of Henry Morgenthau, Containers 50–52, Reel 39/41.
74. AYE, "Note du Secretariat General, Lausanne, le 23 Décembre 1922," 1922–23, A/5, VI (1). The document gives a list of telegrams (together with

a short subject summary) that had been received recently by the Conference.

75. "From İsmet to Hey'et-i Vekile Riyaseti, 6 Kânun-ı Evvel 1338 [December 1922]," in *Lozan Telgrafları,* 172. Here the term "Armenians" refers mainly to those who were living in Istanbul.
76. Ibid.
77. "From Hüseyin Rauf to İsmet Paşa, 28 Teşrin-i Sâni 1338 [November 1922]," in *Lozan Telgrafları,* 143.
78. CA, 494, 5 Kânun-ı Sâni 1337 [January 1921].
79. For details of the discussion on the state of the Patriarchate see Alexandris, *The Greek Minority of Istanbul,* 87–95. Also Dakin, *The Unification of Greece,* 243–245.
80. "From Hüseyin Rauf to İsmet Paşa, 30 Kânun-ı Evvel 1338 [10 December 1922]," in *Lozan Telgrafları,* 296–297.
81. "From Hüseyin Rauf to İsmet Paşa, 2 Kânun-ı Sâni 1339 [2 January 1923]," *in Lozan Telgrafları,* 313–314.
82. *Dr. Rıza Nur'un Lozan Hatıraları,* 113.
83. *T.B.M.M. GZC,* 2 Mart 1339 [March 1923]—25 Teşrin-i Evvel [October] 1934, vol. 4 (Ankara: Türkiye İş Bankası Kültür Yayınları, 1985) 476–477.
84. "From İsmet to Hey'et-i Vekile Riyaseti, 10 Kânun-ı Sâni 1339 [January 1923]," in *Lozan Telgrafları,* 363.
85. "*Bu suretle Patrik münakaşası siyasi ve idari vezaif ve imtiyazatı olmadığının ve ekalliyetler hukuku namı altında tandığımız mevaddan maada bir taahhüde girmediğimizden tasrih ve i'lanı ile hitam bulmuştur.*" See "From İsmet Paşa to Hey'et-i Vekile Riyaseti, 10 Kânun-ı Sâni 1339, [January 1923]," in *Lozan Telgrafları,* 362–363; also "From İsmet Paşa to Hey'et-i Vekile Riyaseti, 20 Kânun-ı Sâni 1339, [January 1923]," in *Lozan Telgrafları,* 415.
86. CA, 744, 3 Ağustos 1340 [August 1924] (030 18 01 01 010 37 1).
87. "From İsmet Paşa to Hey'et-i Vekile Riyaseti, 23 Kânun-ı Evvel 1338 [December 1922]," in *Lozan Telgrafları,* 268–269. Also "From İsmet Paşa to Hey'et-i Vekile Riyaseti, 28 Kânun-ı Evvel 1338 [December 1922]," in *Lozan Telgrafları,* 290.
88. "From İsmet Paşa to Hey'et-i Vekile Riyaseti, 12 Kânun-ı Sâni 1339 [December 1923]," in *Lozan Telgrafları,* 372.
89. *Lozan Telgrafları,* 328.
90. "Up to that date, passport control had remained in the hands of the Allied authorities, who had by that means been able to send out of the country all those who for various reasons were considered well-advised to leave the country." Alexandris, *The Greek Minority of Istanbul,* 79.
91. ΑΥΕ, "Η Αστυνομικη Δ/νσις Θεσσαλονικης προς το Αρχηγειον Χωροφυλακης Τμημα II, Athens, December 31, 1922," 1923, A/2 (7).
92. "From Hüseyin Rauf to İsmet Paşa, 23 Kânun-ı Sâni 1339 [January 1923]," in *Lozan Telgrafları,* 427.
93. "From İsmet Paşa to Hey'et-i Vekile Riyaseti, 22 Kânun-ı Sâni 1339 [January 1923]," in *Lozan Telgrafları,* 425.

94. "From İsmet Paşa to Hey'et-i Vekile Riyaseti, 20 Kânun-ı Sâni 1339 [January 1923]," in *Lozan Telgrafları*, 410.

95. "From İsmet Paşa to Hey'et-i Vekile Riyaseti, 20 Kânun-ı Sâni 1339 [January 1923]," in *Lozan Telgrafları*, 410.

96. AYE, "Anonymous Report, December 20, 1922, Constantinople," 1922–23, A/5 VI (1).

97. AYE, Ibid. The report was wired to Athens and then immediately forwarded to the Greek delegation in Lausanne.

98. "From İsmet Paşa to Hey'et-i Vekile Riyaseti, 25 Kânun-ı Sâni 1339 [January 1923], in *Lozan Telgrafları*, 441–442.

99. AYE, "From A. A. Pallis to the Acting British High Commissioner Henderson, Constantinople, February 4, 1923," A/5, VI (11).

100. AYE, Ibid. A letter from Adnan Bey to the government in Ankara confirms the ongoing violence against the Greeks of the Black Sea region. Adnan Bey asks the government to take measures against the activities of Osman Agha. CA, 102/10, 6 Şubat 1339 [February 1923] (030 10 123 872 10) and see also an attachment to this document dated from 21 Şubat 1339 [February 1923]. There is vast literature in Greek on 'Osman Agha,' known as Topal Osman, a Turkish brigand who was held responsible for most of the atrocities committed against the Greeks, especially during their departure from the Black Sea area. See for example, a two-volume set by Γιώργου Ν. Λαμψίδη, a popular Greek historian of Pontic descent: *Τοπαλ Οσμαν, Η Τραγωδια των Ποντων απο το 1914–1924* (Athens: Εκδοσεις Λαδια και Σια, 1969). The second volume appeared two years later. *Τοπαλ Οσμαν, Η Τελευταια Πραξη, Μικρασιατικη Καταστροφη (1914–1924)* (Athens: Εκδοσεις Λαδια και Σια, 1971). In Turkish popular historiography Topal Osman is portrayed as one of the heroes of the Turkish War of Independence. See for example Cemal Şener, *Topal Osman Olayı* (Istanbul: Ant Yayınları, 1992).

101. AYE, Ibid.

102. AYE, "Η Διοικησις Προκαλυψεως Μακεδονιας προς το Γενικον Στρατηγειον Γραφειον Πον., January 21, 1923," A/2 (7). In the regions of Kalarion, Anaselitsa, and Grevena, the Turkish population did not wait for the signature of the convention and depopulated their settlements in January, having sold "whatever they owned."

103. When the negotiations of the exchange were unfolding, the Mufti of Langada and the representatives of the Muslim community petitioned the Greek state saying that "the decision taken in the Lausanne Congress concerning the exchange of the Christian populations of Asia Minor and the Muslims of Macedonia would cause us great suffering and also that we are not willing to leave the graves of our ancestors and abandon our properties and go elsewhere. Therefore, we by all means object to such an exchange and we announce that we are happy with our Greek government." AYE, "Langada Kazası Kaymakamlığı Canib-i Aliyesine, 13 Kânun-ı Sâni 1923 [Ocak 1923]," A/5, VI (11).

104. AYE, "From the Leaders of Muslim Community in Komotini to the General Administration of Thrace, February 6, 1923," A/5, VI (1).

105. AYE, "From *Επιτροπη Λαου* to the [Greek] Ministry of Foreign Affairs, February 1, 1923," A/5, VI (1). The letter has also been sent to the [Greek] Ministry of Interior.

NOTES TO CHAPTER FOUR

1. Psomiades, *The Eastern Question*, 38.
2. Barton, *Story of Near East Relief*, 166.
3. *Lausanne Conference*, 115.
4. Fridtjof Nansen, "Re-Making Greece," *The Forum* (1923) 23.
5. "The Chargé in Greece (Atherton) to the Secretary of State, Athens, May 17, 1923," in *F.R.U.S*, 337.

NOTES TO CHAPTER FIVE

1. Νικος Καζαντζάκης, *Οι Αδερφοφαδες, μυθιστόρημα*, (Athens: Εκδοσεις Ελ. Καζαντζάκη, 1973) 14–18. (All the Greeks to Greece, all the Turks to Turkey! . . . A cloud of grief rose from within the village. You should know that it's difficult, very difficult, for a soul to unglue itself from familiar waters and lands . . . They are uprooting us! Damned be they who have caused this! Damned be they who have caused this! Damned be they who have caused this! People raised their hands toward the sky and growled:– –Damned be they who caused this! They all rolled down and were kissing the soil, softened by the rain; they were rubbing it on the top of their heads, on their cheeks, on their necks; they were then bending down and were kissing it over and over again.) I thank Dimostenes Yağcıoğlu for his help in rendering this passage to English.
2. The refugee problem—called '*το προσφυγικο προβλημα*' and '*muhacir meselesi*' respectively in Greece and the Ottoman Empire—had been used as a broad category to denote a vortex of issues, particularly with regards to the reception and resettlement of displaced populations in the two countries since the mid-nineteenth century. For qualitative and quantitative aspects of this problem in the Ottoman Empire, see Kemal Karpat, *Ottoman Population, 1830–1914, Demographic and Social Characteristics* (Seattle: Washington University Press, 1985) 60–85; Justin McCarthy, *Muslims and Minorities: the Population of the Ottoman Anatolia and the End of the Empire* (New York: New York University Press, 1983) 117–144; Faruk Kocacık, "Balkanlar'dan Anadolu'ya Yönelik Göçler (1878–1890)" *Osmanlı Araştırmaları*, 1 (1980) 137–190; Bilal Şimşir, *Turkish Emigrations from the Balkans*, Documents, vol. 1, *Turkish Exodus, 1877–1878*, vol. 2, *A Year of Transition, 1879*, (Ankara: T.T.K. Yayınevi, 1989). For the period, 1913–1918, see Dündar, *İttihad ve Terakki'nin Müslümanları İskan Politikası*, 56–62. As for Greece, the studies on the Turco-Greek exchange of populations contain valuable information on the early demographic movements and resettlement policies of the Greek state. See, for example, Pentzopoulos, *The Balkan Exchange of Minorities*, 25–48; Ladas,

The Exchange of Minorities, 1–23; Séfériadès, L'Échange des Populations, 43–64; Mears, Greece Today, 23–36. Lastly, A. A. Παλλης, Στατιστικη Μελετη περι των Φυλετικων Μεταναστευσεων Μακεδονιας και Θρακης, (Athens: Τυπογραφειο Ιωαν. Βαρτσου, 1925) 1–24.

3. T.B.M.M., Kavanin Mecmuası, Devre: IV, İçtima Senesi: 3, Cilt: 13, (Ankara: T.B.M.M. Matbaası, 1934) 69–71.

4. According to Dimitri Kitsikis, "1923 marks the end of the 100 year Greco-Turkish war that had begun in 1821." See Dimitri Kitsikis, "Les Réfugiés Grecs d'Anatolie et le 'Centre d'Études Micrasiatiques' d'Athènes," TUR-CICA 17 (1985) 227. Also his Türk-Yunan İmparatorluğu, Arabölge Gerçeği Işığında Osmanlı Tarihine Bakış, trans. V. Aytar, (Istanbul: İletişim Yayınları, 1996) 205. On the political and military aspects of the Greco-Turkish War of 1920–1922, see K. Jensen, "The Greco-Turkish War, 1920–1922," International Journal of Middle Eastern Studies 10:4 (1974) 553–565.

5. Campbell and Sherrard, Modern Greece, 114–115. Drama, Serres and Kavala remained under Bulgarian occupation until the Treaty of Bucharest (August 10, 1913) made official the secession of these cities to Greece.

6. Upon the signing of the Neuilly Convention for the voluntary exchange of populations in 1919, Greece received 46,000 people from Bulgaria while 123,000 people of Bulgarian descent left Greece. See Αθαν. Νικολ. Πετσαλη, Η Δημοσιονομικη Αντιμετωπισις του Προσφυγικου Ζητηματος, (Athens: Τυπογραφειον ΕΣΤΙΑ, 1930) 7. For a detailed discussion of these figures, see Eddy, Greece and the Greek Refugees, 248–252. The numbers for Cyprus are not included in this discussion, since Cyprus, which had been brought under British administration in 1878 at the time of the Congress of Berlin, was formally annexed by Britain in 1914, when the Ottoman Empire aligned itself with Germany. The island became a crown colony in 1925.

7. Justin McCarthy, "The Population of the Ottoman Empire before and after the Fall of the Empire," in III. Congress on the Social and Economic History of Turkey, eds. H. Lowry and R. Hattox, (Istanbul: The ISIS Press, 1990) 275–288. Also by the same author, "Muslim Refugees in Turkey: the Balkan Wars, WWI, and the Turkish War of Independence," in Humanist and Scholar, Essays on Honor of Andreas Tietze, eds. H. Lowry and D. Quataert, (Istanbul: The ISIS Press, 1993) 87–111. See also Stanford J. Shaw, "Resettlement of Refugees in Anatolia, 1918–1923," The Turkish Studies Association Bulletin 22:1 (1998) 58–90

8. In the immediate aftermath of the second Balkan War, the Ottoman Empire and Bulgaria signed a voluntary exchange of populations according to which some 9,472 Bulgarian families from eastern Thrace and 9,714 Muslim families from Bulgaria were mutually transferred. Pallis, "Exchange of Populations," 3. During this period, the Ottoman Empire signed another agreement (the Treaty of Athens) for a voluntary exchange of populations with Greece. The implementation of this agreement could not be completed due to the outbreak of WWI. See Mourelos, "The 1914 Persecutions and the First Attempt at an Exchange of Minorities," 410–411. From 1913

through 1914, the number of Muslims who departed from the port of Salonica for Istanbul and Anatolia reached between 220,000–250,000. See Πελαγιδης, *Προσφυγικη Ελλαδα*, 119.

9. Justin McCarthy, *Death and Exile: The Ethnic Cleansing of Ottoman Muslims, 1821–1922* (Princeton: The Darwin Press, Inc., 1995) 164; İlhan Tekeli, "Osmanlı İmparatorluğu'ndan Günümüze Nüfusun Zorunlu Yer Değiştirmesi ve İskan Sorunu," *Toplum ve Bilim*, 50 (Summer 1990) 56; Ladas, *The Exchange of Minorities*, 16; Toynbee, *The Western Question in Greece and Turkey: A Study in the Contact of Civilisations* (London, Bombay, Sydney: Constable and Company Ltd., 1922) 138. For a comprehensive coverage of migratory developments in the Ottoman Empire against the background of the political projects of the Committee of Union and Progress during the 1910s, see Adanır and Kaiser, "Migration, Deportation, and Nation-Building," 273–292.

10. *Meclis-i Ayan Zabıt Ceridesi*, Devre: III, İçtima Senesi: 3, Cilt: 2, 14 Şubat 1332 [February 1916]—31 Mart 1333 [March 1917], (Ankara: T.B.M.M. Basımevi, 1990) 213–214.

11. Justin McCarthy, "The Muslim Refugees in Turkey," 96. He also suggests that there were three million Muslim deaths in the course of the period, 1912–1922. See the same article, 87. For a detailed survey of the population of Anatolia (breakdown by religion) prior to the Turco-Greek War, see Γιωργιου Κλεανθους Σκαλιερη, *Λαοι και Φυλαι της Μικρας Ασιας μετα Πινακων και Χαρτων*, (Athens: Τυπογραφειον Τυπος, 1922) (Β' Εκδοση 1990) 235–245. Population figures constituted a major source of controversy between the Ottomans and Greeks prior to the Paris Peace Conference in 1919. See N. Petsalis-Diomidis, *Greece at the Paris Peace Conference (1919)* (Salonica: Institute for Balkan Studies, 1978) 341–347. For a representative sample of the propaganda literature at the time see "Hellenism in the Balkan Peninsula and Asia Minor, An Ethnological Map" by Profesor George Soteriadis of the University of Athens, 1918. Also A. Alexander Papadopoulos, *Persecutions of the Greeks in Turkey Before the European War*, trans. from Greek by Carroll N. Brown (New York: Oxford University Press American Branch, 1919).

12. AYE, "From C. H. Harrington to the League of Nations, 14 July, 1923," 1923, A/5, VI (4). In the autumn of 1920, nearly 130,000 persons (the defeated soldiers of Wrangel's army) together with their dependents sailed from Crimea to Istanbul, which was under the occupation of the Allied troops at the time. By March 1922, the majority of these people are reported to have dispersed to Gallipoli, nearby Greek Islands, Yugoslavia, Bulgaria, Romania, Brazil and other destinations while 24,000 remained in Istanbul. In January 1924, the Turkish government handed over to the Soviets the Russian Embassy and consulates, which resulted in the departure of further Russians from the city. The few remaining Russians melted into the local population. See Marrus, *The Unwanted*, 59–60. See also Mehmet Temel, *İşgal Yıllarında Istanbul'un Sosyal Durumu* (Ankara: Kültür Bakanlığı Yayınları, 1998) 114–148.

13. Toynbee states that during his stay in Istanbul he "came across one family of Turkish refugees from Thrace who had been uprooted no less than six

times since the beginning of the First Balkan War. Three or four successive evictions were not an uncommon experience." Toynbee, *The Western Question*, 139.

14. Cengiz Orhunlu, "Yunan İşgalinin Meydana Getirdiği Göç ve Yunanlıların Yaptıkları "Tehcir" in Sonuçları Hakkında Bazı Düşünceler," *Belleten*, 37 (1973) 488. At the beginning of the Greek administration of the Vilayet of Aydın, the Ottoman government issued a proclamation that when refugees who had come from the territory apply for registration and certification of their abandoned properties, they should be asked to provide a truthful list of the properties and their value. BOA, Dahiliye Nezareti, İdare-i Umumiyye Evrakı, 21/1, 93, 23 M. 1337 [29 October 1918]. But, upon the annexation of this region by Greece, the Greek administration abolished the refugee bureaus there. BOA, Dahiliye Nezareti, İdare-i Umumiyye Evrakı, 20/26, 14/72, 18 C. 1339 [27 February 1921]. See also *Tasvir-i Efkâr*, 22 Teşrin-i Sâni 1335 [November 1919]. The number of Muslims who became refugees through the annexation of this region by Greece is given as 140,000. The newspaper calls the wealthy people of the country to help these people and also suggests that the Ottoman government should organize a national lottery (*piyango*) to raise money for these "helpless people [who have been] separated from their lands and experienced suffering" (*vatancüda ve elemdide biçareler*).

15. Victoria Solomonidis, "Greece in Asia Minor, the Greek Administration of the Vilayet of Aidin, 1919–22," Unpublished Ph.D. Dissertation, (University of London, King's College, 1984) 169. Solomonidis documents that the Greek Administration was involved in a systematic program to repatriate the Greek populations who had left the region after the Balkan Wars through expulsions. Upon the departure of these people, the Ottoman government had ordered the liquidation of their properties in return for their debts to the Agricultural Bank (*Ziraat Bankası*). BOA, Dahiliye Nezareti, Hukuk Müşavirliği Evrakı, 12, 21, 20 Ş. 1333 [03 July 1915]. To replace the Greeks, the Ottoman government had brought a large number of Muslim refugees from Serbia, Macedonia, Albania, Epirus, and the Aegean Islands, and established them in the homes and properties of the Greeks. In the case of Ayvalık for example, the number of resettled Muslims had reached 30,000. The returning Greeks forcibly evicted them, causing further problems for the Greek administration since this would endanger the provisions of the agreement with the Allies for the permanent annexation of these areas. The Greek occupation of Izmir, Menemen, and environs caused the immigration of these areas' Muslim populations to Soma. BOA, Dahiliye Nezareti, İdare-i Umumiyye Evrakı, E/53, 16, 4 N. 1337 [03 June 1921]. See also Berber, *Sancılı Yıllar*, 230–247.

16. AYE, "Untitled Report," 1923, A/5, VI (12).

17. Mears, *Greece Today*, 51. The head of the League of Nations High Commission for Refugees, Dr. Fridtjof Nansen reported that when his office first intervened, deaths were estimated to be 500 per week. Cited by Simpson, *The Refugee Problem*, 14.

18. League of Nations, *Official Journal*, 4th year, No. 8, August 1923, Annex 534. "Greek Loan for Refugees," 644.
19. See N. J. Polyzos, *Essai sur l'Emigration Grecque, étude démographique, economique et sociale* (Paris: Librairie du Recueil Sirey, 1947) 76–77.
20. Claudena M. Skran states that immigration policies in the United States at the time suggest racist and ethnocentric thinking in that debates about immigration quotas reflected a desire to keep out southern and eastern Europeans, including Italians, Greeks, and Jews who were believed to be from inferior races. Skran, *Refugees in Inter-War Europe*, 25.
21. On December 8, 1924, the Consulate General of Greece in Sydney cabled the Ministry of Foreign Affairs in Athens that "the government of Australia is restricting immigration of all foreigners, and will allow one hundred Greeks per month to arrive here, and even those must understand the language and have from twenty to thirty pounds capital, or have a position as soon as they arrive in Australia . . . All refugees especially those unable to speak English [are] impossible to obtain employment; great number of Greeks are already unemployed." AYE, "From Anthony Lekatsas to the Ministry of Foreign Affairs, December 8, 1924," 1923–24, A/2 (6).
22. "The only Greeks who escaped the population exchange in the 1920s were those living on the Northern shore of the Black Sea in the Russian-held areas. But they were rounded up in the late 1940s and sent east, to Siberia and Central Asia. Half a century later, after Abkhazia's capital Sukhumi fell to Abkhazian insurgents in September 1993, the Greek government evacuated some 12,000 of the 15,000 local Greeks" and settled them in northern Greece to the dissatisfaction of the Thracian minority. See Bell-Fialkoff, *Ethnic Cleansing*, 26.
23. Eddy, *Greece and the Greek Refugees*, 245. It should be noted here that some of the Armenian refugees who came to Greece during the Greco-Turkish War and later through the exchange of populations left the country in the following years. For example, in the period from 1921 to 1925, some 15,000 Armenian refugees from Anatolia arrived in Soviet Armenia by way of Greece, Iraq and Iran. Schechtman, *Population Transfers in Asia*, 52.
24. Cevat Geray, "Türkiye'de Göçmen Hareketleri ve Göçmenlerin Yerleştirilmesi," *Orta Doğu Amme İdaresi Dergisi*, 3 (1970) 17.
25. Tekeli, "Osmanlı İmparatorluğu'ndan Günümüze," 62. Turkey concluded on October 18, 1925 another agreement with Bulgaria for a voluntary exchange of populations. Huey Louis Kostanick, *Turkish Settlement of Bulgarian Turks, 1950–1953* (Berkeley: University of California Press, 1957) 66; Geray, "Türkiye'de Göçmen Hareketleri," 13. According to the official census of 1927, the refugees from Greece constituted 61.1% of the refugee population in Turkey. Simpson, *The Refugee Problem*, 26–27.
26. The author adds 130,000 more refugees who had come from Greece after the Balkan Wars and from Western Thrace and the Aegean Islands during the Turco-Greek War, which makes the total number of Muslim refugees subject to the Convention 518,146.

27. Geray provides a more comprehensive coverage of the 1927 census figures. See his "Türkiye'de Göçmen Hareketleri" 11. For an excellent analysis of the demographic conditions in the 1920s and the 1927 census figures see Frederic C. Shorter, "The Population of Turkey After the War of Independence," *International Journal of Middle Eastern Studies* 17 (1985) 417–441. Also see another study by the same author, "Turkish Population in the Great Depression," *New Perspectives on Turkey* 23 (Fall 2000) 103–124.

28. Ladas, *The Exchange of Minorities*, 706. Also see Pallis, "Exchange of Populations," 5. The author states, "abandoned lands and houses of over a million Greeks and Armenians were available. It was therefore sound economic policy to get those waste regions resettled as soon as possible." Also Simpson, *The Refugee Problem*, 27.

29. Pentzopoulos, *The Balkan Exchange of Minorities*, 155–156.

30. Mazower, "The Refugees, the Economic Crisis," 123.

31. Ayhan Aktar has also noted this tendency of the population exchange literature in his "Nüfusun Homojenleştirilmesi ve Ekonominin Türkleştirilmesi," 32–40.

32. Skran, *Refugees in Inter-War Europe*, 1–10; Zolberg, Suhrke, and Aguayo, *Escape from Violence*, 258–282.

33. For a discussion of the situation of the Balkan refugees and the Eastern refugees in the Turkish Grand National Assembly, see *T.B.M.M. ZC*, Devre: II, İçtima Senesi: 2, Cilt: 8/1, 10 Nisan 1340 [April 1924]—22 Nisan 1340 [April 1924], (Ankara: T.B.M.M. Matbaası, 1975) 510–542.

34. For Ottoman institutions and practices concerning the resettlement of refugees see T.M.M.M. Kütüphanesi, No: 73–3109, *Talimatname, 1) Muhacirine Arazi ve Emlak Tevz'ine Dair, 2) Vurud Eden Muhacirine Verilen Bağ, Zeytünlük, Dutluk ve Emsali Yerlerin İmarına ve Hüsn-i Muhafazasına Dair*, Dersaadet [Istanbul]: Garviyan Matbaası, 1333 [1914]. Also T.B.M.M. Kütüphanesi, No: 73–3113, *Muhacirinin Kayd ve İskânlarına ve Muamelat-ı Sairelerine Aid Olarak Muhacirin İdarelerince Tutulacak Kayd ve Defatir Hakkında İzahnamedir*, (Dersaadet [Istanbul]: Hilal Matbaası, 1331 [1912]). The only measure that the Ottoman government took after the Balkan Wars was to encourage Muslim populations in Greece to register the title deeds to their lands and buildings and thereby preserve their claims to these properties. These people were also advised to assign a custodian to look after the properties should they have to leave their lands. BOA, Dahiliye Nezareti, Hukuk Müşavirliği Evrakı, 31, 6, 4 S. 1335 [30 November 1916].

35. Ladas, *The Exchange of Minorities*, 706. A report prepared under the direction of the Historical Section of the British Foreign Office describes the situation of the Muslim refugees in Anatolia c. 1920 as follows: "The muhajirs, who have one and all been induced to migrate to Anatolia, with promises, which are never more than half fulfilled, are unhappy and discontented; they pine for the homes they had left behind." The report also mentions that "the older inhabitants resent the intrusion of these immigrants, who occupy much land formerly available for pasture." *Anatolia*, (Prepared under the Direction of the Historical Section of the

Foreign Office, No: 59) (London: Her Majesty's Stationary Office, 1920) 37.

36. For the property-related problems of the Muslim refugees during the 1913–1918 period. See Dündar, *İttihad ve Terakki'nin Müslümanları İskan Politikası*, 92–173.

37. *T.B.M.M. ZC*, Devre: II, İçtima Senesi: 2, Cilt: 10, 1 Teşrin-i Sâni 1340 [November 1924]—4 Kânun-ı Evvel 1340 [December 1924], (Ankara: T.B.M.M. Matbaası, 1975) 24–38.

38. During the Turco-Greek war, people fled their homes to seek safety elsewhere. Using the special terms of migration studies, both "push" and "pull" factors were at work to affect the internal migrations in Anatolia during this period. For a detailed description of "push" and "pull" factors, see Loescher, *Beyond Charity*, 16–17.

39. İsmail Beşikçi, *Doğu Anadolu'nun Düzeni, Sosyo-Ekonomik ve Etnik Temeller*, (Ankara: Yurt Kitap-Yayın, 1992) 429. Sometimes a whole tribe or a village or a shaiyk with all his followers were expelled to other parts of Anatolia. In the later half of the decade, several laws (e.g., *Bazı Eşhasın Şark Bölgesinden Garp Vilayetlerine Nakli Hakkında Kanun*) were adopted to this effect. For various discussions on this issue see *T.B.M.M. ZC*, Devre: I, İçtima Senesi: 4, Cilt: 28, 1 Mart 1339 [March 1923]—4 Nisan 1339 [April 1923], (Ankara: T.B.M.M. Matbaası, 1961) 252–257. A newspaper reports that the regions depopulated by the Armenians in Çukurova (Adana) were resettled by the refugees from Eastern provinces (*vilayet-i şarkiyye muhacirleri*). *Hâkimiyet-i Milliye*, 3 Kânun-ı Sâni 1340 [January 1924].

40. *T.B.M.M. ZC*, Devre: I, İçtima Senesi: 3, Cilt: 22, 27 Temmuz 1338 [July 1922]—11 Eylül 1338 [September 1922], (Ankara: T.B.M.M. Matbaası, 1959) 163.

41. *Yeni Gün*, 15 Kânun-ı Evvel 1338 [December 1922] and 25 Kânun-ı Evvel 1338 [December 1922]. Some 20,000 houses are reported to have perished in fires. A majority of the people who lost their homes in the neighbouring cities of Aydın, Alaşehir, Manisa, Nazilli, Salihli and Kasaba, moved into Izmir and seized the abandoned properties of the Greeks and Armenians. See also *T.B.M.M. ZC*, Devre: I, İçtima Senesi: 3, Cilt: 25, 20 Teşrin-i Sâni 1338 [November 1922]—21 Kânun-ı Evvel 1338 [December 1922], (Ankara: T.B.M.M. Matbaası, 1960) 240–242, 466–472.

42. The Ankara government passed a number of laws concerning the status of the properties and the procedures carried out to this effect during the period of Greek administration. The government recognized the title deeds, which had been granted through proper legal prodecure. CA, 2555, 246–8, 28 Haziran 1339 [June 1923], [7 22 16 (1)]. Also CA, 2099, 246–7, 24 Kânun-ı Evvel 1338 [December 1922], [6 41 19]. During the same period, the government took measures for the quick Turkification of these areas, to which effect a series of resolutions were immediately passed. A deputy argued that a former law (*Avans Kanunu*) contained an article for the selling of abandoned properties to those whose homes had been destroyed. *T.B.M.M. ZC*, Devre: I, İçtima Senesi: 3, Cilt: 25, 20 Teşrin-i Sâni 1338

[November 1922]—21 Kânun-ı Evvel1338 [December 1922]. The agreement between the Izmir Port and Quay Company (Izmir Liman ve Rıhtım Şirketi) and the Ministry of Public Works was recognized with the provision that all the employees were to be of Turkish citizenship CA, 2500, 161–2, 05 Haziran 1339 [June 1923], [7 20 1 (1)].

43. *T.B.M.M. ZC*, 1 Teşrin-i Sâni 1340 [November 1924]—4 Kânun-ı Evvel 1340 [December 1924], (Ankara: T.B.M.M. Matbaası, 1975) 27.

44. *T.B.M.M. GZC*, 29 Teşrin-i Sâni 1338 [November 1922], vol. 3, (Ankara: İş Bankası Kültür Yayınları, 1985) 1137. For the anti-semitic propaganda at the time, see Rıfat Bali, *Cumhuriyet Yıllarında Türk Yahudileri, Bir Türkleştirme Serüveni, [1923–1945]* (Istanbul: İletişim Yayınları, 1999) 34–54.

45. *T.B.M.M. GZC*, 29 Teşrin-i Sâni 1338 [November 1922], 1138.

46. *T.B.M.M. ZC*, Devre: II, İçtima Senesi: 2, Cilt: 10, 1 Teşrin-i Sâni 1340 [November 1924]—4 Kânun-ı Evvel 1340 [December 1924], 36.

47. "From İsmet to Hey'et-i Vekile Riyaseti, 1 Kânun-ı Evvel 1338 [December 1922]," in *Lozan Telgrafları*, 154.

48. "From Hüseyin Rauf to İsmet Paşa, 2 Kânun-ı Evvel 1338 [December 1922]," in *Lozan Telgrafları*, 155–156.

49. "From Hüseyin Rauf to İsmet Paşa, 23 Kânun-ı Sâni 1339 [January 1923]," in *Lozan Telgrafları*, 428.

50. On September 11, 1922, a deputy (i.e., Dr. Mazhar Bey of Aydın) in the Grand National Assembly announced that "The government has sold my olive grove as abandoned property when a decision was taken to deem as 'abandoned property' unconditionally all the fields found without their owners, including those of the Muslims. Now these very officials will go and settle the question of properties abandoned by the Greeks, a question that involves millions [of liras]" (*Her ne suretle olsun müslümanlar da dahil olduğu halde tegayüp eden yerlerin emvalini emval-i metruke addediniz denildiği vakit efendiler bendenize ait zeytinliği dahi emval-i metruke diye hükümet satmıştır. Aynı memurlar gidecekler bu kadar muazzam işleri milyonları ihtiva eden Rumların Yunanlıların orada bıraktığı emval-i metrukatı da bu zihniyette olan memurlar halledecektir*). *T.B.M.M. ZC*, Devre: I, İçtima Senesi: 3, Cilt: 22, 27 Temmuz 1338 [July 1922]—11 Eylül 1338 [September 1922], (Ankara: T.B.M.M. Matbaası, 1959) 617.

51. The Ankara government had earlier passed a resolution that the abandoned properties, both movable and immovable, of the Greeks in the area of Aydın and other provinces were to be transferred temporarily to the Ministry of Finance. CA, 554, 135–3, 18 Kânun-ı Sâni 1337 [January 1921], [2 29 20]. Another resolution on January 23, 1923 proclaimed that those who had occupied the abandoned properties should pay rent and the other properties should be put on auction. CA, 2201, 103–2, 23 Kânun-i Sâni 1339 [January 1923], [6 47 1]. The populist policies of the government were not limited only to property issues. The government also passed a quick resolution concerning the parity rate of drachma, 27 drachmas to one Turkish lira, and allowed the tax-farmers of the formerly Greek-occupied areas to

pay their debts on the basis of this new rate. CA, 2146, 124–21, 7 Kânun-ı Sâni 1339 [January 1923], [6 44 6 (1)].

52. According to Pallis, consideration of the resettlement of the waste regions along a sound economic policy doubtlessly convinced the Turkish government to accept the population exchange project as proposed. Pallis, "Exchange of Populations," 5.

53. Davison, "Turkish Diplomacy," 204.

54. As early as April 1922, the revolutionary government in Ankara was trying to adopt, with minor modifications, the Ottoman rules and regulations concerning refugee settlement. To this effect, several consecutive resolutions were issued. CA, 1526, 26 Nisan 1338 [April 1922], [4 55 2]. The draft of a document entitled *"Türkiye Büyük Millet Meclisi Hükümeti Murahhıslarıyla Yunan Hükümeti Arasında Mübadele-i Ahaliye ve Emval Hakkında Lozan'da Teati Olunan 30 Kânun-ı Sâni 1923 Tarihli Mukavele-namenin Suret-i Tatbikiyesi Mübeyyin Talimatnamedir."* CA, 2600, 2660, 17 Temmuz 1339 [July 1923], [7 25 2 (5)] provides a list of measures to be taken for the implementation of the Convention. Another document found in the same file also lists a series of measures to this effect. See *"Mübadele-i Ahaliye Dair Lozan Mukavelesinin Suret-i Tatbikiyesini Mübeyyin Olarak Sıhhiye ve Muavenat-i İçtimaiye Vekâletince Tanzim Olunan Birinci Tali-matname."*

55. CA, 1875, 135–14, 1 Teşrin-i Evvel 1338 [October 1922], [5 30 11]. See also *T.B.M.M. GZC,* 2 Mart 1339 [March 1923], Devre: I, İçtima Senesi: 4, Cilt: 4, (Ankara: İş Bankası Kültür Yayınları, 1985) 63–64. The total cost of Greek destruction was estimated to have been around 60,000,000 liras.

56. "Refugee Problem viewed by Haskell," by Walter Duranty, Special Cable to the New York Times, Moscow, February 7, 1923. The Library of Congress, the Papers of Henry Morgenthau, Containers 50–52, Reel 39/41. For the full text of Haskell's report, see "Refugee Problem," AYE, 1923, A/5. VI (11).

57. Ladas, *The Exchange of Minorities,* 708.

58. Ibid, 707.

59. Kitsikis, *Türk-Yunan İmparatorluğu,* 229–230. For the details of the institutional and financial aspects of Greece's engagement with refugee affairs prior to the Turco-Greek War, see Υπουργειον Περιθαλψεως, *Περιθαλψις των Προσφυγων, 1917–1920,* (Athens: Τυπογραφειον Κωνστ. Ι. Θεοδωπουλο, 1920) passim.

60. George Mavrogordatos, "Το Ανεπαναληπτο Επιτευγμα," *ΔΕΛΤΙΟ ΚΜΣ* 9 (1992) 9.

61. For an overview of the institutional arrangements concerning the resettlement of refugees during the 1913–1918 period, see Dündar, *İttihat ve Terakki'nin Müslümanları İskan Politikası,* 62–173.

62. *T.B.M.M. GZC,* 29 Teşrin-i Sâni 1338 [November 1922], vol. 3, (Ankara: İş Bankası Kültür Yayınları, 1985) 1137.

63. *T.B.M.M. ZC,* Devre: I, İçtima Senesi: 3, Cilt: 23, 13 Eylül 1338 [September 1922]—16 Teşrin-i Evvel 1338 [October 1922], (Ankara: T.B.M.M. Matbaası,

1960) 10. The discussion on the Ministry of Liberated Provinces took place on 13 Eylül 1338 [September 1922]. For a general review of this discussion, see Akın, *TBMM Devleti*, 315–318. On April 4, 1923 the government modified article 1 of the law for the abandoned properties (*Emval-i Metruke Kanunu*). This law became the subject of further discussion later on. *T.B.M.M. ZC*, Devre: I, İçtima Senesi: 4, Cilt: 29, 9 Nisan 1339 [April 1923]—16 Nisan 1339 [April 1923], (Ankara: T.B.M.M. Matbaası, 1961) 159–176.

64. *T.B.M.M. ZC*, Devre: I, İçtima Senesi: 3, Cilt: 23, 13 Eylül 1338 [September 1922]—16 Teşrin-i Evvel 1338 [October 1922], 294.

65. *T.B.M.M. ZC*, Devre: I, İçtima Senesi: 3, Cilt: 24, 18 Teşrin-i Evvel 1338 [October 1922]—18 Teşrin-i Sâni 1338 [November 1922], (Ankara: T.B.M.M. Matbaası, 1960) 145.

66. *Tanin*, 3 Temmuz 1339 [July 1923].

67. *Vazife*, 10 Eylül 1339 [September 1923].

68. *Vatan*, 21 Temmuz 1339 [July 1923].

69. *Ahenk*, 16 Eylül 1339 [September 1923].

70. Cf. Robert J. Kleiner et al., "International Migration and Internal Migration: A Comprehensive Theoretical Approach," in *Migration across Time and Nations; Population Mobility in Historical Context*, eds. Ira A. Glazier and Luigu de Rosa, (New York: Holmes and Meier, 1986) 316.

71. Petropoulos, "The Compulsory Exchange of Populations," 135–161.

72. *Yenigün*, 25 Teşrin-i Sâni 1338 [November 1922].

73. CA, 102, 5 Mart 1339 [March 1923]; "Kazım Karabekir'den Ankara İcra Vekilleri Hey'et-i Riyaset-i Celilesine." See also Gündüz Ökçün, ed., *Türkiye İktisat Kongresi, 1923-Izmir, Haberler, Belgeler, Yorumlar*, (Ankara: Ankara Üniversitesi Siyasal Bilgiler Fakültesi Yayınları, 1981) 421.

74. *İsmet Paşa'nın Siyasi ve İçtimai Nutukları*, 78 (*Mübadele meselesi bizim için bir mesele-i hayatiyedir. Devletimizin en mübrem ve en büyük bir meselesidir. Politikamızın asla ihmal edemiyeceği ve bizi ihtiyaç ve ızdırap içinde bulundurduğu bir cihettir*).

75. *T.B.M.M. ZC*, Devre: I, İçtima Senesi: 3, Cilt: 22, 27 Temmuz 1338 [July 1922]—11 Eylül 1338 [September 1922], 127–128.

76. The three-year period immediately following the Treaty of Lausanne is considered by scholars as the period during which the "absorption" (αφομοιωση) of the refugees in Greece was for the most part completed. See in this respect, Mavrogordatos, "Το Ανεπαναληπτο Επιτευγμα," 10–12.

NOTES TO CHAPTER SIX

1. The text of the Exchange Convention, which will be used throughout this section, is the French and English version found in Great Britain, Foreign Office, *Turkey, No. 1 (1923) Lausanne Conference on Near Eastern Affairs, 1922–1923, Records of Proceedings and Draft Terms of Peace* (London: His Majesty's Stationary Office, 1923).

2. By the time such teams were formed, C. G. Ténékides had already been assigned by the Greek government to prepare a report on the legal aspects

of the minority question and the exchange. Ténékidès, "Le Statut des Minorités" passim.

3. Pentzopoulos, *The Balkan Exchange of Minorities*, 78; Ladas, *The Exchange of Minorities*, 621–622. The Sub-Committee consisted of the British, French and Italian members of the Council of the League and a fourth member was to be appointed by the Greek government.

4. The Turkish Grand National Assembly ratified the Lausanne Treaty and the Convention on August 23, 1923, and the Greek side two days later on August 25, 1923. *T.B.M.M. ZC*, Devre: II, İçtima Senesi: 1, Cilt: 1, 11 Ağustos 1339 [August 1923]—8 Eylül 1339 [September 1923], (Ankara: T.B.M.M. Matbaası, 1961) 282. The deposit of the instrument of ratification took place by Greece on February 11, 1924 and by Turkey on March 31, 1924. Psomiades, *The Eastern Question*, 111.

5. The Turkish government issued a decree on June 17, 1923 (no: 2600) for putting into effect "Regulations Prepared in accordance with the Convention Concerning the Exchange of Greek and Turkish Populations." A. Gündüz Ökçün, *A Guide to Turkish Treaties (1920–1964)* (Ankara: Ankara Üniversitesi Basımevi, 1966) 39.

6. The article stated that "all able-bodied men belonging to the Greek population whose families have already left Turkish territory, and who are now detained in Turkey, shall constitute the first installment of Greeks sent to Greece in accordance with the present Convention." *Lausanne Conference*, 818. For the activities of the International Red Cross concerning this matter and the number of Greek war prisoners in Anatolia (breakdown by city) see the report by Lucien Brunel (Adjoint a la Direction Générale de Comite International de la Croix-Rouge). AYE, "From Lucien Brunel to Monsieur Jean Politis (Directeur du secrétariat Hellénique, Geneve) August 7, 1923," A/2. Another report presented by the Greek Légation in Istanbul to the Vice-President of the Turkish Red Crescent reveals that the problem of prisoners-of-war, which involved a total of 30–40,000 people, still had not been resolved by early September of the same year. AYE, "From Greek Légation in Constantinople to Hamid Bey (Vice-President of the Committee of Red Crescent) September 3, 1923," A/2. Some 11,000 civilian prisoners were transferred to Greece and reunited with their families in December 1922 when the Turkish officials reached a compromise with the Greek officials after a stalemate. Barton, *Story of Near East Relief*, 169. For a detailed study of the exchange of prisoners see Mehmet Çanlı, "Milli Mücadele Döneminde Türk-Yunan Esirleri ve Mübadelesi (1920–1923)" Unpublished Ph.D. dissertation (Ankara Üniversitesi, 1994) passim.

7. On April 19, 1923, A. Pallis wrote to Admiral Bristol that "Turkish authorities did not allow any further consignments of food-stuffs etc. intended for the refugees at Constantiople to be imported duty-free . . . Hikmet Bey . . . openly admitted (*bunun maksadi muhajirlerinin tchikarilmasi*) that the object of this measure was to force the removal of the refugees from Constantinople." AYE, "From A. A. Pallis to Admiral Bristol, April 19, 1923," A/5, VI (4). Istanbul was then *de jurie*

under Allied occupation, but the Turkish administration was in the process of installment. The last Allied troops left the city on October 2, 1923 and the official transfer of the city to the Turkish government took place on October 6. See Bilge Criss, *İşgal Altında Istanbul, 1918–1923* (Istanbul: İletişim Yayınları, 1993) 231.

8. AYE, "From the Central Committee of Constantinople Greeks to the Government of Greece, June 11, 1923," A/5, VI (11).

9. An actual observant of the situation reports "why Greeks and Turks oppose being exchanged." See Winthrop D. Lane, "Why Greeks and Turks Oppose Being Exchanged?" *The New York Times Current History* 18 (April 1923) 86–90.

10. CA, 1274, 102/46, 17 Kânun-ı Evvel 1340 [December 1924], [12 63 5]. It is very hard to figure out when applicants filed their original petitions. Given the conditions under which the government in Ankara was functioning, it seems rather plausible that they were filed before the Convention began to be implemented. Similar resolutions continued to be issued long after the signing of the agreement. In 1927, a resolution granted exemption to Nipayot Efendi on the grounds that he was against the "Pontic cause" during the Turco-Greek War. He was spared from the exchange on the condition that he would thenceforward reside in the sections of Istanbul which were not subject to the Convention. CA, 5984, 25 Aralık [December] 1927. Similar resolutions continued to be issued in the early 1930s. On February 17, 1934, a Nikolas Pavlidis Efendi whose permit of residence had been extended for a year was granted another year of extension on the grounds that he was found to have contributed a great deal to the country's economy (*memleket iktisadiyatına çok faydası dokunduğu anlaşıldığından*). CA, 2/138, 17 Şubat [February] 1934.

11. CA, 1277, 102/45, 17 Kânun-ı Evvel 1340 [December 1924] [12 63 8].

12. CA, 1844, 102/58, 29 Nisan 1341 [April 1925]. İstamat Zihni [Özdamar] was a close associate of Papa Eftim. See Alexandris, *The Greek Minority of Istanbul*, 152.

13. CA, 744, 3 Ağustos 1340 [August 1924]. Cf. Alexandris, *The Greek Minority of Istanbul*, 149–154.

14. CA, 2111, 14 Haziran 1341 [June 1925]. A Konstantion asked for 6 months stay in order to train a Turkish tobacco expert (*tütün eksperi*). After the Ankara Agreement of 1930, the Turkish government issued short-term visas to the Greek refugees of Anatolian origin. A Dimitri Kataku-zuni was among the 29 refugees who came to Turkey with a "collective passport" but he fell sick. He was granted special permission to stay until he recovered. CA, 2/4157, 9 Mart [March] 1936. On another occasion, a priest named Amurosion Sumelioti was granted entry visa to go to the Sumela Monastery for uncovering an icon, depicting Virgin Mary, a bible, and a cross, all of which belonged to the Sumela Monastery, which had been buried during the departure from the monastery. CA, 10752, 11 Mart [March] 1931. Visas were issued to the ex-Anatolian Greeks by the Turkish government for a maximum of two months of stay. The reasons for visa applications seem to have varied from person to person. A Greek who had

moved from Izmir to Mithylene was granted two months of visa to come to Izmir for completing his business transactions. CA, 2/1929, 30 Ocak [January] 1935. See also another document, CA, 13964, 4 Mart [March] 1933.

15. The popular literature on the population exchange speaks of the widespread practice of Crypto-Christianity in the Black Sea sections of Anatolia. See Yorgo Andreadis, *Gizli Din Taşıyanlar*, trans. A. Tuygan, (Istanbul: Belge Yayınları, 1999) 57–93. Crypto-Christianity was not a peculiar feature of Greek presence in Asia Minor during the Ottoman Empire. See R. M. Dawkins, "The Crypto-Christianity of Turkey," *Byzantion* 8 (1933) 247–275. It is documented that the number of Crypto-Christian villages increased especially in the northern sections of Anatolia proper (the Pontos) during the nineteenth century. For a brief discussion of this issue and a bibliography of relevant sources, see Anthony M. Bryer, "The Tourkokratia in the Pontos: Some Problems and Preliminary Conclusions," in his *The Empire of Trebizond and the Pontos* (London: Variorum Reprints, 1980) 47–49. Also by the same author, "The Crypto-Christians of the Pontos and Consul William Gifford Palgrave of Trebizond," *ΔΕΛΤΙΟ ΚΜΣ* 4 (1983) 13–68; Peter Mackridge, "Greek-Speaking Moslems of North-East Turkey: Prolegomena to a Study of the Ophitic Sub-Dialect of Pontic," *Byzantine and Modern Greek Studies*, 2 (1987) 115–117. Finally, Alexis Alexandris, "Pontic Greek Refugees in Constantinople 1922–1923, the Human Cost of the Exchange of Populations," *Αρχείον Πόντου* 137 (1982) 292–293.

16. CA, 2615, 22 Temmuz 1339 [July 1923] [7 25 17]. Also 205, 299, 20 Kânun-ı Sâni 1340 [January 1924] [8 49 9 (1)].

17. CA, 213, 732, 20 Kânun-ı Sâni 1340 [January 1924].

18. CA, 299, 22–9, 20 Şubat 1340 [February 1924].

19. CA, 2407, 102–62, 24 Ağustos 1341 [August 1925]. See also another resolution 732, 2407, 27 Temmuz 1340 [July 1924] [10 36 9]. "Women of Greek origin married to Muslim Turks are not subject to the Exchange." A similar resolution was to be issued later, exempting the exchangeable women married to non-exchangeable (établi) men after the Convention for the reason that this would have negative impact on the "enculturation" of their children who are Turkish citizens by law (*Kanunen Türk vatandaşı olan çocuklarının terbiyesine müessir olacağı cihetle*). CA, 13965, 4 Mart [March] 1933.

20. CA, 1916, 102–59, 11 Mayıs 1341 [May 1925] [13 29 9].

21. CA, 2/3633, 19 Kasım [November] 1935.

22. AYE, "Letter from Vayonos Brothers (Oriental Rug Manufacturers in Seljuk) to the Ministry of Foreign Affairs in Athens, April 3, 1923," A/2. A Turkish government resolution dated 8 August 1923 states that "the Oriental Carpet Manufacture Limited and the Eastern (*Istern*) Carpet Limited, which specialize in carpet making, and the *Izmir Sanayi Şirketi* which deals with purchasing, selling and processing roots of the licorice plant (*meyan kökü*) are to be turned into a Turkish Joint Stock Company (*Türk Anonim Şirketi*)." CA, 2654, 184–8, 8 Ağustos 1339 [August 1923] [7 27 15].

23. CA, 2675, 135–51, 19 Ağustos 1339 [August 1923] [7 28 16 1] and also 2737, 2762, 6 Eylül 1339 [September 1923] [7 31 19 (1)].

24. CA, 2762, 135–52, 12 Eylül 1339 [September 1923] [7 33 4 (1)].
25. Rıza Nur speaks of a Muslihiddin Adil, a professor of law in Dar-ül Fünun in Istanbul and the author of *İktisad Dersleri* (Selanik: Zeman Matbaası, 1328) who came to visit him at Lausanne. He forwarded Rıza Nur with the request of the Muslim populations of the Vilayet of Selanik (Salonica) for their exemption from the Convention. Rıza Nur states that this man was representing merely the view of the Dönme community of Salonica not that of the Muslim population. *Dr. Rıza Nur'un Lozan Hatıraları*, 138–139.
26. AYE, "A Letter from the Leaders of Muslim Community in Komotini to the General Administration of Thrace, February 6, 1923," A/5, VI. The letter has been forwarded through Γραφειον Τυπου Θρακης. A similar petition was filed by the *müftü* of Langada (Hafız Ahmed) who stated that "we, Muslims, will never accept this exchange and we declare that we are pleased with our Greek government" (*biz müslümanlar ise bu mübadeleye asla ve kat'a razı olmayacağımızdan ve hükümet-i Yunaniyemizden memnun olduğumuzu bi'l-beyan . . .*). AYE, 13 Kânun-ı Sâni [January] 1923, A/5, VI (11). The letter is written in both Ottoman Turkish and Greek and addressed to "*Langada Kazası Kaymakamlığı Canib-i Aliyesine.*"
27. Interview with Zeliha Bile and Nafia Bilge, October 21, 1994. Kemal Yalçın, a Turkish popular writer, having conducted interviews with Greek and Muslim refugees, published a book entitled *Emanet Çeyiz, Mübadele İnsanları* (Istanbul: Belge Yayınları, 1998). These interviews contain valuable information about the psychological impact of the population exchange and also provide interesting details about the transfer of the refugees. One of the Muslim refugees states that "One day the order for the exchange reached [our village]. Everyone rented two or three mules according to their financial means. Loaded [them] with their belongings. We abandoned out country, village, and properties and set out [our journey]. We were all mourning. It was very difficult to leave" (*Bir gün mübadele emri geldi. Herkes yüküne parasına göre ikişer üçer katır kiraladı. Yükledi yükünü. Memleketimizi, köyümüzü, malımızı, mülkümüzü olduğu gibi bırakıp düştük yola . . . Ağlamaklı olduk. Çok zordu ayrılmak.*). Yalçın, *Emanet Çeyiz*, 174. A similar story is told by a famous Turkish literary figure, namely Necati Cumalı: "When the Treaty of Lausanne was signed and we heard that we were to swap our places with the Greeks, we did not want to believe. We were saying "this can't happen!" When the news was confirmed, my father insisted "I will not leave Florina." "Come on Dad, come on İbrahim Efendi! those days have passed, have you forgotten what we have been suffering through for the [past] three years? I told him, our friends told him. In the meantime, our preparations for the journey continued. One day, we gave up our home to an 'experienced' Greek family that had come from a village nearby Bursa. We set out [our journey]" (*Lozan antlaşması imzalanıp da, bizlerin Rumlar ile yer değiştireceğimiz duyulunca inanmak istemedik. "Olmaz öyle bir şey!" diyorduk. Haber kesinlik kazanınca babam, "Ben Florina'dan ayrılmam" diye tutturdu. "Bre baba, bre İbrahim Efendi yapma, etme, geçti o günler unuttun mu üç*

yıldır çektiklerimizi" . . . *Ben söyledim, dostlarım söyledi, dinletemedik. Bir yandan yol hazırlıklarımız ilerledi. Birgün evimizi Bursa'nın yakın bir köyünden gelen görmüş geçirmiş bir Rum ailesine teslim ettik. Yola çıktık).* Necati Cumalı, *Makedonya 2000* (Istanbul: Can Yayınları, 1981) 27.

28. For the website of the project see http://www.the-unwanted.com/theun-wanted.php

29. Tolga Köker, "Lessons in Refugeehood: The Experience of Forced Migrants in Turkey," in *Crossing the Aegean: An Appraisal of the 1923 Compulsory Population Exchange between Greece and Turkey*, ed. Reneé Hirschon, (New York and Oxford: Berghahn Books, 2003) 193–208. For Greece, we do not have much information about cases of communal conversion. There is scanty information about certain individual cases. For example, Michael Herzfeld speaks of an itinerant vendor known as Tourkoyorgis (Turkish George) who preferred to convert to Christianity in Rethymno, Crete. See Herzfeld, *A Place in History*, 62. Quoting from the actual witnesses, the author also remarks that "most of the Muslims [in Crete] had indeed been very reluctant to leave" 64. This is confirmed by a series of interviews conducted by a Turkish amateur historian. His findings reveal that some male members of Muslim families in Crete avoided the population exchange either by way of converting to Christianity or getting married to the local Greek women. Thereby, it became possible to prevent the properties of their families from confiscation. See Raif Kaplanoğlu, *Bursa'da Mübadele (1923–1930 Yunanistan Göçmenleri)* (Bursa: Avrasya Etnografya Vakfı Yayınları, 1999) 80–81.

30. Reşat D. Tesal, "Yunanistan'da Azınlık Olarak Nasıl Yaşardık?," *Tarih ve Toplum*, 48 (1991) 48–56. See also the interviews published by İskender Özsoy, *İki Vatan Yorgunları, Mübadele Acısını Yaşayanlar Anlatıyor* (Istanbul: Bağlam Yayıncılık, 2003) passim.

31. The assumption that the Muslim populations in Greece welcomed the population exchange decision seems to have dominated the speeches of many deputies in the Turkish Grand National Assembly during the discussions over the Lausanne Treaty. *T.B.M.M. ZC*, Devre: II, İçtima Senesi: 1, Cilt: 1, 22–23 Ağustos 1339 [August 1923], 248–282. Many national and local newspapers also adopted this discourse. See for example, *Ahenk*, 22 Temmuz 1339 [July 1923] which wrote that "Our brethren, a part of whose lives has been corroded and torn away with violence every day for many years, can no longer stay there. They would not want to stay [there]" (*Yıllardan beri her gün hayatının bir kısmı kemirilip koparılan kardeşler orada kalamazlar. Ve kalmak istemezler*). When the news about the reactions of the Turkish populations in Greece to the Convention reached Turkey, it was interpreted as a conspiracy orchestrated by the Greek government to prevent the population exchange from happening and thereby to provide for the repatriation of the Greeks who had left Turkey during the war.

32. Assessments of the provisions of the Convention can be found in the following works: Eddy, *Greece and the Greek Refugees*, 201–226; Ladas, *The*

Exchange of Minorities, 399–419; Penzopoulos, *The Balkan Exchange of Minorities,* 67–68.

33. *Lausanne Conference,* 817–818.

34. In his autobiographical account, the credibility of which has been subject to much discussion among Turkish historians, Rıza Nur credits solely himself for imposing the Turkish definition of the minority (based on faith rather than ethnicity) upon the conference. He narrates the issue in his memoirs as follows: "Franks [Europeans] assume that there are three types of minorities in our country: minorities by race, minorities by language and minorities by religion. This is a great danger for us. When they are against us, these men think so deeply and so well! By the term 'race' they will put Circassians, Abhazes, Bosnians and Kurds in the same category as Greeks and Armenians. By the term 'language' they will turn those Muslims who speak other languages into minorities. By the term 'religion' they will make two million *Kızılbaş,* who are pure Turks, into minorities. That is to say, they will totally tear us apart!" (*Frenkler bizde ekalliyet diye üç nevi biliyorlar: Irkça ekalliyet, dilce ekalliyet, dince ekalliyet. Bu bizim için gayet vahim bir şey, büyük bir tehlike. Aleyhimizde olunca şu adamlar ne derin ve ne iyi düşünüyorlar . . . Irk tabiri ile çerkez, abaza, boşnak, kürt, ilh . . . yi Rum ve Ermenilerin yanına koyacaklar. Dil tabiri ile müslüman olup başka dil konuşanları da ekalliyet yapacaklar. Din tabiri ile halis Türk olan iki milyon Kızılbaşı da ekalliyet yapacaklar. Yani bizi hallaç pamuğu gibi dağıtıp atacaklar.*). Dr. Rıza Nur'un Lozan Hatıraları, 103.

35. *T.B.M.M. GZC,* Devre: I, İçtima: 3, Cilt: 3, 6 Mart 1338 [March 1922]— 27 Şubat 1339 [February 1923], (Istanbul: İş Bankası Kültür Yayınları, 1985) 1159–1163.

36. "From İsmet to Hey'et-i Vekile Riyasetine, 22 Kânun-ı Evvel 1338 [December 1922]," in *Lozan Telgrafları,* 263.

37. For the details of this project, see Chapter Three. For the Turkish understanding of the term "Turkish Orthodox" see Teoman Ergene, *İstiklal Harbinde Türk Ortodoksları* (Istanbul: Milli Mecmua Basımevi, 1951). According to Richard Clogg, Papa Eftim himself wrote this book as an apologia. Clogg, "A Millet Within a Millet," 142.

38. Pallis, "Exchange of Populations," 5. Pallis states that "the test of religion was in the present case well chosen as being the one least likely to give rise to the difficulties of interpretation. Thus, it avoids such thorny questions as, for instance, whether the Pomaks (Slav-speaking Moslems of Macedonia) or the Cretan Moslems, whose mother tongue is Greek and who are undoubted of Hellenic origin, are really Turks. These instances are sufficient to show how difficult it might have been to apply the criterion of race in practice." Psomiades offers a more controversial explanation, "the exchange was based on religious consideration because of the strong loyalty of the Muslim refugees to Islam rather than to the Turkish State . . . The Greeks, one can assume, agreed to the exchange based on religion because the Christians of Anatolia were part of the Byzantine legacy which Turkey rejected outright and which Greece claimed as her own." Psomiades, *The Eastern Question,* 67.

39. The head of the Turkish government, Hüseyin Rauf Bey, presented to Parliament in a closed session a report on the progress of negotiations at Lausanne in which he stated, "We do not accept the thinking of ethnic and linguistic minority. We say non-Muslim minority." (*Irki ve lisani ekalliyet tefrikini kabul etmiyoruz. Gayri Müslim ekalliyyetler diyoruz.*) *T.B.M.M. GZC,* 25 Kânun-ı Evvel 1338 [December 1922], vol. 3, (Ankara: Türkiye İş Bankası Kültür Yayınları, 1985) 1148.

40. The position of the Turkish nationalists concerning the Circassians has not been the subject of a detailed study until now. The Historical Archives of the Greek Ministry of Foreign Affairs contains many files on the Circassians. The available information shows that there were some 9,000 Circassians who had been transferred to Greece following the Armistice of Mudanya in November 1922. AYE, "Report, Thessaloniki, January 10, 1923," 1923, A/2 (7). The report by a Turkish agent, Musa Kazım, provides a detailed account of the Turkish army's stationing in Anatolia and eastern Thrace. As it comes out of the secret reports of the Greek military presented to the Ministry of Foreign Affairs on the situation in eastern Thrace, there were a substantial number of "*αντικεμαλικοι*" (anti-Kemalist) people there and they were ready to cooperate with the Greek forces. Many Circassian bands, which had earlier collaborated with the Greek administration in Izmir, had been fighting against the Turkish army along side the Greek army. They were also involved in a large anti-Kemalist propaganda effort among the populations of Thrace and in other regions that were to be subject to the Convention. On the second day of the Lausanne Conference, Mustafa Kemal himself sent a personal note to İsmet Paşa that Ethem, Eşref, their men and possibly Reşhid and Tevfik had come to Switzerland and they might have been considering a plot against him. "From Hüseyin Rauf to İsmet Paşa, 22 Teşrin-i Sâni 1338 [November 1922]," in *Lozan Telgrafları,* 119.

41. It is widely held, especially by the critics of Lausanne, that the majority of Muslims in Greece spoke Greek and had no ethnic ties with the Muslims in Turkey while the majority of Greeks in Turkey spoke Turkish and were ethnically different from the Greeks in Greece. This polemical assessment requires extensive research to be qualified as a valid argument. See for example, Ahmet Yıldız, *"Ne Mutlu Türküm Diyebilene" Türk Ulusal Kimliğinin Etno-Seküler Sınırları (1919–1938)* (Istanbul: İletişim Yayınları, 2001) 132–133. A Muslim refugee of admittedly Turkish descent writes in his memoirs that "due to the misusage of the term 'Muslim' in the Convention, we had to admit many nomadic people of non-Turkish origins to our country." (*Andlaşmada yanlışlıkla kullanılan "Müslüman" deyimi nedeniyle yurda Türk asıllı olmayan bir hayli göçebeyi de sokmak zorunda kalmıştık*). Tesal, "Yunanistan'da Azınlık Olarak Nasıl Yaşardık?" 54.

42. For a comprehensive survey of the historical development of the Karamanlides, see Clogg, "A Millet Within a Millet," 115–142. The author also provides a synopsis of the discussions concerning this community during the Lausanne Conference. See, 115. Also see Gerasimos Augustinos, *The Greeks of Asia Minor, Confession, Community and Ethnicity in the*

Nineteenth Century (Kent, Ohio and London: The Kent State University Press, 1992) 11–32. A fairly rich information on the Karamanlides can be found in Σια Αναγνωστοπουλου, *Μικρα Ασια, 19ος αι-1919, Οι Ελληνορθοδοξες Κοινοτητες απο το Μιλλετ των Ρωμιων στο Ελληνικο Εθνος*, (Athens: Ελληνικα Γραμματα, 1997) passim.

43. A study by Nikos Marantzidis examines the distinct characteristics of the Turkish-speaking Pontian refugees during the interwar era and the post-WWII period. See his *Γιασασιν Μιλλετ Ζιτω Εθνος, Προσφυγια, Κατοχη και Εμφυλιος: Εθνοτικη Ταυτοτητα και Πολιτικη Συμπεριφορα στους Τουρκοφωνους Ελληνορθοδοξους του Δυτικου Ποντου* (Heraklion: Πενπιστημιακες Εκδοσεις Κρητης, 2001). See also his "Ethnic Identity, Memory and Political Behaviour: The Case of Turkish-Speaking Pontian Greeks," *South European Society and Politics*, 5:3 (Winter 2000) 56–79.

44. Marrus, *The Unwanted*, 104. A petition dated the early months of 1922 reveals that the leaders of the Israélite community in Rodosto (Tekirdağ) had appealed on behalf of the entire Jewish population of Thrace to the Greek authorities that they not be associated with the views of a journalist (Behor Habib) in Istanbul, who published an article in a journal (Stamboul) accusing the Greek authorities, among other things, of persecuting the Jewish populations of Thrace. The community leaders protested the author and expressed their allegiance to the Greek administration. AYE, "Résolution adoptée dans la Séance Extraordinaire du Conseil Communal Israélite de Rodosto, 5/18 Mai 1922," A/5, VI (12). Similarly the leaders of the *dönme* community in Salonica tried to convince the Greek authorities that they were not Muslims but were "Crypto-Jews."

45. AYE, "From British Legation in Athens to the Ministry of Foreign Affairs, September 27, 1923," A/5, VI (10). The British Legation informed the Greek government authorities that they had prepared a survey so as to provide regular disposition of these refugees. Interestingly enough, the survey, entitled "Declarations made by the refugees concerning damages suffered by them owing to Greek occupation," includes such questions as "were there any persons, living in his own house at home, outraged by Greek soldiers or native Greeks, killed or wounded or perished in any other way? If so, who were they? Describe the outrage and its consequences."

46. *Lozan Konferansı*, 86. Both groups were included in the quantification of the arguments offered by the two sides in support of their demographic theses.

47. On the religious divisions among Albanians and their role in the belated development of Albanian nationalism during the Ottoman period, see Stavro Skendi's *The Albanian National Awakening, 1878–1912*, (Princeton: Princeton University Press, 1967) 365–390 and 464–472. For the linguistic aspects of Albanian nationalism and whether Arabic or Italian script should be adopted, which resulted in the creation of Bashkimi Committee, see Hanioğlu, *Preparation for a Revolution*, 254–257. Also see *The Memoirs of Ismail Kemal Bey*, ed. Sommerville Story, (London: Constable and Company Ltd., 1920).

48. Pallis, "Exchange of Populations," 6. Bernard Lewis, who considered the population exchange "as the brutal but effective method to settling the ancient disputes between Turks and Greeks," was the first scholar to note the confusion of concepts and loyalties that went into the Greco-Turkish exchange of populations. According to Lewis, "what took place was not an exchange of Greeks and Turks but rather an exchange of Greek Orthodox Christians and Ottoman Muslims." Bernard Lewis, *The Emergence of Modern Turkey*, 2nd Edition, (Oxford: Oxford University Press, 1968) 255 and 354–355. Cf. Elie Kedourie, *Nationalism*, (New York: Frederick A. Praeger, 1961) 62–91. Another Lewis, Geoffrey Lewis, a linguist, sees the population exchange as a source of problems from a linguistic point of view: "this exchange of populations . . . though well-meant, was responsible for a great deal of unhappiness, because the criterion of "Greek" and "Turkish" was religion: as a result of it, many Greek speaking Muslims and Turkish speaking Christians found themselves living in virtual exile among their co-religionists of alien speech." Geoffrey L. Lewis, *Turkey*, 3rd Edition, (New York, Praeger, 1965) 75–76. In their assessment of the demographic changes in the Middle East following WWI, Owen and Pamuk distinguish the Greeks of Anatolia from the other groups by referring to their European origins. The authors squarely state that "after the expulsion of the Greek population from Anatolia in 1922, the only large group of persons of European origin was in Egypt." See their *A History of Middle East Economies*, 3.

49. AYE, "From Délégation de Paramythia et environs to Légation des Pay-Bas in Athens, August 24, 1923," A/5, VI (10).

50. Pallis, "Exchange of Populations." Pallis states, "The Mixed Commission which has been entrusted to deciding who are the persons of Albanian origin entitled to exemption, has found it [a] very tough nut to crack. Thus a conflict has arisen as to the exact origin of the Moslem inhabitants of Chamouria, a district in Epirus, opposite Corfu. By religion Moslems, by descent Greek Epirotes who were converted to Islam in the seventeenth century, they are linguistically Albanian, and by political sympathy Turkish, as is shown by the desire of many of them to emigrate to Turkey and by that fact that during the numerous Albanian insurrections against Turkey, they have invariably sided with the Turks." 6. Pallis adds that 1,700 Muslim Albanians were exempted from being transferred with the intervention of the Mixed Commission. Pallis, "Exchange of Populations," footnote 1. For a polemical view of the question of Muslim Albanians, see Dimitris Michalopoulos, "The Moslems of Chamuria and the Exchange of Populations between Greece and Turkey," *Balkan Studies* 27:2 (1986) 303–313.

51. As part of his unique style, Rıza Nur relates the settlement of these districts by the Albanians to the special efforts of two leading politicians of Albanian origin, namely Mustafa Abdülhalik and Besim Ömer Paşa. *Dr. Rıza Nur'un Lozan Hatıraları*, 146–150.

52. CA, 1936, 97–82, 6 Mayıs 1341 [May 1925].

53. By the time the Convention was signed, the great majority of Pomak populations in Greece had been living a nomadic way of life in areas along the

Bulgarian border. According to oral sources, many of them converted to Christianity in the first half of the 1920s. Kaplanoğlu, *Bursa'da Mübadele*, 70–71. For the recent situation of the Pomaks in Greece, see Hugh Poulton, "The Turks and Pomaks," in his "The Balkans, Minorities and Governments in Conflict," http://www.armory.com/~thrace/back.html

54. *T.B.M.M.* ZC, Devre: II, İçtima Senesi: 2, Cilt: 10, 1 Teşrin-i Sâni 1340 [November 1924]—4 Kânun-ı Evvel 1340 [December 1924], (Ankara: T.B.M.M. Matbaası, 1975) 34.

55. Kaplanoğlu, *Bursa'da Mübadele*, 71–72. Also Reşat D. Tesal, *Selanik'ten Istanbul'a* (Istanbul: İletişim Yayınları, 1998) 27.

56. CA, 623, 102–34, 18 Haziran 1340 [June 1924] [10 20 19 (1)].

57. Ironically, the Bulgarian inhabitants of Kurfalli sent a petition to the Turkish government on January 17, 1935 and requested to be exchanged with the Turkish inhabitants of a village, namely Kediören (in the prefecture of Popova) in Bulgaria. They had apparently corresponded with the inhabitants of Kediören and reached an agreement to this effect. The government approved their request. CA, 2/1992, 16 Şubat [February] 1935.

58. CA, 1314, 28 Kânun-ı Evvel1340 [December 1924].

59. CA, 1188, 2 Kânun-ı Evvel1340 [December 1924] [030 18 1.1/012 59 3]. For a brief discussion of the situation of the Cypriot refugees, see Hikmet Öksüz, "Kıbrıs Türkleri'nin Anavatana Göçleri," *Tarih ve Toplum* 32:187 (1999) 35–38. The number of these refugees reached 20,000 by the end of 1925. CA, 2871, 1 Kânun-ı Evvel 1341 [December 1925].

60. *Oriente Moderno*, 8 (1928) 6–7, cited in Nada Zimova, "The Minority Question and the Lausanne Convention of 1923 (Historical Context and Religious-Ethnic Aspects of the Exchange of Greek and Turkish Populations)," *Asian and African Studies* 25 (1990) 165.

61. *Lausanne Conference*, 818. The Treaty of Lausanne also has an attachment, Declaration IX, made by the Greek representatives at the conference. This document prescribes the terms for the protection of the property rights of the Muslim populations who had left Greece, including Crete, before October 18, 1912. The understanding on the part of the Greek representatives was that the Turkish government would grant reciprocity to Greek property owners who had left before October 18, 1912 what are now the Turkish areas. See the text of the document, a brief appraisal of which can be found in Eddy, *Greece and the Greek Refugees*, 209.

62. For details of the établi problem, see Alexandris, *The Greek Minority of Istanbul*, 112–117 and Baskın Oran, "Kalanların Öyküsü (1923 Mübadele Sözleşmesinin Birinci ve Özellikle de İkinci Maddelerinin Uygulanmasından Alınacak Dersler," in *Uluslararası Konferans: Atatürk ve Modern Türkiye*, Ankara, 22–23 October 1998, (Ankara: Ankara Üniversitesi Siyasal Bilgiler Fakültesi Yayınları, 1998) 162–163. According to the Convention, the entire Greek population (those with Greek passports included) in Istanbul was exempted from the Convention as long as they could comply with the terms of residence.

63. *T.B.M.M.* GZC, Devre: 1, İçtima Senesi: 4, Cilt: 2, 2 Mart 1339 [March 1923], (Ankara: İş Bankası Kültür Yayınları, 1985) 476–477.

64. AYE, "From Politis to the Ministry of Foreign Affairs, November 10, 1923," A/5, VI (10). This incident is also cited by Ladas. See his *The Exchange of Minorities*, 497. The Mixed Commission had decided that the collection of all the taxes was to be suspended until further notification.

65. CA, 252, 102–33, 10 Şubat 1340 [February 1924] [8 51 16 (1)] Another development concerning the non-exchangeable Greeks that had to be incorporated into the Convention was related to the status of the Greek inhabitants on the Islands, İmbros (Gökçeada) and Tenedos (Bozcaada). The ceding of these islands to Turkey was decided long after the formulation of the Convention, thus the fate of the Greek inhabitants of these places which amounted to 9,000 remained pending until the ratification of the Lausanne Treaty. Once Article 14 of the Lausanne Treaty clarified the status of these islands, and they were considered within the borders of the Istanbul prefecture, the Greek residents were considered établis and exempted from the Convention.

66. Turkish authorities informed the Mixed Commission that refugees who were engaged in commerce and industry or who were well-to-do in Greece would settle these districts. These refugees were to come from Salonica, Serez, Janina, Kavala, Hania, Rethymno, and Thessaly. They would not be subjected to temporary settlement (*iskân-ı adi*) but would be permanently resettled on the condition that they would be granted 25% of their declared properties. The rest would be granted at the end of the population exchange process. *Hilal-i Ahmer*, Akşam Nüshası, 13 Temmuz 1340 [July 1924].

67. *Hilal-i Ahmer*, Akşam Nüshası, 13 Temmuz 1340 [July 1924].

68. Cumhuriyet, 3 Eylül 1340 [September 1924]. "No matter how long ago they started living and engaging in commerce in Istanbul, it does not constitute a reason for exemption from the Exchange" (*Istanbul'da ikamet ve ticaret ne kadar eski bir zamandan beri başlamış olursa olsun mübadeleden istisnayı teşkil etmez*).

69. Psomiades, *The Eastern Question*, 74. Alexis Alexandris quotes from the records of the Patriarchate that in March 1923, there were "250,000 Greeks in Constantinople and about 150,000 Greeks are going." "Certainly some 60,000 Hellene Greeks, about 40,000 non-exchangeable Greeks, 38,000 Greeks established in the city after 1918 and about 20,000 Greeks from the suburbs left Istanbul during the period 1922–24." Alexandris, *The Greek Minority of Istanbul*, 104. Another striking development arose concerning around 30,000 Greeks living in Constantinople. They were established in the city before October 30, 1918 and had left the city prior to the declaration of the Turkish Republic on October 29, 1923. Though they held Ottoman passports, the Turkish authorities would not permit them to return. These people were considered "fugitives" and their properties could be liquidated only after the Ankara Convention of 1930.

70. On October 22, 1923, a group of 30 deputies submitted a proposal *(takrir)* to the Turkish Grand National Assembly that "the Greek government is not complying with the terms of agreement concerning the exchange of

populations and properties and it continues to expose the helpless Muslims
to various kinds of pain and suffering. Therefore, we propose to exercise
a reciprocal act by way of requisitioning the movables and immovables,
stores and storages, factories and institutions that belong to the Greeks
and people of Greek nationality." The Turkish Ministry of Foreign Affairs
appealed to the Mixed Commission for taking action on this matter on
February 13, 1924. *Cumhuriyetin İlk On Yılı ve Balkan Paktı (1923–
1934)* 155–156. Similar discussions concerning this issue appeared later
on. See *T.B.M.M.* ZC, Devre: II, İçtima Senesi: 2, Cilt: 11, 6 Kânun-ı Evvel
1340 [December 1924]—3 Kânun-ı Sâni 1341 [January 1925], (Ankara:
T.B.M.M. Matbaası, 1975) 282. "The properties of non-exchangeable
Turks in Western Thrace and those who are currently in Turkey are subject to restrictive measures of the Greek government, which does not allow
any action to be taken by the non-exchangeables." A letter dated 20 June
1923 by a Greek official in Komotini (Gümülcine) report to the Ministry of Foreign Affairs in Athens the complaint of the Italian Consulate
in Salonica concerning the ever-increasing pressure on the local Muslim
populations, which included among other things the payment on the part
of the Muslims for the housing expenses of the incoming Greek refugees
from Asia Minor. AYE, "From Pakhnos to the Ministry of Foreign Affairs,
June 20, 1923," A/5, VI (11).

71. *Hâkimiyet-i Milliye,* 9 Eylül 1339 [September 1923].
72. *İsmet Paşa'nın Siyasi ve İçtimai Nutukları,* 77.
73. AYE, "From Adnan Bey to Monsieur Advocaat, Ministre de Sa Majesté la
    Reine des Pays-Bas in Athens, November 12, 1923," A/5, VI (10).
74. AYE, "Note Verbale (from Légation Royale de Pays Bas) November 27,
    1923," A/5, VI (10).
75. Παλλης, *Στατιστικη Μελετη,* 17–18. Campbell and Sherrard indicate that the
    Greeks amounted to 17% of the region's total population at the time of the
    Paris Peace Conference (1919). Campbell and Sherrard, *Modern Greece,*
    143.
76. Alexandris, *The Greek Minority of Istanbul,* 120–122. Cf. Pentzopoulos,
    The Balkan Exchange of Minorities, 136.
77. Greece was represented by H. E. M. Politis while Turkey was represented
    by Tevfik Rüşdü Bey. The president of the Session was M. M. Huber. "The
    Proceedings of the Sixth Session (Extraordinary) First Public Sitting held
    at the Peace Palace, the Hague on Friday January 16, 1925." CA, 1283,
    1739, 18 Kânun-ı Evvel 1340 [December 1924], [12 63 14]. For a discus-
    sion of the decisions taken in Athens see *T.B.M.M.* ZC, Devre: II, İçtima
    Senesi: 4, Cilt: 30, 2 Mart [March] 1927—28 Mart [March] 1927, (Ankara:
    T.B.M.M. Matbaası, n.d.) 48–65.
78. Publication of the Permanent Court of International Justice, Series B, 21
    February 1925. *Collection of Advisory Opinions,* No. 10, "Exchange of
    Greek and Turkish Populations," 25–26.
79. *Cumhuriyetin İlk On Yılı ve Balkan Paktı,* 170–171.
80. Ladas, *The Exchange of Minorities,* 408–409; Psomiades, *The Eastern
    Question,* 79.

81. The files of the cases against the Turkish government are presently held in storage at the Republican Archives in Ankara. I had a chance to see some samples from those cases, which seem to have been concluded in favor of the Turkish government. They are not accessible to researchers. Certain files in the Historical Archives of the Ministry of Foreign Affairs in Athens contain information about the cases of Greeks who were considered "fugitives" by the Turkish authorities and had not been compensated for their properties.
82. AYE, "The minutes of the Mixed Commission, August 22, 1927," 1926–27, B/61. See also Mazower, "The Refugees, the Economic Crisis," 122.
83. Eddy, *Greece and the Greek Refugees*, 207.
84. *Lausanne Conference*, 818.
85. CA, 1344, 28 Kânun-ı Evvel 1340 [December 1924].
86. CA, 2201, 23 Kânun-ı Sâni1339 [January 1923]. The resolution states that "Rents are to be exacted in proportion to their salaries, their social standings and the size of their households from the families of soldiers and those salaried [officials] who own no other houses in return for the [abandoned] houses that they have occupied, and the rest of the houses will be auctioned" (*zabitan aileleriyle maaşlarına nazaran, başka süknası olmayanlara maaş ve mevki-i içtimaiyelerine ve aded-i nüfuslarına göre işgal eyledikleri hanelerin irad-i gayri safisi üzerinden icarın tahakkuk ettirilmesi ve bunun dışında kalanların müzayedesi*).
87. Ömer Dürrü Tesal, "Türk-Yunan İlişkilerinin Geçmişinden Bir Örnek: Azınlıkların Mübadelesi," *Tarih ve Toplum*, 9:53 (1988) 51.
88. Some 300,000 *kıyye* (1 *kıyye* = 1300 grams) currants abandoned by the Greeks were sold in auction and the Turkish government even auctioned the transportation rights of this produce. *Türk Sesi*, 6 Temmuz 1339 [July 1923].
89. CA, 2001, 2039 16 Teşrin-i Sâni 1338 [November 1922] [6 37 1]. "The sacks and boxes, containing the seeds of the silk cocoons of the departed Greeks, are to be sold before they get rotten and their receipts to be transferred to the Ministry of Finance" (*Giden Rumların ipek böceği tohumlarını havi torba ve kutuların satılıp mevsimi geçmeden parasının Maliye Vekâleti'ne tahsili*).
90. T.B.M.M. GZC, Devre: I, İçtima Senesi: 4, Cilt: 2, 2 Mart 1339 [March 1923], (Ankara: İş Bankası Kültür Yayınları, 1985) 532. See also *T.B.M.M ZC*, Devre: II, İçtima Senesi: 2, Cilt: 18, 14 Nisan 1341 [April 1925]—22 Nisan 1341 [April 1925], (Ankara: T.B.M.M. Matbaası, 1976) 42, 56–62. The Greek government signed an agreement with the National Bank of Greece on May 5, 1925, which passed the administration and liquidation of the abandoned Muslim properties (with the exception of the rural and urban estates handed over to the Refugee Settlement Commission) on to the hands of the Bank. This agreement cancelled out the sales of property and other transactions concluded since October 1922. See League of Nations, *Greek Refugee Settlement*, 171–172.
91. Tesal, "Türk-Yunan İlişkilerinin Geçmişinden Bir Örnek," 50.

92. CA, 291, K488, 13 Şubat 1340 [February 1924] [9 14 8 (1)]. This is confirmed by the information found in a letter written on 24 March 1924 by Cemil Zeki (Yoldaş) to the members of his family who were preparing for evacuation in Florina. He says "The lands that are currently being granted to the refugees are not well-arranged. That is, they do not match the land that they have vacated; approximately 17 percent of it" (*Muhacire şimdi verilen arazi gayri muntazam. Yani terk ettiği emlaka mukabil değildir. On yedi buçuk nispetinde*). See *Kendi Kaleminden Teğmen Cemil Zeki (Yoldaş) Anılar-Mektuplar*, ed. E. Berber, (Istanbul: ARBA, 1994) 75.

93. *T.B.M.M.* ZC, Devre: II, İçtima Senesi: 2, Cilt: 7/1, 16 Mart 1340 [March 1924]—20 Mart 1340 [March 1924], (Ankara: T.B.M.M. Matbaası, 1968) 1043.

94. *Cumhuriyetin İlk On Yılı ve Balkan Paktı*, 169. "In practice, the valuation [of properties] did not take place as stipulated by the Convention" (*Tatbikatta, ekseriya kıymetlerin tevzii sözleşmede öngörüldüğü şekilde olmamıştır*).

95. CA, 1/7693, 20 Şubat [February] 1929.

96. CA, "Copy of the Crypto Message (by Hamdi Bey)" 132, 15 Kânun-ı Sâni 1340 [January 1924].

97. CA, 6/5430, 102/137, 11 Mart 1341 [March 1925].

98. CA, 329, 97–68, 9 Mart 1340 [March 1924] [9 16 6 (1)].

99. *Anadolu*, 2 Teşrin-i Evvel 1340 [October 1924]. *T.B.M.M.* ZC, Devre: II, İçtima Senesi: 3, Cilt: 19, 26 Teşrin-i Evvel 1341 [October 1925]—30 Teşrin-i Sâni 1341 [November 1925], (Ankara: T.B.M.M. Matbaası, 1977) 172, 186–187.

100. *Anadolu*, 8 Nisan [April] 1932.

101. CA, 11997, 9 Aralık [December], 1931.

102. *T.B.M.M.* ZC, Devre: I, İçtima Senesi: 3, Cilt: 26, 23 Kânun-ı Evvel 1338 [December 1922]—25 Kânun-ı Sâni1339 [January 1923], (Ankara: T.B.M.M. Matbaası, 1960) 104–114.

103. AYE, "Note Verbal to the British Ministry of Foreign Affairs, April 3/4, 1923," A/5, VI (3). Also "Note-verbal to the Quai d'Orsay, April 3, 1923," A/5, VI (3). It is worth mentioning here that the Greek Ministry of Foreign Affairs formulated each letter to be sent to the British and French Foreign Ministries with a very careful language in that the letter to the British characterizes the Kemalist act as "directly opposed to the obligation of respecting private property . . . elementary spirit of respect of acquired rights" while the letter to the French Ministry is characterized by the grave situation of French establishments such as the Credit Lyonnaise and Credit Focier d'Algerie et de Tunisie.

104. AYE, "From Lancelot Oliphant to M.C. Collas, Greek Légation, April 6, 1923," A/5, VI (3).

105. AYE, "From Meletopoulos to the Ministry of Foreign Affairs, Constantinople, November 16, 1922," A/5, VI (10). The letter reads "*J'a apprends de bonne source que á la situation Banque ottomane aurait décidé envoyer Paris Somme un million livres or. Cet argent provient en partie des dépôts allemands durant la guerre.*"

106. AYE, Note Verbale, "From the Greek Légation in Paris to the French Ministry of Foreign Affairs, October 25, 1923," A/5, VI (10).
107. *T.B.M.M. Kavanin Mecmuası*, Devre: 3, İçtima Senesi: 3, Cilt: 8, (Ankara: T.B.M.M. Matbaası, 1930) 897.
108. CA, 712, 136/5, 20 Temmuz 1340 [July 1924].
109. The full text of the Athens Agreement, see CA, [123 878 3], "*Atina'da 1 Kânun-ı Evvel 1926 Tarihinde İmza Olunan Emlake Mütedair İtilafname, Emlake Mütedair 1 Kânun-ı Evvel 1926 Tarihli İtilafname Melfufu, Nihai Protokol, Beyanname, Bir Nümerolu Protokol, İki Nümerolu Protokol, İmza Zabıtnamesi, Saracoğlu Şükrü Beyfendi ile Argiroplos Beyninde Teati Olunan Mektup Sureti.*"
110. *İsmet Paşa'nın Siyasi ve İçtimai Nutukları*, 70.

NOTES TO CHAPTER SEVEN

1. On the plight of the Greek populations in Izmir and its environs, certain insights can be gained from the following books: Michael Llewellyn Smith, *Ionian Vision: Greece in Asia Minor, 1919–1922* (London: Allen Lane, 1973); Bilge Umar, *Izmir'de Yunanlıların Son Günleri* (Ankara: Bilgi Yayınevi, 1974) 257–334; Marjorie Housepian Dobkin, *Smyrna 1922: The Destruction of a City* (New York: Newmark Press, 1998) (first edition appeared in 1972). The last two books, in particular, contain much imaginary material and therefore should be used with caution.
2. It was not until September 26, 1922 that the refugees and Greek soldiers were allowed to land, for political reasons, at the ports of "Old Greece" (Λιμανια της Παλαιας Ελλαδας). The Revolutionary government of Plastiras and Gonatas repudiated this order. See Αρετης Τουντα-Φεργαδη, *Το Προσφυγικο Δανειο του 1924*, (Salonica: Παρατηρητης, 1986) 25.
3. AYE, "From Dasios (quoting from a telegram by the mayor of Drama) to the Ministry of Foreign Affairs, Komothene, 31 May 1923," A/5, VI (4). Interview with Zeliha Bilge, Izmir, October 21, 1994. Also Tesal, *Selanik'ten Istanbul'a*, 59–71.
4. Before the Greek populations left eastern Thrace, especially the territories on the east bank of the Maritsa River, the Greek government seems to have registered their properties including their stocks of agricultural produce and bulk merchandise. See a series of reports in the AYE, A/5, VI (11). One of the journalists who were reporting about the plight of the Greek refugees from eastern Thrace was Ernest Hemingway, who was at the time the correspondent for a Canadian newspaper. See *The Toronto Daily Star*, October 20, 1922.
5. *İsmet Paşa'nin Siyasi ve İçtimai Nutukları*, 70–71.
6. One of the points common to the testimonies held in the archives of the Centre for Asia Minor Studies (KMS) in Athens is that all the refugees who came before and after Lausanne believed that this was a temporary solution, another armistice, and they would be eventually be allowed to return home with the cessation of hostilities. Moreover, the refugees were unaware as to when the war was over. KMS, Files 291, 293, and 295.

7. AYE, "From Dr. Adnan to Ministre des Pays-Bas in Athens, August 4, 1923," A/5, VI (4). Dr. Adnan explains the policy of his government as "Un grande nombre d'habitants grecs de Turquie, par leur propre désir et se basant surtout aux promesses qui leur furent faites de quelques parts, s'étaient, bien avant, rassemblés au port de Samsoun pour être transportés en Grèce." For the situation in Mersin, see in the same file "Near East Relief, Mersin(e) report of Refugee Station, Mersin(e) April 3, 1923." There are many documents showing the mounting pressure on the male Greeks in the interior of Asia Minor. On November 10, 1923, the British Legation in Athens notified the Greek Ministry of Foreign Affairs that "58 young men of Greek race succeeded in embarking on a British steamer at Constantinople and were not discovered until the arrival of vessel at Alexandria on October 3. As it was impossible to land these men in Eygpt, they were taken to Cyprus where they are now being maintained at the expense of His Majesty's government." They asked for permission to land in Greece at the expense of the Greek government. AYE, "From British Legation to Ministry of Foreign Affairs, November 10, 1923," A/5, VI (10).

8. CA, 558, 2391, 28 Mayıs 1340 [May 1924] [9 27 15 (1)]

9. CA 271, 181–18, 13 Şubat 1340 [Şubat 1924] [9 13 8].

10. Melville Chater, "History's Greatest Trek," *The National Geographic Magazine* 48 (1925) 533–590.

11. AYE, "From the Greek Red Cross to Henderson, Constantinople, February 22, 1923," A/5, VI (11).

12. AYE, "From the Ministry of Health to the Ministry of Foreign Affairs, March 27, 1923, A/5, VI (3).

13. Alexandris, "Pontic Greek Refugees," 287.

14. *Times*, 17 January 1923, cited in Alexandris, "Pontic Greek Refugees," 283. The article provides a detailed list of organizations and individuals in Istanbul that assisted the Greek refugees from the Pontos.

15. Morgenthau, *I Was Sent to Athens*, 101.

16. Παλλης, Στατιστικη Μελετη, 8.

17. These four ports were designated as the "exit gates" (*ihraç kapıları*) for the Muslim refugees. In Turkey, the "entry gates" (*kabul kapıları*) were Urla, Tuzla, Mersin, Antalya, Sinop and Trabzon. See CA, 102/16, [123 572 16], "*Mübadelei Ahaliye Dair Lozan Mukavelenamesinin Suret-i Tatbikiyesini Mübeyyin Olarak Sıhhiye ve Muavenet-i İçtimaiye Vekaletince Tanzim Olunan Birinci Talimatname*," Article 12, 2 Temmuz 1339 [July 1923].

18. Since the early summer of 1923, many refugees from eastern sections of Anatolia were transferred to the western provinces. Two newspapers, *Hâkimiyet-i Milliye* and *Türk Sesi*, are full of news about the eastern refugees (*vilayet-i şarkiyye muhacirleri*). See for example, *Hâkimiyet-i Milliye*, 29 Mayıs 1339 [May 1923] *Türk Sesi*, 18 Temmuz 1339 [July 1923], and 19 Temmuz 1339 [July 1923]. Those refugees from Greece who could afford their passage began to arrive in Izmir during the same period. See for example, *Tanin*, 11 Temmuz 1339 [July 1923], 12 Ağustos 1339 [August 1923], *Hâkimiyet-i Milliye*, 1 Ağustos 1339 [August 1923].

19. *Hâkimiyet-i Milliye*, 15 Teşrin-i Sâni 1339 [October 1923].

20. In one of his speeches, Mustafa Necati said "Since our brothers, coming to our country from Rumelia, will be traveling under our flag and with our own ships, and the owners of these ships are Muslim and Turkish, they [refugees] will be given maximum assistance on board. There are presently some 17 Turkish ships in the possession of our Ministry. The Ministry, which has adopted the development of our national economy as its job and responsibility, will pay utmost attention to this particular matter during its operation. However, both the Administration of Navigation and the national companies should acquire new ships through the revenues that they will gain from transportation. It would be the manifestation of our goal to watch ships under our own banner operating throughout our coasts. I look forward to seeing the owners of ships fulfill this goal." *Ayın Tarihi*, 2:4 (Kânun-ı Evvel 1923) [December 1923].

21. *Türkiye İktisat Mecmuası*, 2:36 (28 Teşrin-i Sâni 1339) [November 1923] 377.

22. The names of these boats were Gülcemal, Akdeniz, Reşit Paşa, Kızılırmak, Şam, Giresun, Ümit, Gülnihal, Bahricedit, Altay, Gelibolu, Bandırma, İnebolu, Nimet, Canik, Millet and Ereğli. *İstanbul Ticaret ve Sanayi Odası Mecmuası*, Teşrin-i Sâni 1339 [October 1923] 25. Nearly half of the forty refugees interviewed by İskender Özsoy mention that their ships experienced mechanical problem during the trip to Turkey. See Özsoy, *İki Vatan Yorgunları*, 36–39, 50–51, 79–80, 92–93.

23. Yorğaki Effimianidis, *Cihan İktisad Buhranı Önünde Türkiye*, vol. 2, (Istanbul: Kaadçılık ve Matbaacılık Anonim Şirketi, 1936) 114.

24. CA, 11, 204–4, 07 Teşrin-i Sâni 1339 [November 1923] [8 39 11 (1)].

25. *Hâkimiyet-i Milliye*, 7 Kânun-ı Sâni1340 [January 1924].

26. Kosova, *Ben İşçiyim*, 14–15.

27. Tülay Alim Baran, "İzmir'de Çiftçi Mübadiller," *Kebikeç*, 4 (1996) 181. She quotes this information from the Register, *1340 Tarihli Canlı Malları Gösteren Defter*. Her research is based on the archives of the Provincial Bureau of Village Affairs (*Köy Hizmetleri İşleri Müdürlüğü*) in Izmir, now transferred in its entirety to the Republic Archives in Ankara, which provide very rich information as to various aspects of the refugee situation. The transportation of livestock was regulated by a decree issued on March 9, 1924. "The payment for the transportation of the livestock is to be made by the refugees themselves . . . but in case the owners declare that they are unable to afford the full fare, of the kinds of livestock such as sheep and goats, they should pay only for three in each category and they should pay for the rest in multiple installments after arrival." CA, 329, 9 Mart 1340 [March 1924].

28. *Hâkimiyet-i* Milliye, 21 Mart 1340 [March 1924].

29. *Hâkimiyet-i Milliye*, 21 Mart 1340 [March 1924] and Yeni Gün, 21 Mart 1340 [March 1924].

30. *Açıksöz*, 26 Mayıs 1340 [May 1924].

31. Παλλης, *Στατιστικη Μελετη*, 4.

32. For the appeal of Venizelos to the international public for refugee relief, see Pentzopoulos, *The Balkan Exchange of Minorities*, 76–77. For a general

overview of the experiences of Greek refugees see Dimitra Giannuli,
"Greeks or "Strangers at Home": The Experiences of Ottoman Greek
Refugees during their Exodus to Greece, 1922–1923," *Journal of Modern
Greek Studies* 13: 2 (1995) 271–287.

33. AYE, "Anonymous Report Presented to the Ministry of Foreign Affairs,
    June 9, 1923," A/5, VI (4). See also Barton, *The Story of Near East Relief*,
    169.

34. AYE, "Refugee Problem Viewed by [the Head of the American Red Cross]
    William Haskell, Walter Duranty, Special Cable to New York Times, Mos-
    cow, February 7, 1923," A/5, VI (11).

35. AYE, "Report of the Relief Work in Aegean Sea by B. D. MacDonald.
    October 1922," 1923, A/5, VI (11). Dr Esther Lovejoy, President of the
    International Medical Women's Association, who was in Symrna in Sep-
    tember 1922 writes: "Smyrna's misery exceeds the saddest episode of war.
    The most vivid incident in Dante's Inferno" are but ordinary happenings
    in comparison with the sufferings of the thousands of Smyrna refugees."
    Extracts from N.E.R. (Near East Relief) Cables.

36. AYE, "Report of the Relief Work in Aegean Sea by B. D. MacDonald,
    October 1922," A/5, VI (11). The report attests that the Greek government
    was providing shelter for 90 per cent of the refugees but had no food or
    funds for relief.

37. The offices of the Near East Relief in Geneva played a significant role in
    this respect. See AYE, "To Americans Abroad, Near East Relief, Geneva,
    October 17, 1922," A/5 VI (3). "From J. H. Crutger, Director of Samsun
    Unit, to Managing Director of N.E.R. in Constantinople, June 6, 1923,"
    A/5, VI (4). This report provides detailed figures about Armenian and
    Greek refugees in Asia Minor.

38. The Vatican donated to the archbishop of Istanbul around 3,000 Turkish
    liras for the relief of the refugees from Pontus. The Greek officials in Istan-
    bul instructed the Ministry of Foreign Affairs in Athens not to reveal this
    information to the public. AYE, "From the Greek Legation in Istanbul to
    the Ministry of Foreign Affairs, September 26, 1923," A/5, VI (10).

39. Campbell and Sherrard, *Modern Greece*, 166. The Greek government had
    apparently resettled some 7,500 refugees in Corfu; 2,000 of these refu-
    gees had been brought over from Thrace (probably eastern Thrace). AYE,
    "Note-Verbale from the Ministry of Foreign Affairs to La Legation Royale
    d'Italie, September 14, 1923," A/5, VI (10). The file contains several letters
    concerning the Greek-Italian dispute on Corfu.

40. AYE, "From Kondres to the Ministry of Foreign Affairs, October 1, 1923,"
    1923–24, A/2. The passage roughly reads "Wishing to appease the uni-
    versal outrage that resulted from the extortion of 50 million from Greece,
    Mussolini made an offer of 10 million in favor of the refugees. It must not
    be forgotten, among other things, that the military order in Malta which is
    charged to distribute money is a catholic unit that wants to use our money
    in order to make Italian and catholic propaganda among us and to intro-
    duce in Corfu a form of moral occupation almost as dangerous as a mili-
    tary one."

41. AYE, "From General Directorate of Macedonia in Salonica to the Ministry of Foreign Affairs, November 19, 1924," 1925, A/4, (7). Also in the same file, "From Dendramis to the Ministry of Foreign Affairs, November 23, 1924, Berne," and "From the General Directorate of Macedonia in Salonica to the Ministry of Foreign Affairs, July 17, 1925."
42. AYE, "Near East Relief, Report of Refugee Situation by Joseph W. Beach, April 3, 1923," A/5, VI (3). See especially the section "The Situation in the Interior."
43. AYE, "From Anninos to the Ministry of Foreign Affairs in Athens, Constantinople, April 19, 1923," A/5 VI (4). In April, the number of Greek refugees was roughly as follows: 21,000 in Constantinople; 12,000 in Samsun; several thousands at the other Black Sea Ports and Mersin; and several thousands in Syria. In March, 3,000 were removed from Constantinople; 5,000 from Mersin and Beyrouth; and when the document was being written, another ship left Istanbul to take 2,000 from Samsun. In the same month some 10,000 prisoners of war had also been repatriated.
44. The above report has an appendix that contains the translation of an order posted on the gates of Armenian and Greek churches in Mersin. The order, issued by the acting Mutasarrıf of Mersin on March 15, 1923, is addressed "to those families that have come to Mersin(e) from different parts of Anatolia of their will and demand, with the intention of leaving the country and have been prolonging their stay in Mersin(e)." It states, "since the city is not desirous of more people, and because a contagious disease has broken out lately among these people, therefore all those who intend to leave the country ought to do so in a few days time. Otherwise they will be compelled to return their homes in order to protect the health of the public."
45. AYE, "From Pallis to Admiral Bristol, Constantinople, April 19, 1923," A/5 VI (4).
46. AYE, "From Stellakis to the Ministry of Foreign Affairs, Beyrouth, May 31, 1923," A/5, VI (3).
47. AYE, "A Note from the French Ministry of Foreign Affairs to the Greek Legation in Paris, July 10, 1923," and "From Romanos to the Greek Ministry of Foreign Affairs, July 11, 1923," A/5, VI (3). "Les autorités Françaises ne peuvent continuer à nourrir ces émigrés qui refusent de travailler, ils constituent, en outre, un danger pour l'hygiène publique."
48. AYE, "Facts Relating to the Refugee(s) Situation in Greece," A/5, VI (10). The number of refugees already arrived in Greece amounted to 1,150,000, which consisted of 1,040,000 Greeks, 100,000 Armenians, 1,000 Assyrians, and 9,000 Circassians.
49. AYE, "From Politis to the Prime Minister, August 1, 1923," A/5, VI (11).
50. Pentzopoulos, *The Balkan Exchange of Minorities*, 77.
51. AYE, "From Brainerd Salmon to Mr. A. Politis, October 3, 1923," A/5, VI (10).
52. AYE, "From Lancelot Oliphant to Monsieur Collas, June 1, 1923," A/5, VI (4).
53. AYE, "From the Near East Relief to the Ministry of Foreign Affairs, September 29, 1923," A/5, VI (10).

54. AYE, "From the Minister of Health Doksiadis to the Director of the Near East Relief Ralph Knoff, October 5, 1923," A/5, VI (10).

55. AYE, "From K. Gondikas to the Ministry of Foreign Affairs, August 30, 1923," A/5, VI (10).

56. Like many other issues, the fate of the refugees was from the early months of 1920 influenced by the nature of alliances between the countries involved. The Turkish rapproachment with France and Russia had important effects on the policies of the Ankara government concerning the status of Greek populations in Anatolia. A resolution issued on June 29, 1921 illustrates this point best. This resolution allowed the Greeks of Russian nationality to stay in their places while it granted ample time to the Greeks of Italian and French nationalities for evacuation. The Greeks of British nationality, on the other hand, were ordered to be arrested. CA, 1003, 95–14, 29 Haziran 1337 [June 1921] [3 27 14 1]. Alexis Alexandris notes that "despite their extensive facilities [in Istanbul], [the French/Catholic] Missionaries, anxious not to offend the Turkish authorities, refused to offer any assistance to the Pontic Greek refugees." Alexandris, "Pontic Greek Refugees," 285.

57. AYE, "Dr. Vidal, Compte rendu à la Commission des Refugiés Grecs d'une visite au camp des emigrés de San Stefano, Constantinople, May 17, 1923," A/5, VI (4). The passage roughly translates "Those arriving at the camp are deloused; given a shower; have their hairs cut; their clothes, their luggage, their undergarment are disinfected, and they are installed with other refugees only after these operations. The place of shower and disinfection is found at the entry of the camp. In the vicinity of the pavilion of disinfection is found an infirmary for the ordinary patients; the contagious patients are not kept in the camp but are transferred immediately to the Greek hospital of Yedikule . . . Notwithstanding occasional mishaps, Turkish authorities provide them with an effective cooperation and we have the impression that the whole enterprise is directed with firmness and intelligence."

58. "Freedom to travel" was one of the major issues that were discussed at Lausanne. The Turkish authorities, who were trying to detain the anti-revolutionary elements and those who cooperated with the occupying forces, closely watched over the railways and roads.

59. AYE, "From A. Pallis to the Ministry of Foreign Affairs, Constantinople, February 22, 1923," A/5, VI (4).

60. AYE, "From Pallis to the Ministry of Foreign Affairs, Constantinople, April 29, 1923," A/5, VI (4).

61. Interview with Zeliha Bilge, Izmir, October 21, 1994. Also see Köker, "Lessons in Refugeehood" passim.

62. The archival collections of the Red Crescent have only recently come to the attention of researchers. See Çapa, "Kızılay (Hilal-i Ahmer) Cemiyeti."

63. Çapa, "Kızılay (Hilal-i Ahmer) Cemiyeti," 296. A newspaper indicates the total amount of funds reserved for the refugees and given to the Red Crescent for the whole year of 1923 as 500,000 Turkish liras. *Hâkimiyet-i Milliye*, 4 Eylül 1339 [September 1923].

64. AYE, "From A. Anninos to the Ministry of Foreign Affairs, Constantinople, October 22, 1923," A/5, VI (10).
65. AYE, "From H. Hyppan to the General Directorate of Macedonia, November 10, 1923," A/5, VI (10).
66. *Yeni Gün*, 27 Teşrin-i Evvel 1338 [October 1922].
67. CA, 1985, 137–20, 12 Teşrin-i Sâni 1338 [November 1922] [6 36 5]. (*Yunan istilasından kurtarılan livalarda kısmen veya kamilen yanan şehirler ve kasabaların haritalarını ahz ve tersim ve şekli müstakbellerinin tayin ve tesbit eylemek üzre bir reisin taht-ı nezaretinde sekiz hey'et-i fenniyye teşkil edilecektir*). As stated earlier, the principal objective of this policy was to map out the properties of Greeks (especially those belonging to people of Greek nationality) which could be used as security against the war reparations to be demanded from Greece during the upcoming peace conference. CA, 1875, 135–4, 1 Teşrin-i Evvel 1338 [October 1922] [5 30 11]. (*Sulh müzakeratında nazarı dikkate alınmak üzre gerek Yunan tebaasına ve gerekse muhaceret iden Rum ve Ermenilere aid emval ve emlakın Hükümet-i mahalliyelerce şimdiden tayin ve tesbiti . . .*). See also *T.B.M.M. ZC*, Devre: I, İçtima Senesi: 3, Cilt: 25, 20 Teşrin-i Evvel 1338 [October 1922]— 21 Kânun-ı Evvel 1338 [December 1922] (Ankara: T.B.M.M. Matbaası, 1960) 23 and 473.
68. AYE, 1923, A/5, VI (11) 29/1/1923. The Greek Embassy in Sofia and the Consulate in Phillipoupolis kept Athens updated about the number of Turkish armed forces and their activities in Thrace. On January 29, 1923 it was reported that "a new Turkish division of 12,000 men is moving from Bizyis to Uzunköprü."
69. CA, 1526, 26 Nisan 1338 [April 1922] [4 55 2].
70. The draft of the document is entitled "*Türkiye Büyük Millet Meclisi Hükümeti Murahhıslarıyla Yunan Hükümeti Arasında Mübadele-i Ahaliye ve Emval Hakkında Lozan'da Teati Olunan 30 Kânun-ı Sâni 1923 Tarihli Mukavelenamenin Suret-i Tatbikiyesi Mübeyyin Talimatnamedir.*" CA, 2600, 2660, 17 Temmuz 1339 [July 1923] [7 25 2 (5)]. The second document found in the same file is "*Mübadele-i Ahaliye Dair Lozan Mukavelesinin Suret-i Tatbikiyesini Mübeyyin Olarak Sıhhiye ve Muavenat-i İçtimaiye Vekaletince Tanzim Olunan Birinci Talimatname.*"
71. CA, 102/19M, 25 Mart 1339 [March 1923] [123 873 18], "Muhacir İskânına Müsait Olan Mahalleri İrae Eder Cedvel." Based on the information obtained from local officials, this is an incomplete list of available houses in various provinces (*vilayets*) which were available for the incoming refugees. The list also indicates the number of refugees to be resettled in each province. No such information has been obtained from the provinces of Trabzon, Edirne, Bursa and Istanbul. See also CA, 102/1 [123 872 2] "Mübadeleten Gelecek Ahali İskan Mıntıkalarına Aid 2 Numaralı Cedvel." According to this document, the country had been divided into eight "resettlement regions." Each region consisted of multiple *sancak*s (e.g., Gümüşhane Sancağı, Adana Sancağı etc.) and vilayets (e.g., Sivas Vilayeti, Izmir Vilayeti etc.) with their towns (*kazalar*) and smaller administrative units (*nahiyeler*). The Resettlement Scheme (*İskân Cetveli*) mentioned in

the text as having been attached, was not found in the pertaining file in CA. A facsimile copy of this table was located in *İskan Tarihçesi*, (İstanbul: Hamit Matbaası, 1932) 18.

72. *T.B.M.M. ZC*, Devre: II, İçtima Senesi: 2, Cilt: 10, 1 Teşrin-i Sâni 1340 [November 1924]—4 Kânun-ı Evvel 1340 [December 1924], 83–84.

73. İskan ve Teavün Cemiyeti, *Umumi Kongre Mübadele Encümeni Mazbatası*, *İskân ve Teavün Cemiyeti Mübadele Rehberi* (İzmir: Ahenk Matbaası, 1339 [1923]).

74. Another organization that prompted the government to take social and economic measures before the resettlement of the refugees began was Makedonya Cemiyeti. *Vatan*, 30 Temmuz 1339 [July 1923] For the views of various journalists, see *Ahenk*, 19 Teşrin-i Sâni 1339 [November 1923] *Türk Sesi*, 27 Eylül 1339 [September 1923].

75. CA, "Mübadele İmar ve İskân Kanunu," 2867, 23 Teşrin-i Evvel 1339 [October 1923].

76. See İpek, *Mübadele ve Samsun*. Also by the same author "Köy Hizmetleri İl Müdürlüğü Arşivlerinden Mübadil Göçmenlerle İlgili Defterler," *Tarih ve Toplum* 144 (1995) 15–18. İpek does not include the two registers, namely the Registers of Greek Buildings (*Rum Bina Defteri*), in the inventory of registers he provides in the article.

77. Baran, "Bir Kentin Yeniden Yapılanması," 105–115.

78. There are two types of registers in which the values of the allotted properties were recorded. Registers of Assessed Values of Estates (*Arazi Kıymet Tesbit Defteri*) and the Registers of Assessed Values of Buildings (*Bina Kıymet Tesbit Defteri*).

79. Such transfers can be traced through the Daily Registers of Refugee Transfer (*Mübadil Sevk Jurnal Defteri*).

80. Kosova, *Ben İşçiyim*, 16. For similar problems experienced by the refugees who came to Kayaköy (Livisi) see Barbaros Tanç, "Where Local Trumps National: Christian Orthodox and Muslim Refugees since Lausanne," *Balkanologie* 5:1–2 (2001) 273–289.

81. A certain group of homeless refugees who obtained permission to resettle in İzmit went there with the provision that they would build their own houses. But this apparently did not happen. The local offices of the Ministry took over the case and resettled the refugees according to its own plans. *T.B.M.M. ZC*, Devre: II, İçtima Senesi: 2, Cilt: 10, 1 Teşrin-i Sâni 1340 [Kasım 1924]—4 Kânun-ı Evvel 1340 [December 1924], 75–76.

82. Baran, "Bir Kentin Yeniden Yapılanması," 133.

83. *T.B.M.M. ZC*, Devre: II, İçtima Senesi: 2, Cilt: 10, 1 Teşrin-i Sâni 1340 [Kasım 1924]—4 Kânun-ı Evvel 1340 [December 1924], 41–42.

84. Ibid, 77.

85. *Hâkimiyet-i Milliye*, 28 Teşrin-i Evvel 1339 [October 1923].

86. *T.B.M.M. ZC*, Devre: II, İçtima Senesi: 2, Cilt: 10, 1 Teşrin-i Sâni 1340 [Kasım 1924]—4 Kânun-ı Evvel 1340 [December 1924], 34–35.

87. Ibid, 78.

88. *Celal Bayar Diyor ki, 1920–1950, Nutuk-Hitabe-Beyanet-Hasbıhal*, ed. Nazmi Sevgen, (İstanbul: n. p., 1951) 29.

89. CA, 102/8, 3 Kânun-ı Evvel 1338 [December 1922] [123 872 8].
90. Kemal Arı, "1923 Türk-Rum Mübadele Anlaşması Sonrasında Izmir'de 'Emval-i Metruke' ve 'Mübadil Göçmenler,'" *Atatürk Araştırma Merkezi Dergisi* 6:18 (1990) 627–657.
91. According to government estimates, there were 20,000 empty houses and 50,000 refugees were to be resettled in these houses. A local newspaper published a series of articles on this issue and pointed out that there were not enoough vacant houses and the number of such houses could not exceed 5,000. The great majority of abandoned properties had already been occupied by government officials, soldiers, needy, victims of disaster, and refugees (*memurin, zabitan, erbabı ihtiyaç, felaketzedegan ve muhacir*). *Ahenk*, 28 Ağustos 1339 [August 1923] and 19 Teşrin-i Evvel 1339 [October 1923].
92. *Hâkimiyet-i Milliye*, 3 Ağustos 1339 [August 1923].
93. *Düstur*, Üçüncü Tertip, Vol. 15, Ankara, 1934, 1165–1166.
94. As late as 1925, certain resolutions were passed to this effect. Such a resolution stipulated that people who had moved to the interior of Anatolia but had not permanently resettled during the Greek occupation were granted the right to return to their former territories and secure compensation for their properties from those abandoned by the Greeks. CA, 2867, 7 Kânun-ı Evvel 1341 [December 1925].
95. As early as February 1922, the nationalist leaderhip in Ankara passed a resolution that the Greeks who departed from the formerly Greek-occupied areas were considered as traitors and that their properties would be distributed among those who suffered under Greek occupation. CA, 1394, K209, 15 Şubat 1338 [February 1922] [4 48 10 1]. Almost a year later, the government issued another resolution allowing the people, especially government officials and families of the soldiers who had occupied the abandoned Greek properties in Izmir, to hold onto these properties in return for a certain amount of rent (*geliri üzerinden icar tahakkuk ettirilmesi*) and the rest of the abandoned properties to be leased to interested parties in auction. CA, 2201, 103/2, 23 Kânun-ı Sâni 1339 [January 1923] [6 47 1]. In this regard, certain measures were taken. A Priştineli Mehmed who had occupied a factory was evicted and asked to pay rent for the period of his occupation. CA, 2458 135–23, 03 Mayıs 1339 [May 1923] [7 17 19 (1)].
96. *İstimlak Kanunları, 1339* [1923]. Also see in the same volume *İşgal Kanunu. Şark*, 4 Teşrin-i Evvel 1338 [October 1922].
97. CA, 554, 135–3, 18 Kânun-ı Sâni 1337 [January 1921] [2 29 30].
98. *Tanin*, 30 Teşrin-i Sâni 1338 [November 1922].
99. *Yenigün*, 30 Teşrin-i Sâni 1338 [November 1922].
100. *T.B.M.M. ZC*, Devre: I, İçtima Senesi: 3, Cilt: 25, 20 Teşrin-i Sâni 1338 [November 1922]—21 Kânun-ı Evvel 1338 [December 1922] (Ankara: T.B.M.M. Matbaası, 1960) 200. Government efforts to prevent the seizure of abandoned properties proved ineffective. In some cases, government policies caused more problems. As in the case of turning large buildings into governmental offices, the government ordered the evacuation of all refugees from these buildings. CA 426, 133–21, 3 Nisan 1340 [April 1924]

[9 21 4 (1)]. For a government decree that ordered the evacuation of an abandoned Greek building so that it could be turned into a "School for the Mute and the Blind" (*Dilsiz ve Körler Mektebi*) in Izmir, see CA., 2193, 145–15, 1 Temmuz [July] 1925 [14 435].

101. Later developments would show that the government continued to distribute Greek properties among war veterans and political and cultural institutions. At the peak of the refugee influx, the government granted some of the abandoned properties in Izmir, to the Turkish Hearths (*Türk Ocakları*) in return for an insignificant rent. CA, 679, 1887, 2 Temmuz 1340 [July 1924] [10 33 16].

102. *Ahenk*, 30 Ağustos 1339 [August 1923].

103. Ibid

104. It is reported that there were many refugees in Izmir whose official destination was originally Samsun or other interior towns of Anatolia. The following statistics are offered by the director of National Property, Hasan Fehmi Bey as to the number of houses and other properties deserted by the Greeks in the city: 12,287 houses, 271 shops, 89 factories, 2 baths, 1 hospital. *Anadolu*, 18 Haziran 1340 [June 1924]. According to the practice, Greek property was granted to exchangeables while the Armenian property was offered to those who had lost their houses to the great fire. The newspaper *Şark* reports on September 25, 1922 that those who seized abandoned properties should return them in a week to the local bureau of Ministry of Finance (i.e., *defterdarlık*). Otherwise, they will be subjected to a trial in the 'Court Martial' (*Divan-i Harb*). People who provided information on the people who appropriated these properties would be rewarded 10% of the sale value of these properties.

105. *Ahenk*, 14 Teşrin-i Evvel 1339 [October 1923].

106. *Ahenk*, 4 Eylül 1339 [September 1923].

107. *Yeni Gün*, 15 Kânun-ı Evvel1338 [December 1923].

108. *Hâkimiyet-i Milliye*, 2 Eylül 1339 [September 1923]. This paper reports that the rent of a house with three bedrooms jumped to 670 liras due to the abolition of the *Sekene Kanunu*.

109. *Hâkimiyet-i Milliye*, 27 Haziran 1339 [June 1923].

110. *Türk Sesi*, 26 Eylül 1339 [September 1923].

111. *Ahenk*, 2 Teşrin-i Evvel 1341 [October 1925].

112. *İstatistik Yıllığı*, vol. 3, 1930, (Ankara: İstatistik Umum Müdürlüğü, 1930) 100.

113. (*Bir Türk kasaba veya köyünde lisan ve adeti başka diğer bir ırka mensup muhacirinin miktarı yüzde yirmiyi asla tecavüz etmeyecektir.*) *Ahali Mübadelesi Hakkında Talimatname*, 17 Temmuz 1339 [July 1923]. See also *Vatan*, 1 Ağustos 1339 [August 1923].

114. BOA, Dahiliye Nezareti, Hukuk Müşavirliği Evrakı, 30, 60, 7.2.1332 [1913]; "villages with 50 households to be constructed for the resettlement of the refugees" (*muhacirlerin iskânı için en az elli hanelik karyelerin teşkili*).

115. CA, 2417, 3582, 26 Ağustos 1341 [August 1925] [15 154 11]. The government decided to establish 14 villages (Samsun: 7, Izmir: 2, Bursa: 2, Izmit:

1, Adana: 1) each with 50 households. *T.B.M.M.* ZC, Devre: II, İçtima Senesi: 2, Cilt: 10, 1 Teşrin-i Sâni 1340 [Kasım 1924]—4 Kânun-ı Evvel 1340 [December 1924]. A recent study offers a preliminary investigation of the government attempts to establish new villages for the incoming refugees. See Ali Cengizkan, *Mübadele Konut ve Yerleşimleri* (Ankara: ODTÜ Mimarlık Fakültesi and Arkadaş Yayıncılık, 2004) see especially 32–51 and 75–77.

116. CA, 1522, 12 Şubat 1341 [February 1925].
117. *T.B.M.M.* ZC, Devre: II, İçtima Senesi: 2, Cilt: 10, 1 Teşrin-i Sâni 1340 [Kasım 1924]—4 Kânun-ı Evvel 1340 [December 1924], 75–78.
118. CA, 2604, 30 Eylül 1341 [September 1925]; CA, 3206, 26 Ağustos 1341 [August 1925] [15 63 20].
119. *T.B.M.M.* ZC, Devre: II, İçtima Senesi: 2, Cilt: 13, 31 Kânun-ı Sâni 1341 [January 1925] (Ankara: T.B.M.M. Matbaası, 1975) 453.
120. *Hilal-i Ahmer*, 14 Temmuz 1340 [July 1924]. *Haber*, 23 Haziran 1340 [June 1924].
121. CA, 118/109, 757, 102/156, 17 Mart [March] 1937, [123 879 6]. The document also provides certain figures about the properties whose official registration was completed and the owners were granted the title deeds. According to these figures, 684,202 pieces of property were registered with the cadastral offices and their owners received title deeds. The total number of property appears as 745,686 pieces. The status of 61,484 pieces remained pending due to their large size or the problems concerning indemnification.
122. CA, 2/5308, 22 Temmuz [July] 1936 [030 18 01 68 75 7]; CA., 2/4708, 29 Mayıs [May] 1936 [030 18 01 65 45 13].
123. A concise bibliography in English would include: League of Nations, *Greek Refugee Settlement*, passim; Mears, *Greece Today*, 53–129; Morgenthau, *I Was Sent to Athens*, 236–280; Eddy, *Greece and the Greek Refugees*, 71–170. All these people were affiliated with the RSC, and they tend to depict the whole resettlement process as a success story.
124. A comprehensive list of the Greek literature on the subject would include: Devedji, *L'echange obligatoire des minorites*; Séfériadès, *L'Échange des Populations*; Kiosséoglou, *L'echange forcé des minorités*; Ténékidès, "Le statut de minorités et l'échange obligatoire," 72–88; Γουναρακη, "Περι της Συνθηκης της Λωζανης," 1–39; Πρωτονοταριου, *Το Προσφυγικον Προβλημα*; Μιχ. Νοταρα, *Η Αγροτικη Αποκαταστασις των Προσφυγων*, (Athens: n.p., 1934); Πετσαλη, *Η Δημοσιονομικη Αντιμετωπισις*; Ε. Ι. Τσουδερος, *Η Αποζημιωσις των Ανταλλαξιμων*, (Athens, 1927). Also Pentzopoulos, *The Balkan Exchange of Minorities*, 75–119; Perhaps the most neutral assessment of the resettlement process from Greek point of view is provided by Ladas, *The Exchange of Minorities*, 618–704; A hybrid view can be found in Campbell and Sherrard, *Modern Greece*, 138–144.
125. My own research in the Historical Archives of the Ministry of Foreign Affairs yielded plenty of information about the issues of liquidation but very little about the impediments experienced domestically by the refugees during the early phases of resettlement. Similarly, the testimonies of the

refugees in the Center for Asia Minor Studies in Athens do not present any information regarding this issue due to the organization of the interview questionnaire, which seems to have been focused on the pre-Convention experiences of refugees.

126. Karakasidou, *Fields of Wheat*, 164–173. Her research is based on the documents from Historical Archives of Macedona/General Directorate of Macedonia in Salonica.

127. Ibid, 164.

128. Elisabeth Kontogiorgi, "The Rural Settlement of Greek Refugees in Macedonia: 1923–30," Unpublished Ph.D. dissertation, (St. Anthony's College, Oxford University, 1996) 106. The author has conducted a major portion of her research in the national and local archives in Greece and the archives of the League of Nations in Geneva.

129. The Greek government established, within the structure of the Ministry of Agriculture, the General Administration of the Exchange (*Γενικη Διευθυνσις Ανταλλαγης*) to address the questions and grievances over the property rights of Muslims on May 2/3, 1924. Kontogiorgi, "The Rural Settlement of Greek Refugees," 108.

130. Mavrogordatos, *Stillborn Republic*, 196, footnote 36. The author states that "the settlement remained forever incomplete," 191.

131. Τουντα-Φεργαδη, *Το Προσφυγικο Δανειο του 1924*, 27.

132. Βικα Δ. Γκιζελη, *Κοινωνικοι Μετασχηματισμοι και Προελευση της Κοινωνικης Κατοικιας στην Ελλαδα (1920–1930)* (Athens: Εκδοσεις Επικαιροτητα, 1984) 132–141. Renée Hirschon speaks of a Refugee Relief Fund (*Το Ταμειον Προστασιας Προσφυγων*) as an ad hoc body designated by the Greek government to deal with the emergency of the refugee situation. This must have been the Refugee Assistance Fund (*Το Ταμειον Περιθαλψεως Προσφυγων*) which had been established by the government in November 1922. Cf. Hirschon, *Heirs of the Greek Catastrophe*, 36–39. This institution dealt with the emergent sheltering and feeding problems of the refugees in urban areas. Through this institution, certain compact houses were constructed for the refugees in the outskirts of main cities such as Athens and Piraeus as well as small towns such as Volos, Edessa and Eleusis. The work of this institution seemed to have been limited only to a small of group of refugees due to the shortage of funds at its disposal. Although it remained in operation until May of 1925, most of its functions and responsibilities had been transferred, in the meantime, to the RSC.

133. Mears, *Greece Today*, 51.

134. Ibid, 112.

135. Χαρης Κουτελακης—Αμαντα Φωσκολου, *Πειραιας και Συνοικισμοι (Μαρτυριες και Γεγονοτα απο τον 14ο Αιωνα μεχρι Σημερα)* (Athens: Βιβλιοπωλειον της ΕΣΤΙΑΣ, 1991) 121–213.

136. For the later developments concerning the resettlement of urban refugees, especially with reference to the housing projects undertaken by the RSC in Piraeus and Athens, see Γκιζελη, *Κοινωνικοι Μετασχηματισμοι*, 151–292. For Salonica, see *Βιλμα Χασταογλου* and *Αλεξανδρα Καραδημου-Γερολυμπου,*

"Η Θεσσαλονικη, 1900–1940, απο τις Αντιφανεις του Κοσμοπολιτισμου στην Ομογενεια της Νεοελληνικης Πολης," in *Η Θεσσαλονικη μετα το 1912, Συμποσιο*, Salonica, November 1–3, 1985, (Salonica: Δημος Θεσσαλονικης, 1986) 449–473.

137. Hirschon, *Heirs of the Greek Catastrophe*, 49–55.
138. Charles Howland, "Greece and Her Refugees," *Foreign Affairs*, 4:4 (1926) 622.
139. Violet Markham, "Greece and the Refugees from Asia Minor," *The Fortnightly Review*, 117 (1925)182–184.
140. On the motives of Greek government behind the resettlement of northern Greece see the section "Why Resettlement in Macedonia" in Kontogiorgi, "The Rural Settlement of Greek Refugees," 77–90. The author emphasizes, among other factors, the importance of the Communist threat, 86.
141. Kontogiorgi, "The Rural Settlement of Greek Refugees," 107.
142. Mavrogordatos, *Stillborn Republic*, 187–188. For a detailed picture of the resettlement scheme in the region of Salonica, see Μ. Μαραβελακη—Α. Βακαλοπουλου, *Οι Προσφυγικες Εγκαταστασεις στην Περιοχη της Θεσσαλονικης*, (Salonica: Εκδοσεις Βανιας, 1993) passim. For the corresponding situation in the Western Macedonian provinces of Florina, Kastoria and Kozani, see the statistical tables in Πελαγιδης, *Η Αποκατασταση των Προσφυγων*, 109–183.
143. Hirschon, *Heirs of the Greek Catastrophe*, 39–42.
144. Ibid, 2 and 40–41. See also note 1, 257. According to the author, the settlement of Kokkinia occurred without regard to the place of origin, which was one of the principles of the policy observed in the settlement of rural refugees in northern Greece, 24.
145. Hirschon, *Heirs of the Greek Catastrophe*, 41.
146. Mavrogordatos, *Stillborn Republic*, 196. According to the author, the great portion of the refugee populations suffered from the arbitrary policies of the government in regards to compensation for their lost properties, the estimation of which "gave rise to abuses and frauds of great proportions." Much like the Muslim refugees in Turkey, the Greek refugees were entitled to a small fraction (5–25%) of the estimated value of their lost property. See 190.
147. The author states that "in towns and cities, natives illegally took possession of Turkish properties, which were supposed to house refugees or to be liquidated for their ultimate benefit." Mavrogordatos, *Stillborn Republic*, 196.
148. Ibid, 190.
149. Karakasidou, *Fields of Wheat*, 154 and 165–167; Hirschon, *Heirs of the Greek Catastrophe*, 41–42.
150. *Anadolu*, 28 Temmuz 1340 [July 1924].

NOTES TO CHAPTER EIGHT

1. The general literature on population transfers often confuses this institution with the Greek RSC. See, for example, Marrus, *The Unwanted*, 104–106. In other studies, this institution is not even included in the discussion

of the population exchange. See, for example, Skran, *Refugees in Inter-War Europe*, 156–167.

2. Jean Papas (Minister Plenipotentiary) Alexander Pallis (former delegate of the Greek government in Istanbul for the assistance of refugees) Antonius Calvo-coressi (former Director of the Mediterranean Bank in Istanbul) and Canaginis (Director of Immigration at the Ministry of Agriculture) were the first Greek members of the Commission. Jean Papas was replaced by G. Exintaris on September 24, 1924; Sovvidas replaced A. Pallis on December 20, 1924; J. Politis, K. Diamantopoulos and Aristide Phocas served on the Commission in later years. Ladas, *The Exchange of Minorities*, 354–355. The Turkish government organized a special ceremony for the departure of A. Pallis from Istanbul. CA, uncatalogued document, 20 Kânun-ı Evvel 1340 [December 1924].

3. Tevfik Rüşdü Bey (former Minister of Health) Hamid Bey (Minister of Health) Senieddin Efendi (Inspector of Finance) and İhsan Bey (from the Ministry of Pious Foundations) were the first Turkish members of the Commission. Şükrü Saraçoğlu and Cemal Hüsnü Bey served on the Commission in later years. Ladas, *The Exchange of Minorities*, 354–356.

4. Erik Einar Ekstrand (high functionary in the Ministry of Foreign Affairs of Sweden) Don Manuel Manrique de Lara (Spanish general) and Karl Marius Widding (Danish diplomat) were the first neutral members of the Commission. The presidency of the Commission was to be exercised in a rotating manner, every four months, by these three neutral members. Captain Hans Holstad (Norwegian lawyer and businessman) replaced Erik Einar Ekstrand on April 17, 1926; Senor Manuel de Rivas Vicuna Sperlier (Chilean) took the seat of Karl Marius Widding on February 27, 1929; Holger Andersen (Dane) succeeded General de Lara in December 1929. Ladas, *The Exchange of Minorities*, 354–356.

5. The Turkish government, in particular, seems to have had serious doubts about the neutral position of the Commission. İsmet Paşa received harsh criticism in the Grand National Assembly for allowing the Council of the League of Nations to choose Athens as the seat of the Commission. The dailies of the period in Turkey published long criticisms regarding this matter. See for example, *Hâkimiyet-i Milliye*, 11 Teşrin-i Evvel 1339 [October 1923], *Hâkimiyet-i Milliye*, 10 Kânun-ı Sâni 1340 [January 1924], and *Ahenk*, 7 Teşrin-i Evvel 1339 [October 1923]. In defense, İsmet Paşa stated that "in the character of this institution, the League of Nations put itself on a litmus test" and "he himself had fears that the meetings and negotiations might lead to no beneficial results." Accordingly, he asked the Turkish members of the Mixed Commission to "find out whether the operation of the Mixed Commission will produce quick and efficient results." See *İsmet Paşa'nın Siyasi ve İçtimai Nutukları*, 74–80. For a series of correspondence between the Ministry of Foreign Affairs in Ankara and the Turkish members of the Mixed Commission, see the documents published in *Türkiye Dış Politikasında 50 Yıl*, 154–160.

6. The question concerning the seat of the Commission became the subject of constant conflict between the Turkish and Greek members of the Commission. As Ladas shows, in the late 1920s, when the Commission was

seated in Istanbul, the Turkish delegation wanted to move the seat of the Commission to Komotini in Western Thrace where the problems concerning the Muslim minority in the region would be more practically handled. The Turks were prompted by the concern that when the Commission was stationed in Istanbul, the Greeks of Constantinople had better access to the offices of the Commission. Ladas, *The Exchange of Minorities*, 357–358.

7. For a detailed discussion of the functions of the Commission, see Ladas, *The Exchange of Minorities*, 355–364.

8. See the three letters dated respectively 2, 13, 21 February 1924, AYE, 1925, Γ/68 II, 3. These refugees are referred to as Greeks of Ottoman nationality (Ελλινων Οθωμανων Υπικοων).

9. See Ayşe Nükhet Adıyeke and Nuri Adıyeke, "Newly Discovered in Turkish Archives: Kadı Registers and Other Documents on Crete," *TURCICA* 22 (2000) 453.

10. Dimitri Timoleondos Ambelas, *Yeni Onbinlerin İnişi* (Istanbul: Askeri Matbaası, 1943) 16–17.

11. CA, 2593, 146/19, 27 Eylül 1341 [September 1925] [15 63 9]. This material was transferred to a library located in the courtyard of Hacı Bayram Mosque in Ankara.

12. Concerning these sub-commissions, see Ladas, *The Exchange of Minorities*, 365–366.

13. The Mixed Commission created a sub-commission, known as "the Commission of Non-Exchangeables" (*Gayri Mübadiller Komisyonu*) in Turkey to handle the affairs of the non-exchangeables. CA, 2738, 2825, 11 Teşrin-i Sâni 1341 [November 1925]. The country where sub-commissions were created provided the funds and provisions of all sub-commissions. In this specific case, the Turkish Ministry of Finance was obliged to finance the operation of the Commission of Non-Exchangeables.

14. Mehmed Esat Altuner (translator and editor) *Mübadeleye Dair Türkiye ve Yunanistan Arasında İmza Olunan Mukavelenameler, Muhtelit Mübadele Komisyonu Kararları, Bitaraf Azaların Hakem Kararları* (Istanbul: Damga Matbaası, 1937) passim.

15. CA, 1314, 28 Kânun-ı Evvel 1340 [December 1924].

16. AYE, "Letter dated January 20, 1923," 1923-A (1).

17. AYE, "From Venizelos to the Secretary of the League of Nations, August 6, 1923," 1923-A (1).

18. Altuner, *Mübadeleye Dair Türkiye ve Yunanistan Arasında İmza Olunan*, 245.

19. AYE, "Echange des populations entre la Grèce et la Turquie–Musulmans d'origine Albanaise en Grèce, December 9, 1925," B/1, 2. See also the proceedings of the Mixed Commission, December 10, 1925, AYE, 1925-A (1). For Mehdi Frasheri's speech, see "Echange des populations entre la Grèce et la Turquie: Musulmans d'origine Albanaise en Grèce, December 4, 1925." The speech provides a long historical overview of the Albanian community in Greece and an analysis of the Albanian situation in regard to the Convention. For a discussion of the subject from Greek point of view, see Michalopoulos, "The Moslems of Chamuria," 303–313.

20. Altuner, *Mübadeleye Dair Türkiye ve Yunanistan Arasında İmza Olunan*, 233–247. Altuner quotes a number of cases which show that the Greek government continued to violate the decision of the Mixed Commission until 1931.

21. *Oriente Moderno*, 8 (1928) 6–7, cited by Zimova, "The Minority Question and the Lausanne Treaty Convention of 1923," 165.

22. CA, 1283, 1739, 18 Kânun-ı Evvel 1340 [December 1924] [12 63 14]; CA, 881, 1283 14 Eylül 1340 [September 1924] [11 43 17].

23. Ladas, *The Exchange of Minorities*, 390–419, also,476–495. See "Sixth Session (Extraordinary) First Public Sitting Held at the Peace Palace on Friday, January 16, 1925, at 10 a.m., the President M. Huber Presiding." Including this particular one, the minutes of the Permanent Court of International Justice are found scattered through various files in the Historical Archives of the Greek Ministry of Foreign Affairs and the Republic Archives (CA).

24. AYE, 1925, B/40 (1). This report, entitled "Le minorité Grecque le Turquie," was prepared after 1928 and placed in a file, dated 1925, that contains all kinds of statistical information about the number of Greeks and the size of their properties prior to the population exchange. These numbers were often quoted during the meetings of the Mixed Commission and more concretely during the negotiations in Ankara (1925) and Athens (1926). The Turkish government, in the meantime, was involved with the compilation of all statistical figures about the Greeks of Constantinople. See *Tevhid-i Efkâr*, 10 Nisan 1340 [April 1924].

25. *Cumhuriyet*, 10 Teşrin-i Evvel 1340 [October 1924]. For the appeals of the Turkish government to the Mixed Commission on the situation of Muslims in Western Thrace, see the documents reprinted in *Türkiye Dış Politikasında 50 Yıl*, 154–160. Also see *T.B.M.M. ZC*, Devre: II, İçtima Senesi: 3, Cilt: 24, 1 Nisan [April] 1926–28 Nisan [April] 1926, (Ankara: T.B.M.M. Matbaası, n.d) 176–181.

26. For the problems involved in the activities of the Mixed Commission in Turkey, see Ahmed Emin Yalman, *Yakın Tarihte Gördüklerim ve Geçirdiklerim, (1922–1944)* vol. 3, (Istanbul: Rey Yayınları, 1970) 126. According to Yalman, Muslim refugees were exposed to numerous injustices committed by the Turkish members of the Mixed Commission in Turkey. In this regard, it should also be noted that before the transfer of refugees was completed, the Turkish government sold a great portion of the properties of the exchangeable Greeks through the state-owned Agricultural Bank (*Ziraat Bankası*). On July 27, 1924, the government issued a decree to repudiate the sale of these properties. CA, 731, 1162, 27 Temmuz 1340 [July 1924] [10 36 8].

27. CA, 2135, 2136, 18 Haziran 1341 [June 1925] [14 40 7].

28. For details on the Turkish view, see the proceedings of the Turkish Grand National Assembly in which the government representatives openly acknowledged that the size and value of the properties of the Muslims in Greece and those of the Greeks in Turkey were not precisely known. They believed that the value of the abandoned properties of Muslims far exceeded that of Greek abandoned properties in Turkey. *T.B.M.M. ZC*, Devre: II,

İçtima Senesi: 2, Cilt: 8/1, 10 Nisan 1340 [April 1924]—22 Nisan 1340 [April 1924], (Ankara: T.B.M.M. Matbaası, 1975) 794–795.

29. The Turkish government seems to have adopted the proposals of the Mixed Commission in regard to the principles to which the incoming refugees from Greece under the Convention were to be subjected. CA, 2135, 2136, 18 Haziran 1341 [June 1925] [14 40 7]. This contradicts many decisions of the government concerning the fate of abandoned properties throughout the country.

30. CA, [123 878 3], "*Atina'da 1 Kânun-ı Evvel 1926 Tarihinde İmza Olunan Emlake Mütedair İtilafname, Emlake Mütedair 1 Kânun-ı Evvel 1926 Tarihli İtilafname Melfufu, Nihai Protokol, Beyanname, Bir Nümerolu Protokol, İki Nümerolu Protokol, İmza Zabıtnamesi, Saracoğlu Şükrü Beyfendi ile Argiroplos Beyninde Teati Olunan Mektup Sureti.*" Following this agreement, the Permanent Court of International Justice continued to issue advisory opinions in favor of the refugees. See The Permanent Court of International Justice, *Collection of Advisory Opinions*, Series B, No. 16, Interpretation of the Greco-Turkish Agreement of December 1st, 1926, Final Protocol, Article IV.

31. The Turkish government issued a decree on December 9, 1925 that the properties of non-exchangeable Greeks, which had been retained by the government, registered with the Treasury, and then distributed to the refugees, were to stay in the possession of the people who were granted these properties. CA, 2892, K622, 9 Kânun-ı Evvel 1341 [December 1925] [16 78 7].

32. For the full text of the Ankara Convention, see T.T.K. Kütüphanesi, B/2250-b, *Türkiye Cumhuriyeti Hariciye Vekâleti, Mübadelei Ahaliye Mütedair Lozan Muahedenamesile Atina İtilafnamesinin Tatbikatından Mütevellit Mesailin Sureti Katiyede Halli Hakkında Mukavelename*. For an overall assessment of this Convention, see Ladas, *The Exchange of Minorities*, 567–588.

33. For the series of decisions taken by the Mixed Commission between 1930 and 1934, see Altuner, *Mübadeleye Dair Türkiye ve Yunanistan Arasında İmza Olunan*, 260–308.

34. Charles Howland, "Greece and Her Refugees," 620. Also see League of Nations, *The Greek Refugee Settlement*, 7.

35. League of Nations, *The Greek Refugee Settlement*, 8. For the details of this plan, see Τουντα-Φεργαδη, *Το Προσφυγικο Δανειο του 1924*, 77.

36. Elisabeth Kontogiorgi argues that the RSC was not intended "to substitute for the international private agencies which were assisting the Greek government to meet the urgent situation." Kontogiorgi, "The Rural Settlement of Greek Refugees," 66. Evidence suggests that a few foreign relief agencies, such as the Save the Children Fund, were still conducting some relief work in major Greek cities like Salonica. See a newspaper article by W. H. H. Sams, the Save the Children Fund Administrator, "The Refugees in Macedonia," *The Yorkshire Observer*, October 5, 1925. AYE, 1925-A/4, 4. As was mentioned previously, the Greek government adopted a stiff position on the relief work of certain Italian Catholic orders in northern Greece.

37. Kontogiorgi, "The Rural Settlement of Greek Refugees," 71.
38. Richard Clogg, *A Concise History of Greece*. (Cambridge: Cambridge University Press, 1992) 103.
39. On this issue, see the discussion by Karakasidou, *Fields of Wheat*, 146–157 and 167–173.
40. League of Nations, *The Greek Refugee Settlement*, 31; Pentzopoulos, *The Balkan Exchange of Minorities*, 103,153. Also see Eddy, *Greece and the Greek Refugees*, 88. Eddy points out that there was a considerable delay in the performance of the redistribution task.
41. Petropoulos, "The Compulsory Exchange of Populations," 153. George Mavrogordatos states that when the RSC terminated its operations in 1930, 90% of the total refugee population had been resettled in Greek Macedonia and Thrace. See Mavrogordatos, *Stillborn Republic*, 187–188.
42. The attacks of the Internal Macedonian Organization (IMRO) against Greeks in Bulgaria, especially around Melnik, Nevrekop, and Asenovgrad, increased the tension between Greece and Bulgaria, causing the Pangalos government to invade Bulgaria in October 1925. For details of this conflict and its impact on Greeks on Bulgaria, see Theodora Dragostinova, "Between Two Motherlands: Changing Memories of the Past within the Greek-Bulgarian Minority and Refugee Communities, 1906–1939," presented to the Conference "Voice or Exit: Comparative Perspectives on Ethnic Minorities in Twentieth Century Europe," Humboldt University, Berlin, June 14–16, 2001. For the political aspects of this conflict, see Howland, "Greece and Her Refugees," 622, and Clogg, *A Concise History of Greece*, 108. When the RSC's presence was questioned in the Council of the League of Nations in late 1925, one of the principal arguments offered by the chairman of the RSC in defense was that the RSC's operations were crucial to bringing about peace and political stability in the Balkans. See "Sociéte des Nations, Sous-Comite Grec du Conseil, Séanse tenué le 5 Septembre 1925 à 17 heures sous la présidence de M. Chamberlain," AYE, 1925-A/4, 5.
43. Freme, "The Refugee Settlement in Greece: Some Facts and Figures," Rodman Wanamaker Collection, Firestone Library of Princeton University, 2. The National Bank of Greece was responsible for granting loans to urban refugees. According to Freme, by March 31, 1925, the National Bank had granted about 150,000,000 drachmas in loans to urban refugees. Cf. League of Nations, *The Greek Refugee Settlement*, 175–182. The representatives of the RSC give this figure as 33,000,000 drachmas by December 31, 1925. For a general discussion of the economic conditions of urban refugees, see Mazower, "The Refugees, the Economic Crisis," 129. Also Kritikos, "State Policy and Urban Employment of Refugees," 189–206.
44. Members of the RSC furnished the Council of the League of Nations with quarterly reports about the progress of their activities. See "Travaux de l'Office Autonome des Réfugies Grecs, presented by Henry Morgenthau and Colocotronis, 11 Mars 1924," and "Report on the Operations of the Refugee Settlement Commission for the Second Three Months, prepared by the Chairman of the RSC, John Campbell, 25 May 1924," AYE, 1925-A/4,

4. "Septième Rapport Trimestriel sur L'Œuvre de l'Office Autonome pour l'Établissement des Réfugiés, Genève, le 31 Août 1925," AYE, 1925-A/4, 5. Also "Huitième Rapport Trimestriel sur l'œuvre de l'Office Autonome pour l'Etablissement des Réfugiés, Genève, le 7 décembre 1925," AYE, 1925-A/4, 4. Ladas has shown that only one tenth of the first refugee loan was spent on urban resettlement. See Ladas, *The Exchange of Minorities*, 674.

45. "Septième Rapport Trimestriel sur L'Œuvre de l'Office Autonome pour l'Établissement des Réfugiés, Genève, le 31 Août 1925," AYE, 1925-A/4, 5. See the section "établissement urbain," 4–5. Also League of Nations, *The Greek Refugee Settlement*, 118.

46. "Société des Nations, Sous-Comite Grec du Conseil, Séance tenue le 5 Septembre 1925 à 17 heures sous la présidence de M. Chamberlain," AYE, 1925-A/4, 5.

47. Campbell and Sherrard, *Modern Greece*, 139.

48. The Commission at the beginning composed of Henry Morgenthau as the chairman and John Campbell as the vice-chairman. The Greek members were Etienne Delta (then the president of the Greek Red Cross) and Pericles Argyropoulos. When Henry Morgenthau resigned as the Chairman, Alfred Bonzon succeeded him and he was then replaced by Charles Howland. A year later, Argyropoulos resigned and Theodore Eustathopoulo became chairman. Many other substitutions took place until the abolition of the Commission in 1930. The initial organization of the Commission remained unchanged until then. See League of Nations, *The Greek Refugee Settlement*, 9.

49. Greece experienced eight governments during the period 1924–1925: The Revolutionary Administration, to January 2, 1924; Venizelos, January 2, for a few days; Kaphandaris, to March 10; Papanastassiou, March 10 to July 20; Kaphandaris (summoned to form a new cabinet but failed); Sophoulis, July 20, for ten days; Michaelacopolous, to June 25, 1925; General Pangalos, June 1925 to August 1926. See Howland, "Greece and the Greeks," 458. An "ecumenical" (all party) government was in power in Greece from August 1926 to July 1928. Venizelos came to power again on July 1928. For a chronological overview of the political developments with special emphasis on the role of the military see Evangelos Spyropoulos, *The Greek Military (1908–1941) and the Greek Mutinies in the Middle East (1941–1944)* (Boulder: East European Monographs, 1993) 32–39.

50. Morgenthau made this remark in his speech in the Council of the League of Nations on March 11, 1924. See "Travaux de l'Office Autonome des Réfugies Grecs, presented by Henry Morgenthau and Colocotronis, 11 Mars 1924," AYE, 1925-A/4, 4.

51. Morgenthau, *I Was Sent to Athens*, 229–230.

52. Ibid, 80–81. Morgenthau provides a full report of his loan negotiations in London. Morgenthau's next two stops were Paris and Geneva. In Paris, he met with Venizelos to exchange views on the settlement of the refugees.

53. Ibid, 93. It is important to note here that the Governor of the National Bank of Greece, Alexandros Diomides, also played a significant role in

the loan negotiations in various European capitals. Fergadi provides a full account of Diomides' activities on the basis of his private archives. See Τουντα-Φεργαδη, *Το Προσφυγικο Δανειο του 1924*, 111–124 and 133–149.

54. Morgenthau, *I Was Sent to Athens*, 97.
55. Mazower, *Greece and the Inter-War Economic Crisis*, 77–78.
56. League of Nations, *The Greek Refugee Settlement*, 52–54.
57. "Société des Nations, Sous-Comite Grec du Conseil, Séance tenue le 5 Septembre 1925 à 17 heures sous la présidence de M. Chamberlain," AYE, 1925-A/4, 5. See the annexed document, "Réfugiés Grecs, Rapport spécial de l'Office Autonome pour l'établissement des réfugiés grecs, présenté au Conseil de la Société des Nations, 1 Septembre 1925," 4–7.
58. AYE, "From Vikol Makridis to the Department of Health, June 8, 1925," 1925, A/4 (1).
59. "Εξετασις Μαρτυρος" in AYE, 1925, A/4, 5. Some 22 interviews (each an average of 20 pages) are found in this file. A brief summary of this incident can also be found in Eddy, *Greece and the Greek Refugees*, 79–82.
60. AYE, "From the President of the Council, Pangalos, to the Governor General of Salonica, July 14, 1925," 1925, A/4, (1). The government passed a law to this effect, a French translation of which can be found in AYE, 1925-A/4, 5. "Décret-loi du 20 Juillet 1925 Ayant pour Objet de Faire Rentrer Certains Délits dans la Compétence de Cours Martiales."
61. "Mémorandum au sujet de récent incident survenu dans les rapports entre la Commission d'Etablissement des réfugies et le Gouvernement Hellénique." AYE, 1925, A/4, 5.
62. *The Times*, July 31, 1925; *Financial News*, August 15, 1925. AYE, 1925, A/4, 5.
63. The eighth quarterly report of the RSC provides detailed information about the developments following the decision of the Council. According to this report, "the government had promulgated a decree under which judicial proceedings could in future be instituted against persons employed by the Commission, except at the instance of the Commission or of the Ministry of Justice. This decree applied to the cases then pending." "Huitième Rapport Trimestriel sur l'œuvre de l'Office Autonome pour l'Etablissement des Réfugies, Genève, le 7 Décembre 1925," AYE, 1925-A/4, 4. For a recount of these developments, see Eddy, *Greece and the Greek Refugees*, 81.
64. Ladas, *The Exchange of Minorities*, 636.
65. Ibid, 672–673.
66. Kontogiorgi, "The Rural Settlement of Greek Refugees," 117. When the refugees were resettled in quarters, these places were organized according to the refugees' place of origin and named after the city or town from which they originated. A report, prepared by an official of the Ministry of Health on the sanitary conditions of the refugees, quotes the names of certain quarters which all carry the names of places in Anatolia, such as Σαφραμπολεως (Saframbolu). AYE, "From Nikol Makridis to the Department of Health, June 1, 1925," 1925-A/4, (1).
67. Karakasidou, *Fields of Wheat*, 152.
68. Mears, *Greece Today*, 231.

69. Morgenthau, *I Was Sent to Athens*, 264–266.
70. Mazower, "The Refugees, the Economic Crisis," 127. By the time the effects of the Depression began to be felt in Greece, a great number of refugees lacked the proper title deeds to their lands. The RSC held these lands with full ownership until the refugees had settled their debts and also paid the value of the land in question. According to Mazower, the provisional character of the allocation of the land discouraged the refugees from cultivating their holdings to the fullest extent.
71. Ibid, 123.
72. The Ottoman State established the High Commission of Refugees (*Muhacirin Komisyon-ı Âlisi*) in 1878 and instituted many refugee commissions (*muhacirin komisyonları*) during the late nineteenth and early twentieth centuries. Especially in the Ottoman Rumeli, in centers like Skopje and Salonica, these commissions functioned well into the Balkan Wars, and in urban centers in Anatolia later on. After the Balkan Wars, refugee affairs were entrusted to a general directorate, namely the General Directorate for the Resettlement of Tribes and Refugees (*İskân-ı Aşair ve Muhacirin Müdüriyeti Umumisi*)–originally established in 1860–as a branch of the Ministry of Interior. The archives of these specific institutions are not found in the Ottoman Archives in Istanbul. Recent attempts to get the microfilms of the Ottoman material from the Macedonian Archives have proved successful and the records of the Refugee Commission of Skopje from 19/S/1295 [February 22, 1878] to 8/R/1295 [April 11, 1878] seem to have survived, though very scantily. There are apparently 21 files on the subject. The documents in this collection include information from the "food provisioning of refugees" to the "attempts at locating the missing refugees" and "immoral behaviors among refugees." See "Makedonya Arşivindeki Osmanlı Dönemine Ait Arşiv Malzemesinin Kataloğu" (The Catalogue of Archival Documents from the Ottoman Period in Macedonian Archives) with archival number 29/A, 29/1. A comprehensive list of refugee-related institutions in the Ottoman Empire during the period 1856–1913 can be found in the following publications: Abdullah Saydam, *Kırım ve Kafkas Göçleri (1856–1876)* (Ankara: T.T.K. Basımevi, 1997) 101–119; İpek, *Rumeli'den Anadolu'ya*, 68–78 and 159–172; and Dündar, *İttihad ve Terakki'nin Müslümanları İskan Politikası*, 57–62.
73. *T.B.M.M. ZC*, Devre: I, İçtima Senesi: 2, Cilt: 11, 23 Haziran 1337 [June 1921]–3 Ağustos 1337 [August 1921], (Ankara: T.B.M.M. Matbaası, 1958) 39–40.
74. A recent study provides details of discussions on the establishment of this directorate. See Akın, *TBMM Devleti*, 312–323.
75. *T.B.M.M. ZC*, Devre: II, İçtima Senesi: 2, Cilt: 2, 9 Eylül 1339 [September 1923]–21 Teşrin-i Evvel 1339 [October 1923], (Ankara: T.B.M.M. Matbaası, n.d.) 428 and 630–637.
76. CA, 2867, 23 Teşrin-i Evvel 1339 [October 1923]. Also *Düstur*, Üçüncü Tertip, Vol. 5, (Istanbul, 1931) 165–167. For the discussions on this law, see *T.B.M.M. ZC*, Devre: II, İçtima Senesi: 2, Cilt: 7/1, 16 Mart 1340 [March 1924]–20 Mart 1340 [March 1924], 1059–1074.

77. *Düstur*, 407–410, and 428.
78. Ibid, 401. For details of the budget discussions, see *T.B.M.M. ZC*, Devre: II, İçtima Senesi: 1, Cilt: 10, 1 Teşrin-i Sâni 1340 [November 1924]—4 Kânun-ı Evvel 1340 [December 1924], 73–85. The budget of the Ministry was decided to be 6,125,277 liras for the year 1923. CA, 2868, 102/7, 23 Teşrin-i Evvel 1339 [October 1923] [7 38 10 (1)]. According to a foreign observer, a considerable proportion of this money was spent on the salaries of the officials. Macartney, "The New Opposition in Turkey," 785.
79. *Düstur*, 444–446. In the cities, the members of these commissions consisted of the Governor, an accountant (*muhasebeci*) the Director of Health (*sihhiye müdürü*) the Mayor and two refugees. *Düstur*, Üçüncü Tertip, vol. 2 (Istanbul, 1929) 74–76. In reality, written and oral sources do not mention any refugee participation in these commissions.
80. *Hâkimiyet-i Milliye*, 23 Teşrin-i Evvel 1339 [October 1923].
81. *Yeni Gün*, 21 Teşrin-i Evvel 1339 [October 1923].
82. For biographical details of Mustafa Necati Bey, see Mustafa Eski, *Cumhuriyet Döneminde Bir Devlet Adamı* (Ankara: Atatürk Kültür, Dil ve Tarih Yüksek Kurumu, 1999) 72–95. Before he took over the job, Mustafa Necati had prepared surveys on resettlement and reconstruction programs and related-legal regulations of countries like Belgium, Germany and France. *Tanin*, 10 Teşrin-i Evvel 1339 [October 1923].
83. For details of Celal Bayar's term in the MERR see, *Celal Bayar Diyor ki*, 29–39.
84. *T.B.M.M. ZC*, Devre: II, İçtima Senesi: 2, Cilt: 10, 1 Teşrin-i Sâni 1340 [November 1924]—4 Kânun-ı Evvel 1340 [December 1924], 42–51.
85. *T.B.M.M. ZC*, Devre: II, İçtima Senesi: 2, Cilt 9, 18 Teşrin-i Evvel 1340–30 Teşrin-i Evvel 1340 [October 1924], (Ankara: T.B.M.M. Matbaası, 1975) 75. A month later, several deputies joined to submit an interpellation (*istizah takriri*) to the government for the report of its resettlement and reconstruction activities. *T.B.M.M. ZC*, Devre: II, İçtima Senesi: 2, Cilt: 10, 1 Teşrin-i Sâni 1340 [November 1924]—4 Kânun-ı Evvel 1340 [December 1924], 24–25.
86. *T.B.M.M. ZC*, Devre: II, İçtima Senesi: 2, Cilt: 10, 1 Teşrin-i Sâni 1340 [November 1924]—4 Kânun-ı Evvel 1340 [December 1924], 26–28.
87. *T.B.M.M. ZC*, Devre: II, İçtima Senesi: 2, Cilt 9, 18 Teşrin-i Evvel 1340–30 Teşrin-i Evvel 1340 [October 1924], 86–88.
88. Ibid.
89. *Anadolu*, 23 Temmuz 1340 [July 1924]; 28 Eylül 1340 [September 1924].
90. *T.B.M.M. ZC*, Devre: II, İçtima Senesi: 2, Cilt: 10, 1 Teşrin-i Sâni 1340 [November 1924]—4 Kânun-ı Evvel 1340 [December 1924], 26–27.
91. CA, 2201, 23 Kânun-ı Sâni1339 [January 1923]. A year later the situation was the same. See CA, 659, 29 Haziran 1340 [June 1924] [010 32 17].
92. Interview with Nafia and Zeliha Bilge, October 21, 1994.
93. Macartney, "The New Opposition in Turkey," 786.
94. *T.B.M.M. ZC*, Devre: II, İçtima Senesi: 2, Cilt: 10, 1 Teşrin-i Sâni 1340 [November 1924]—4 Kânun-ı Evvel 1340 [December 1924], 31–32, and 41–42.

95. CA, 1027, 102–57, 3 Teşrin-i Sâni 1340 [November 1924] [11 50 19].
96. *Hizmet*, 23 Temmuz 1930.
97. CA, 10545, 1 Şubat [February] 1931.
98. CA, 12098, 3 Ocak [January] 1932 [25 1 16]; 2/796, 26 Mayıs [May] 1934 [45 37 6]; 2/1059, 19 Temmuz [July] 1934 [26 14 13]; 2/2349, 17 Nisan [April] 1935 [53 28 5]; 2/5308, 22 Temmuz [July] 1936 [68 75 7].
99. Dertilis, *La Réconstruction de la Grèce et la Société des Nations* (Paris: Rousseau & Cie, 1929) 25.
100. Greece was experiencing a major inflation rate as best reflected in the parity value of paper drachma against the US dollar. "The average yearly value of the paper drachma as distinguished from the gold drachma was 18 cents in 1919; 10.5 cents in 1920; 5.5 cents in 1921; 3 cents in 1922; and from then until 1928 between 1.8 and 1.25. In May 1928, a legislative decree stabilized the drachma value at 3755 to the pound sterling or 77 to the dollar, making the new parity value 1.3 cents." Mears, *Greece Today*, sf. ix.
101. For a full discussion of the negotiation process, see Τουντα-Φεργαδη, *Το Προσφυγικο Δανειο του 1924*, 50–55. The summer of 1923 witnessed an all-out campaign in the British press to convince the government that "Great Britain can not divest herself of some measure of responsibility for the deplorable condition in which these people [Greeks] found themselves . . . We believe that if the people of this country realized the appalling condition of the refugees from Asia Minor now in Greece and the moral responsibility which rests on Great Britain, they would respond generously to an appeal for funds to relieve this distress." *The Nottingham Guardian*, 30 July 1923, see also *The Times*, 26 July 1923 and *Morning Post*, 21 August 1923. The newspaper clippings are found in AYE, 1925-A/5, VI (10).
102. For the full text of the agreement, see Τουντα-Φεργαδη, *Το Προσφυγικο Δανειο του 1924*, 147–163.
103. James R. Mood, "Public Debt of Greece," United States Department of Commerce, Supplement to Commerce Reports Published by the Bureau of Foreign and Domestic Commerce, Trade Information Bulletin, No. 321, February 1925, 1–3. This report is found in the AYE, 1925, A/7. The Turkish government authorities, who were apparently keeping a close eye on Greek efforts to secure a refugee loan, immediately transmitted information to the government. CA, 579/883, 102/95, 21 Teşrin-i Sâni 1339 [November 1923] [123 875 18].
104. For the highlights of this debate, see Kontogiorgi, "The Rural Settlement of Refugees," 63–65.
105. Nicos Mouzelis, *Modern Greece, Facets of Underdevelopment* (London: The MacMillan Press, 1978) 21.
106. Ladas, *The Exchange of Minorities*, 635.
107. Τουντα-Φεργαδη, *Το Προσφυγικο Δανειο του 1924*, 123–124 and 166.
108. Mears, *Greece Today*, vii. The United States did not extend loans to any other states experiencing problems with the resettlement of refugees. According to Skran, the US remained in the background on refugee issues.

Since it did not belong to the League of Nations, it did not even participate in the annual discussions on refugee affairs, held each September at the Assembly sessions. Skran, *Refugees in Inter-War Europe*, 207.

109. Ladas, *The Exchange of Minorities*, 715. This is one of the many points demonstrating the utterly optimistic and peaceful stance of the author.

110. "The Lausanne Treaty and Kemalist Turkey," 70 and 72.

111. *Hâkimiyet-i Milliye*, 23 Teşrin-i Evvel 1339 [October 1923]; *T.B.M.M. ZC*, Devre: II, İçtima Senesi: 1, Cilt: 3, 24 Teşrin-i Evvel 1339 [October 1923]— 1 Kânun-ı Evvel 1339 [December 1923], 28. The funds for refugee settlement were to be used not only for incoming refugees from Greece but also for those refugees (*vilayet-i şarkiyye muhacirleri*) who had been displaced in the eastern sections of the country.

112. *Hâkimiyet-i Milliye*, 28 Eylül 1339 [September 1923]; *Ayın Tarihi*, Vol. 2, No. 4, Kânun-ı Evvel 1339 [December 1923].

NOTES TO CHAPTER NINE

1. *Lausanne Conference*, 115.

2. Ibid.

3. Zehra Kosova says that "we came to Turkey through the law of exchange, but the next few years people lived with the hope that they would return to our homes in Greece. This hope lasted until 1930. In the meantime our permits of residence expired. People then were scattered all around the country." Kosova, *Ben İşçiyim*, 24.

4. Pentzopoulos, *The Balkan Exchange of Minorities*, 206.

5. Kaplanoğlu, *Bursa'da Mübadele*, 127–134; Yalçın, *Emanet Çeyiz*, 150–270.

6. Ömer Lütfü Barkan, "Türkiye'de Muhacir İskanı İşleri ve bir İç Kolonizasyon Planına Olan İhtiyaç," *İstanbul Üniversitesi İktisat Fakültesi Mecmuası* 10:1–4 (1948–49) 204–223. Barkan emphasized the significance of a systematic plan for the settlement of the refugees. He also indicated that such a plan should take into consideration the psychological aspects of the refugee problem that would make the resettlement more effective.

7. Campbell and Sherrard, *Modern Greece*, 141. Cf. Morgenthau, *I Was Sent to Athens*, 134.

8. Mazower, "The Refugees, the Economic Crisisis," passim.

9. Ibid, 120.

10. Ελεφάντης, *Η Επαγγελια της Αδυνατης Επαναστασης*, 55.

11. The 1926 elections were held under a proportional system of representation of the country.

12. Carabott, "The Greek 'Communists," 100. "The Comintern insisted that the Greek party [KKE] support the idea of separate Macedonian state, the creation of which would have entailed the detachment of a large area of northern Greece." See Clogg, *A Concise History of Greece*, 106. Clogg argues that "few among the newly settled refugees, having

had their worlds turned upside down once, were inclined to repeat the experience."

13. In a conversation with the leading Greek politicians, Morgenthau remarks that there are three roads from which Greece could choose. The Left Road, the Right Road, and the Central Road—which the Greeks should take because it was "a fine, broad highway, on which the United States was serenely traveling peacefully to and fro, in pleasant competition with Great Britain." The Left Road or the Russian Road, on the other hand belonged to "the Bolsheviks, the Mexicans and Turks, and as they could see it was in very bad shape and quite unsafe for travelers." Morgenthau, *I Was Sent to Athens*, 155.

14. *Ahenk*, 4 Haziran 1341 [June 1925]. The minister of Interior, Cemil Bey, makes it clear in a public speech that "the mass resettlement of the refugees like the resettlement of the Circassians would cause them to live independent of the Turkish culture. Therefore, the resettlement of the refugees in small groups, such as in the form of one or two families, is more appropriate."

15. Among these organizations were *Muhacirin-i İslamiye Muavenet Yurdu*, *Mülteci ve Muhacirin Amele Cemiyeti*, *Muhacirin-i İslamiye İskan ve Teavün Cemiyeti*. See *Yenigün*, 26 Eylül 1339 [September 1923]. The last organization had prepared an alternative scheme of resettlement and published it.

16. *T.B.M.M. ZC*, Devre: II, İçtima Senesi: 2, Cilt: 10, 1 Teşrin-i Sâni 1340 [November 1924]—4 Kânun-ı Evvel 1340 [December 1924], 86.

17. Ibid.

18. Eric J. Zürcher, *Political Opposition in the Early Turkish Republic, the Progressive Republican Party, 1924–1925* (Leiden: E.J. Brill, 1991) 52–94; Nevin Yurdusever Ateş, *Türkiye Cumhuriyet'nin Kuruluşu ve Terakkiperver Cumhuriyet Fırkası* (Istanbul: Sarmal Yayınevi, 1994) 103–242.

19. Kosova, *Ben İşçiyim*, 17.

20. Çetin Yetkin, *Serbest Cumhuriyet Fırkası Olayı* (Istanbul: Karacan Yayınları, 1982) 111–125; Osman Okyar and Mehmet Seyitdanlıoğlu, eds., *Fethi Okyar'ın Anıları, Atatürk, Okyar ve Çok Partili Türkiye* (Istanbul: İş Bankası Kültür Yayınları, 1997) 73–77; Asım Us, *Gördüklerim, Duyduklarım, Duygularım, Meşrutiyet ve Cumhuriyet Devirlerine Ait Hatıralar ve Tetkikler* (Istanbul: Vakit Matbaası, 1964) 127–149.

21. Mehmet Ali Gökaçtı, *Nüfus Mübadelesi: Kayıp Bir Kuşağın Hikayesi* (Istanbul: İletişim Yayınları, 2002) 278–280.

22. *Hizmet*, 1 İkinci Kanun [January] 1929.

23. Cem Emrence, "Politics of Discontent in the Midst of the Great Depression: the Free Republican Party of Turkey (1930)," *New Perspectives on Turkey* 23 (2000) 31–52

24. Ibid.

25. Samet Ağaoğlu, *Serbest Fırka Hatıralarım* (Istanbul: İletişim Yayınları, 1994) 62. Okyar and Seyitdanlıoğlu, *Fethi Okyar'ın Anıları*, 77.

26. Ağaoğlu, *Serbest Fırka Hatıralarım*, 88.

27. For a brief discussion on the composition of the electorate that supported the Democratic Party, see Keyder, *State and Class*, 128–129.

28. Hanioğlu, *The Young Turks in Opposition*, 207. Also, Robert Bianchi, *Interest Groups and Political Development in Turkey* (Princeton: Princeton University Press, 1984) 100–107.

NOTES TO THE EPILOGUE

1. See, for example, H. Yıldırım Ağanoğlu, *Osmanlı'dan Cumhuriyet'e Balkanlar'ın Makus Talihi: Göç* (Istanbul: Kum Saati, 2001). Perhaps the best indicator of the growing interest in the subject is the recent discovery, translation and publication of Mihri Belli's masters' thesis on the subject which had been submitted to the Missouri University in 1940. See Mihri Belli, *Türkiye ve Yunanistan Nüfus Mübadelesi: Ekonomik Açıdan Bir Bakış*, trans. M. Pekin (Istanbul: Belge Yayınları, 2004). A recent bibliographic compilation also attests to this interest, see Müfide Pekin and Çimen Turan, eds. *Mübadele Bibliyografyası: Lozan Nüfus Mübadelesi ile İlgili Yayınlar ve Yayımlanmamış Çalışmalar* (Istanbul: Lozan Mübadilleri Vakfı, 2002). Finally see Pekin, *Yeniden Kurulan Yaşamlar*. This volume is a compilation of papers presented to the conference organized by the Association of the Lausanne Refugees for commemorating the 80th anniversary of the Exchange Convention.
2. Pentzopoulos, *The Balkan Exchange of Minorities*.
3. For a review of the shifts in the refugee protection policies of the UNHCR, see Howard Adelman, "From Refugees to Forced Migration: The UNHCR and Human Security," *International Migration Review*, 35:1 (2001) 18–30.
4. For the reflections of an experienced journalist on these issues, see Bruce Clark, *Twice A Stranger: How Mass Expulsion Forged Modern Greece and Turkey* (London: Granta Books, 2006) xi–xviii.
5. See Norman Cigar, *Genocide in Bosnia: The Policy of "Ethnic Cleansing"* (College Station: Texas A & M University Press, 1995) 11–21. Cf. Michael Mann, *The Dark Side of Democracy: Explaining Ethnic Cleansing* (Cambridge: Cambridge University Press, 2005) 502–529.
6. Petropoulos, "The Compulsory Exchange of Populations," 149–156.
7. Μαραντζίδης, *Γιασασιν Μιλλετ, Ζητω Εθνος*, passim. The author shows how a Turkish-speaking refugee community from Bafra, transferred by the Exchange Convention to northern Greece, struggled to rationalize and reconcile their conflicting sources of identity by aligning themselves with the political right during the inter-war era.
8. For a representative publication of this view see Ramazan Tosun, *Türk-Yunan İlişkileri ve Nüfus Mübadelesi* (Ankara: Berikan, 2002) especially 57–88.
9. The concept is borrowed from Eric Wolf. See his *Europe and the People without History* (Berkeley: University of California Press, 1982) 5.

Bibliography

1- PRIMARY SOURCES

a- Archives and Libraries

Ankara

    Cumhuriyet Arşivi (CA) (Republican Archives)

    T.B.M.M. Arşivi (Archives of the Turkish Grand National Assembly)

    Türk Tarih Kurumu Kütüphanesi (Library of the Turkish Historical Association)

    Milli Kütüphane (The National Library)

    Askeri Tarih ve Stratejik Etütler Başkanlığı (ATASE) (Archives of the Turkish General Chief of Staff

Athens

    Ιστορικο Αρχειο του Υπουργειου Εξωτερικων της Ελλαδας (AYE) (Historical Archives of the Ministry of Foreign Affairs of Greece)

    Αρχειο του ΚεντρουΜικρασιατικων Σπουδων (ΚΜΣ) (Archives of the Centre for Asia Minor Studies)

Istanbul

    Başbakanlık Osmanlı Arşivi (BOA) (Prime Ministry's Ottoman Archives)

    Hariciye Nezareti Hukuk Müşavirliği İstişare Odası Evrakı

    Dahiliye Nezareti İdare-i Umumiye Evrakı

Izmir

    Milli Kütüphane (National Library)

Samsun

    Köy Hizmetleri İl Müdürlüğü Arşivi (Archives of the Provincial Bureau of Village Affairs)

Washington, D.C.

    The Library of Congress

    The Papers of Henry Morgenthau.

b- Official Publications

Düstur, III. Tertip.
Great Britain, Foreign Office. Anatolia (London: Published by H. M. Stationary
     Office, 1920).
"Influence of Pan-Turkish Political Aims on Turkish Military Policy, 1914–1918"
     (official report prepared by the British Foreign Intelligence).
İstatistik Yıllığı 1929 (Ankara: İstatistik Umum Müdürlüğü, 1929).
İstatistik Yıllığı 1930 (Ankara: İstatistik Umum Müdürlüğü, 1930).
Kavanin Mecmuası.
Meclis-i Mebusan Zabıt Ceridesi.
Meclis-i Ayan Zabıt Ceridesi.
Meclis-i Mebusan-ı Osmani Rum Azasının Siyasi Programı. (n.d., n.p.)
T.B.M.M. Zabıt Ceridesi.
T. C. Dışişleri Bakanlığı, Araştırma ve Siyaset Planlama Genel Müdürlüğü. Türkiye
     Dış Politikasında 50. Yıl, Cumhuriyetin İlk On Yılı ve Balkan Paktı 1923–
     1934) (Ankara: T. C. Dışişleri Bakanlığı, 1974).
T. C. Dışişleri Bakanlığı, Araştırma ve Siyaset Planlama Genel Müdürlüğü Tür-
     kiye Dış Politikasında 50 Yıl: Lozan (1922–1923) (Ankara: T. C. Dışişleri
     Bakanlığı, 1974).

c- Newspapers and Journals

Açıksöz
Ahenk
Akbaba
Akşam
Anadolu
Ayın Tarihi
Cumhuriyet
Daily Telegraph
Haber
Hakimiyet-i Milliye
Hilal-i Ahmer
Hizmet
İkdam
Istanbul Ticaret ve Sanayi Odası Mecmuası
The New York Times
Sabah
Şark
Tanin
Tasvir-i Efkar
Tevhid-i Efkar
The Toronto Daily Star
Türk Sesi
Türkiye İktisat Mecmuası
Yenigün
Vakit

Vatan,
Vazife

d- Pamphlets

[The] American Hellenic Society. *Memorandum Presented by the Greek Members of the Turkish Parliament to the American Commission on Mandates Over Turkey.* (New York: Columbia University, 1919).

"Greek Refugees, Report on the Operations of the Refugees Settlement Commission for the First Three Months," (Washington, D.C.: American Friends of Greece Incorporated, 1924).

"Hellenism in the Balkan Peninsula and Asia Minor, An Ethnological Map" by Professor George Soteriadis of the University of Athens, 1918.

Hüseyin Kazım. *Rum Patrikhanesine Açık Mektup, Boykot Müslümanların Hakkı Değil midir?* (Istanbul: Yeni Turan Matbaası, 1330 [1914/1915]).

"La Question d'Orient, vue pa les socialistes grecs, Memoire soumis par les socialistes grecs a la Conference socialiste interalliee de Londres," (Paris, 1918).

[The] *Lausanne Treaty and Kemalist Turkey.* (A Collection of Pamphlets and Articles written by the well-known American politicians, journalists, academics etc. in 1920's.)

Papadopoulos, A. Alexander. *Persecutions of the Greeks in Turkey Before the European War*, trans. from the Greek by Carroll N. Brown (New York: Oxford University Press American Branch, 1919).

e- Published Documents

Altuner, Mehmed Esad (trans.). *Mübadeleye Dair Türkiye ve Yunanistan Arasında İmza Olunan Mukavelenameler, Muhtelit Mübadele Komisyonu Kararları.* ([Istanbul]: Damga Matbaası, 1937).

Atina Konvensiyonu, 1913.

Great Britain, Foreign Office. *Turkey, No. 1 (1923) Lausanne Conference on Near Eastern Affairs, 1922–1923, Records of Proceedings and Draft Terms of Peace.* (London: His Majesty's Stationary Office, 1923).

Η Δίκη των Εξ, Τα Εστεσογραφημένα Πρακτικα, 31 Οκτωβρίου-15 Νοεμβρίου 1922. Athens: Δημιουργια, 1996.

İskan ve Teavün Cemiyeti Umumi Kongre Mübadele Encümeni Mazbatası, İskan ve Teavün Cemiyeti Mübadele Rehberi. (Izmir: Ahenk Matbaası, 1339 [1923]).

İstimlak Kanunları (1923).

League of Nations. *Greek Refugee Settlement.* (Geneva: Publications of the League of Nations, 1926).

Lozan Barış Konferansı, Tutanaklar, Belgeler. ed. Seha L. Meray, 8 vols. (Ankara: Ankara Üniversitesi Siyasal Bilgiler Fakültesi Yayınları, 1969–1973).

Lozan Telgrafları (1922–1923). 2 vols. ed. Bilal N. Şimşir (Ankara: T.T.K. Basımevi, 1990).

Matbuat. (Dersaadet [Istanbul]: Matbaa-i Askeriye, 1335 [1919]).

Papers Relating to Foreign Relations of the United States 1923. Vol. 2. (Washington: United States Government Printing Office, 1938).

Publication of the Permanent Court of International Justice, Series B, 21 February 1925. *Collection of Advisory Opinions*, No. 10, "Exchange of Greek and Turkish Populations."

Publication of the Permanent Court of International Justice, Series B, No. 16, *Collection of Advisory Opinions*, Interpretation of the Greco-Turkish Agreement of December 1ˢᵗ, 1926, Final Protocol, Article IV.

Şimşir, Bilal, ed. *Turkish Emigrations from the Balkans, Documents*, vol. 1, *Turkish Exodus, 1877–1878*, vol. 2, *A Year of Transition, 1879*. (Ankara: Türk Tarih Kurumu Yayınevi, 1989).

———. *İngiliz Belgelerinde Atatürk (1919–1938)*, vol. 1 (Ankara: Türk Tarih Kurumu Basımevi, 1979).

Talimatname, 1-Muhacirine Arazi ve Emlak Tevzi'ne 2-Muhacirine Verilen Bağ, Zeytünlük, Dutluk ve Emsali Yerlerin İmarına ve Hüsn-ü Muhafazasına Dair. Dersaadet ([Istanbul]: Garuyan Matbaası, 1333 [1914]).

Turkey and the United Nations, prepared under the auspices of the Institute of International Relations of the Faculty of Political Science of the University of Ankara for the Carnegie Endowment for International Peace. (New York: Manhattan Publication Co., 1961).

Υπουργειον Περιθαλψεως. *Περιθαλψις των Προσφυγων, 1917–1920.* (Athens: Τυπογραφειον Κωνστ. Ι. Θεοδωρoπoυλo, 1920).

Vurud Eden Muhacirinin Kayd ve İskanlarına ve Muamalat-ı Sayirelerine Aid Olarak Muhacirin İdarelerince Tutulacak Kayd ve Defatirr Hakkında İzahnamedir. (Dersaadet [Istanbul]: Hilal Matbaası, 1331 [1912]).

f- First Person Narratives (Interviews, Biographies, Speeches, Memoirs)

Ağaoğlu, Samet. *Serbest Fırka Hatıraları.* (Istanbul: İletişim Yayınları, 1994).

Ambelas, Dimitri Timoleondos. *Yeni Onbinlerin İnişi.* (Istanbul: Askeri Matbaası, 1943).

Atay, Falih Rıfkı. *Eski Saat, 1917–1933.* (Istanbul: Akşam Matbaası, 1933).

Barton, James L. *Story of Near East Relief (1915–1930), An Interpretation.* (New York: The MacMillan Company, 1930).

Berber, Engin, ed. *Kendi Kaleminden Teğmen Cemil Zeki (Yoldaş).* (Istanbul: ARBA, 1994).

Bilge, Zeliha and Nafia Bilge, Interview, October 21, 1994.

Bilsel, M. Cemil. *Lozan*, 2 vols. Reprint of 1932–1933 Edition. (Istanbul: Sosyal Yayınlar, 1998).

Celal Bayar Diyor ki, 1920–1950, Nutuk-Hitabe-Beyanet-Hasbıhal, ed. Nazmi Sevgen. (Istanbul: n.p. 1951).

Cumalı, Necati. *Makedonya 2000.* (Istanbul: Can Yayınları, 1981).

Djemal Pasha. *Memoirs of a Turkish Statesman-1913–1919.* (New York: George H. Doran Company, 1922).

Dr. Rıza Nur. *Dr. Rıza Nur'un Lozan Hatıraları.* (Istanbul: Boğaziçi Yayınları, 1992).

Early of Ronaldhay. *The Life of Lord Curzon, Being the Authorized Biography of George Nathaniel Marquess Curzon of Kedleston, K. G.*, vol. 3. (London: Ernest Benn Limited, 1928).

Eddy, Charles B. *Greece and the Greek Refugees.* (London: George Allen and Unwin Ltd., 1931).

Grew, Joseph. *Turbulent Era, A Diplomatic Era of Forth Years, 1904–1945,* 2 vols. (London: Hammond, Hammond & Co., 1953).

Innes, Kathleen E. *The Story of Nansen and the League of Nations.* (London: Friends of Peace Committee, 1931).

İnönü, İsmet. *Hatıralar,* 2 vols. (Ankara: Bilgi Yayınevi, 1985–1987).

İsmail Habib Sevük'ün Açıksöz'deki Yazıları, Makaleler, Fıkralar, ed. Mustafa Eski. (Ankara: Atatürk Kültür, Dil ve Tarih Yüksek Kurumu, Atatürk Araştırma Merkezi, 1998).

İsmet Paşa'nın Siyasi ve İçtimai Nutukları. (Ankara: Başvekalet Matbaası, 1933).

Καζαντζάκης, Νικος. *Οι Αδερφοφαδες.* (Athens: Εκδοσεις Ελ. Καζαντζάκη, 1973).

Karacan, Ali Naci. *Lozan Konferansı ve İsmet Paşa.* (Istanbul: Milliyet Yayınları, 1971).

Kosova, Zehra. *Ben İşçiyim.* (Istanbul: İletişim Yayınları, 1996).

Μαζαρακη-Αινιανος, Αλεξανδρου. *Απομνημονευματα.* (Athens: Ικαρος, 1948).

Morgenthau, Henry (in Collaboration with French Strother). *I Was Sent to Athens.* Garden City (NewYork: Doubleday, Doran & Company, Inc., 1929).

Nansen, Fridjof. "Re-making Greece," *The Forum* (1923) 18–25.

Nicolson, Harold. *Curzon, the Last Phase, 1919–1925, A Study in the Post War Diplomacy.* (Boston and New York: Houghton Mifflin Company, 1934).

Osman Okyar and Mehmet Seyitdanlıoğlu eds. *Fethi Okyar'ın Anıları, Atatürk, Okyar ve Çok Partili Türkiye.* (Istanbul: İş Bankası Kültür Yayınları, 1997).

Özsoy, İskender. *İki Vatan Yorgunları: Mübadele Acısını Yaşayanlar Anlatıyor.* (Istanbul: Bağlam, 2003).

[Söylemezoğlu], Galip Kemali. *Hatıraları,* Canlı Tarihler 5. (Istanbul: Türkiye Yayınevi, 1946).

Story, Sommerville, ed. *The Memoirs of Ismail Kemal Bey.* (London: Constable and Company LTD., 1920).

Streit, M. G. (Address before the Academy of Athens), *Messager d'Athènes,* February 7, 1930.

Tesal, Reşat D. *Selanik'ten Istanbul'a.* (Istanbul: İletişim Yayınları, 1998).

———. "Yunanistan'da Azınlık Olarak Nasıl Yaşardık," *Tarih ve Toplum* 48 (1991): 48–56.

Tesal, Ömer Dürrü. "Türk-Yunan İlişkilerinin Geçmişinden Bir Örnek: Azınlıkların Mübadelesi," *Tarih ve Toplum,* 9:53 (1988): 46–52.

Uran, Hilmi. *Hatıralarım.* (Ankara: H. Uran, 1959).

Us, Asım. *Gördüklerim, Duyduklarım, Duygularım, Meşrutiyet ve Cumhuriyet Devirlerine Ait Hatıralar ve Tetkikler.* (Istanbul: Vakit Matbaası, 1964).

[Yalçın], Hüseyin Cahit. *Siyasal Anılar.* (Istanbul: İş Bankası Kültür Yayınları, 1976).

Yalçın, Kemal. *Emanet Çeyiz, Mübadele İnsanları.* (Istanbul: Belge Yayınları, 1998).

Yalman, Ahmed Emin. *Yakın Tarihte Gördüklerim ve Geçirdiklerim, (1922–1944),* vol. 3. (Istanbul. Rey Yayınları, 1970).

[Yalman], Ahmed Emin *Turkey in the World War.* (New Haven: Yale University Press, 1930).

2- SECONDARY SOURCES

a- Unpublished (Dissertations and Conference Papers)

Beriker, F. Nimet. "Negotiating Styles of the Minor Parties in Multilateral Peace Negotiations: Greece and Turkey at the Lausanne Peace Conference, 1922–1923," Ph.D. Dissertation, George Mason University, 1993.

Çanlı, Mehmet. "Milli *Mücadele Döneminde Türk-Yunan Esirleri ve Mübadelesi (1920–1923)*," Ph.D. Dissertation, Türk İnkilap Tarihi Enstitüsü, Ankara Üniversitesi, 1994.

Çapa, Mesut. "Kızılay Hilal-i Ahmer Cemiyeti (1914–1925)," Ph.D. Dissertation, Türk İnkılap Tarihi Enstitüsü, Ankara Üniversitesi, Ankara, 1989.

Dark, Michael. "The Comparative Politics of the Greco-Turkish Exchange," Unpublished Paper presented at *Turkey and Greece: Assessment of the Consequences of the Treaty of Lausanne Convention 1923 (75th Anniversary)*, hosted by the Refugee Studies Programme, Queen Elizabeth House, Oxford University, September 17–20, 1998.

Dragostinova, Theodora. "Between Two Motherlands: Changing Memories of the Past within the Greek-Bulgarian Minority and Refugee Communities, 1906–1939," presented to the Conference "Voice or Exit: Comparative Perspectives on Ethnic Minorities in Twentieth Century Europe," Humboldt University, Berlin, June 14–16, 2001.

Giannuli, Dimitra M., "American Philonthrophy in the Near East: Relief to the Ottoman Greek Refuges, 1922–1923," Ph.D. Dissertation, Kent State University, 1992.

Kontogiorgi, Elisabeth. "The Rural Settlement of Greek Refugees in Macedonia: 1923–30," Ph.D. Dissertation, the University of Oxford, St. Antony's College, 1996.

Kritikos, George, "Greek Orthodox Refugees and the Making of a New Greek Community (1923–1930)," Ph.D. Dissertation, European University Institute, Florence, 2001.

Solomonidis, Victoria. "Greece in Asia Minor, the Greek Administration of the Vilayet of Aidin, 1919–22," Ph.D. Dissertation, University of London, King's College, 1984.

Triadafilopoulos, Triadafilos. "Debating 'Engineered Unmixing': Partition and Transfers of Populations in 20th Century," Lecture in a series on "Minorities and Minority Conflicts in Transition: Central and Eastern Europe in the Era of Post Socialism," Humboldt University, Berlin, October 24, 2000.

Ζαμπατα, Ευστρατιου Χρ. "Οι εκ Μικρας Ασιας Ελληνορθοδοξοι Προσφυγες," Ph.D. Dissertation, University of Athens, 1969.

b- Published (Books and Articles)

Adanır, Fikret and Hilmar Kaiser. "Migration, Deportation, and Nation-Building: The Case of the Ottoman Empire," in *Migrations et Migrants dans une Perspective Historique. Permanences et Innovations*, ed. René Leboutte. (Brussels: Peter Lang, 2000) 273–292.

Adanır, Fikret. "Lo Scambio Greco-Turco di Populazioni nella Storiografica Turca," in *Esodi: Transferimenti Forzati di Populazioni nel Novecento Europeo*, eds. M. Cattaruzza, M. Dogo and Raoul Pupo. (Napoli: Edizioni Scientifiche Italiane, 2000) 89–101.

———. "The Macedonians in the Ottoman Empire, 1878–1912," in *The Formation of National Elites: Comparative Studies on Governments and Non-Dominant Ethnic Groups in Europe, 1850–1940*, vol. 6, ed. A. Kappeler (in collaboration with F. Adanır and A. O'Day). (Dartmouth: New York University Press, 1992) 161–191.

Adelman, Howard. "From Refugees to Forced Migration: The UNHCR and Human Security," *International Migration Review* 35:1 (2001): 7–32.

Adıyeke, Ayşe N. and Nuri Adıyeke. "Newly Discovered in Turkish Archives: Kadı Registers and Other Documents on Crete," *TURCICA* 22 (2000): 447–463.

Ağanoğlu, Yıldırım H. *Osmanlı'dan Cumhuriyet'e Balkanlar'ın Makus Talihi: Göç*. (Istanbul: Kum Saati, 2001).

Ahmad, Feroz and Dankwart Rustow. "İkinci Meşrutiyet Döneminde Meclisler," *Güney-Doğu Avrupa Araştırmaları Dergisi*, 4–5 (1976): 250–283.

Akın, Rıdvan. *TBMM Devleti, (1920–1923), Birinci Meclis Döneminde Devlet Erkleri ve İdare*. (Istanbul: İletişim Yayınları, 2001).

Aktar, Ayhan. "Türk-Yunan Nüfus Mübadelesi'nin İlk Yılı: Eylül 1922-Eylül 1923," in *Yeniden Kurulan Yaşamlar, 1923 Türk-Yunan Zorunlu Nüfus Mübadelesi*, ed. M. Pekin (Istanbul: Bilgi Üniversitesi Yayınevi, 2005) 41–84.

———. "Nüfusun Homojenleştirilmesinde ve Ekonominin Türkleştirilmesi Sürecinde Bir Aşama: Türk-Yunan Nüfus Mübadelesi, 1923–1924," in his *Varlık Vergisi ve 'Türkleştirme' Politikaları*. (Istanbul: İletişim Yayınları, 2000) 17–69.

Alexandris, Alexis. *The Greek Minority of Istanbul and Greek-Turkish Relations, 1918–1974*. (Athens: Centre for Asia Minor Studies, 1992).

———. "Pontic Greek Refugees in Constantinople 1922–1923, the Human Cost of the Exchange of Populations," *Αρχείον Πόντου* 137 (1982): 280–293.

Αναγνωστοπούλου, Σία. *Μικρά Ασία, 19ος αι-1919, Οι Ελληνορθοδοξες Κοινοτητες απο το Μιλλετ των Ρωμιων στο Ελληνικο Εθνος*. (Athens: Ελληνικα Γραμματα, 1997).

Anderson, M. S. *The Eastern Question, 1774–1923, A Study in International Relations*, (Reprint of 1966 Edition). (London: Macmillan, 1991).

Andreadis, Yorgo. *Gizli Din Taşıyanlar*, (trans.) A. Tuygan. (Istanbul: Belge Yayınları, 1999).

Arı, Kemal. *Büyük Mübadele, Türkiye'ye Zorunlu Göç (1923–1925)*. (Istanbul: Tarih Vakfı 1995).

———. "1923 Türk-Rum Mübadele Anlaşması Sonrasında Izmir'de 'Emval-i Metruke' ve 'Mübadil Göçmenler,'" *Atatürk Araştırma Merkezi Dergisi* 6:18 (1990): 627–657.

Armaoğlu, Fahir. *20. Yüzyıl Siyasi Tarihi (1914–1980)*. (Ankara: T.T.K. Basımevi, 1988).

Armstrong, Hamilton Fish. "The Unredeemed Isles of Greece," *Foreign Affairs* 4:1 (1925): 154–157.

Ateş, Nevin Yurdusever. *Türkiye Cumhuriyet'nin Kuruluşu ve Terakkiperver Cumhuriyet Fırkası*. (Istanbul: Sarmal Yayınevi, 1994).

Augustinos, Gerasimos. *The Greeks of Asia Minor: Confession, Community, and Ethnicity in the Nineteenth Century.* (Kent: The Kent State University Press, 1992).

Bali, Rıfat. *Cumhuriyet Yıllarında Türkiye Yahudileri, Bir Türkleştirme Serüveni (1923–1945).* (Istanbul: İletişim Yayınları, 1999).

Baran, Tülay Alim. "Izmir'de Çiftçi Mübadiller," *Kebikeç*, 4 (1996): 175–183.

———. *Bir Kentin Yeniden Yapılanması Izmir, 1923–1938.* (Istanbul: ARMA, 2003).

Barkan, Ömer Lütfi. "Türkiye'de Muhacir İskan İşleri ve Bir İç Kanalizasyon Planına Olan İhtiyaç," *Istanbul Üniversitesi İktisat Fakültesi Mecmuası* 10:1–4 (1948/49): 204–223.

Bayur, Yusuf Hikmet. *Yeni Türkiye Devletinin Harici Siyaseti.* (Istanbul: Burhaneddin, 1935).

———. *Türk İnkilabı Tarihi.* (Istanbul: T.T.K. Basımevi, 1940).

Bell-Fialkoff, Andrew. *Ethnic Cleansing.* (New York: St. Martin's Press, 1996).

Belli, Mihri. *Türkiye-Yunanistan Nüfus Mübadelesi: Ekonomik Açıdan Bir Bakış,* tran. M. Pekin. (Istanbul: Belge Yayınları, 2004).

Berber, Engin. *Sancılı Yıllar, Izmir 1918–1922, Mütareke ve İşgal Döneminde Izmir Sancağı.* (Ankara: Ayraç Yayınevi, 1997).

Beşikçi, İsmail. *Doğu Anadolu'nun Düzeni, Sosyo-Ekonomik ve Etnik Temeller.* (Ankara: Yurt Kitap-Yayın, 1992).

Bianchi, Robert. *Interest Groups and Political Development in Turkey.* (Princeton: Princeton University Press, 1984).

Black, Richard. "Fifty Years of Refugee Studies: From Theory to Policy," *International Migration Review* 35:1 (2001): 57–78.

Boura, Katherina. "The Greek Millet in Turkish Politics: Greeks in the Ottoman Parliament (1908–1918)," in *Ottoman Greeks in the Age of Nationalism: Politics, Economy, and Society in the Nineteenth Century,* eds. Dimitri Gondicas and Charles Issawi. (Princeton: The Darwin Press, Inc., 1999) 193–206.

Braudel, Fernand. *The Identity of France,* vol. 1: *History and Environment.* trans. S. Reynolds. (New York: Harper & Row Publishers, 1988).

Brown, L. Carl. *International Politics and the Middle East, Old Rules Dangerous Game.* (Princeton: Princeton University Press, 1984).

Brubaker, Rogers. *Nationalism Reframed: Nationhood and the National Question in the New Europe.* (Cambridge: Cambridge University Press, 1996).

Bryer, Anthony M. "The Tourkokratia in the Pontos: Some Problems and Preliminary Conclusions," in his *The Empire of Trebizond and the Pontos.* (London: Variorum Reprints, 1980) 47–49.

———. "The Crypto-Christians of the Pontos and Consul William Gifford Palgrave of Trebizond," *ΔΕΛΤΙΟ ΚΜΣ,* 4 (1983): 13–68.

Busch, Briton Cooper. *Mudros to Lausanne: Britain's Frontier in West Asia, 1918–1923.* (Albany, N.Y.: SUNY Press, 1976).

Can, Bülent Bilmez. *Demiryolundan Petrole Chester Projesi (1908–1923).* (Istanbul: Tarih Vakfı Yurt Yayınları, 2000).

Carabott, Philip. "The Greek Communists and the Asia Minor Campaign," *ΔΕΛΤΙΟ ΚΜΣ* 9 (1992): 99–118.

Campbell, John and Philip Sherrard. *Modern Greece.* (London: Ernest Benn Limited, 1968).

Cengizkan, Ali. *Mübadele ve Konut Yerleşimleri.* (Ankara: ODTÜ Mimarlık Fakültesi and Arkadaş Kitapevi, 2004)

Chater, Melville. "History's Greatest Trek: Tragedy Stalks through the Near East as Greece and Turkey Exchange Two Million of Their People," *The National Geographic Magazine* 48 (1925): 533–590.

Cigar, Norman. *Genocide in Bosnia: The Policy of "Ethnic Cleansing"* (College Station: Texas A & M University Press, 1995)

Clark, Bruce. *Twice a Stranger: How Mass Expulsion Forged Modern Greece and Turkey* (London: Granta Books, 2006).

Clogg, Richard. "A Millet within a Millet: the Karamanlides," in *Ottoman Greeks in the Age of Nationalism: Politics, Economy, and Society in the Nineteenth Century,* eds. Dimitri Gondicas and Charles Issawi. (Princeton: The Darwin Press, Inc., 1999) 115–142.

———. *A Concise History of Greece.* (Cambridge: Cambridge University Press, 1992).

———. "The Byzantine Legacy in the Modern Greek World: The Megali Idea," in *The Byzantine Legacy in Eastern Europe,* ed. Lowell Clucas (Boulder: East European Monographs, 1988) 253–281

———. *Parties and Elections in Greece: The Search for Legitimacy.* (London: C. Hurst & Co., 1987).

Criss, Bilge. *İşgal Altında Istanbul, 1918–1923.* (Istanbul: İletişim Yayınları, 1993).

Çanlı, Mehmet. "Yunanistan'daki Türklerin Anadolu'ya Nakledilmesi, II," *Tarih ve Toplum* 130 (1994): 51–59

Δαφνη, Γρηγοριου. *Η Ελλας μεταξύ Δυο Πολεμων, 1923–1940.* vol. 1. (Athens: Εκδοσεις Κακτος, 1997).

Dakin, Douglas. "The Importance of the Greek Army in Thrace during the Conference of Lausanne, 1922–1923," in *Greece and Great Britain during World War I, First Symposium Organized in Salonica by the Institute for Balkan Studies and King's College.* (Salonica: Institute for Balkan Studies, 1985) 210–232.

———. *The Unification of Greece, 1770–1923.* (London: Ernest Benn Limited, 1973).

Daniel, E. Valentine and John Chr. Knudsen, eds. *Mistrusting Refugees.* (Berkeley: University of California Press, 1995).

Davison, Roderic H. "Turkish Diplomacy from Mudros to Lausanne," in *The Diplomats, 1919–1939,* eds. Gordon A. Craig and F. Gilbert, First Princeton Paperback Printing. (Princeton: Princeton University Press, 1994) 172–209.

Dawkins, R. M. "The Crypto-Christianity of Turkey," *Byzantion* 8 (1933): 247–275.

Demirel, Ahmet. *Birinci Meclis'te Muhalefet, İkinci Grup.* (Istanbul: İletişim Yayınları, 1994).

DeNovo, John A. *American Interests and Policies in the Middle East, 1900–1939.* (Minneapolis: University of Minnesota Press, 1963).

Devedji, Alexandre. *L'échange obligatoire des minorités grecquès et turques.* (Paris: Imprimerie du Montparnasse et de Persan-Beaumont, 1929).

Dertilis, P. *La Réconstruction de la Grèce et la Société des Nations.* (Paris: Rousseau & Cie, 1929).

Dobkin, Marjorie Housepian. *Smyrna 1922: The Destruction of a City.* (New York: Newmark Press, 1998) (first edition appeared in 1972).

Dodd, Clement H. *The Cyprus Imbroglio.* (Cambridgeshire: The Eothen Press, 1998).

Doumanis, Nicholas. *Myth and Memory in the Mediterranean: Remembering Fascism's Empire.* (London: Macmillan, 1998).

Δριτσα, Μαργαριτα. "Πολιτικες και Οικονομικες Οψεις του Προσφυγικου Προβληματος," *Συμποσιο για τον Ελευθεριο Βενιζελο, Πρακτικα,* December 3–5, 1986. (Athens: Εταιρεια Ελληνικου Λογοτεχνικου και Ιστορικου Αρχειου, Μουσειο Μπενακη, 1988) 133–144.

Dündar, Fuad. *İttihad ve Terakki'nin Müslümanları İskan Politikası (1913–1918).* (Istanbul: İletişim Yayınevi, 2001).

Effimianidis, Yorğaki. *Cihan İktisad Buhranı Önünde Türkiye,* 2 vols. (Istanbul: Kaadçılık ve Matbaacılık Anonim Şirketi, 1936).

Ελευθεριαδου, Ν. Π. *Τα Μετα την Συνθηκην Αθηνων περι των εν ταις Νεαις Χωραις Εγκαταλειμμενων Κτηματων.* (Athens: Τυπογραφειον της Αυλης Α. Ραφτανη, 1915).

———. *Οι Μουσουλμανοι εν Ελλαδη.* (Athens: εκ του Τυπογραφειου Π. Α. Πετρακου, 1913).

———. *Μελεται Μουσουλμανικου Δικαιου Οθωμανικης Νομοθεσιας και Δικαιων των εν Τουρκια Χριστιανων.* (Mytilene: Τυποις Σαλπιγγος, 1912).

Ελεφαντης, Αγγελος Γ. *Η Επαγγελια της Αδυνατης Επαναστασης, Κ.Κ.Ε. και Αστισμος στον Μεσοπολεμο.* (Athens: Εκδοσεις Ολκος, 1976).

Emrence, Cem. "Politics of Discontent in the Midst of the Great Depression: the Free Republican Party of Turkey (1930)," *New Perspectives on Turkey* 23 (2000): 31–52.

Eski, Mustafa. *Cumhuriyet Döneminde Bir Devlet Adamı, Mustafa Necati.* (Ankara: Atatürk Kültür, Dil ve Tarih Yüksek Kurumu, Atatürk Araştırma Merkezi, 1999).

Ergene, Teoman. *İstiklal Harbinde Türk Ortodoksları.* (Istanbul: Milli Mecmua Basımevi, 1951).

Eroğlu, Hamza. *70. Yıldönümünde Lozan.* ([Ankara]: T. C. Kültür Bakanlığı, 1993).

Feder, Don. "Israel Should Prepare for Armageddon," http://www.townhall.com/

Finefrock, Michael Martin. "The Second Group in the First Grand National Assembly," *Journal of South Asian and Middle Eastern Studies* 3 (1979): 3–20.

Gabbay, Rony E. *A Political Study of the Arab-Jewish Conflict: The Arab Refugee Problem (A Case Study).* (Geneve: Librairie E. Droz, 1959).

Gallant, Thomas W. "Greek Exceptionalism and Contemporary Historiography: New Pitfalls and Old Debates," *Journal of Modern Greek Studies* 15:2 (1997): 209–216.

Geray, Cevat. "Türkiye'de Göçmen Hareketleri ve Göçmenlerin Yerleştirilmesi," *Orta Doğu Amme İdaresi Dergisi* 3 (1970): 8–37.

Γιαννακοπουλος, Γιοργος Α. "Οι Μικρασιατες Προσφυγες στην Ελλαδα, Βιβλιογραφικο Δοκιμιο," *ΔΕΛΤΙΟ ΚΜΣ* 9 (1992): 283–291.

Giannuli, Dimitra. "Greeks or "Strangers at Home": The Experiences of Ottoman Greek Refugees during their Exodus to Greece, 1922–1923," *Journal of Modern Greek Studies*, 13: 2 (1995): 271–287.

Γκιζελη, Βικα Δ. *Κοινωνικοι Μετασχηματισμοι και Προελευση της Κοινωνικης Κατοικιας στην Ελλαδα (1920–1930).* (Athens: Εκδοσεις Επικαιροτητα, 1984).

Glenny, Misha. *The Balkans, 1804–1999, Nationalism, War and the Great Powers.* (London: Granta Books, 1999).

Goodwin-Gil, Guy S. *The Refugee in International Law*, 2nd Edition. (Oxford: Clarendon Press, 1996).

Γουναρακη, Πετρου Ν. "Περι της Συνθηκης της Λωζανης, της Συμβασεως περι Ανταλλαγης των Πληθυσμων και των Συναφων προς αυτας Διαταξεων της Ελληνικης Νομοθεσιας," εν Βεβηλοι Κενοφωνιαι του Κ. Ν. Λουβαρη Υπομνημα προς την Δ. Ιεραν Συνοδον της Εκκλησιας της Ελλαδος. (Athens: n.p. 1930) 1–39.

Gökaçtı, Mehmet Ali. *Nüfus Mübadelesi: Kayıp Bir Kuşağın Hikayesi.* (Istanbul: İletişim Yayınları, 2002).

Gökalp, Ziya. *Türkçülüğün Esasları.* (Istanbul: Varlık Yayınları, 1973).

Gökay, Bülent. *A Clash of Empires: Turkey between Russian Bolshevism and British Imperialism, 1918–1923.* (London: I. B. Tauris, 1997).

Gürel, Ş. Sina. "Turkey and the Newly Independent States," Special Seminar Report, The Washington Institute for Near East Policy, www.washingtoninstitute.org/media

Hale, William. *Turkish Foreign Policy, 1774–2000.* (London: Frank Cass, 2000).

Hanioğlu, M. Şükrü. *Preparing for a Revolution, The Young Turks, 1902–1908.* (New York: Oxford University Press, 2000).

———. *The Young Turks in Opposition.* (New York: Oxford University Press, 1995).

———. *Bir Siyasal Düşünür Olarak Doktor Abdullah Cevdet ve Dönemi.* (Istanbul: Üçdal Neşriyat, [1981]).

Haraven, Tamara. "The Search for Generational Memory," in *Oral History; An Interdisciplinary Anthology*, eds. David K. Dunaway and Willa K. Baum. (London: Altamira Press, 1996) 241–256.

Hatipoğlu, Murat. *Yakın Tarihte Türkiye ve Yunanistan, 1923–1954.* (Ankara: Siyasal Kitapevi, 1997).

Herzfeld, Michael. "Displaced: The Spaces of the Refugee Identity in Greece," *Anthropological Quarterly* 64:2 (1991): 92–95.

———. *A Place in History: Social and Monumental Time in a Cretan Town.* (Princeton: Princeton University Press, 1991).

———. *The Poetics of Manhood, Contest and Identity in a Cretan Mountain Village.* (Princeton: Princeton University Press, 1985).

Hirshon, Renée. *Heirs of the Greek Catastrophe, the Social Life of Asia Minor Refugees in Piraeus.* (Oxford: Clarendon Press, 1989).

Hirshon, Renée, ed. *Crossing the Aegean: An Appraisal of the 1923 Compulsory Population Exchange Between Greece and Turkey.* (New York, Oxford: Berghahn Books, 2003).

Howard, Harry N. *Turkey, the Straits and U. S. Policy.* (Baltimore and London: The Johns Hopkins University Press, 1974).

———. *The Partition of Turkey, A Diplomatic History, 1913–1923*. (Norman: University of Oklahoma Press, 1931).

Howland, C. "Greece and the Greeks," *Foreign Affairs* 4:3 (1926): 454–464.

———. "Greece and Her Refugees," *Foreign Affairs* 4:4 (1926): 613–623.

İpek, Nedim. *Mübadele ve Samsun*. (Ankara: T.T.K.Basımevi, 2000).

———. "Köy Hizmetleri İl Müdürlüğü Arşivlerinden Mübadil Göçmenlerle İlgili Defterler," *Tarih ve Toplum* 144 (1995): 15–18.

———. *Rumeli'den Anadolu'ya Türk Göçleri*. (Ankara: T.T.K. Basımevi, 1994).

İskan Tarihçesi. (Istanbul: Hamit Matbaası, 1932).

Jaeschke, Gotthard. *Türk Kurtuluş Savaşı Kronolojisi, Mondros'tan Mudanya'ya Kadar (30 Ekim 1918–11 Ekim 1922)*. (Ankara: T.T.K. Basımevi, 1989).

Jensen, P. K. "The Greco-Turkish War, 1920–1922," *International Journal of Middle East Studies* 10:4 (1974): 553–565.

Kaplan, İsmail. *Türkiye'de Milli Eğitim İdeolojisi*. (Istanbul: İletişim Yayınları, 2000).

Kaplanoğlu, Raif. *Bursa'da Mübadele (1923–1930 Yunanistan Göçmenleri)*. (Bursa: Avrasya Etnografya Vakfı Yayınları, 1999).

Kappeler, A., ed. (in collaboration with F. Adanır and A. O'Day), *The Formation of National Elites: Comparative Studies on Governments and Non-Dominant Ethnic Groups in Europe, 1850–1940*. (Dartmouth: New York University Press, 1992).

Karakasidou, Anastasia N. *Fields of Wheat, Hills of Blood, Passages to Nationhood in Greek Macedonia, 1870–1990*. (Chicago: The University of Chicago Press, 1997).

Karal, Enver Ziya. *Türkiye Cumhuriyeti Tarihi, (1918–1944)*. (Istanbul: Milli Eğitim, 1945).

Karpat, Kemal. *The Politicization of Islam: Reconstructing Identity, Faith and Community in the Late Ottoman State* (New York: Oxford University Press, 2001)

———. "Historical Continuity and Identity Change or How to Be Modern Muslim, Ottoman, and Turk" in *Ottoman Past and Today's Turkey*, ed. K. Karpat. (Leiden: E.J. Brill, 2000) 1–28.

———. *Ottoman Population, 1830–1914: Demographic and Social Characteristics*. (Wisconsin: University of Wisconsin Press, 1985).

Kaufmann, Chaim D. "When All Else Fails: Ethnic Population Transfers and Partitions in the Twentieth Century," *International Security* 23:2 (1998): 120–156.

———. "Possible and Impossible Solutions to Ethnic Civil Wars," *International Security* 20:4 (1996): 136–175.

Katz, Yossi. "Transfer of Population as a Solution to International Disputes; Population Exchanges between Greece and Turkey as a Model for Plans to Solve the Jewish–Arab Dispute in Palestine during the 1930s," *Political Geography* 11:1 (1992): 55–72.

———. *Partner to Partition: The Jewish Agency's Partition Plan in the Mandate Era*. (London, Portland, Or.: Frank Cass, 1998).

Kedourie, Elie. *Nationalism*. (New York: Frederick A. Praeger, 1961).

Κεντρο Μικρασιατικων Σπουδων. *Ο Τελευταιος Ελληνισμος της Μικρας Ασιας, Εκθεση του Εργου του Κεντρου Μικρασιατικων Σπουδων (1930–1973), Καταλογος*. (Athens: Εκδοσεις του Κεντρου Μικρασιατικων Σπουδων, 1974).

Keyder, Çağlar. "Whither the Project of Modernity? Turkey in the 1990s," in *Rethinking Modernity and National Identity in Turkey*, eds. Sibel Bozdoğan and Reşat Kasaba. (Seattle and London: University of Washington Press, 1997) 37–51.

———. *State and Class in Turkey, A Study in Capitalist Development*. (London, New York: VERSO, 1987).

Kiosséoglou, Th. P. *L'échange forcé des minorités d'après la traite de Lausanne*. (Nancy: Imprimerie Nancéinne, 1926).

Kitroeff, Alexander. "Continuity and Change in Contemporary Greek Historiography," in *Modern Greece, Nationalism and Nationality*, eds. M. Blinkhorn and T. Veremis. (London: Sage-ELIAMEP, 1986) 143–172.

Kitsikis, Dimitri. *Türk-Yunan İmparatorluğu, Arabölge Gerçeği Işığında Osmanlı Tarihine Bakış*. (Istanbul: İletişim Yayınları, 1996).

———. "Les Réfugies grecs d'Anatolie et le 'Centre d'Etudes Micrasiatiques' d'Athènes," *TURCICA* 17 (1985): 227–244.

Kleiner, Robert J., Tom Sorensen et al. "International Migration and Internal Migration: A Comprehensive Theoretical Approach," in *Migration across Time and Nations, Population Mobility in Historical Contexts*, eds. Ira A. Glazier and Luigi De Rosa. (New York: Holmes & Meier, 1986) 305–317.

Kocacık, Faruk. "Balkanlar'dan Anadolu'ya Yönelik Göçler (1878–1890)," *Osmanlı Araştırmaları* 1 (1980): 137–190.

Kofas, John V. *Authoritarianism in Greece, the Metaxas Regime*. (Boulder, Colorado: East European Monographs, 1983).

Koliopoulos, John S. and Thanos M. Veremis, *Greece: The Modern Sequel from 1821 to the Present*. (New York: New York University Press, 2002).

Koraltürk, Murat. "Mübadelenin İktisadi Sonuçları Üzerine Bir Rapor," *Çağdaş Türkiye Tarihi Araştırmaları Dergisi* 2:6–7 (1996–97): 183–198.

Κορδάτος, Γιαννης. "Οικονομικη Χρισις που Γεννηθηκε απο τον Πολεμο Γινεται καθε Μερα Μεγαλυθερη και Βαθυτερη," in *Κομμουνιστικη Επιθεωρησις*, 1:1 (1921).

Kostanick, Huey Louis. *Turkish Resettlement of Bulgarian Turks, 1950–1953*. (Berkeley: University of California Press, 1957).

Koulouri, Christina, ed. *Teaching the History of Southeastern Europe*. (Salonica: Center for Democracy and Reconciliation in Southeast Europe, 2001).

Κουτελακης, Χαρης—Αμαντα Φωσκολου. *Πειραιας και Συνοικισμοι (Μαρτυριες και Γεγονοτα απο τον 14° Αιωνα μεχρι Σημερα)*. (Athens: Βιβλιοπωλειον της ΕΣΤΙΑΣ, 1991).

Köker, Tolga (with Leyla Keskiner) "Lessons in Refugeehood: The Experience of Forced Migrants in Turkey," in *Crossing the Aegean: An Appraisal of the 1923 Compulsory Population Exchange between Greece and Turkey*, ed. Reneé Hirschon, (New York and Oxford: Berghahn Books, 2004) 193–208.

Krasner, Stephen D. "Structural Causes and Regime Consequences: Regimes as Intervening Variables," *International Organization* 36:2 (1982): 185–205.

Kritikos, George. "State Policy and Urban Employment of Refugees: the Greek Case (1923–30)," *European Review of History* 7:2 (2000): 189–206.

———. "Motives for Compulsory Population Exchange in the Aftermath of the Greek-Turkish War," *ΔΕΛΤΙΟ ΚΜΣ*, 13 (1999–2000): 209–224.

Κωστης, Κωστας. "Η Ιδεολογια της Οικονομικης Αναπτυξης, Οι Προσφυγες στο Μεσοπολεμο," *ΔΕΛΤΙΟ ΚΜΣ* 9 (1992): 31–46.

Ladas, Stephan. *The Exchange of Minorities Bulgaria, Greece and Turkey*. (New York: The MacMillan Co., 1932).

Λαμψιδη, Γιωργου Ν. *Οι Προσφυγες του 1922, Η Προσφορα τους στην Αναπτυξη της Χωρας,* (3rd Edition). (Salonica: Εκδοτικος Οικος Αδελφων Κυριακιδη, 1992).

———. *Τοπαλ Οσμαν, Η Τελευταια Πραξη, Μικρασιατικη Καταστροφη (1914–1924).* (Athens: Εκδοσεις Λαδια και Σια, 1971).

———. *Τοπαλ Οσμαν, Η Τραγωδια των Ποντων απο το 1914–1924.* (Athens: Εκδοσεις Λαδια και Σια, 1969).

Landau, Jacob M. *Tekinalp, Turkish Patriot, 1883–1961.* (Istanbul: Nederlands Historisch Archaeologisch Instituut, 1984).

Lane, Winthrop D. "Why Greeks and Turks Oppose Being Exchanged?" *The New York Times Current History*, 18 (April 1923): 86–90.

LeGoff, Jacques. *History and Memory*. Trans. S. Rendall and E. Claman. (New York: Columbia University Press, 1992).

Lenczowski, George. *The Middle East in World Affairs*. (Ithaca, N. Y.: Cornell University Press, 1953).

Levi, Giovanni. "The Distant Past: On the Political Use of History," *Mediterranean Historical Review* 16:1 (2001): 61–73.

Lewis, Bernard. *The Emergence of Modern Turkey*, 2nd Edition. (London, Oxford, New York: Oxford University Press, 1968).

Lewis, Geoffrey L. *Turkey*, 3rd Edition. (New York: Praeger, 1965).

Loescher, Gil. *Beyond Charity, International Cooperation and the Global Refugee Crisis*. (New York, Oxford: Oxford University Press, 1993).

Loizos, Peter. "Ottoman Half-lives: Long term Perspectives on Particular Forced Migrations," *Journal of Refugee Studies* 12:3 (1999): 237–263.

Lowenthal, David. *The Past is A Foreign Country*. (Cambridge: Cambridge University Press, 1985).

Lozan Barış Antlaşması'nın 70. Yıldönümü. (Ankara: T. C. Dışişleri Bakanlığı, 1993).

Mackridge, Peter. "Greek-Speaking Moslems of North-East Turkey: Prolegomena to a Study of the Ophitic Sub-Dialect of Pontic," *Byzantine and Modern Greek Studies* 2 (1987): 115–137.

Macartney, Maxwell H. H. "The New Opposition in Turkey," *The Fortnightly Review*, 117 (1925): 781- 793.

Macartney, C. A. *National States and National Minorities*. (New York: Russell & Russell, 1968) (first published in 1934).

Mann, Michael. *The Dark Side of Democracy: Explaining Ethnic Cleansing* (Cambridge: Cambridge University Press, 2005).

Μαραβελακη, Μ.—Α. Βακαλοπουλου. *Οι Προσφυγικες Εγκαταστασεις στην Περιοχη της Θεσσαλονικης*. (Salonica: Εκδοσεις Βανιας, 1993).

Μαραντζιδης, Νικος. *Γιασασιν Μιλλετ, Ζητω Εθνος, Προσφυγια, Κατοχη και Εμφυλιος: Εθνοτικη Ταυτοτητα και Πολιτικη Συμπεριφορα στους Τουρκοφωνους Ελληνορθοδοξους του Δυτικου Ποντου*. (Heraklion: Πανεπιστημιακες Εκδοσεις Κρητης, 2001).

———. "Ethnic Identity, Memory and Political Behaviour: The Case of Turkish-Speaking Pontian Greeks," *South European Society and Politics* 5:3 (2000): 56–79.

Markham, Violet, R. "Greece and the Refugees from Asia Minor," *The Fortnightly Review* 117 (1925): 176–184.

Marrus, Michael R. *The Unwanted, European Refugees in the Twentieth Century.* (New York and Oxford: Oxford University Press, 1985).

Mavrogordatos, George T. "Το Ανεπαναληπτο Επιτευγμα," *ΔΕΛΤΙΟ ΚΜΣ* 9 (1992): 9–12.

———. *Stillborn Republic: Social Coalitions and Party Strategies in Greece, 1922–1936.* (Berkeley: University of California Press, 1983).

———. "Party and Society in Modern Greece," in *New Trends in Modern Greek Historiography*, Occasional Papers 1, eds. A Lily Macracis and P. Nikiforos Diamandouros. (Athens; The Modern Greek Studies Association in Cooperation with Anatolia College, 1982) 105–111.

Mazower, Mark. *Salonica, City of Ghosts: Christians, Muslims and Jews, 1430–1950.* (New York: Knopf, 2005)

———. *The Balkans.* (London: Weidenfeld & Nicolson, 2000).

———. "The Refugees, the Economic Crisis and the Collapse of Venizelist Hegemony, 1929–1932," *ΔΕΛΤΙΟ ΚΜΣ* 9 (1992): 119–134.

———. *Greece and the Inter-War Economic Crisis.* (Oxford: Clarendon Press, 1991).

McCarthy, Justin. *Death and Exile: The Ethnic Cleansing of Ottoman Muslims, 1821–1922.* (Princeton: The Darwin Press, Inc., 1995).

———. "Muslim Refugees in Turkey: The Balkan Wars, World War I and the Turkish War of Independence," in *Humanist and Scholar, Essays in Honor of Andreas Tietze*, eds. D. Quataert and H. Lowry. (Istanbul: The Isis Press, 1993) 87–111.

———. "The Population of the Ottoman Empire before and after the Fall of the Empire," in *III. Congress on the Social and Economic History of Turkey*, eds. H. Lowry and R. Hattox. (Istanbul: The ISIS Press, 1990) 275–288.

———. *Muslims and Minorities, the Population of the Ottoman Anatolia and the End of the Empire.* (New York: New York University Press, 1983).

Mears, Eliot Grinnel. *Greece Today-The Aftermath of the Refugee Impact.* (Stanford: Stanford University Press, 1929).

Michalopoulos, Dimitris. "The Moslems of Chamuria and the Exchange of Populations between Greece and Turkey," *Balkan Studies* 27:2 (1986): 303–313.

Mourelos, Yannis G. "The 1914 Persecutions and the First Attempt at an Exchange of Minorities between Greece and Turkey," *Balkan Studies* 26:2 (1985): 389–413.

Mouzelis, Nicos P. *Modern Greece, Facets of Underdevelopment.* (London: The MacMillan Press, 1978).

Naimark, Norman M. *Fires of Hatred: Ethnic Cleansing in Twentieth-Century Europe* (Cambridge, MA and London: Harvard University Press, 2002)

Νοταρα, Μιχ. *Η Αγροτικη Αποκαταστασις των Προσφυγων.* (Athens: n.p., 1934).

Oran, Baskın. "Kalanların Öyküsü (1923 Mübadele Sözleşmesinin Birinci ve Özellikle de İkinci Maddelerinin Uygulanmasından Alıncak Dersler)," in *Uluslararası Konferans, Atatürk ve Modern Türkiye.* (Ankara: Ankara Üniversitesi Siyasal Bilgiler Fakültesi Yayını, 1998) 155–173.

———. *Türk-Yunan İlişkilerinde Batı Trakya Sorunu*, 2nd Edition. (Ankara: Bilgi Yayınevi, 1991).

Orhunlu, Cengiz. "Yunan İşgalinin Meydana Getirdiği Göç ve Yunanlıların Yaptıkları "Tehcir" in Sonuçları Hakkında Bazı Düşünceler," *Belleten*, 37 (1973): 485–495.

Ortaylı, İlber. "Atatürk Döneminde Türkiye'de Tarihçilik Üzerine Bazı Gözlemler," in his *Gelenekten Geleceğe*. (Istanbul: Hil Yayınları, 1982) 72–79.

Owen, Roger and Şevket Pamuk. *Middle East Economies in the Twentieth Century*. (Cambridge, M.A.: Harvard University Press, 1999).

Ökçün, Gündüz, ed. *Türkiye İktisat Kongresi, 1923-İzmir, Haberler, Belgeler, Yorumlar*. (Ankara: Ankara Üniversitesi Siyasal Bilgiler Fakültesi Yayınları, 1981).

———. *A Guide to Turkish Treaties (1920–1964)*. (Ankara: Ankara Üniversitesi Basımevi, 1966).

Öke, Mim Kemal. *The Armenian Question, 1914–1923*. (Nicosia: K. Rüstem & Brother, 1988).

Öksüz, Hikmet. "Kıbrıs Türkleri'nin Anavatana Göçleri," *Tarih ve Toplum* 32:187 (1999): 35–38.

Özcan, Azmi. *Pan-Islamism, Indian Muslims, the Ottomans and Britain (1877–1924)*. (Leiden; E. J. Brill, 1997).

Öztürkmen, Arzu. *Türkiye'de Folklor ve Milliyetçilik*. (Istanbul: İletişim Yayınları, 1998).

Pallis, A. Alexander. *Συλλογη των Κυριωτερων Στατιστικων των Απορησων τη Ανταλλαγην των Πληθυσμων και Προσφυγικων Αποκαταστασιν μετα Αναλυσεως και Επεχηγησεως* (Athens: n.p., 1929).

———. "The Exchange of Populations in the Balkans," *The Nineteenth Century and After* 47: 576 (1925): 1–8.

———. *Στατιστικη Μελετη περι των Φυλετικων Μεταναστευσεων Μακεδονιας και Θρακης*. (Athens: Τυπογραφειο Ιωαν. Βαρτου, 1925).

Pekin, Müfide. ed., *Yeniden Kurulan Yaşamlar: 1923 Türk-Yunan Zorunlu Mübadelesi* (Istanbul: Bilgi Üniversitesi Yayınları, 2005).

Pekin, Müfide and Çimen Turan, eds. *Mübadele Bibliyografyası: Lozan Nüfus Mübadelesi ile İlgili Yayınlar ve Yayımlanmamış Çalışmalar* (Istanbul: Lozan Mübadilleri Vakfı, 2002).

Πελαγιδης, Ευσταθιος. *Προσφυγικη Ελλαδα (1913–1930), Ο Πονος και Η Δοξα*. (Salonica: Εκδοτικος Οικος Αδελφων Κυριακιδη Α. Ε., 1997).

———. *Η Αποκατασταση των Προσφυγων στη Δυτικη Μακεδονια (1923–1930)*. (Salonica: Εκδοτικος Οικος Αδελφων Κυριακιδη Α. Ε., 1994).

Pentzopoulos, Dimitri. *The Balkan Exchange of Minorities and its Impact upon Greece*. (Paris: Moulton, 1962).

Penwith, Lord Courtney. *Nationalism and War in the Near East*. (Oxford: Clarendon Press, 1915).

Petropulos, John A. "The Compulsory Exchange of Populations: Greek-Turkish Peace-making, 1922–1930," *Byzantine and Modern Greek Studies* 2 (1976): 135–160.

Πετσαλη, Αθαν. Νικολ. *Η Δημοσιονομικη Αντιμετωπισις του Προσφυγικου Ζητηματος*. (Athens: Τυπογραφειον ΕΣΤΙΑ, 1930).

Petsalis-Diomidis, N. *Greece at the Paris Peace Conference 1919*. (Salonica: Institute for Balkan Studies, 1978).

Polyzos, N. J. *Essai sur l'Emigration grecque, Etude démographique économique et sociale*. (Paris: Libraire du Recueil Sirey, 1947).

Poulton, Hugh. "The Turks and Pomaks," in his "The Balkans, Minorities and Governments in Conflict," http://www.armory.com/~thrace/back.html.

Πρωτονοταριου, Αθανασιου. *Το Προσφυγικον Προβλημα απο Ιστορικης, Νομικης και Καρατικης Αποψεως*. (Athens: Τυποις Πυρσου Ανων. Εταιριας, 1929).

Psomiades, Harry J. "Thrace and the Armistice of Mudanya, October 3–11, 1922," *ΔΕΛΤΙΟ ΚΜΣ* 12 (1997–1998): 213–247.

———. *The Eastern Question: the Last Phase-A Study in Greek-Turkish Diplomacy*. (Salonica: Institute for Balkan Studies, 1968).

Ρηγος, Αλκης. *Η Β' Ελληνικη Δημοκρατια, 1924–1935, Κοινωνικες Διαστασεις της Πολιτικης Σκηνης*, 2nd Edition. (Athens: ΘΕΜΕΛΙΟ, 1992).

Ροδοπουλου, Γ. Α. *Περι Θρησκευτικης Ανεξαρτησιας των Μουσουλμανων και περι Διοικησεως και Διαχειρισεως των Οθωμανικων Βακουφιων εν Ελλαδη*. (Athens: Τυπογραφειον Δ. Γ. Ευστρατιου και Δ. Δελη, 1913).

Roddy, Michael. "Horn Angrily Rejects Slovak Plan to Move Hungarians," Reuters, Sept. 9, 1997. http://www.house.gov/csce/slovakia97.htm.

Sadiq, Muhammed. *The Turkish Revolution and the Indian Freedom Movement*. (Delhi: Macmillan India Limited, 1983).

Sander, Oral. *Siyasi Tarih, İlkçağlardan 1918'e*. (Ankara: İmge Kitabevi, 2000).

Saydam, Abdullah. *Kırım ve Kafkas Göçleri (1856–1876)*. (Ankara: T.T.K. Basımevi, 1997).

Saylavi, Prof. Sinop [Yusuf Kemal Tengirşenk]. *Türk İnkilabı Dersleri—Ekonomik Değişmeler*. (Istanbul: Resimli Ay Matbaası, 1935).

Σβολοπουλου, Κωνσταντινου. *Η Αποφαση για την Υποχρεωτικη Ανταλλαγη των Πληθυσμων μεταξυ Ελλαδος και Τουρκιας*. (Salonica: Εθνικη Βιβλιοθηκη, 1981).

Schechtman, Joseph B. *Postwar Population Transfers in Europe, 1944–55*. (Philadelphia: University of Pennsylvania Press, 1962).

———. *Population Transfers in Asia*. (New York: Hallsby Press, 1949).

———. *European Population Transfers, 1939–1945*. (New York: Russell & Russell, 1946).

Sefériadès, Stelio. *L'Échange des Populations*. (Paris: Librairie Hachette, 1929).

Seton-Watson, R. W. *The Rise of Nationality in the Balkans*. (New York: E. P. Dutton and Company, 1918).

Shaw, Stanford J. "Resettlement of Refugees in Anatolia, 1918–1923," *The Turkish Studies Association Bulletin* 22:1 (1998): 58–90.

Shorter, Frederic C. "Turkish Population in the Great Depression," *New Perspectives on Turkey* 23 (2000): 103–124.

———. "The Population of Turkey After the War of Independence," *International Journal of Middle Eastern Studies* 17 (1985): 417–441.

Simpson, Sir John Hope. *The Refugee Problem, Report of a Survey*. (London, New York, Toronto, Oxford University Press, 1939).

———. *Refugees, Preliminary Report of a Survey*. (London: The Royal Institute of International Affairs, 1938).

Σκαλιερη, Γιωργιου Κλεανθους. *Λαοι και Φυλαι της Μικρας Ασιας μετα Πινακων και Χαρτων*. (Athens: Τυπογραφειον Τυπος, 1922) (Β' Εκδοση 1990).

Skendi, Stavro. *The Albanian National Awakening, 1878–1912*. (Princeton: Princeton University Press, 1967).

Skran, Claudena M. *Refugees in Inter-War Europe, the Emergence of a Regime*. (Oxford: Clarendon Press, 1995).

Smith, Michael Llewllyn. *Ionian Vision, Greece in Asia Minor, 1919–1922*. (London: Allen Lane, 1973).

Soğuk, Nevzat. *States and Strangers, Refugees and Displacement of Statecraft*. (Minneapolis: University of Minnesota Press, 1999).

Solomonidis, Victoria. "Greece in Asia Minor 1919–1922, A Historiographic Survey," in *New Trends in Modern Greek Historiography*, Occasional Papers 1, eds. A Lily Macracis and P. Nikiforos Diamandouros. (Athens: The Modern Greek Studies Association in Cooperation with Anatolia College, 1982) 121–128.

Sonyel, Salahi R. *Türk Kurtuluş Savaşı ve Dış Politika*, 2 vols. (Ankara: T.T.K. Basımevi, 1986).

———. *Turkish Diplomacy, Mustafa Kemal and the Turkish National Movement*. (London: Sage Publications Ltd., 1975).

Spyropoulos, Evangelos. *The Greek Military (1909–1941) and the Greek Mutinies in the Middle East (1941–1944)*. (Boulder: East European Monographs, 1993).

Stavrianos, L. S. *The Balkans since 1453*. (New York: Holt, Rinehart and Winston, 1958).

Stola, Dariusz. "Forced Migrations in Central European History," *International Migration Review* 26: 2 (1992) 324–341.

Şener, Cemal. *Topal Osman Olayı*. (Istanbul: Ant Yayınları, 1992).

Tanç, Barbaros. "Where Local Trumps National: Christian Orthodox and Muslim Refugees since Lausanne," *Balkanologie* 5:1–2 (2001): 273–289.

Tarih Eğitimi ve Tarihte "Öteki" Sorunu. (Istanbul: Tarih Vakfı Yurt Yayınları, 1998).

Tekeli, İlhan. "Osmanlı İmparatorluğu'ndan Günümüze Nüfusun Zorunlu Yer Değiştirmesi ve İskan Sorunu," *Toplum ve Bilim* 50 (1990): 49–71.

Tekin Alp, *The Turkish and Pan-Turkish Ideal*, Constantinople, Admiralty War Staff, Intelligence Division, March 1917.

Temel, Mehmet. *İşgal Yıllarında Istanbul'un Sosyal Durumu*. (Ankara: Kültür Bakanlığı Yayınları, 1998).

Temperley, H. W. V. ed. *A History of the Peace Conference of Paris*, vol. VI, Reprint of 1924 Edition. (London: Oxford University Press, 1969).

Ténékidès, C. G. "Le statut de minorités et l'échange obligatoire des populations Gréco-Turques," *Revue Générale de Droit International Public* 31 (1924): 72–88.

Thomas, Lewis V. "The National and International Relations of Turkey," in *Near Eastern Culture and Society*, ed. T. Cuyler Young. (Princeton: n.p., 1951) 167–187.

Toprak, Zafer. *İttihat-Terakki ve Devletçilik, Türkiye'de Ekonomi ve Toplum (1908–1950)*. (Istanbul: Tarih Vakfı Yurt Yayınları, 1995).

———. *Milli İktisat, Milli Burjuvazi, Türkiye'de Ekonomi ve Toplum (1908–1950)*. (Istanbul: Tarih Vakfı Yurt Yayınları, 1995).

Tosun, Ramazan. *Türk-Yunan İlişkileri ve Nufüs Mübadelesi* (Ankara: Berikan, 2002)

Τουντα-Φεργαδη, Αρετης. *Το Προσφυγικο Δανειο του 1924.* (Salonica: Παρατηρητης, 1986).

Toynbee, Arnold. *The Western Question in Greece and Turkey: A Study in the Contact of Civilisations.* (London, Bombay, Sydney: Constable and Company Ltd., 1922).

Triandafyllidou, A., et al. " New Greek Nationalism," *Sociological Research Online*, 2:1 http://www.socresonline.org.uk/socresonline/2/1/7/html.

Τσουδερος, Ε. Ι. *Η Αποζημιωσις των Ανταλλαξιμων.* (Athens: n.p., 1927).

Τσουλουφη, Αγγελου. *Η Ανταλλαγη Ελληνικων & Τουρκικων Πληθυσμων και η Εκτιμηση των Εκατερωθεν Εγκαταλειφθεισων Περιουσιων.* (Athens: Εκδοσεις Ενωσεως Σμυρναιων, 1989) (first edition appeared in 1982).

Tuchman, Barbara. "Distinguishing the Significant from the Insignificant," in *Oral History, An Interdisciplinary Anthology*, eds. David K. Dunaway and Willa K. Baum, 2nd Edition. (Walnut Creek, London and New Delhi: Altamira Press, 1996) 94–98.

Turfan, Naim. *Rise of the Young Turks, Politics, the Military and Ottoman Collapse.* (London: I. B. Tauris, 2000).

Umar, Bilge. *İzmir'de Yunanlıların Son Günleri.* (Ankara: Bilgi Yayınevi, 1974).

Üstel, Füsün. *İmparatorluktan Ulus-Devlete Türk Milliyetçiliği, Türk Ocakları, (1912–1931).* (Istanbul: İletişim Yayınları, 1997).

Vaner, Semih, ed. *Türk-Yunan Uyuşmazlığı.* (Istanbul: Metis Yayınları, 1990).

Vansina, Jan. "Oral Tradition and Historical Methodology," in *Oral History, An Interdisciplinary Anthology*, eds. David K. Dunaway and Willa K. Baum, 2nd Edition. (Walnut Creek, London and New Delhi: Altamira Press, 1996) 121–125.

Βερεμης, Θανος. *Οι Επεμβασεις του Στρατου στην Ελληνικη Πολιτικη, 1916–1936.* (Athens: Εξαντας, 1977).

Βεργετη, Μαρια. "Η Ποντιακη Ταυτοτητα της Τριτης Γενιας," *ΔΕΛΤΙΟ ΚΜΣ* 9 (1992): 80–96.

Χατζημωυσης, Παυλος. *Βιβλιογραφια 1919–1978, Μικρασιατικη Εκστρατεια-Ηττα Προσφυγια.* (Athens: ΕΡΜΗΣ, 1981).

Χασταογλου, Βιλμα and Αλεξανδρα Καραδημου-Γερολυμπου. "Η Θεσσαλονικη, 1900–1940, απο τις Αντιφανεις του Κοσμοπολιτισμου στην Ομογενεια της Νεοελληνικης Πολης" in *Η Θεσσαλονικη μετα το 1912, Συμποσιο*, Salonica, November 1–3, 1985. (Salonica: Δημος Θεσσαλονικης, 1986) 449–473.

Xydis, Stephen G. "Modern Greek Nationalism," in *Nationalism in Eastern Europe*, eds. Peter F. Sugar and Ivo J. Lederer. (Seattle: University of Washington Press, 1969) 207–258.

Valensi, Lucette. "Notes on Tow Discordant Histories: Armenia during World War I," *Mediterranean Historical Review* 16:1 (2001): 49–60.

Volkan, Vamık D. and Norman Itzkowitz. *Turks and Greeks, Neighbours in Conflict.* (London: The Eothen Press, 1994).

Voutira, Eftihia. "Population Transfers and Resettlement Policies in Inter-War Europe: the Case of Asia Minor Refugees in Macedonia from an International and National Perspective," in *Ourselves and Others, the Development of a Greek Macedonian Cultural Identity since 1912*, eds. Peter Mackridge and Eleni Yannakis. (Oxford, New York: Berg, 1997) 111–131.

Wenner, Manfred W. *Modern Yemen, 1918–1966.* (Baltimore: The Johns Hopkins Press, 1968).

Wolf, Eric. *Europe and the People without History.* (Berkeley: University of California Press, 1982).

Wolff, Stefan. *Disputed Territories: The Transnational Dynamics of Ethnic Conflict Settlement.* (New York: Berghahn Books, 2003).

Yapp, M. E. *The Making of the Modern Near East, 1792–1923.* (London and New York: Longman, 1987).

Yeşilkaya, Neşe Gürallar. *Halkevleri: İdeoloji ve Mimarlık.* (Istanbul: İletişim Yayınları, 1999).

Yetkin, Çetin. *Serbest Cumhuriyet Fırkası Olayı.* (Istanbul: Karacan Yayınları, 1982).

Yıldız, Ahmet. *"Ne Mutlu Türküm Diyebilene" Türk Ulusal Kimliğinin Etno-Seküler Sınırları (1919–1938).* (Istanbul: İletişim Yayınları, 2001).

Yetmişinci Yılında Lozan Barış Antlaşması, Uluslararası Seminer, October 25–26, 1993, The Marmara Oteli, Istanbul.

Zimova, Nada. "The Minority Question and the Lausanne Treaty Convention of 1923 (Historical Context and Religious-Ethnic Aspects of the Exchange of Greek and Turkish Populations)," *Asian and African Studies* 25 (1990): 159–165.

Zolberg, Aristide, Astri Suhrke and Sergio Aguayo. *Escape from Violence: Conflict and the Refugee Crisis in the Developing World.* (New York and Oxford: Oxford University Press, 1989).

Zürcher, Erik J. "Young Turks, Ottoman Muslims and Turkish Nationalists: Identity Politics, 1908–1938," in *Ottoman Past and Today's Turkey*, ed. Kemal Karpat. (Leiden: E. J. Brill, 2000) 150–179.

———. *Turkey, A Modern History.* (London & New York: I.B. Tauris, 1993).

———. *Political Opposition in the Early Turkish Republic, the Progressive Republican Party, 1924–1925.* (Leiden: E.J. Brill, 1991)

———. *The Unionist Factor: The Role of the Committee of Union and Progress in the Turkish National Movement, 1905–1926.* (Leiden: E. J. Brill, 1984).

Index

For Product Safety Concerns and Information please contact our EU
representative GPSR@taylorandfrancis.com Taylor & Francis Verlag GmbH,
Kaufingerstraße 24, 80331 München, Germany

Printed and bound by CPI Group (UK) Ltd, Croydon, CR0 4YY
08/05/2025
01864420-0001